MW00780057

Finding the Light

A Mother's Journey from Trauma to Healing

Marian Henley

Andrews McMeel
PUBLISHING®

A Note to the Reader

This book contains scenes of rape, violence, and
graphic language. Please read with care.

One

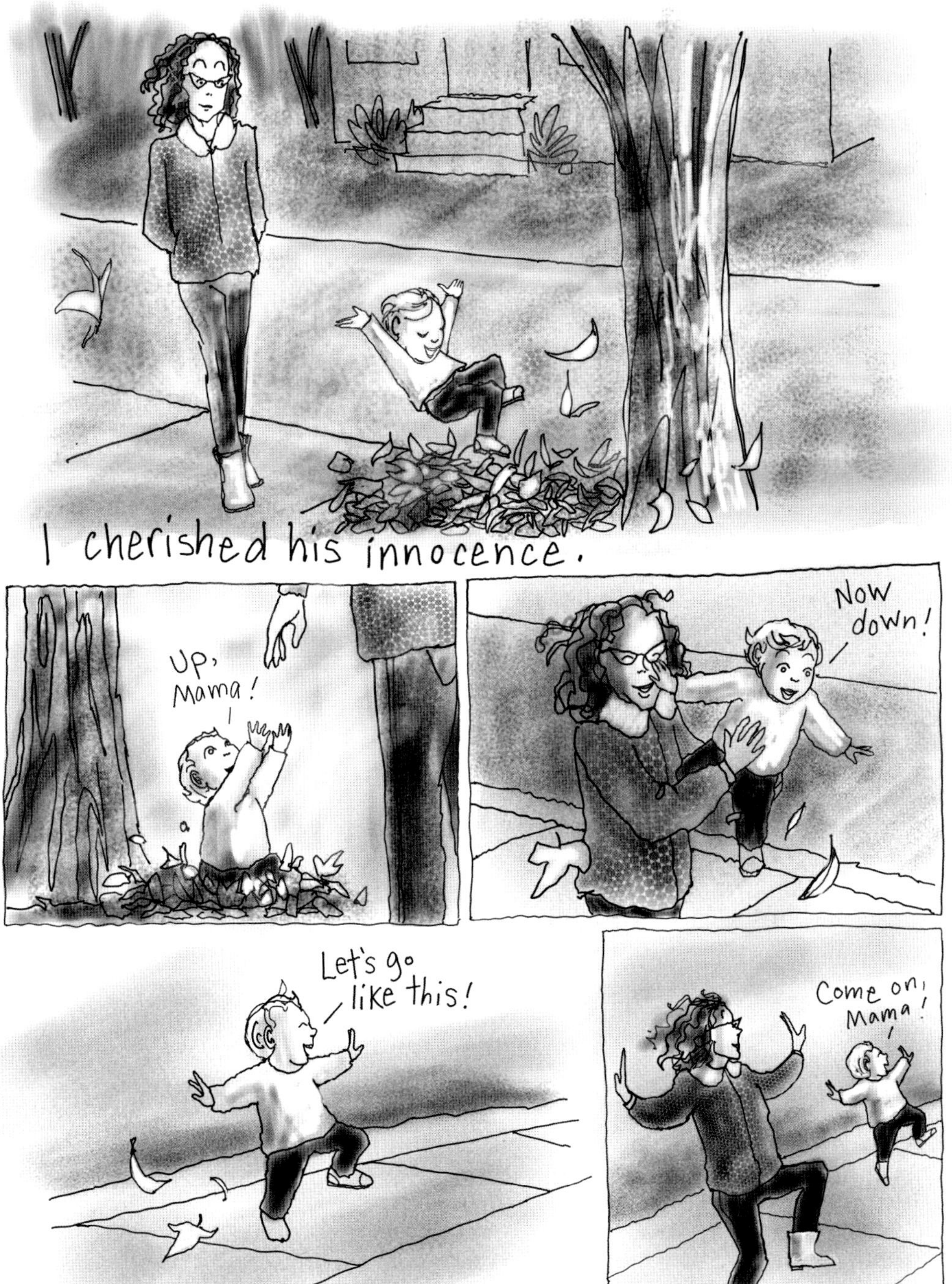

I cherished his innocence.
Up, Mama!
Now down!
Let's go like this!
Come on, Mama!

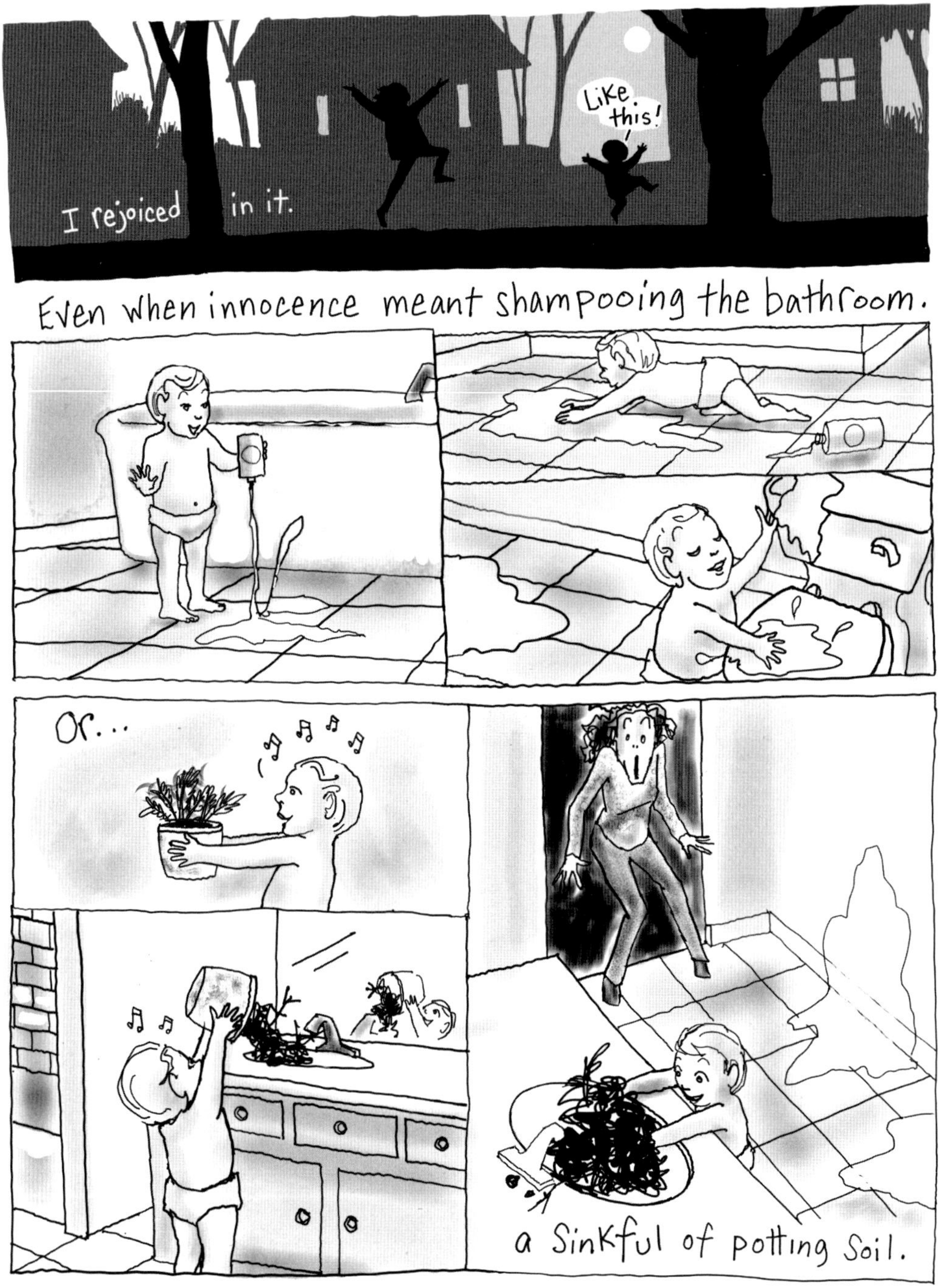
I rejoiced
in it.
Like this!
Even when innocence meant shampooing the bathroom.
Or...
a Sinkful of potting Soil.

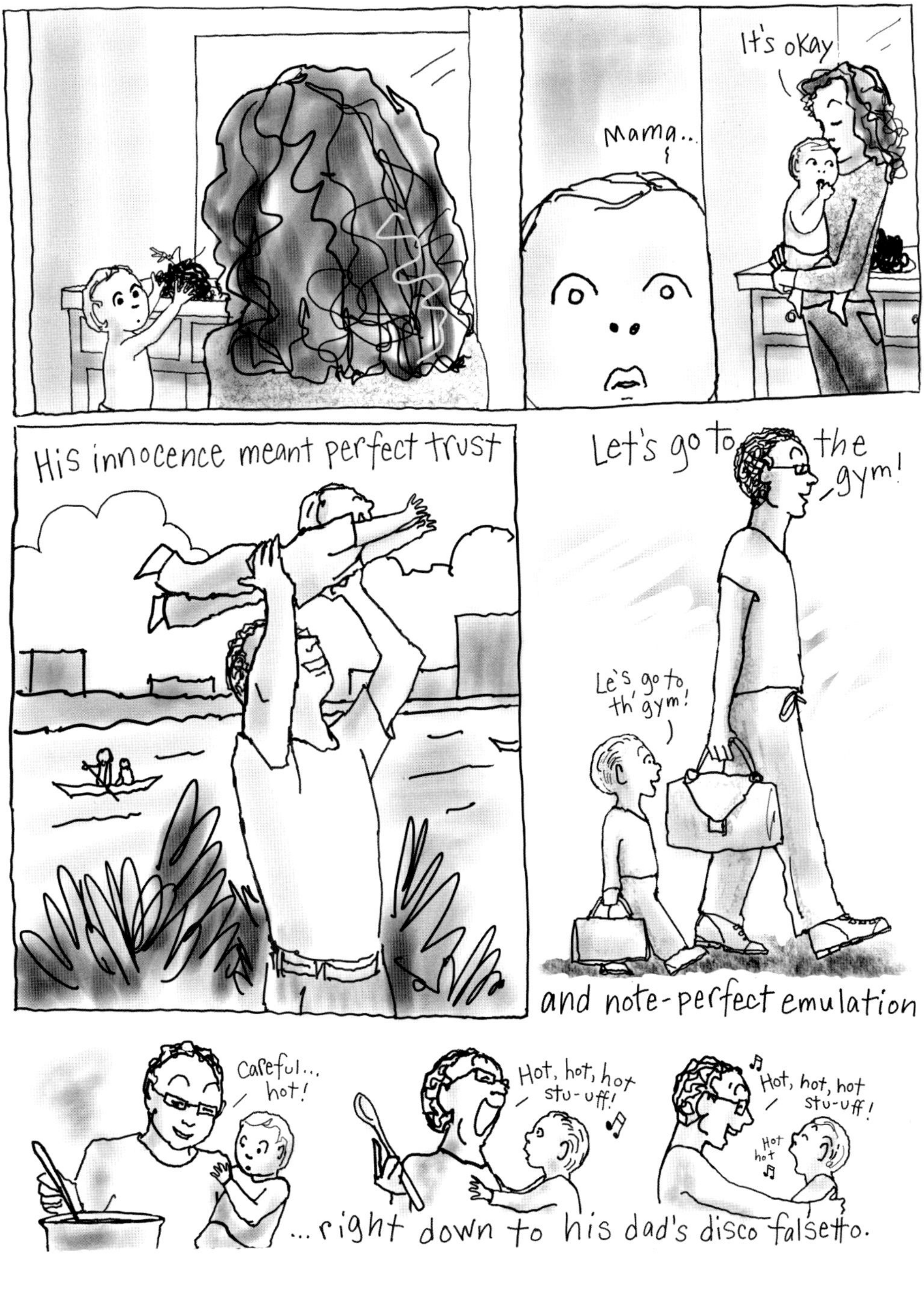
Mama...
It's okay
His innocence meant perfect trust
Let's go to the gym!
Le's go to th' gym!
and note-perfect emulation
Careful... hot!
Hot, hot, hot stu-uff!
Hot, hot, hot stu-uff!
Hot hot
...right down to his dad's disco falsetto.

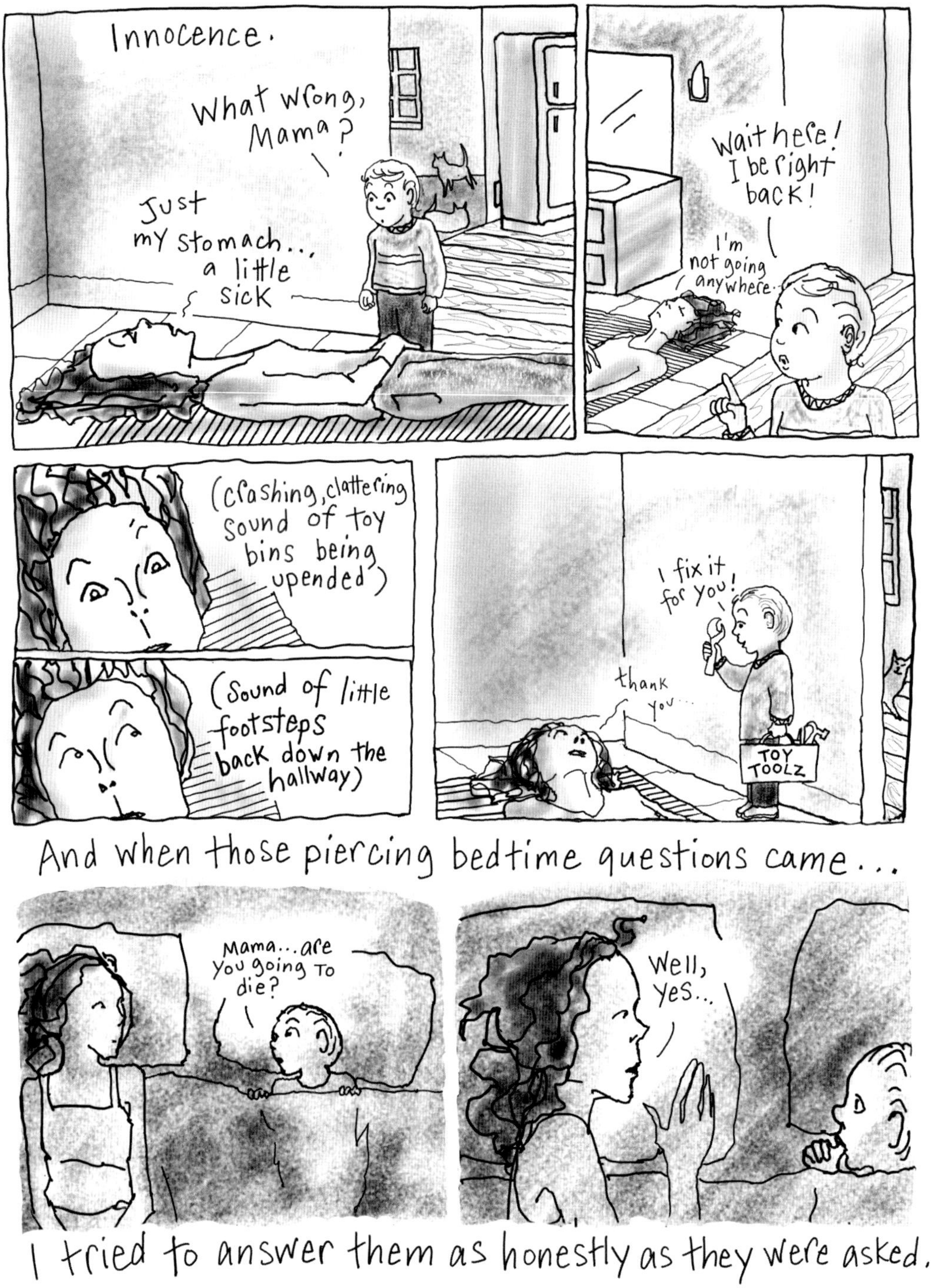
Innocence.
What wrong, Mama?
Just my stomach... a little sick
Wait here! I be right back!
I'm not going anywhere.
(crashing, clattering sound of toy bins being upended)
(Sound of little footsteps back down the hallway)
I fix it for you!
thank you...
TOY TOOLZ
And when those piercing bedtime questions came...
Mama... are you going to die?
Well, yes...
I tried to answer them as honestly as they were asked.

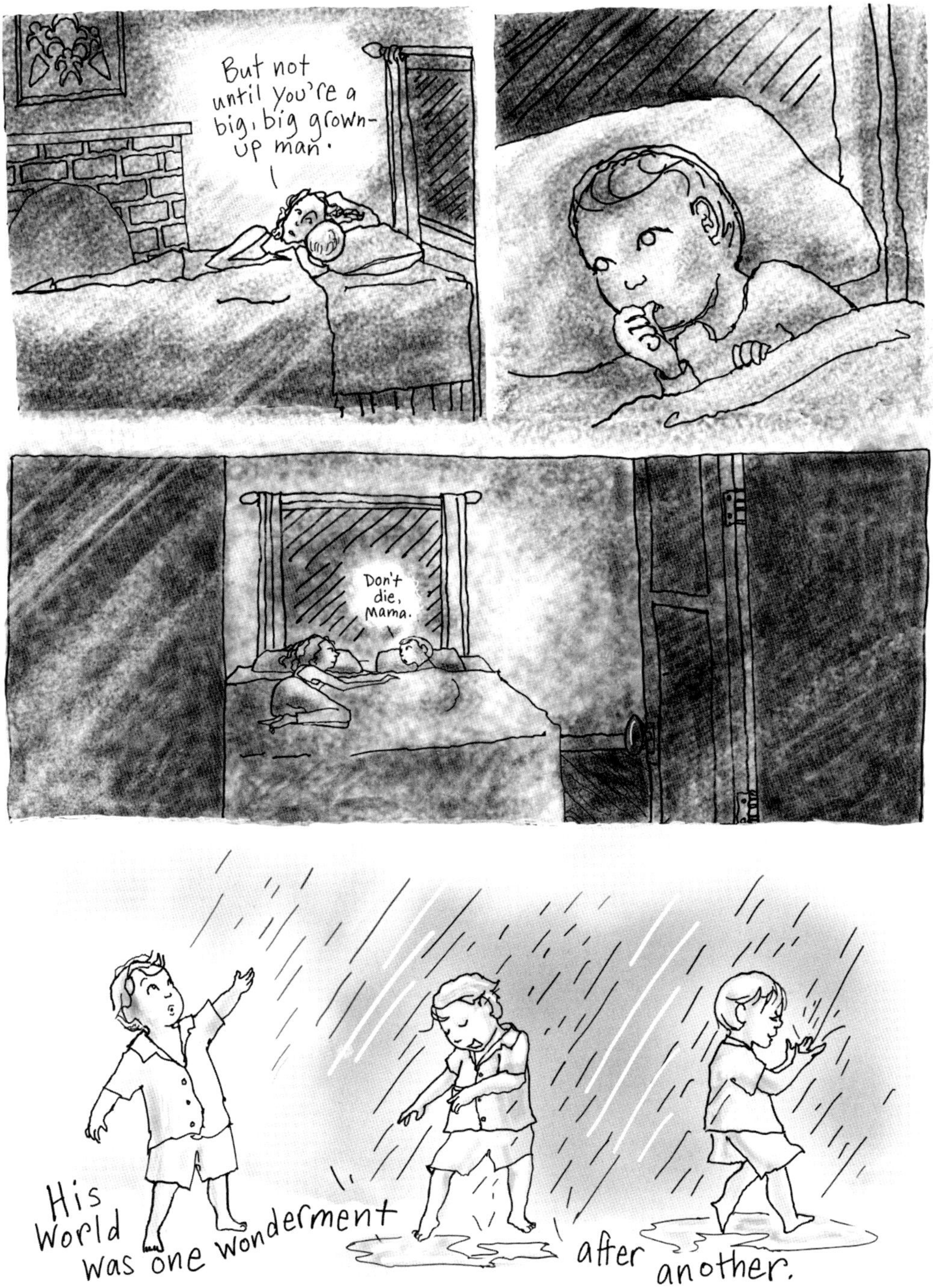
But not until you're a big, big grown-up man.
Don't die, Mama.
His world was one wonderment after another.

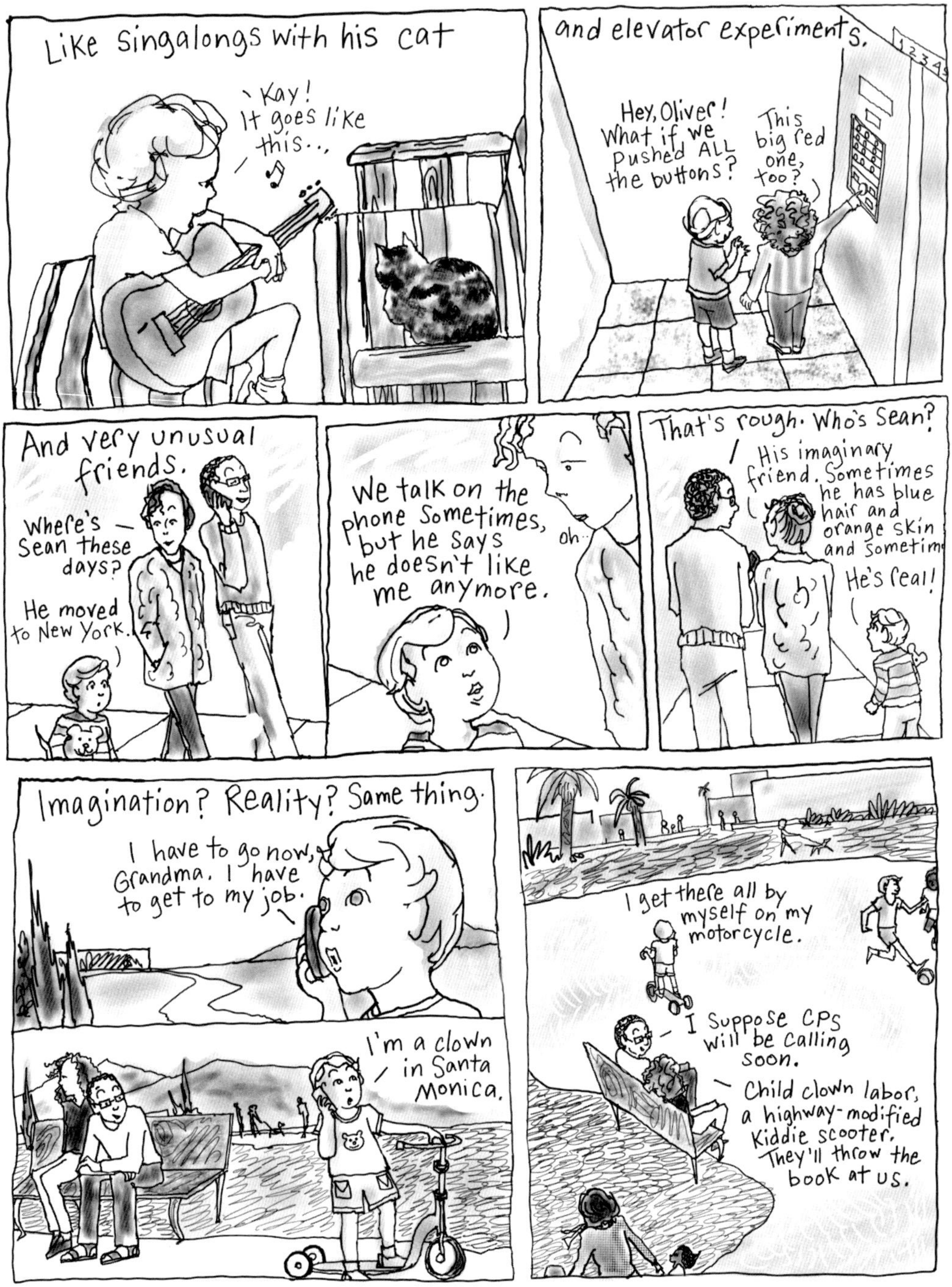
Like singalongs with his cat
'Kay! It goes like this...
and elevator experiments.
Hey, Oliver! What if we pushed ALL the buttons?
This big red one, too?
And very unusual friends.
Where's Sean these days?
He moved to New York.
We talk on the phone sometimes, but he says he doesn't like me anymore.
oh...
That's rough. Who's Sean?
His imaginary friend. Sometimes he has blue hair and orange skin and sometim
He's real!
Imagination? Reality? Same thing.
I have to go now, Grandma. I have to get to my job.
I'm a clown in Santa Monica.
I get there all by myself on my motorcycle.
I suppose CPS will be calling soon.
Child clown labor, a highway-modified kiddie scooter. They'll throw the book at us.

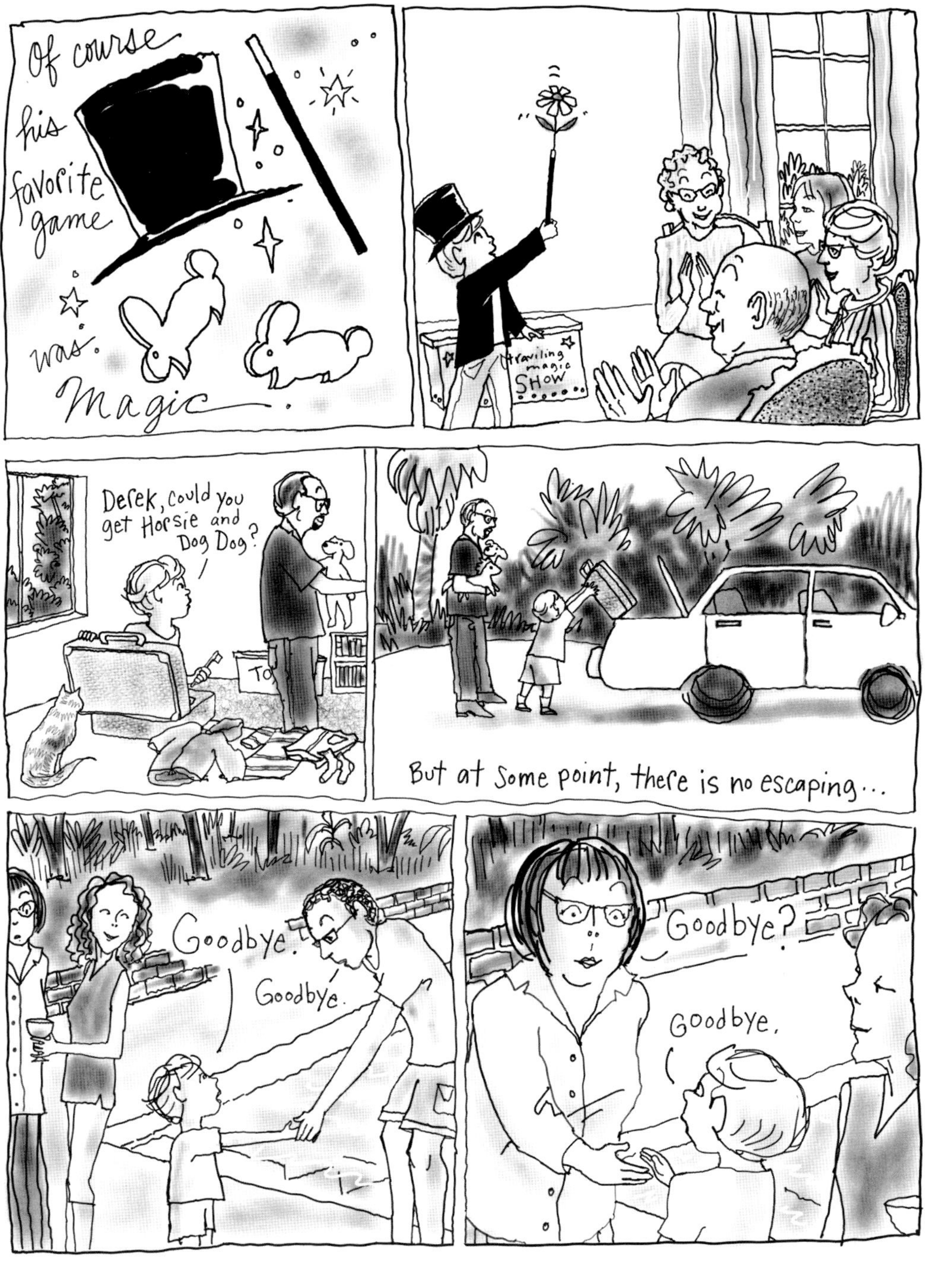
Of course his favorite game was Magic
traviling magic SHOW
Derek, could you get Horsie and Dog Dog?
To
But at some point, there is no escaping...
Goodbye.
Goodbye.
Goodbye?
Goodbye.

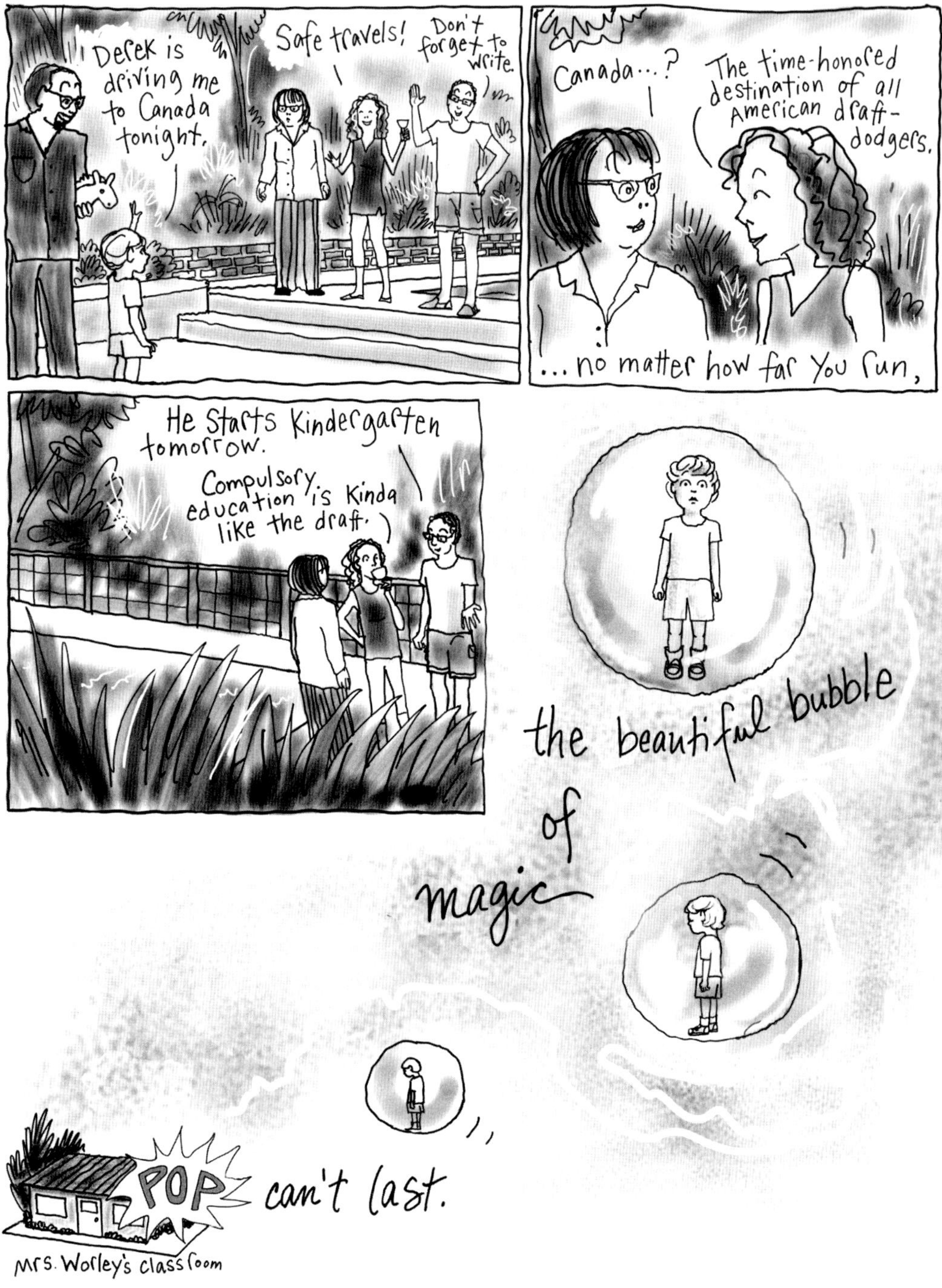

Derek is driving me to Canada tonight.
Safe travels!
Don't forget to write.
Canada...?
The time-honored destination of all American draft-dodgers.
... no matter how far you run,
He starts kindergarten tomorrow.
Compulsory education is kinda like the draft.
the beautiful bubble of magic
POP
can't last.
Mrs. Worley's classroom

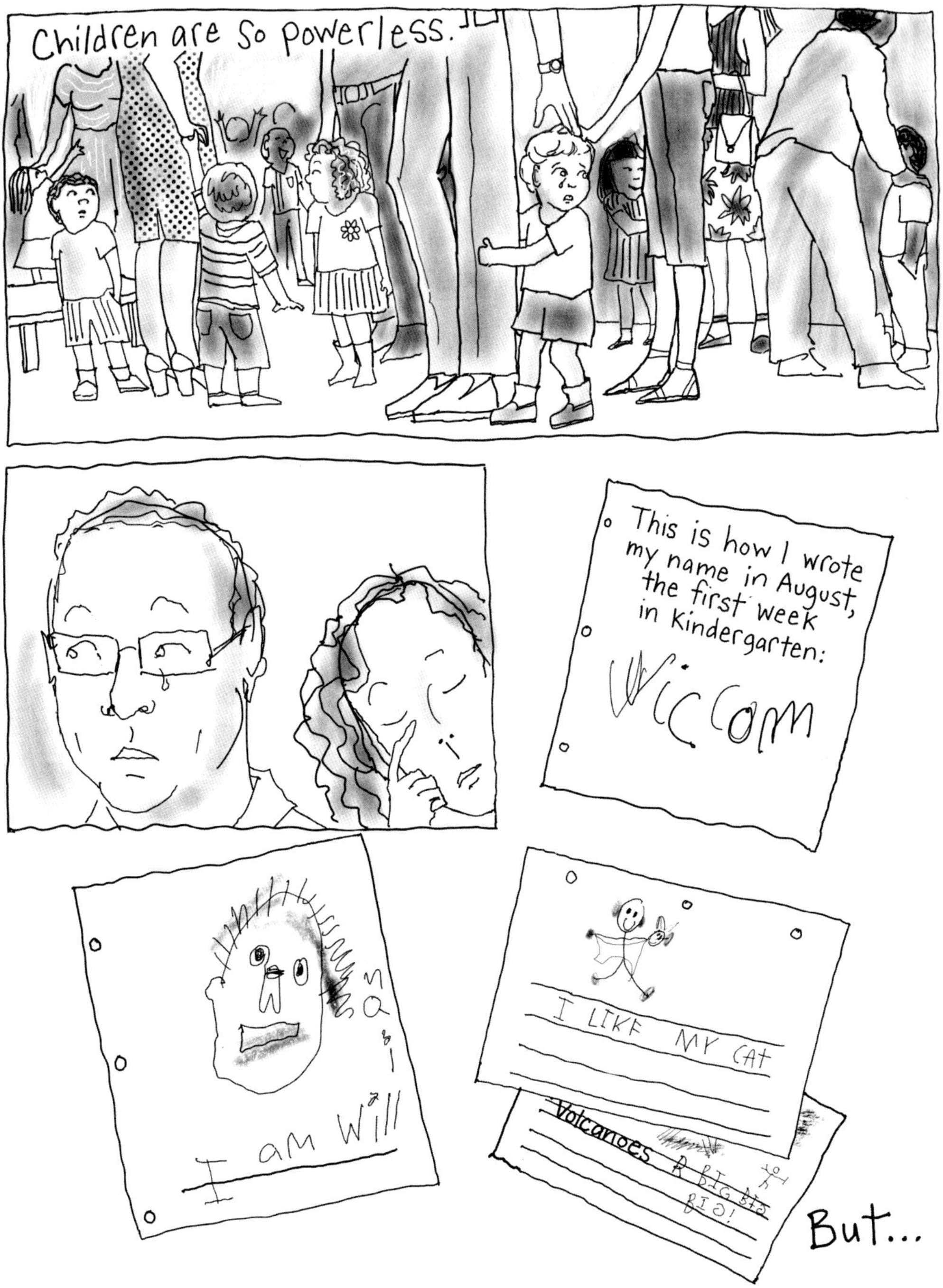
Children are so powerless.
This is how I wrote my name in August, the first week in Kindergarten:
I am Will
I LIKE MY CAT
Volcanoes
But...

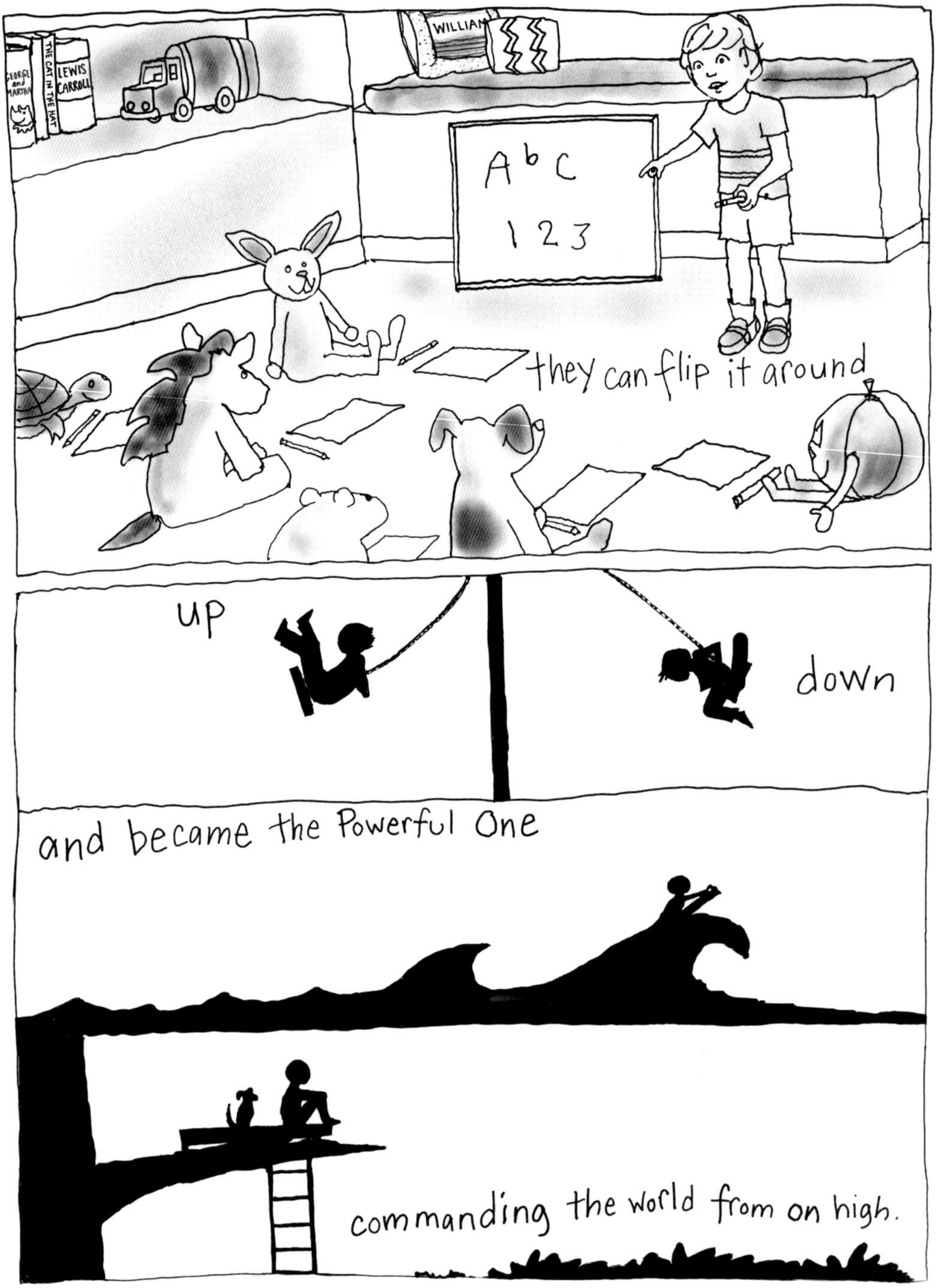
GEORGE and MARTHA
THE CAT IN THE HAT
LEWIS CARROLL
WILLIAM
A b C
1 2 3
they can flip it around
up
down
and became the Powerful One
commanding the world from on high.

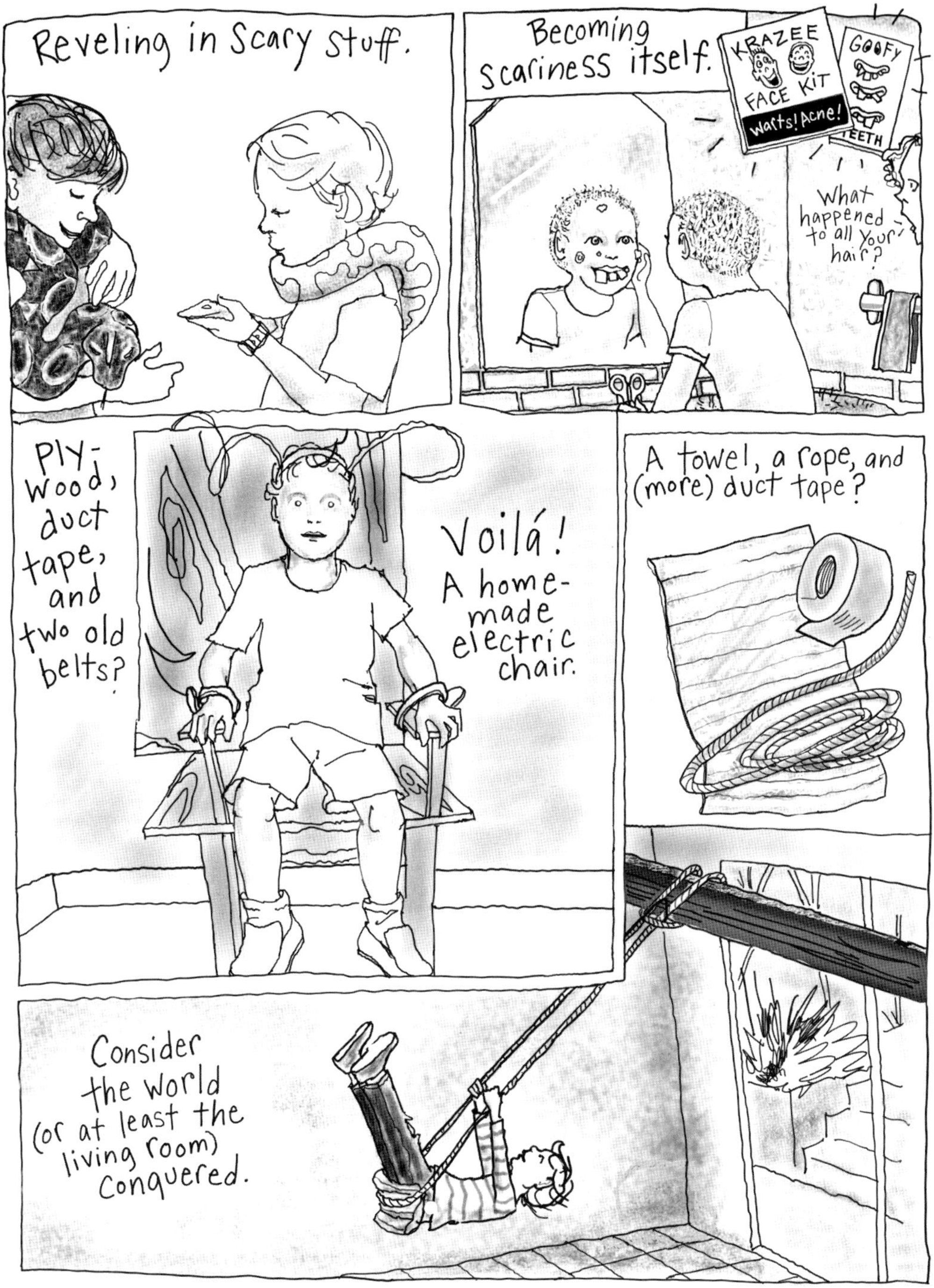
Reveling in Scary stuff.
Becoming Scariness itself.
KRAZEE FACE KIT
Warts! Acne!
GOOFY TEETH
What happened to all your hair?
Ply-wood, duct tape, and two old belts?
Voilá! A home-made electric chair.
A towel, a rope, and (more) duct tape?
Consider the world (or at least the living room) Conquered.

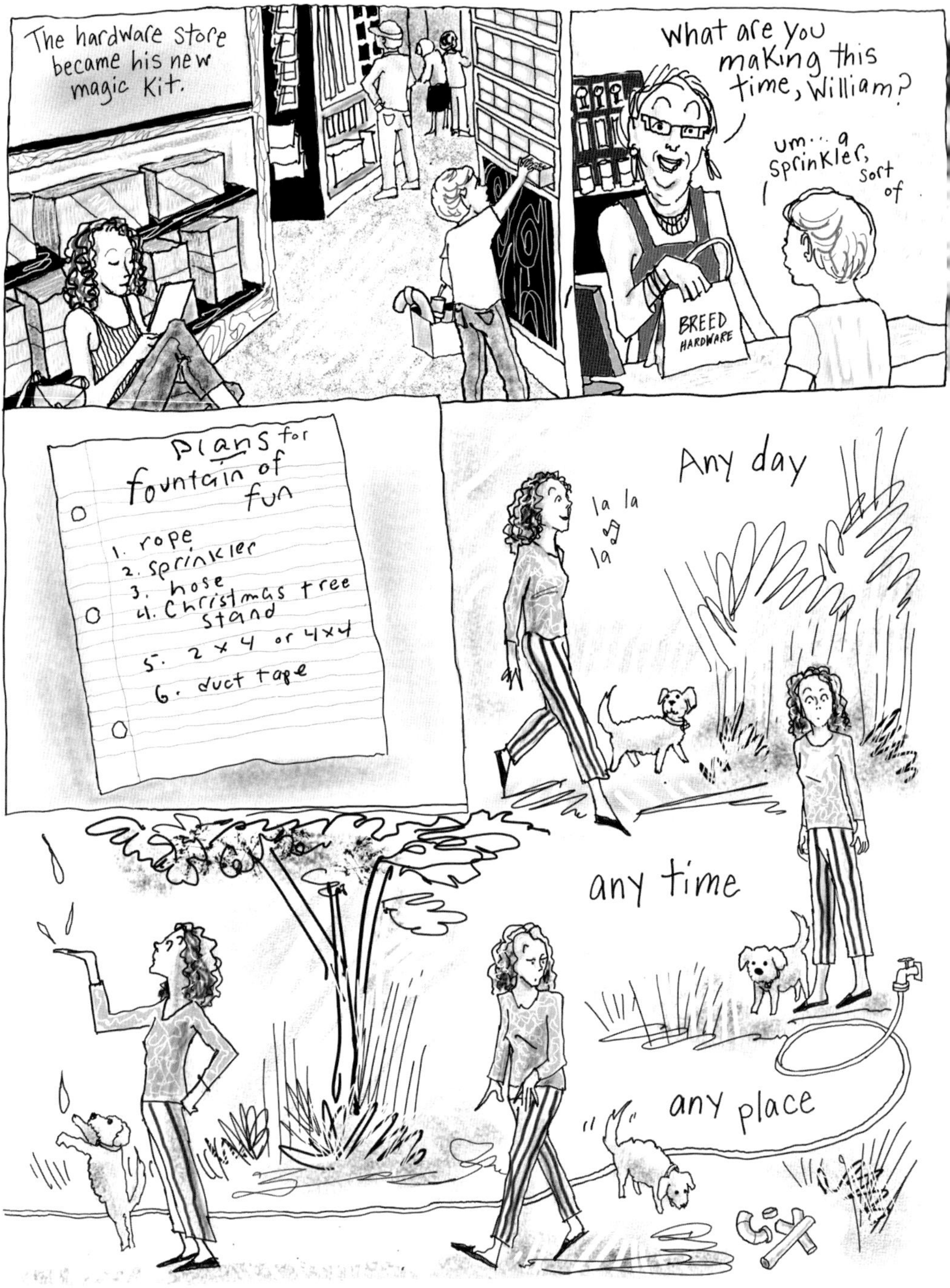
The hardware store became his new magic kit.
What are you making this time, William?
um... a sprinkler, sort of
BREED HARDWARE
Plans for fountain of fun
1. rope
2. sprinkler
3. hose
4. Christmas tree stand
5. 2 x 4 or 4x4
6. duct tape
Any day
la la
la
any time
any place

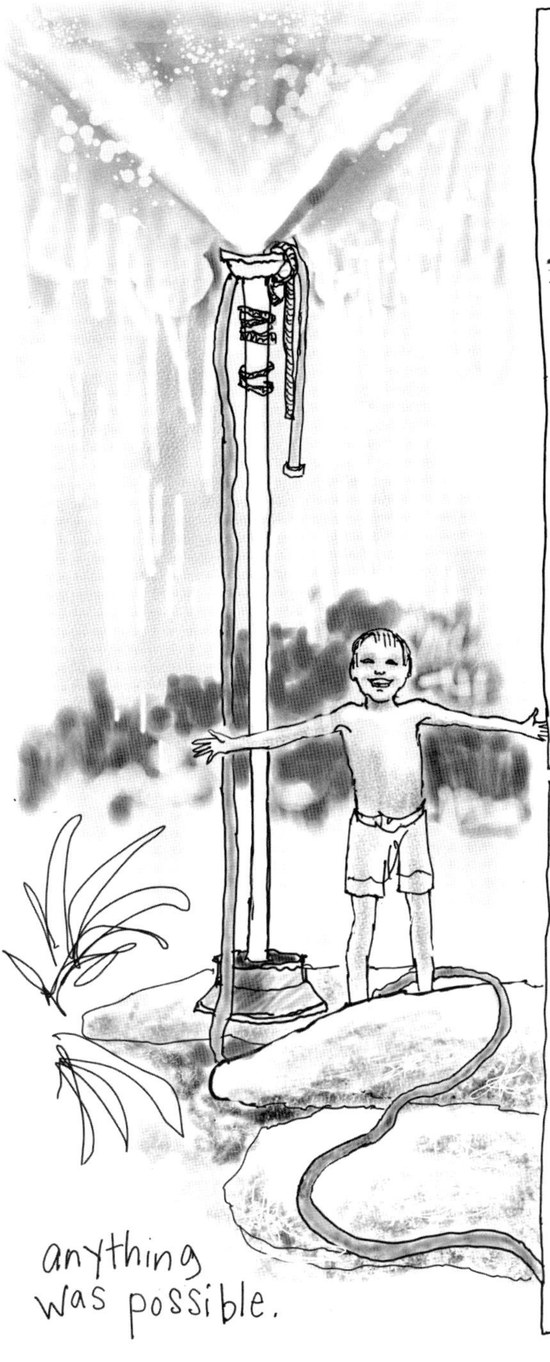
anything
was possible.

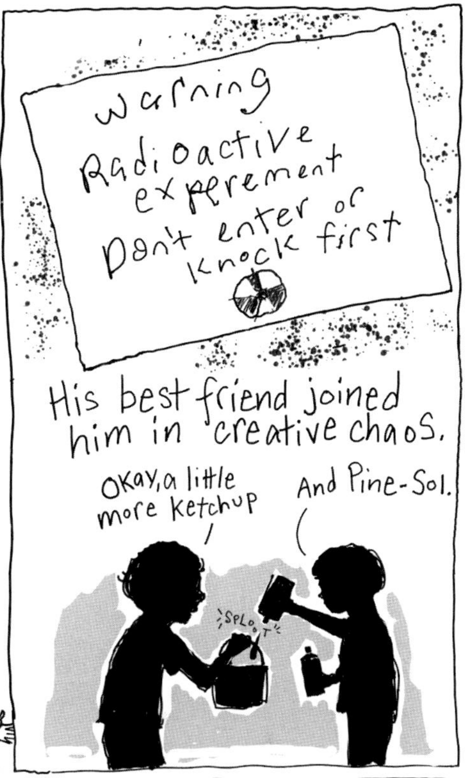
warning
Radioactive
experement
Don't enter or
knock first
His best friend joined
him in creative chaos.
Okay, a little
more ketchup
And Pine-Sol.
SPLOOT

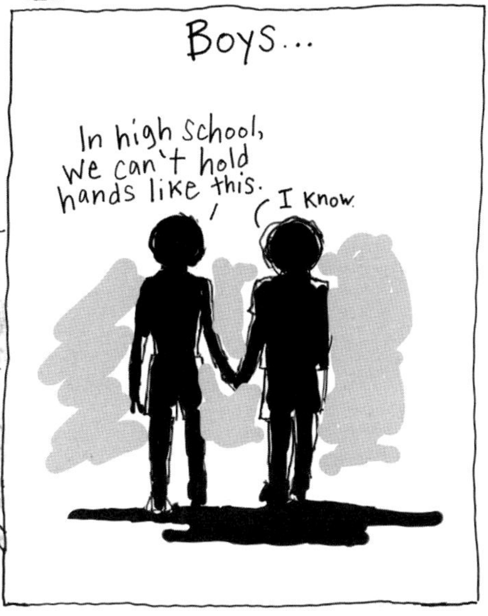
Boys...
In high school,
we can't hold
hands like this.
I know.

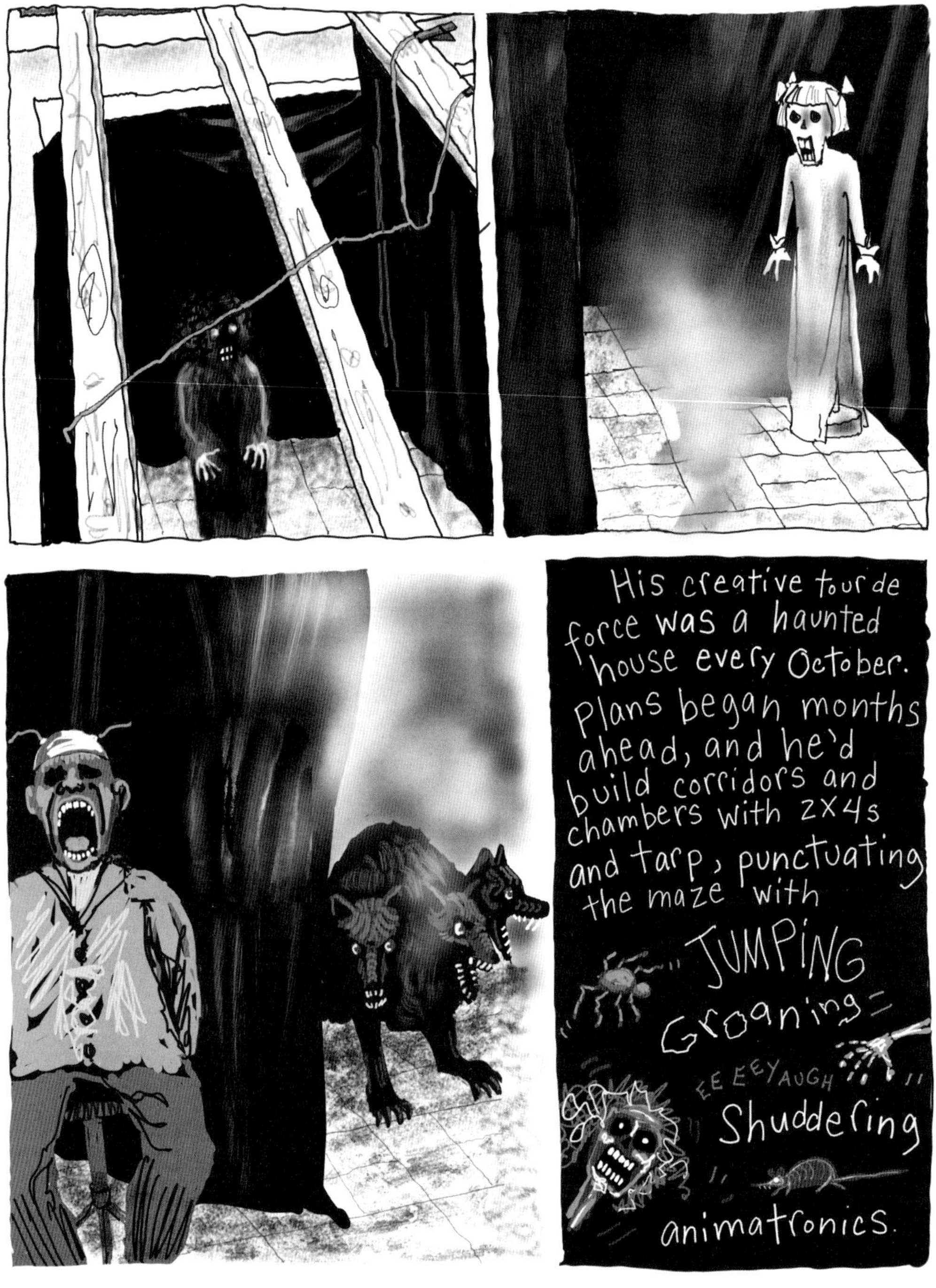
His creative tour de force was a haunted house every October. Plans began months ahead, and he'd build corridors and chambers with 2x4s and tarp, punctuating the maze with
JUMPING
Groaning
EEEEYAUGH
Shuddering
animatronics.

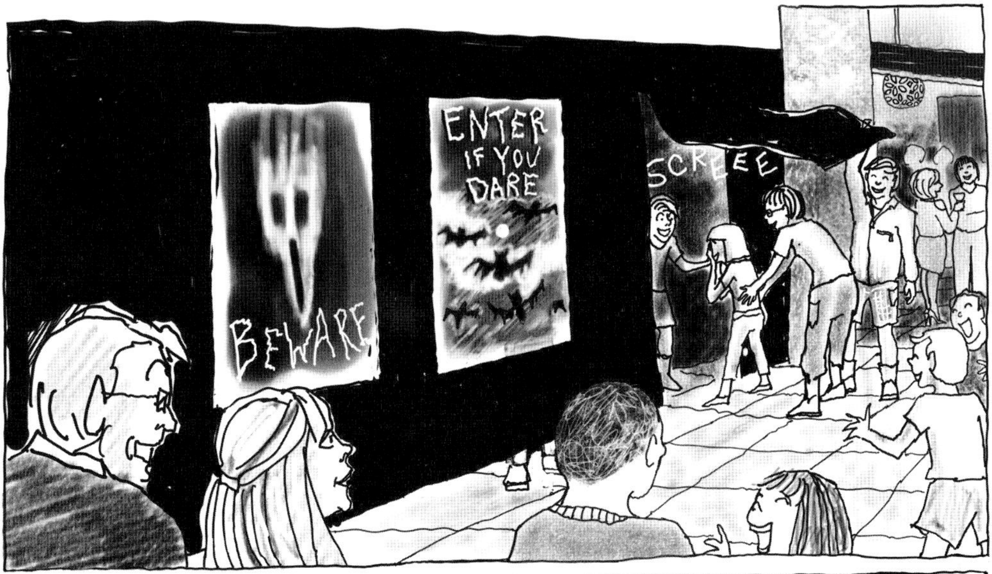
BEWARE
ENTER IF YOU DARE
SCREEE

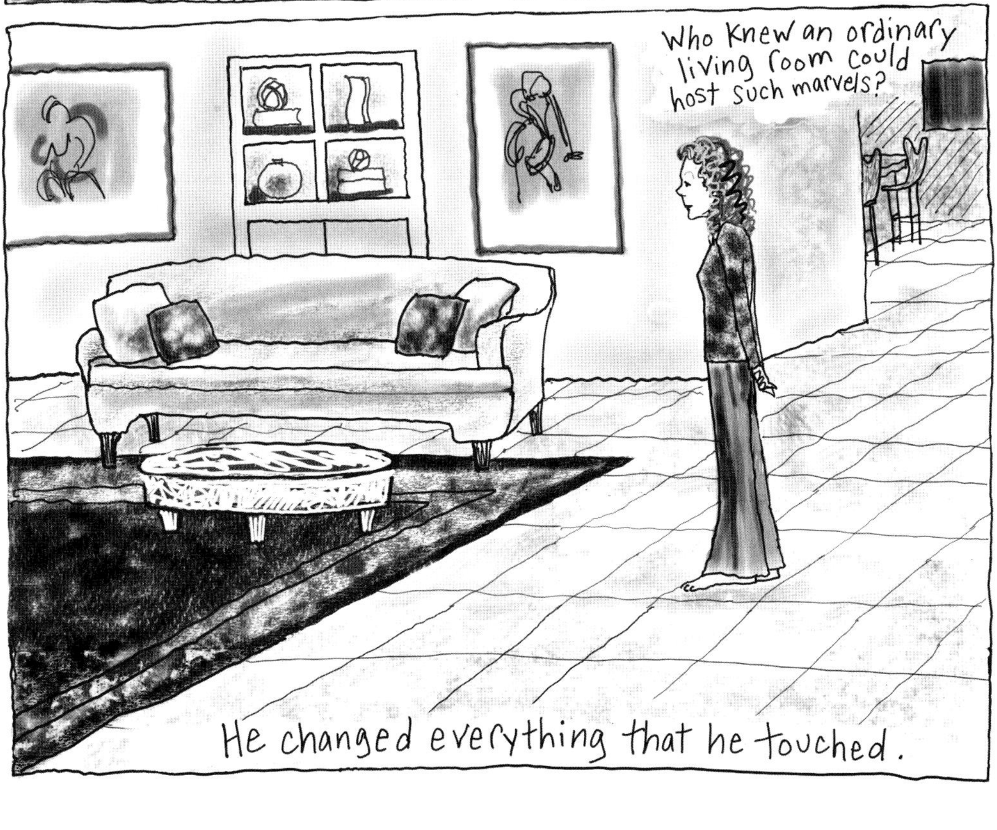
Who knew an ordinary living room could host such marvels?
He changed everything that he touched.

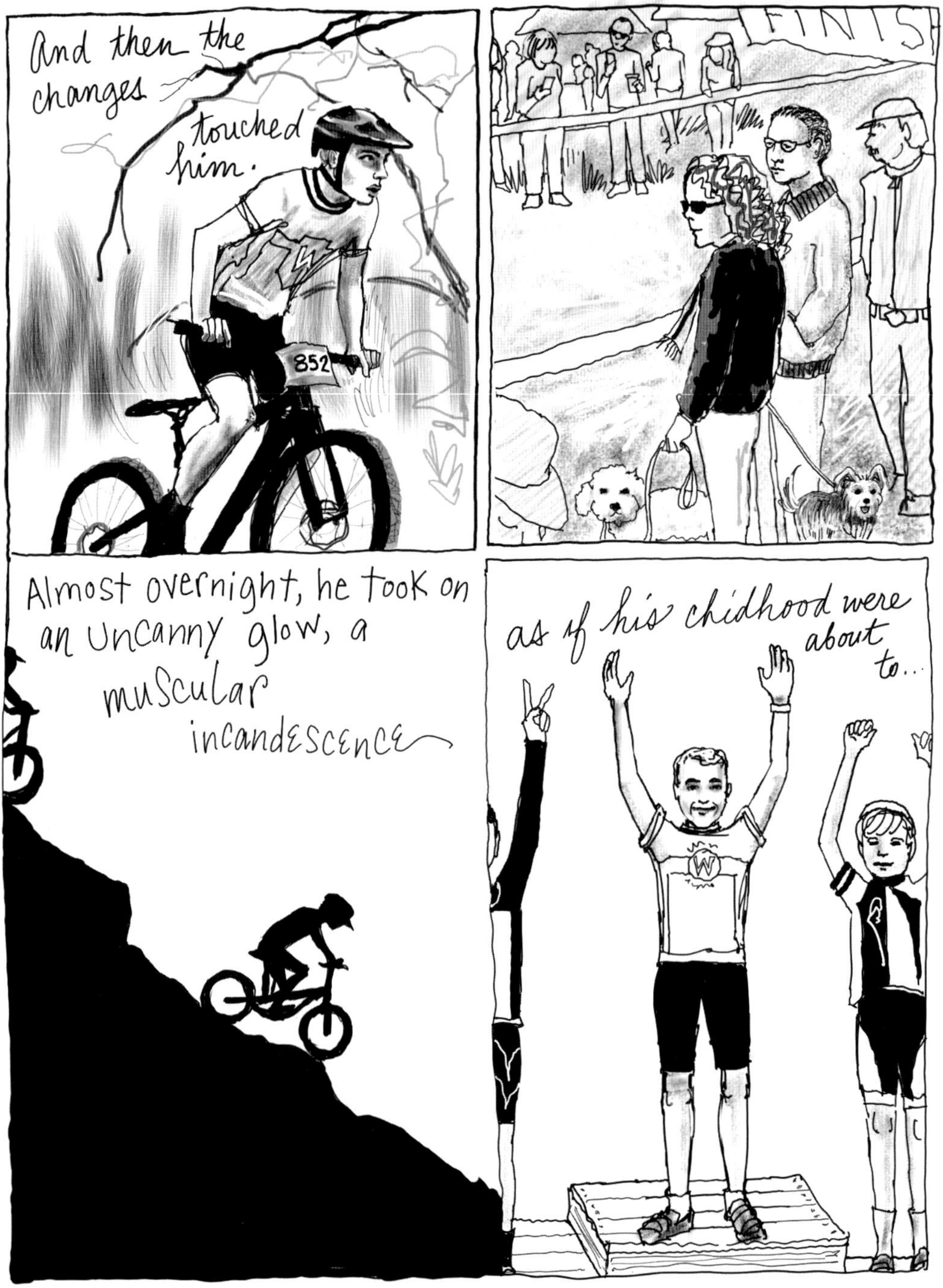
And then the changes touched him.
852
FINISH
Almost overnight, he took on an uncanny glow, a muscular incandescence
as if his chidhood were about to...

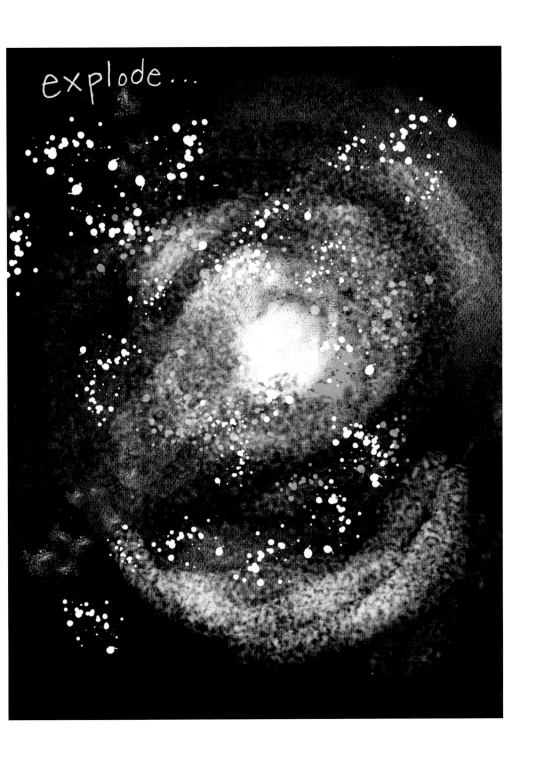

explode...

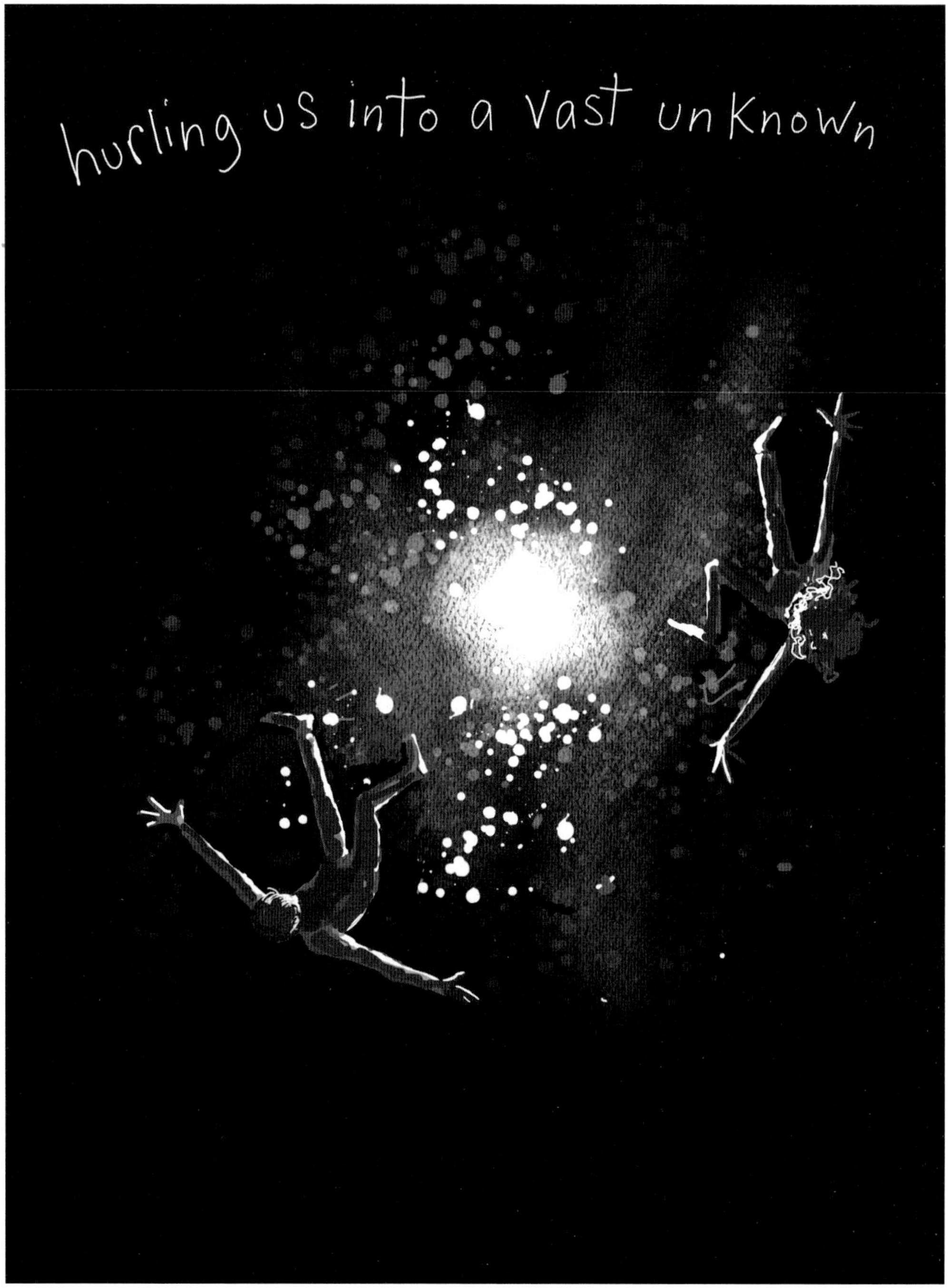
hurling us into a vast unknown

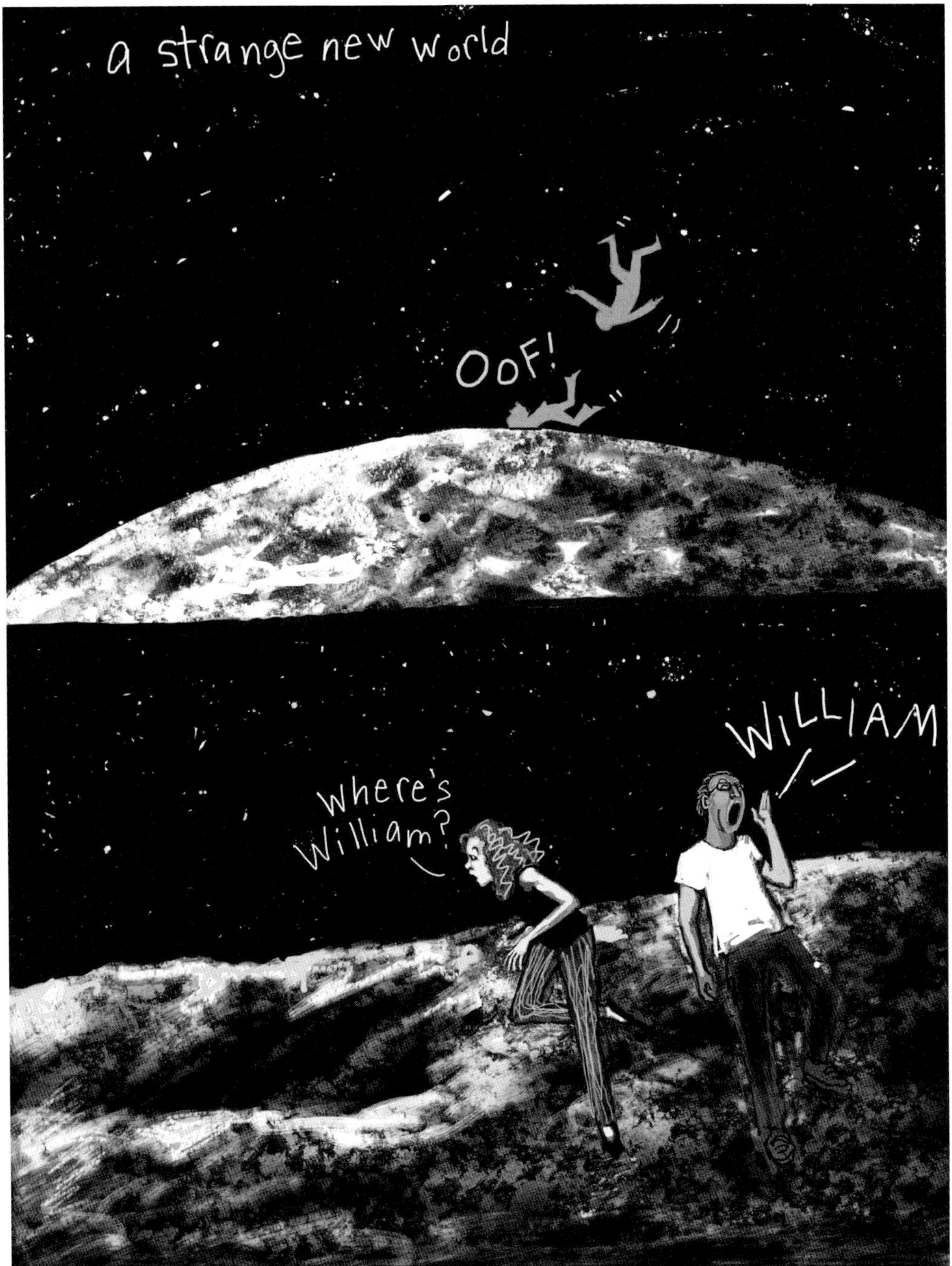
a strange new world
OOF!
where's William?
WILLIAM

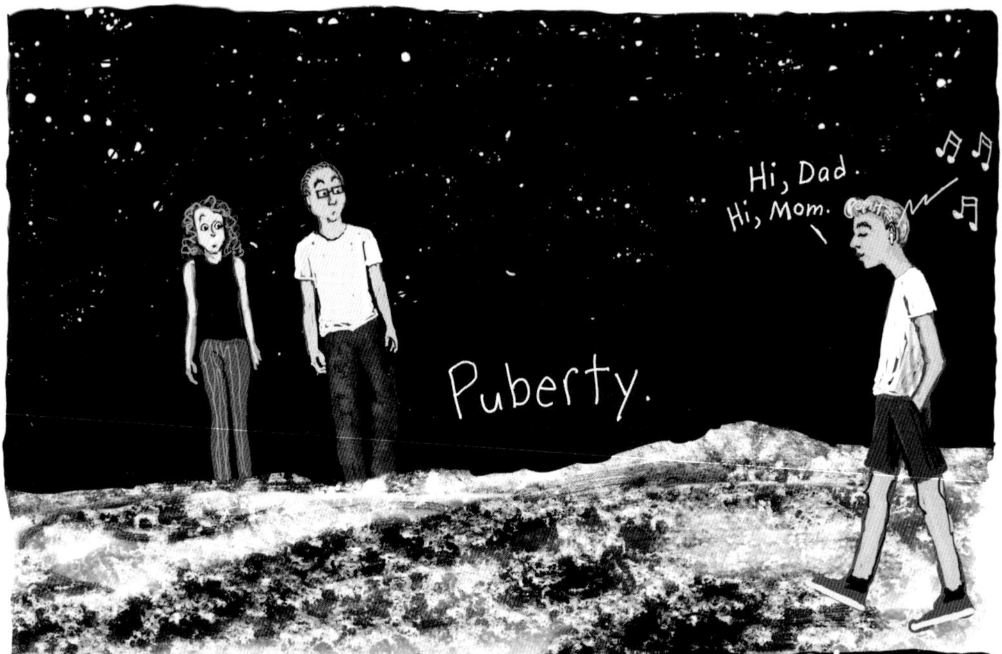
Hi, Dad.
Hi, Mom.
Puberty.

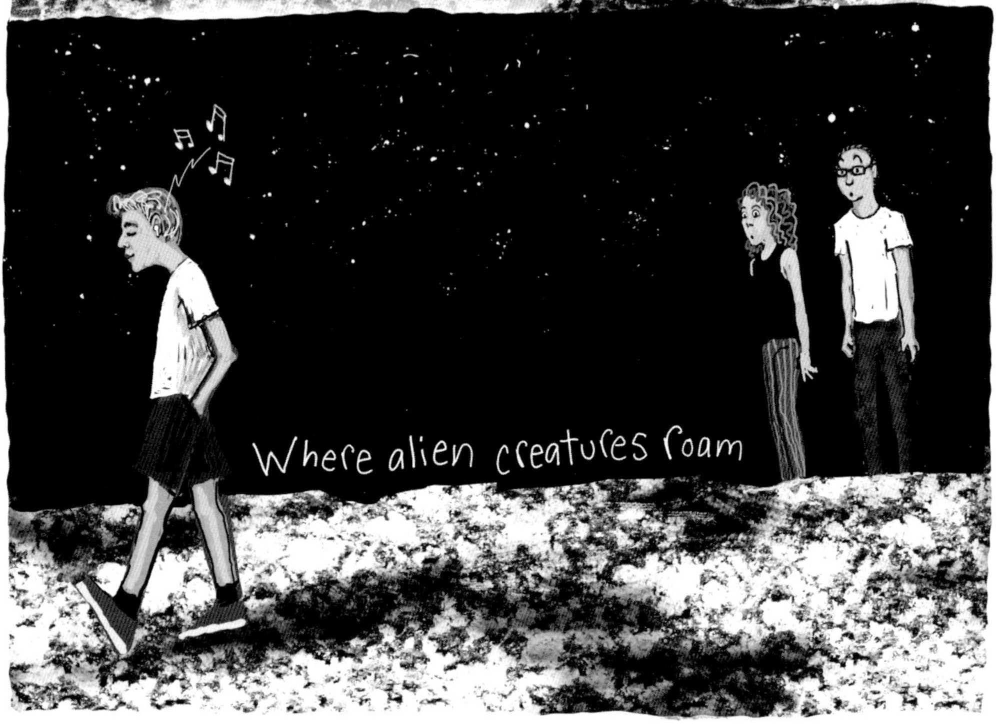
Where alien creatures roam

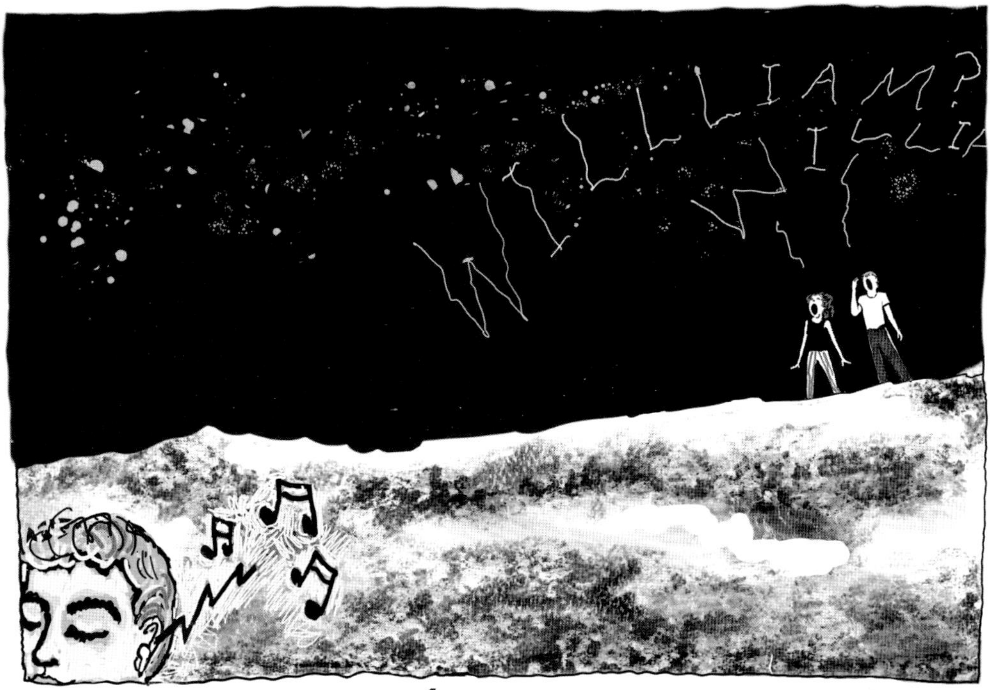
WILLIAM?
WILLIA
WI
WI

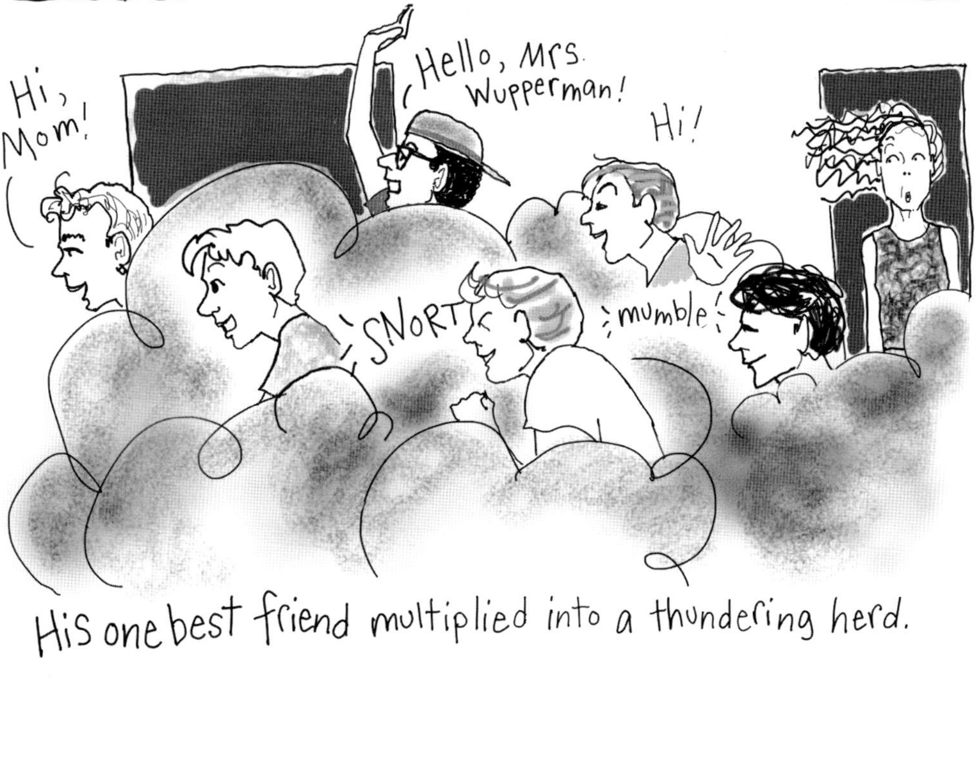
Hi, Mom!
Hello, Mrs. Wupperman!
Hi!
SNORT
mumble

His one best friend multiplied into a thundering herd.

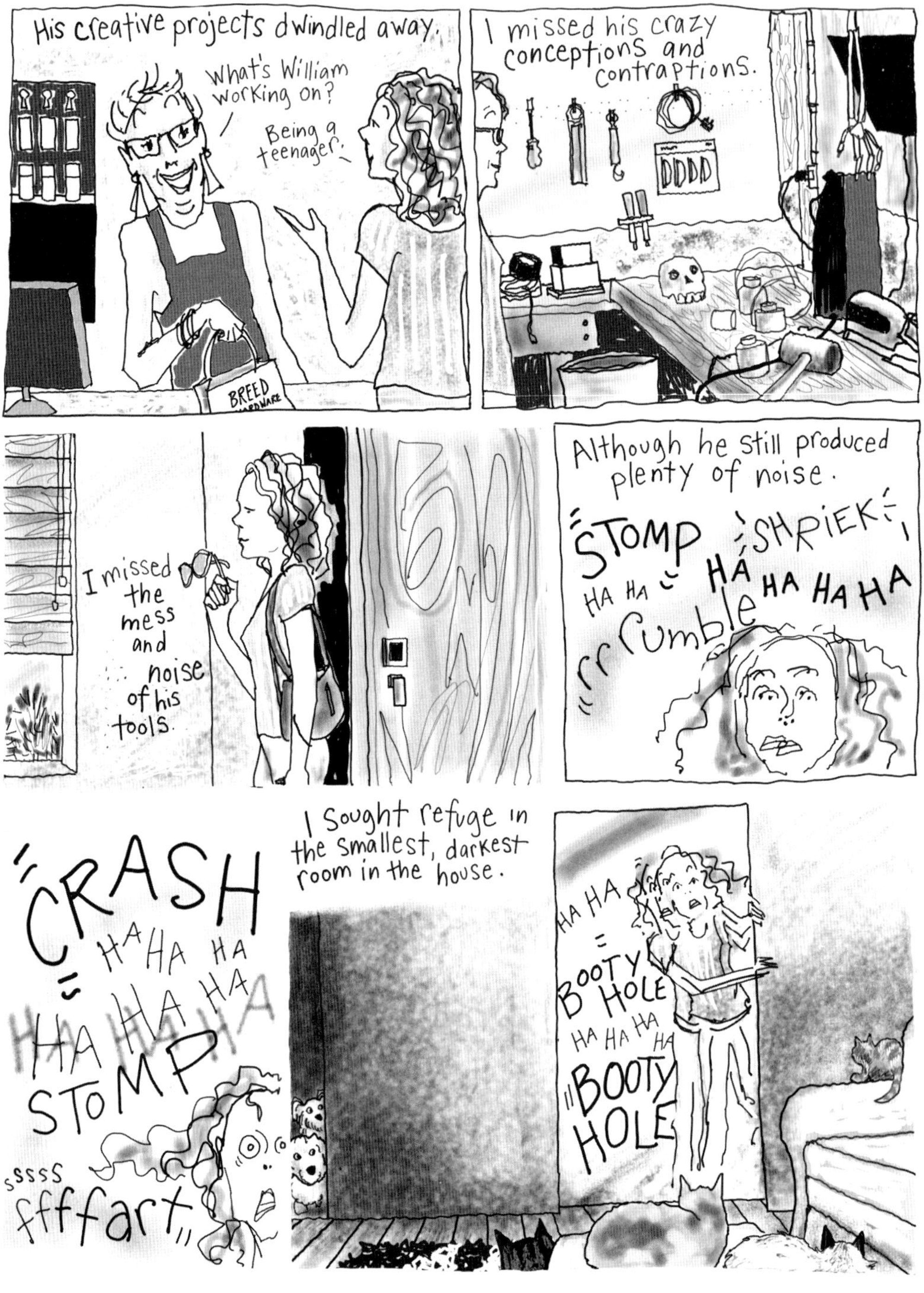
His creative projects dwindled away.
What's William working on?
Being a teenager.
BREED
I missed his crazy conceptions and contraptions.
I missed the mess and noise of his tools.
Although he still produced plenty of noise.
STOMP
SHRIEK
HA HA
HA HA HA HAHA
rrrumble
CRASH
HA HA HA
HA HA HA
HA HA HA
STOMP
sssss
fffart
I sought refuge in the smallest, darkest room in the house.
HA HA
BOOTY HOLE
HA HA HA HA
BOOTY HOLE

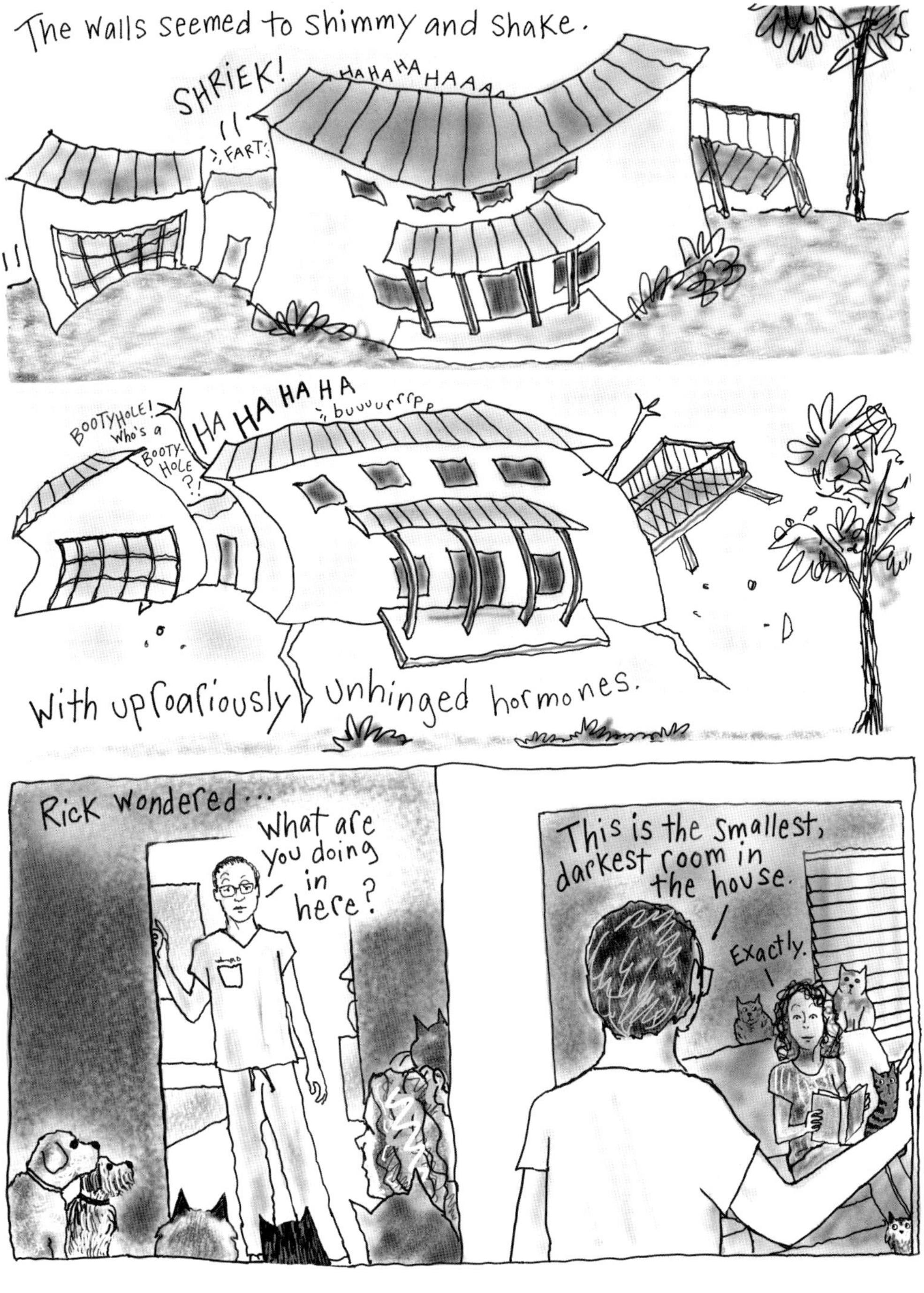
The walls seemed to shimmy and shake.
SHRIEK!
HAHAHAHAAA
FART
BOOTYHOLE! Who's a BOOTY-HOLE ?!
HA HA HA HA
buuuurrrpp
With uproariously unhinged hormones.
Rick wondered...
What are you doing in here?
This is the smallest, darkest room in the house.
Exactly.

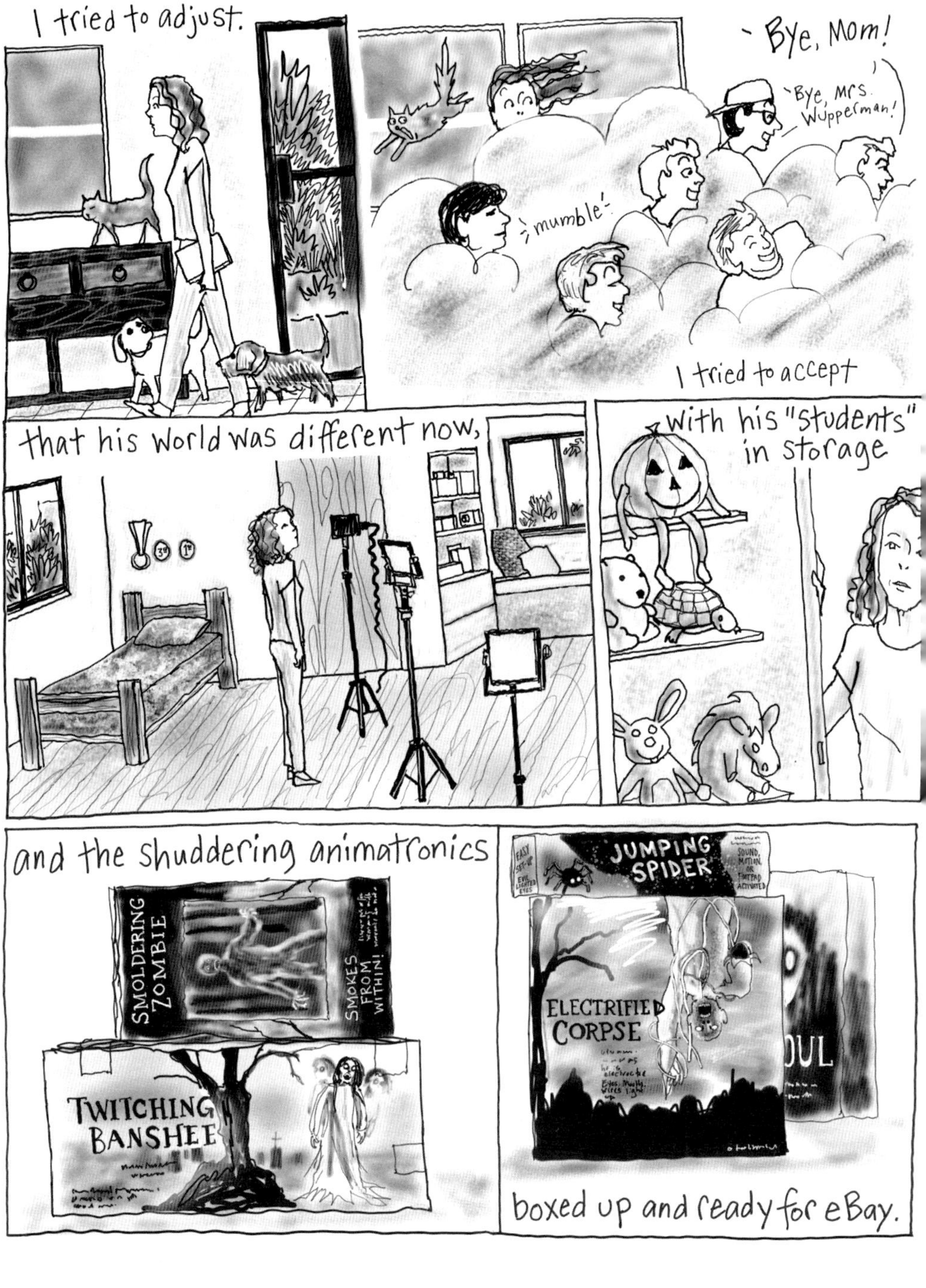
I tried to adjust.
Bye, Mom!
Bye, Mrs. Wupperman!
mumble
I tried to accept
that his world was different now,
with his "students" in storage
and the shuddering animatronics
SMOLDERING ZOMBIE
SMOKES FROM WITHIN!
TWITCHING BANSHEE
JUMPING SPIDER
EASY SET-UP
EVIL LIGHTED EYES
SOUND, MOTION, OR FOOTPAD ACTIVATED
ELECTRIFIED CORPSE
OUL
boxed up and ready for eBay.

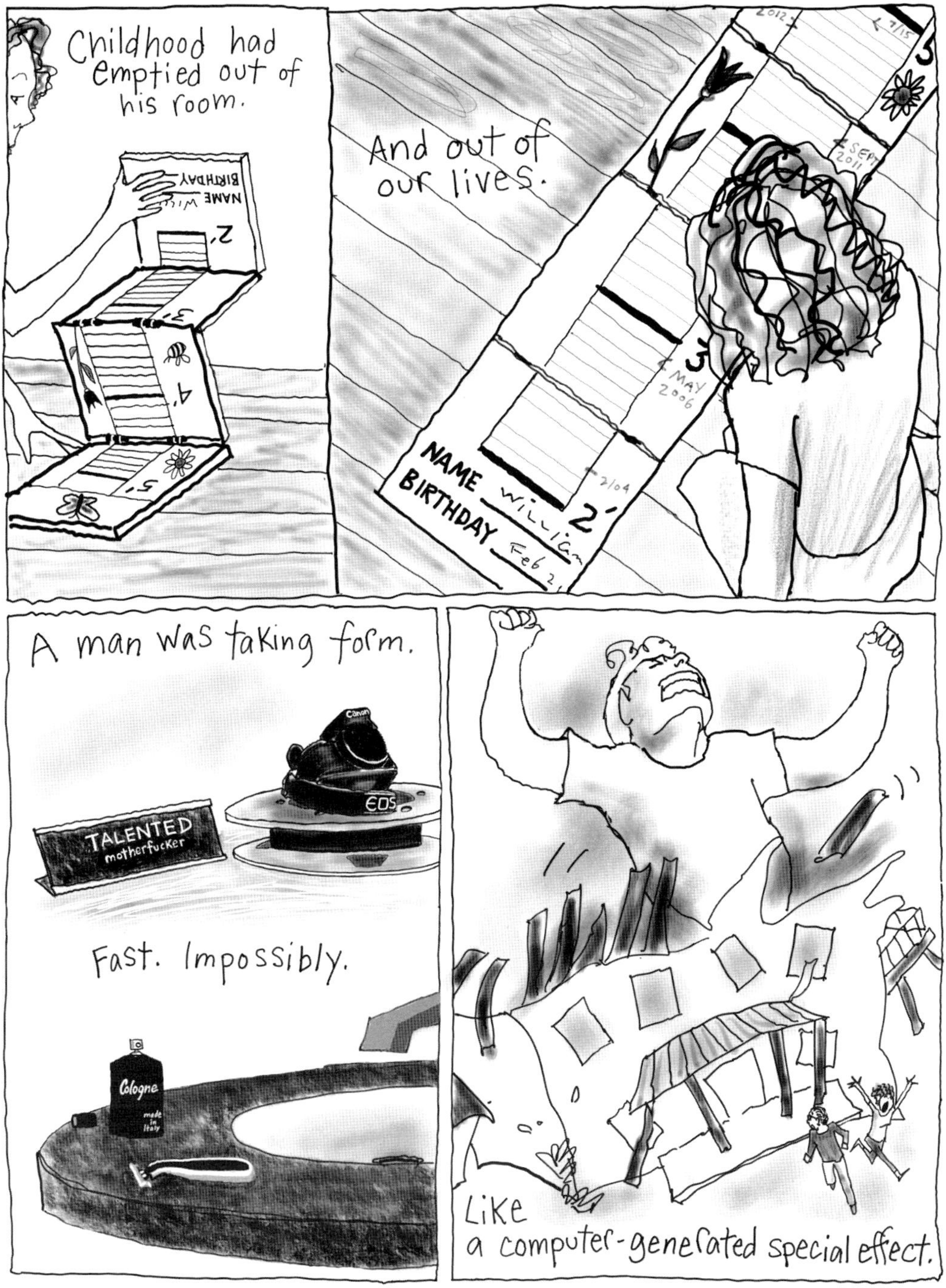
Childhood had emptied out of his room.
NAME
BIRTHDAY
And out of our lives.
NAME William
BIRTHDAY Feb 2
MAY 2006
SEPT 2011
2012
A man was taking form.
Canon
EOS
TALENTED motherfucker
Fast. Impossibly.
Cologne
made in Italy
Like a computer-generated special effect.

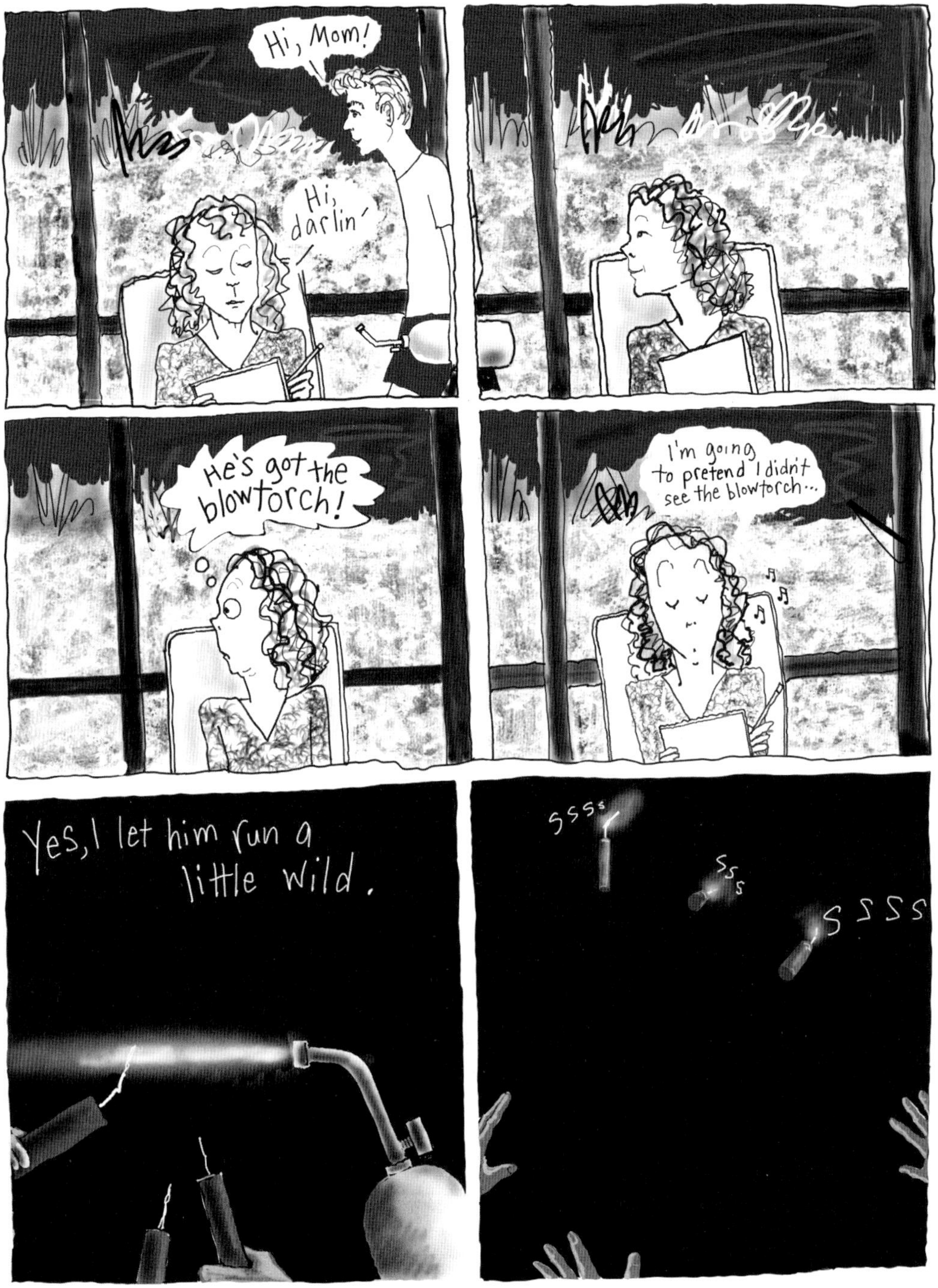
Hi, Mom!
Hi, darlin'
He's got the blowtorch!
I'm going to pretend I didn't see the blowtorch...
Yes, I let him run a little wild.
ssss
sss
ssss

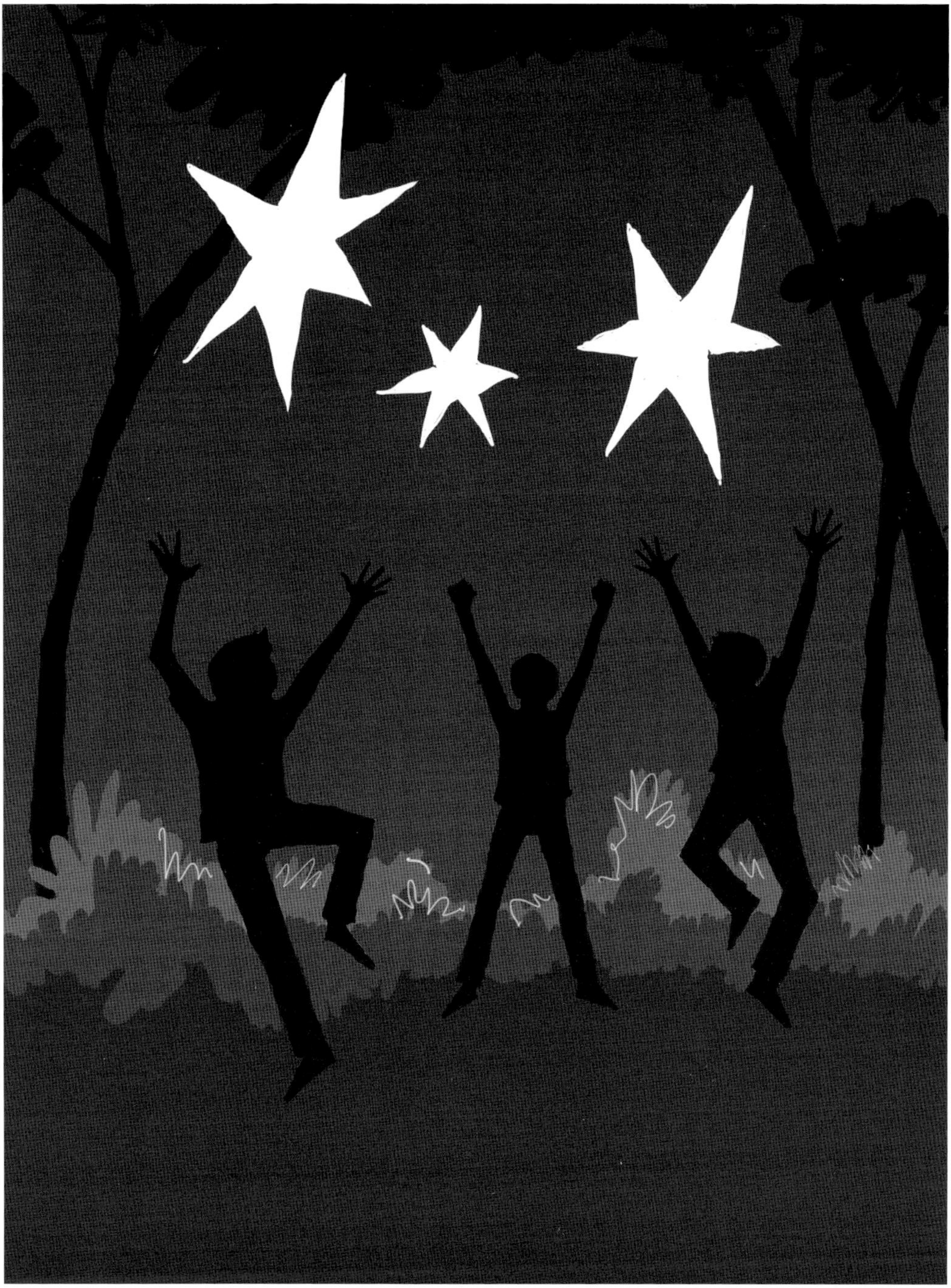

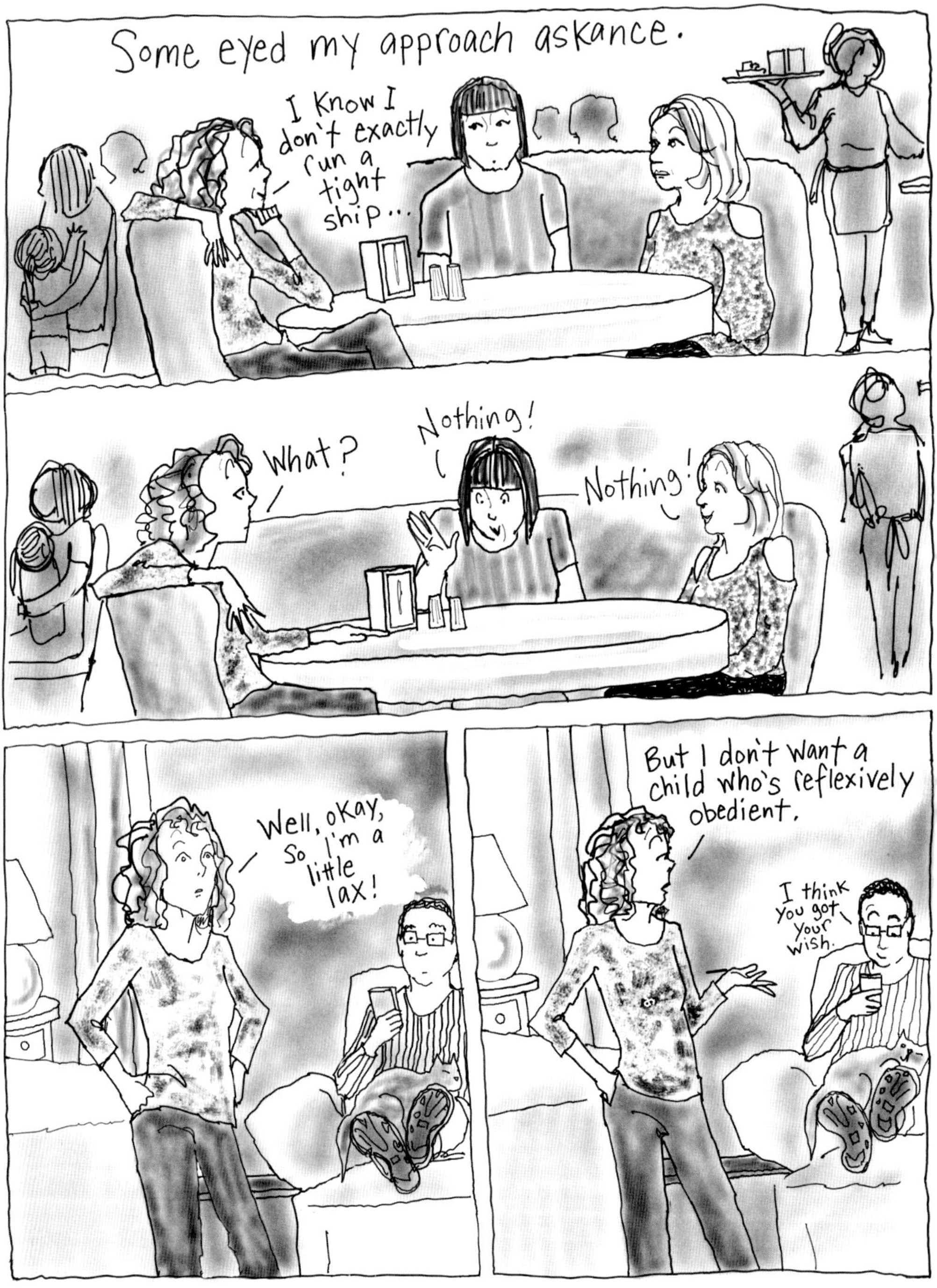

Some eyed my approach askance.
I know I don't exactly run a tight ship...
What?
Nothing!
Nothing!
Well, okay, so I'm a little lax!
But I don't want a child who's reflexively obedient.
I think you got your wish.

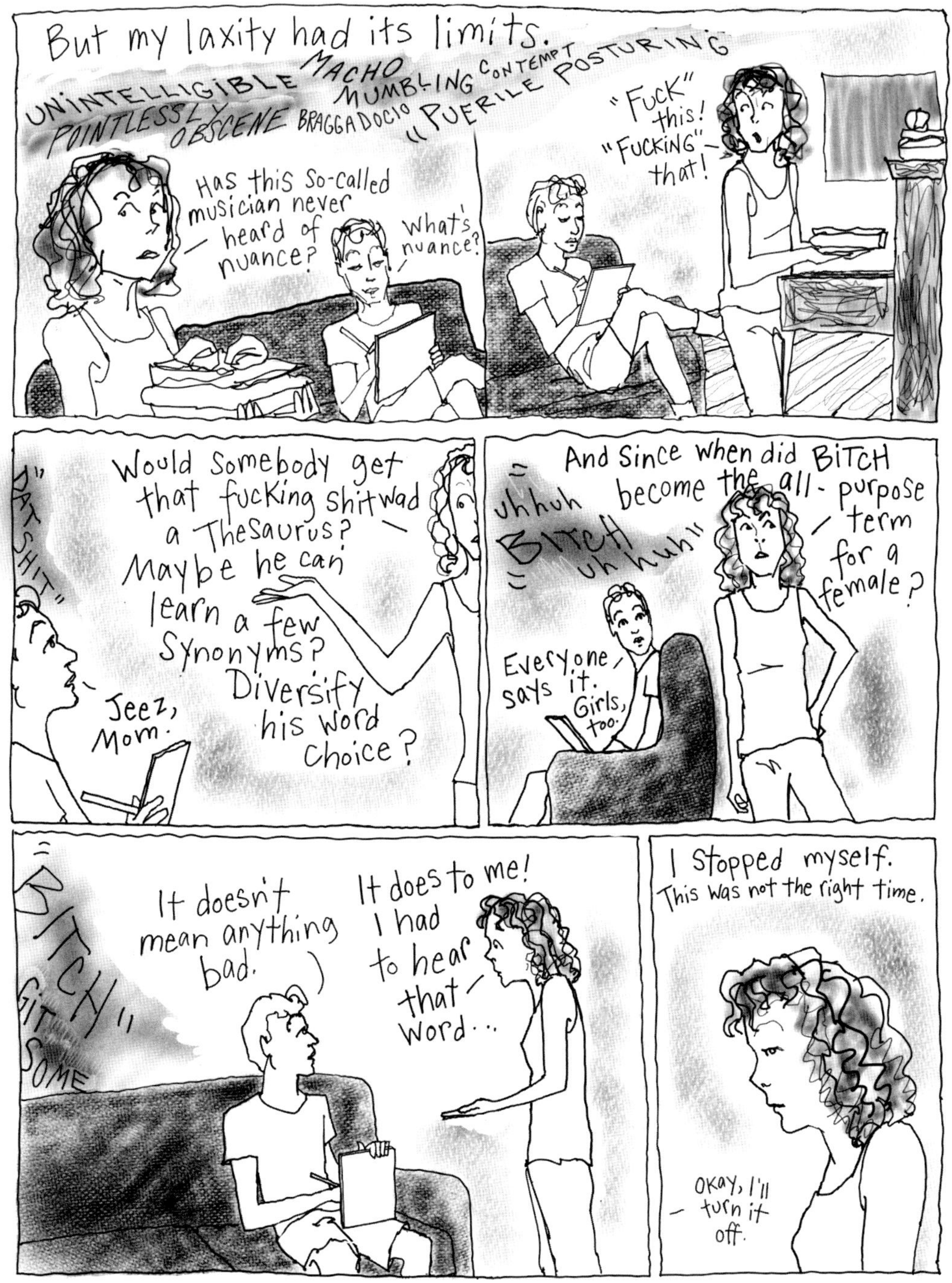

But my laxity had its limits.
UNINTELLIGIBLE MACHO MUMBLING CONTEMPT POINTLESSLY OBSCENE BRAGGADOCIO "PUERILE POSTURING"
Has this so-called musician never heard of nuance?
What's nuance?
"FUCK" this! "FUCKING" that!
Would somebody get that fucking shitwad a Thesaurus? Maybe he can learn a few synonyms? Diversify his word choice?
"DAT SHIT"
Jeez, Mom.
And since when did BITCH become the all-purpose term for a female?
"uhhuh BITCH uh huh"
Everyone says it.
Girls, too.
"BITCH" GIT SOME
It doesn't mean anything bad.
It does to me! I had to hear that word...
I stopped myself. This was not the right time.
Okay, I'll turn it off.

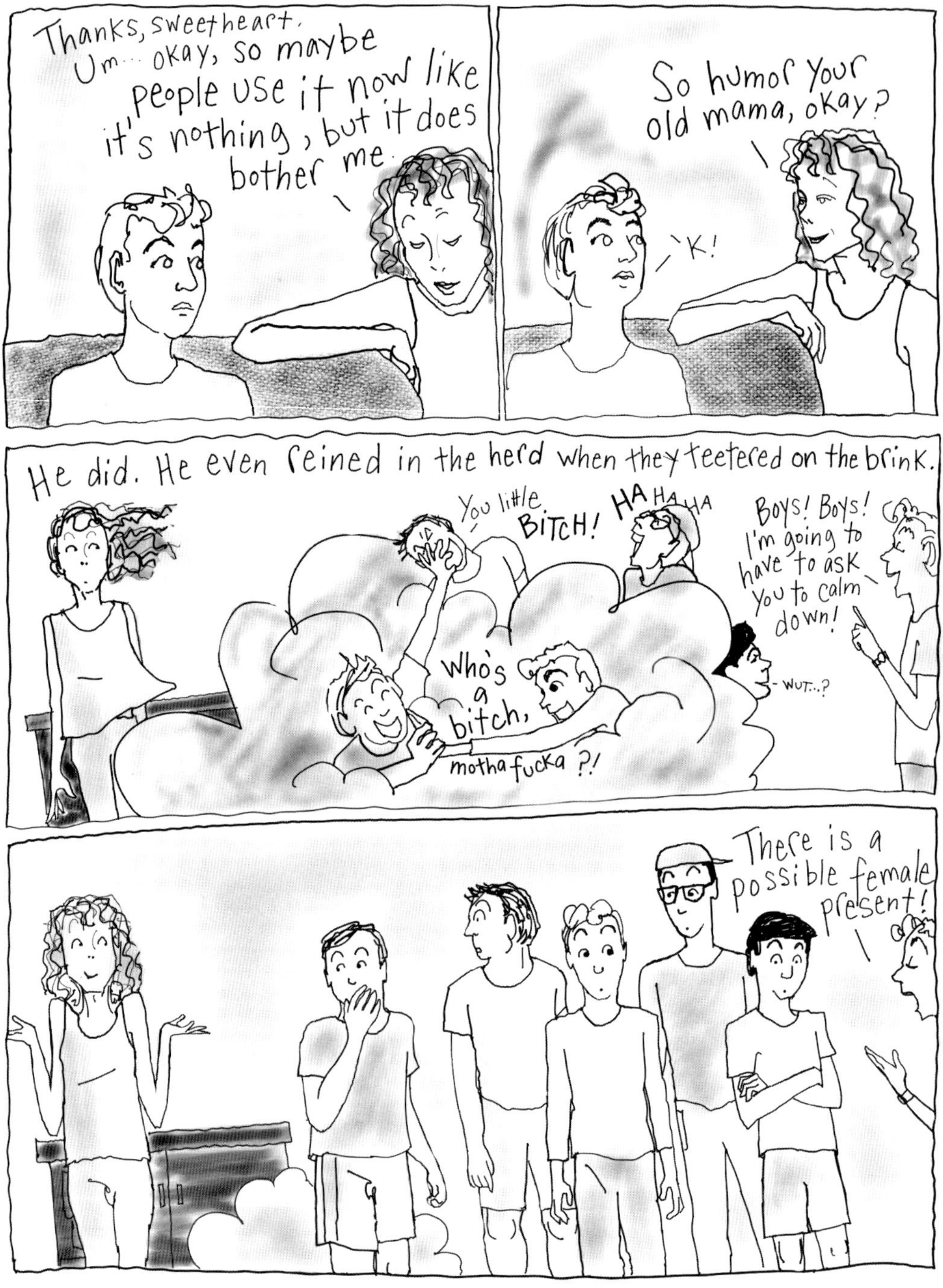
Thanks, sweetheart. Um... okay, so maybe people use it now like it's nothing, but it does bother me.
So humor your old mama, okay?
'K!
He did. He even reined in the herd when they teetered on the brink.
You little BITCH!
HA HA HA HA
Boys! Boys! I'm going to have to ask you to calm down!
Who's a bitch, motha fucka ?!
- WUT...?
There is a possible female present!

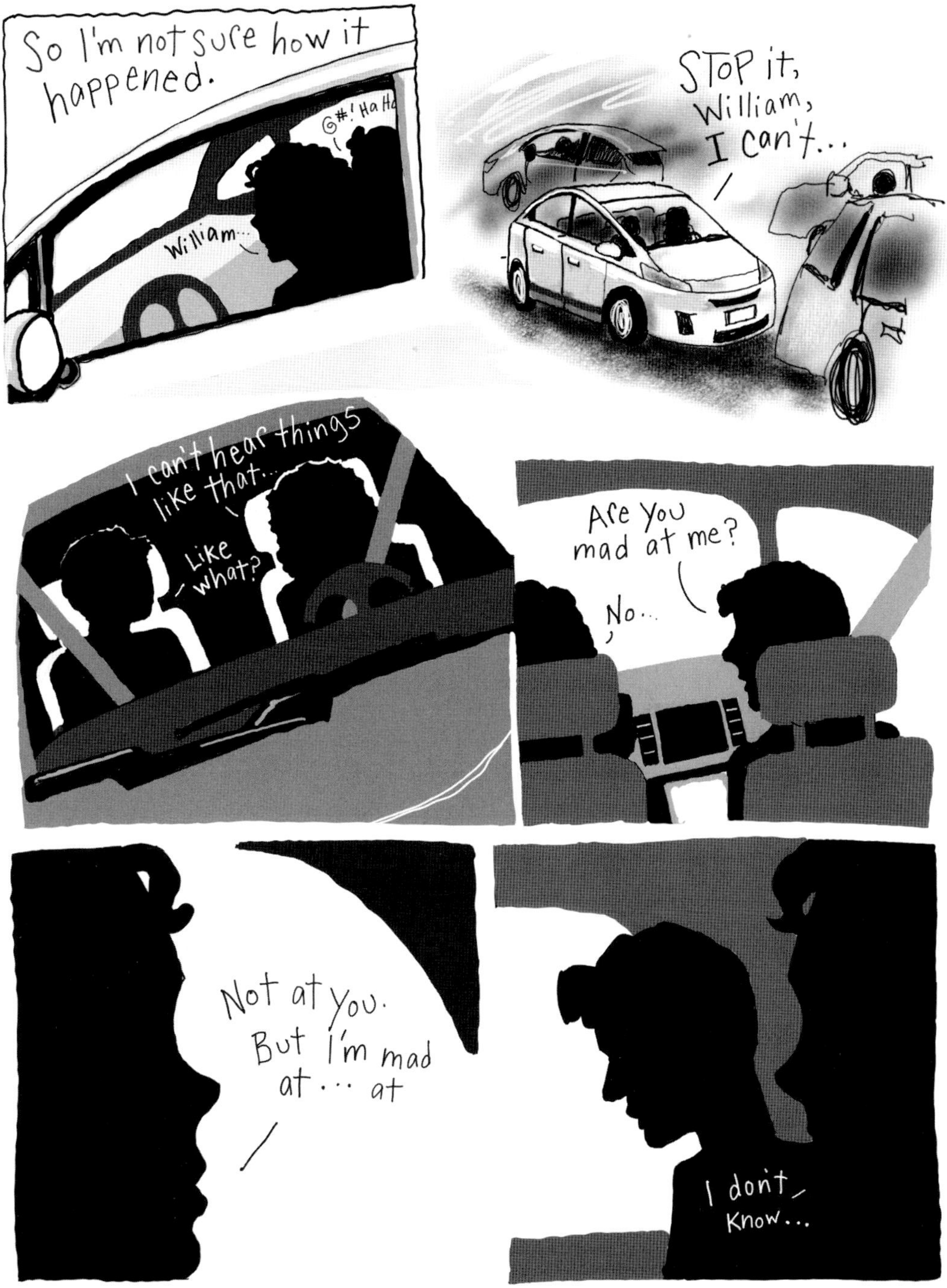

So I'm not sure how it happened.
@#! Ha Ha
William...
STOP it, William, I can't...
I can't hear things like that...
Like what?
Are you mad at me?
No...
Not at you. But I'm mad at... at
I don't know...

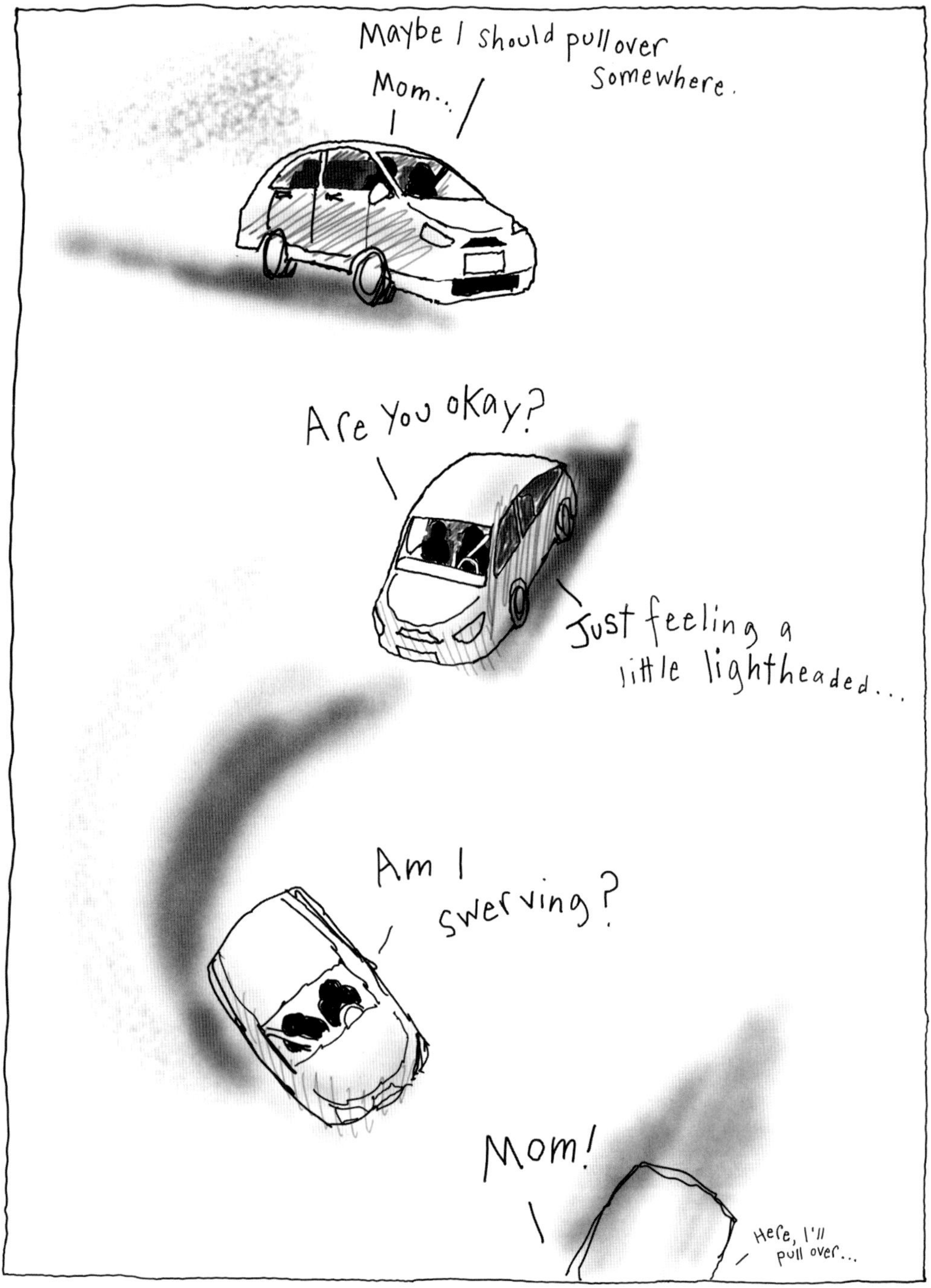
Maybe I should pull over somewhere.
Mom...
Are you okay?
Just feeling a little lightheaded...
Am I swerving?
Mom!
Here, I'll pull over...

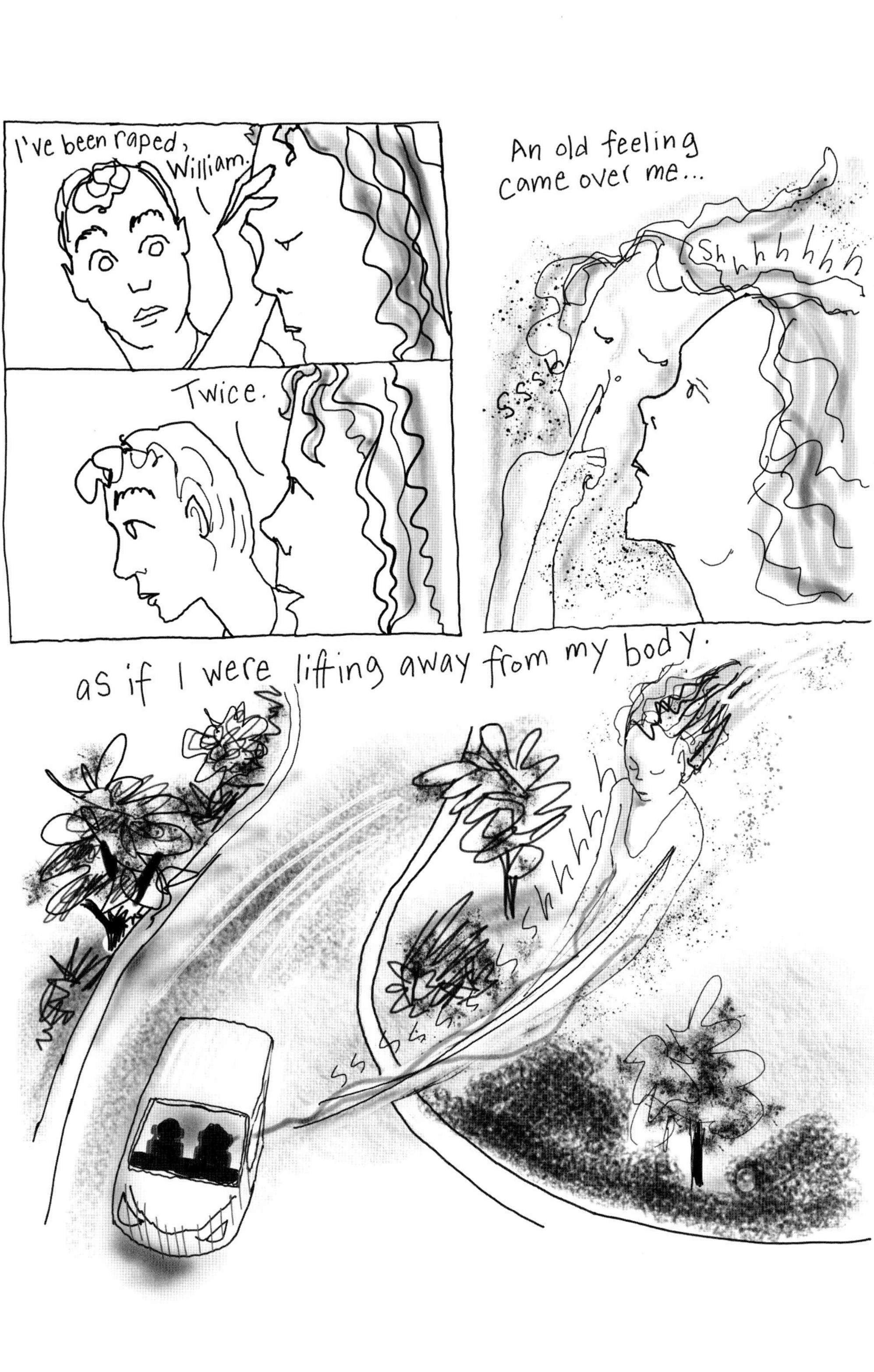
I've been raped, William.
Twice.
An old feeling came over me...
Shhhhhhh
sssh
as if I were lifting away from my body.
sssssshhhhhhh

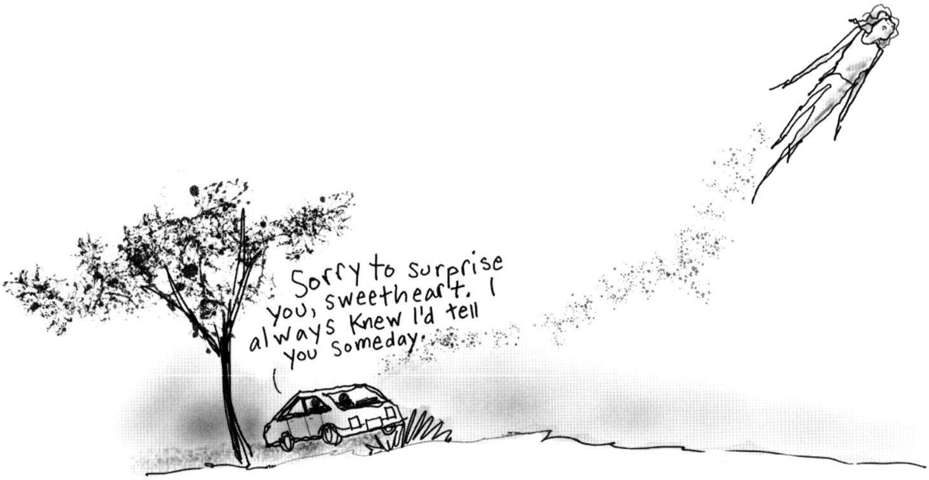
Sorry to surprise you, sweetheart. I always Knew I'd tell you someday.

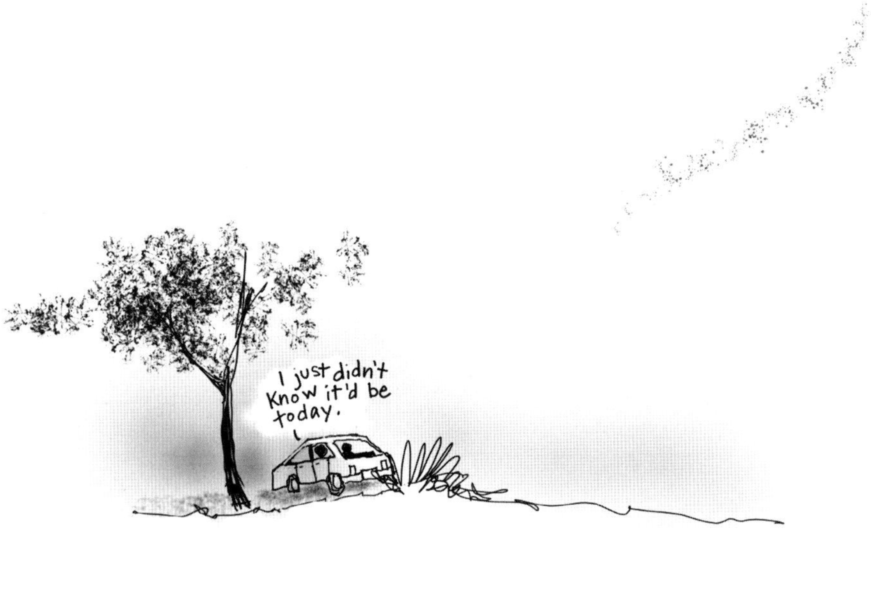
I just didn't Know it'd be today.

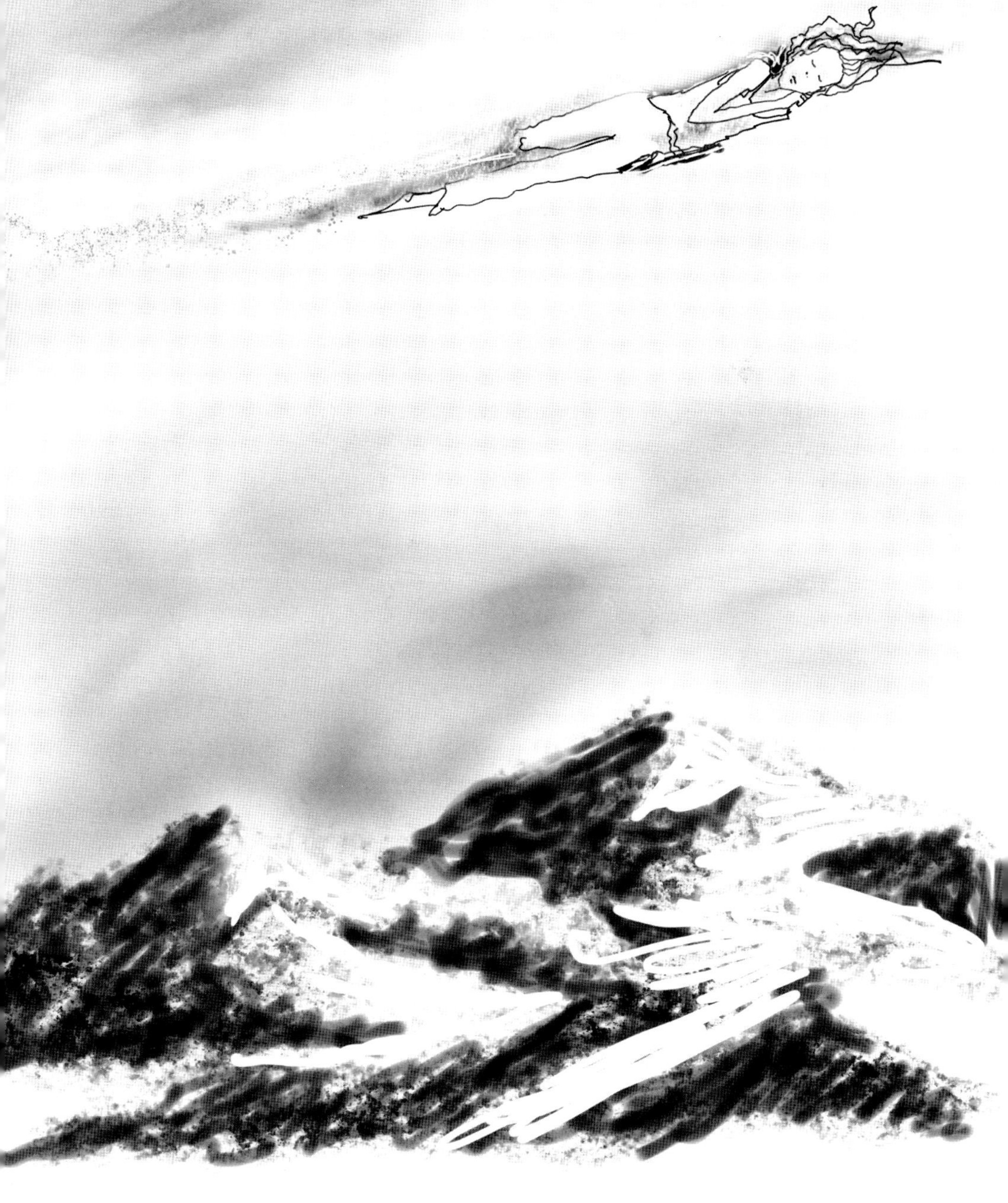

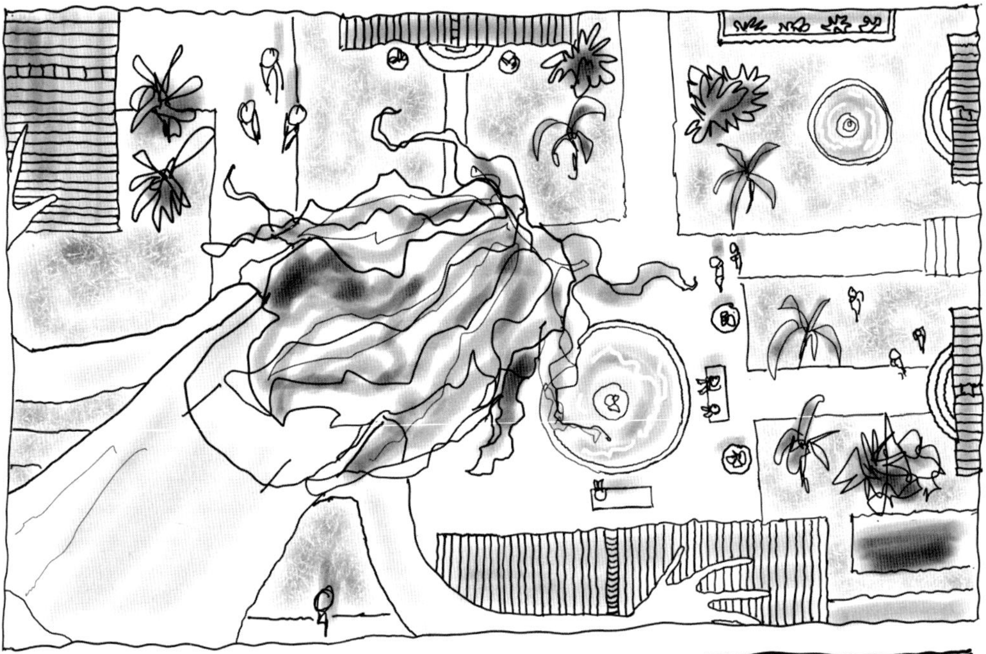

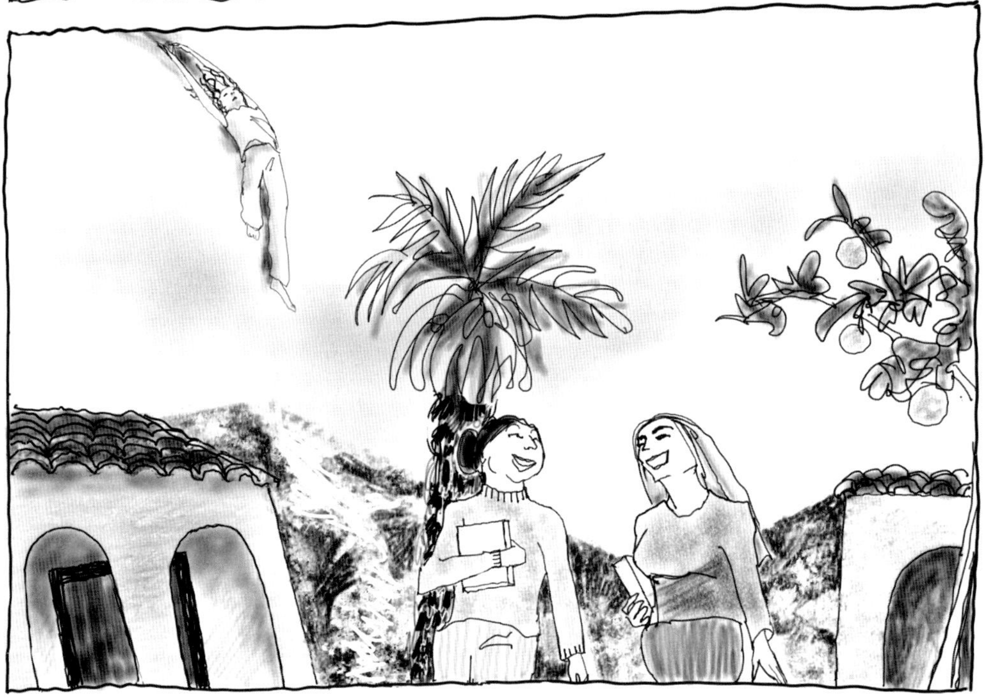

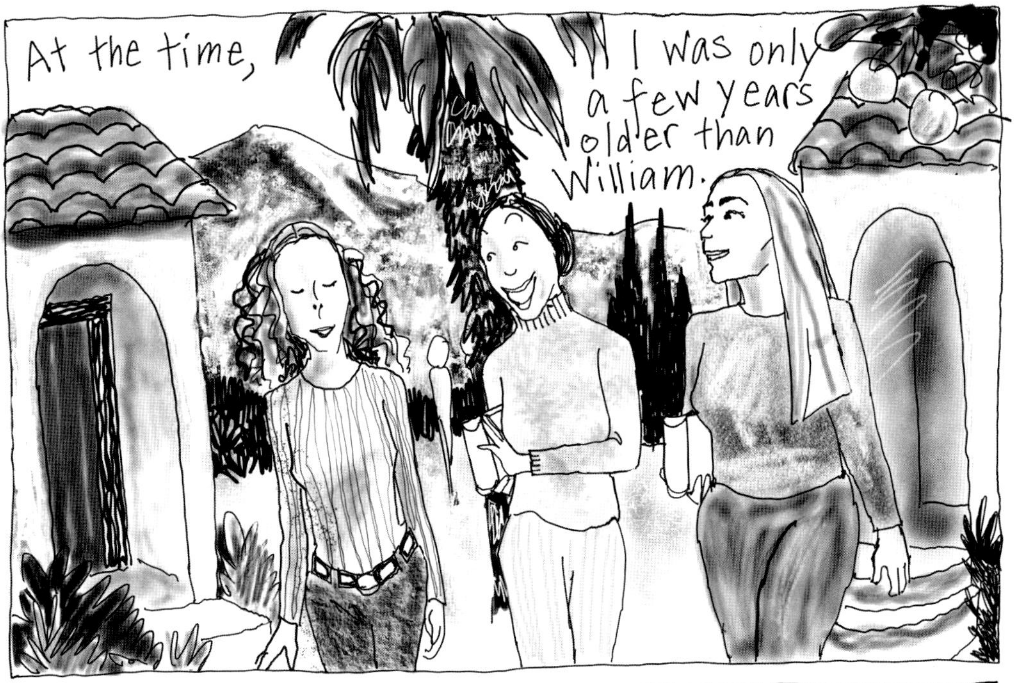
At the time,
I was only a few years older than William.

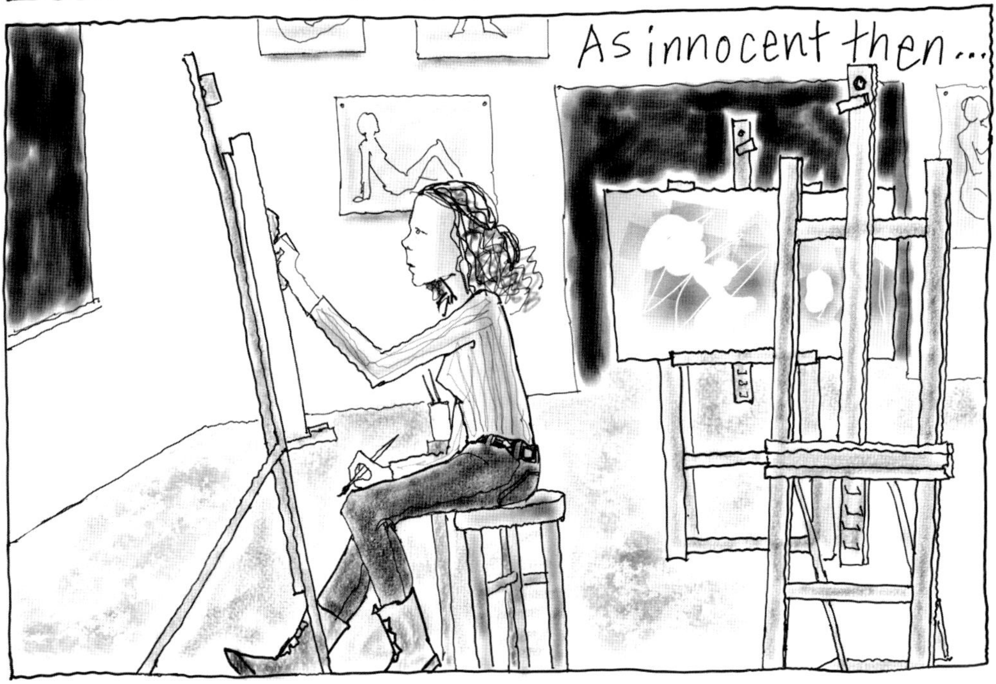
As innocent then...

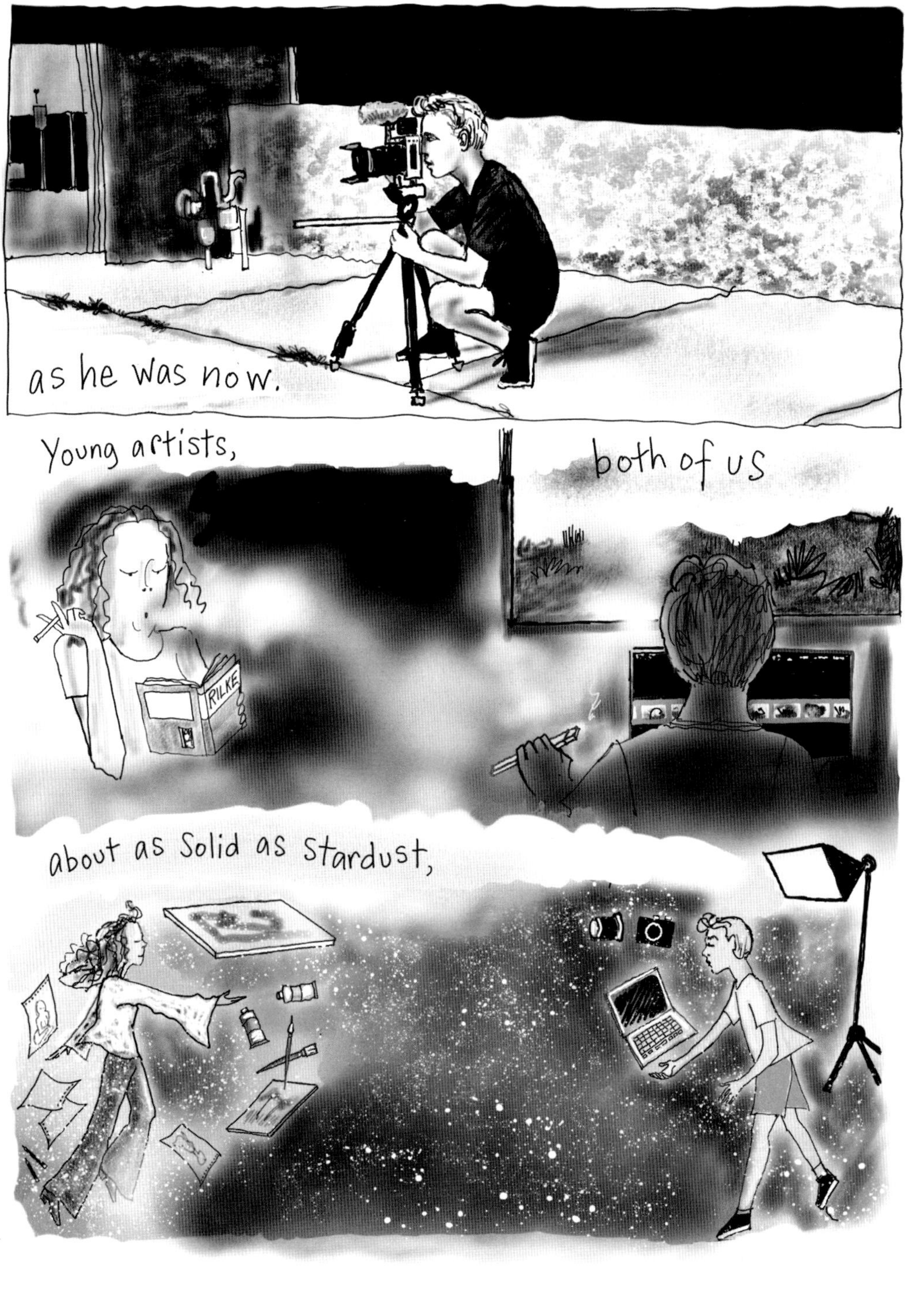
as he was now.
Young artists,
both of us
RILKE
about as Solid as Stardust,

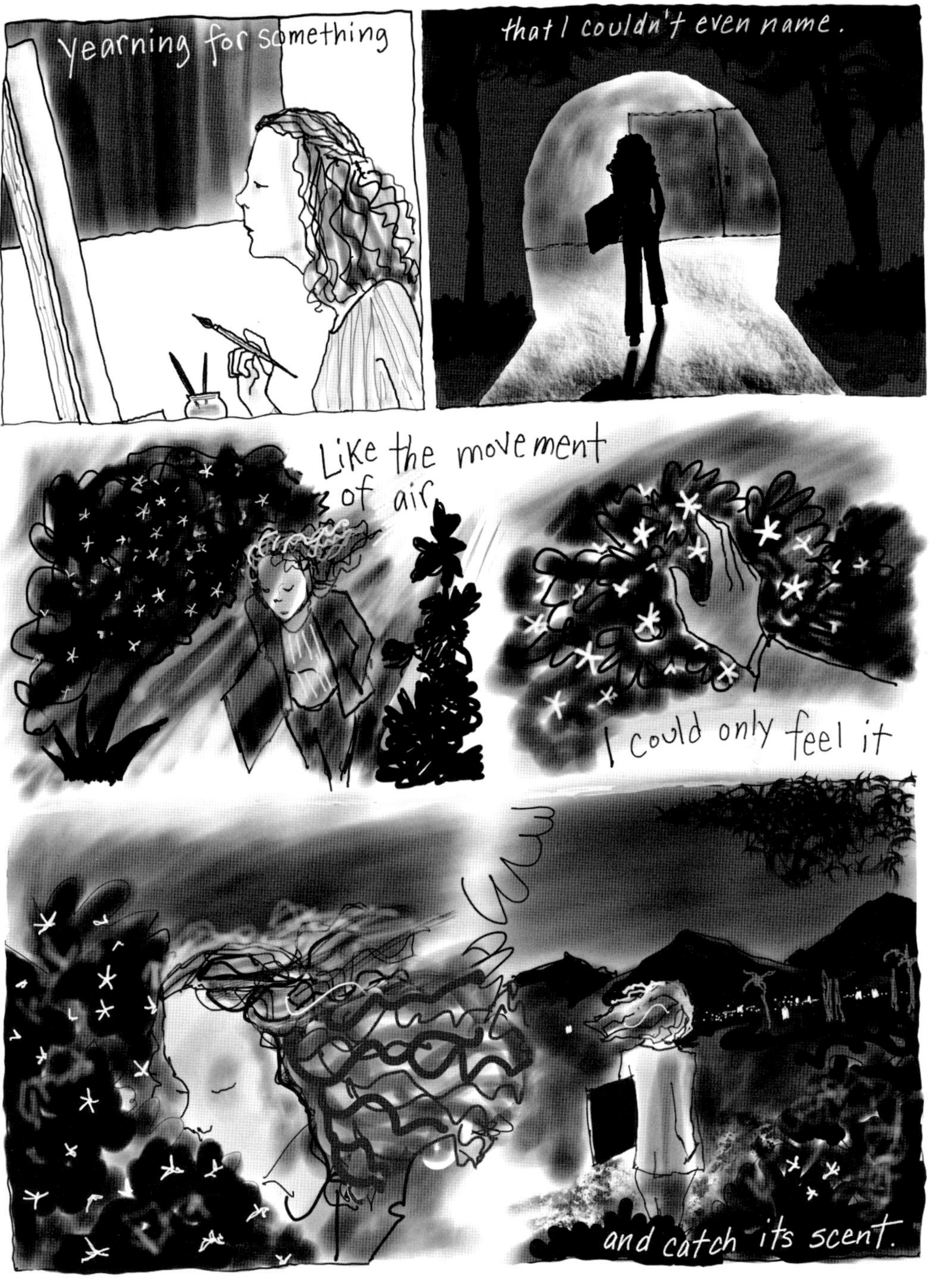
yearning for something
that I couldn't even name.
Like the movement of air
I could only feel it
and catch its scent.

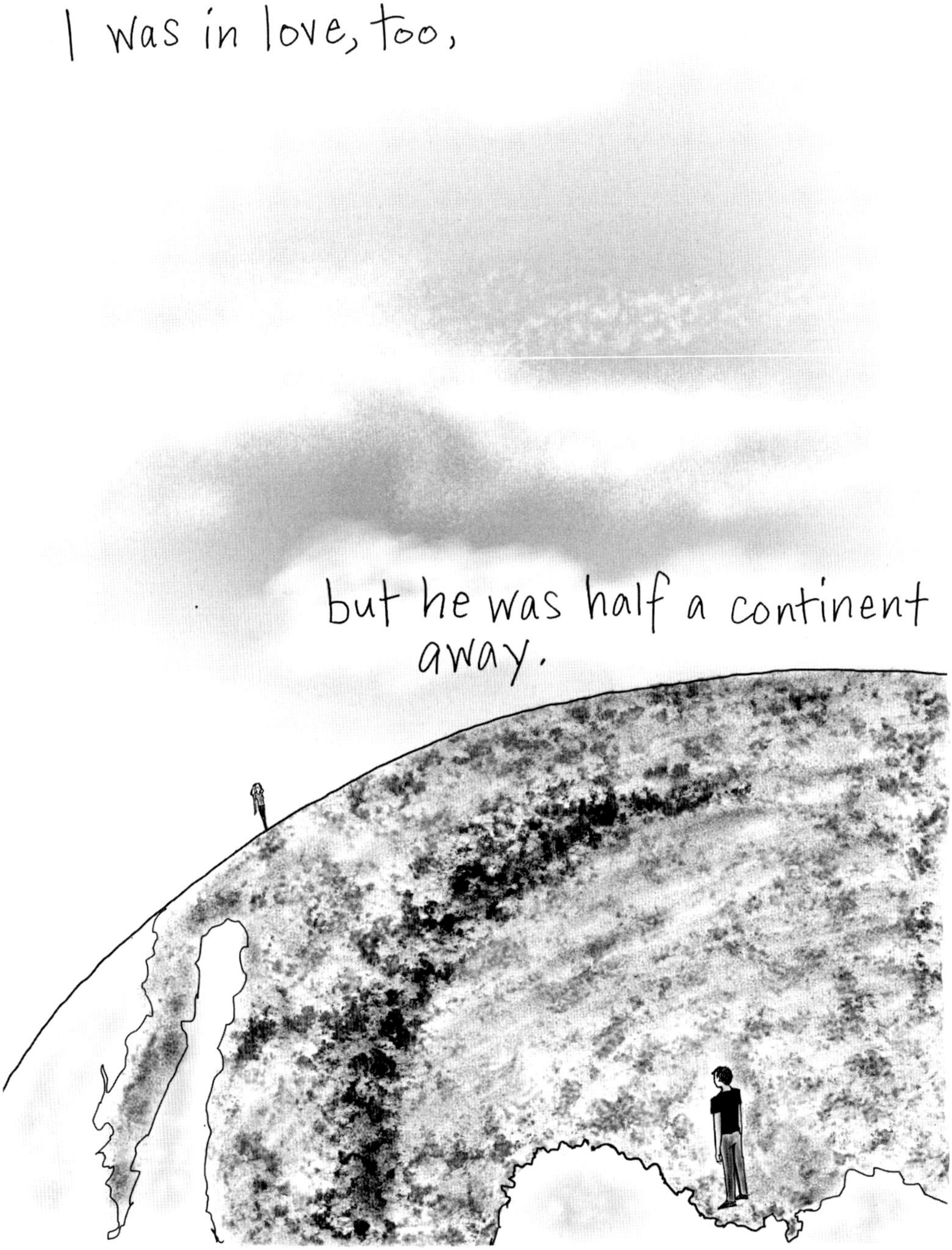
I was in love, too,
but he was half a continent away.

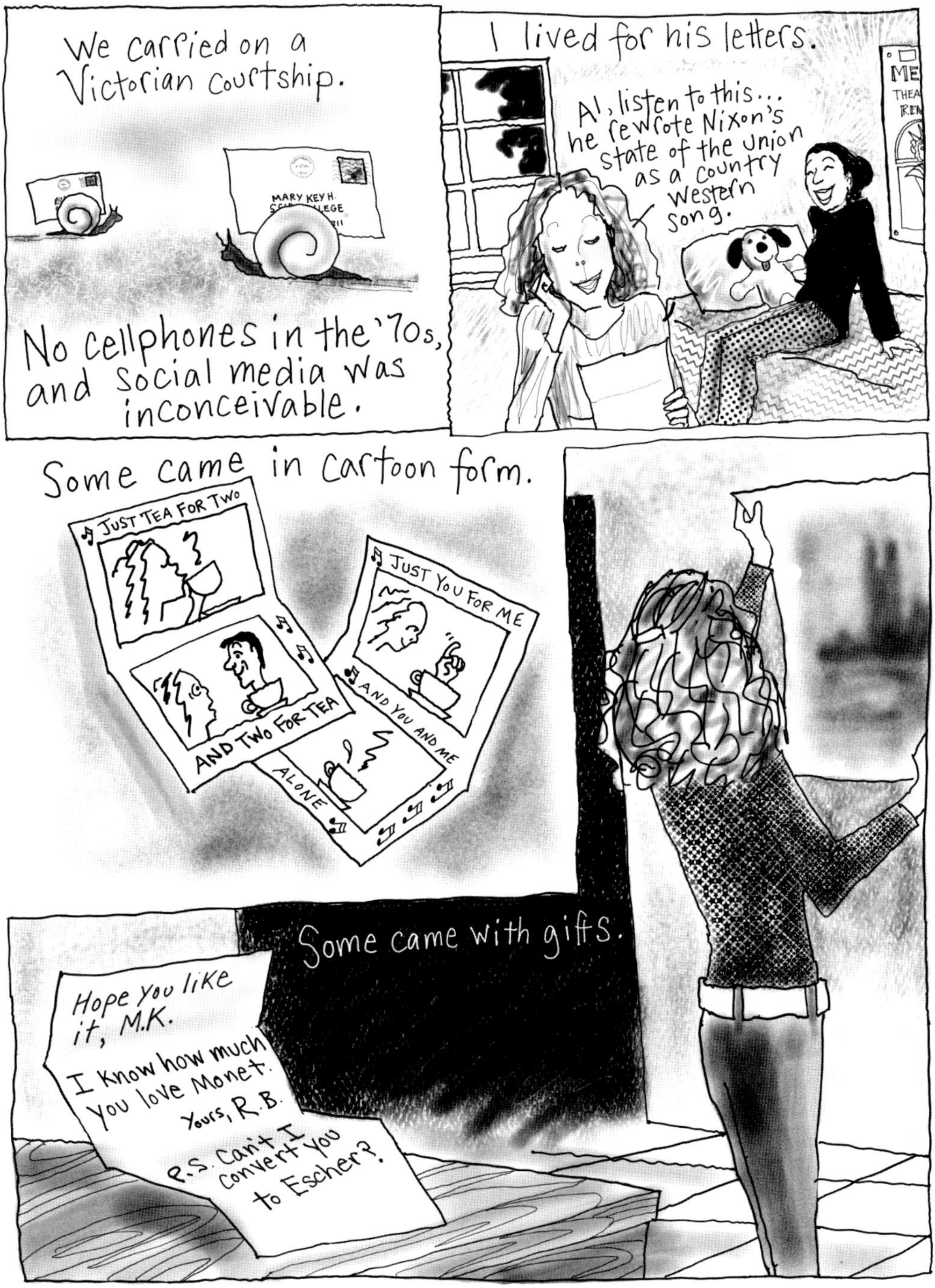
We carried on a Victorian courtship.
MARY KEY H.
No cellphones in the '70s, and social media was inconceivable.
I lived for his letters.
Al, listen to this... he rewrote Nixon's state of the union as a country western song.
Some came in cartoon form.
JUST TEA FOR TWO
AND TWO FOR TEA
JUST YOU FOR ME
AND YOU AND ME
ALONE
Some came with gifts.
Hope you like it, M.K.
I know how much you love Monet.
Yours, R.B.
P.S. Can't I convert you to Escher?

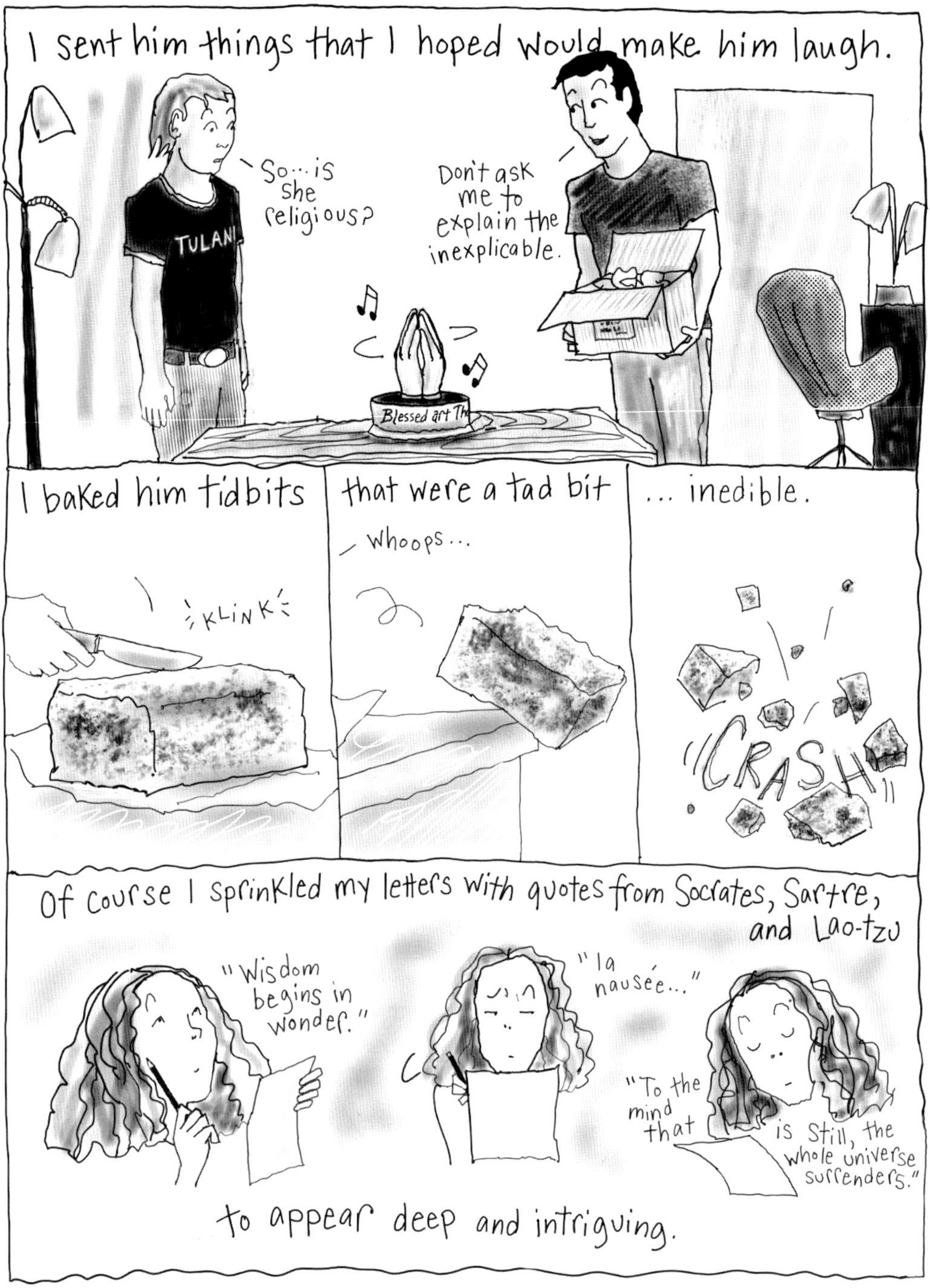
I sent him things that I hoped would make him laugh.
So... is she religious?
Don't ask me to explain the inexplicable.
TULAN
Blessed art Th
I baked him tidbits
KLINK
that were a tad bit
Whoops...
... inedible.
CRASH
Of course I sprinkled my letters with quotes from Socrates, Sartre, and Lao-tzu
"Wisdom begins in wonder."
"la nausée..."
"To the mind that is still, the whole universe surrenders."
to appear deep and intriguing.

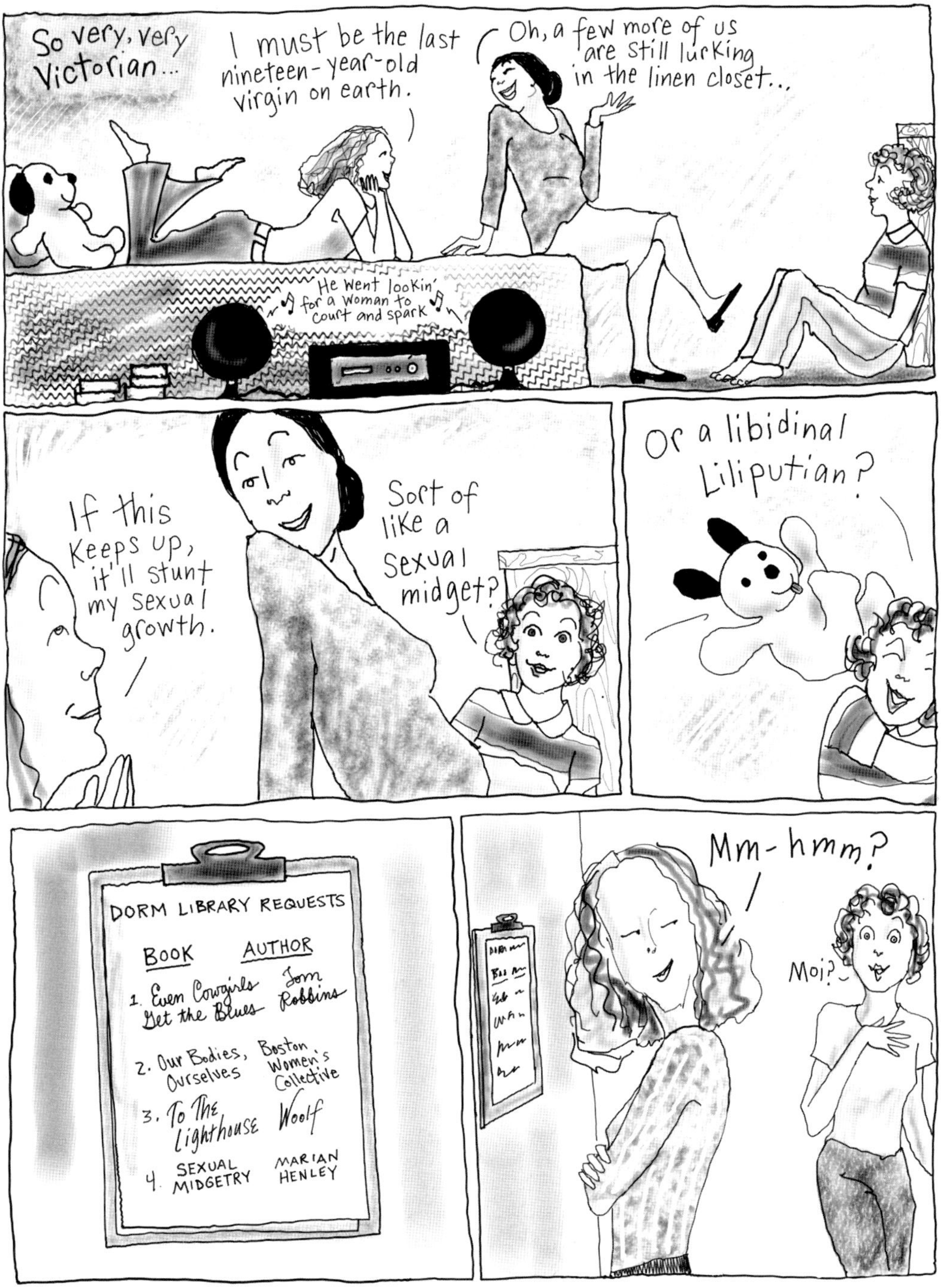
So very, very Victorian...
I must be the last nineteen-year-old virgin on earth.
Oh, a few more of us are still lurking in the linen closet...
He went lookin' for a woman to court and spark
If this keeps up, it'll stunt my sexual growth.
Sort of like a sexual midget?
Or a libidinal Liliputian?
DORM LIBRARY REQUESTS
BOOK AUTHOR
1. Even Cowgirls Get the Blues Tom Robbins
2. Our Bodies, Ourselves Boston Women's Collective
3. To The Lighthouse Woolf
4. SEXUAL MIDGETRY MARIAN HENLEY
Mm-hmm?
Moi?

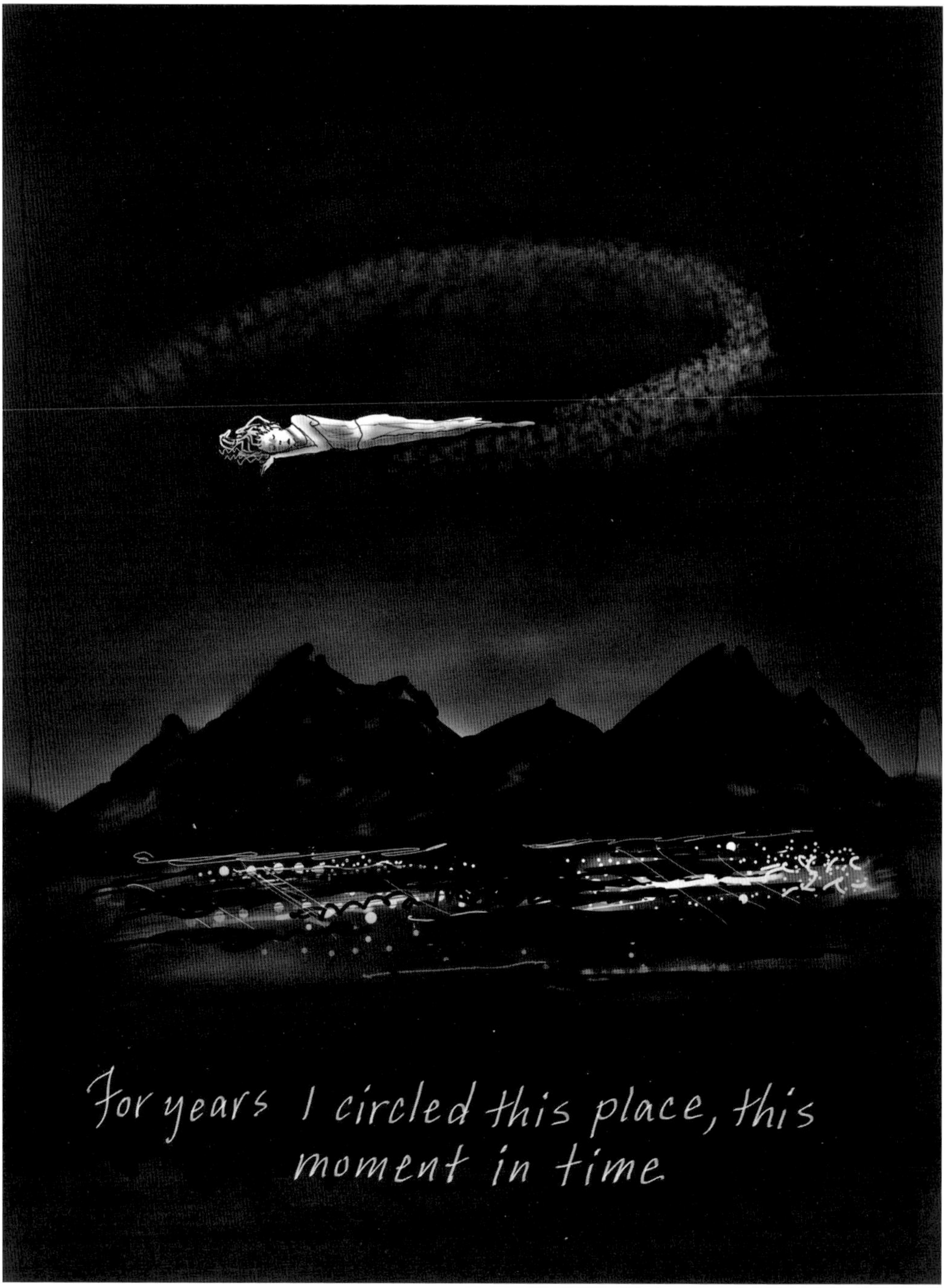
For years I circled this place, this moment in time.

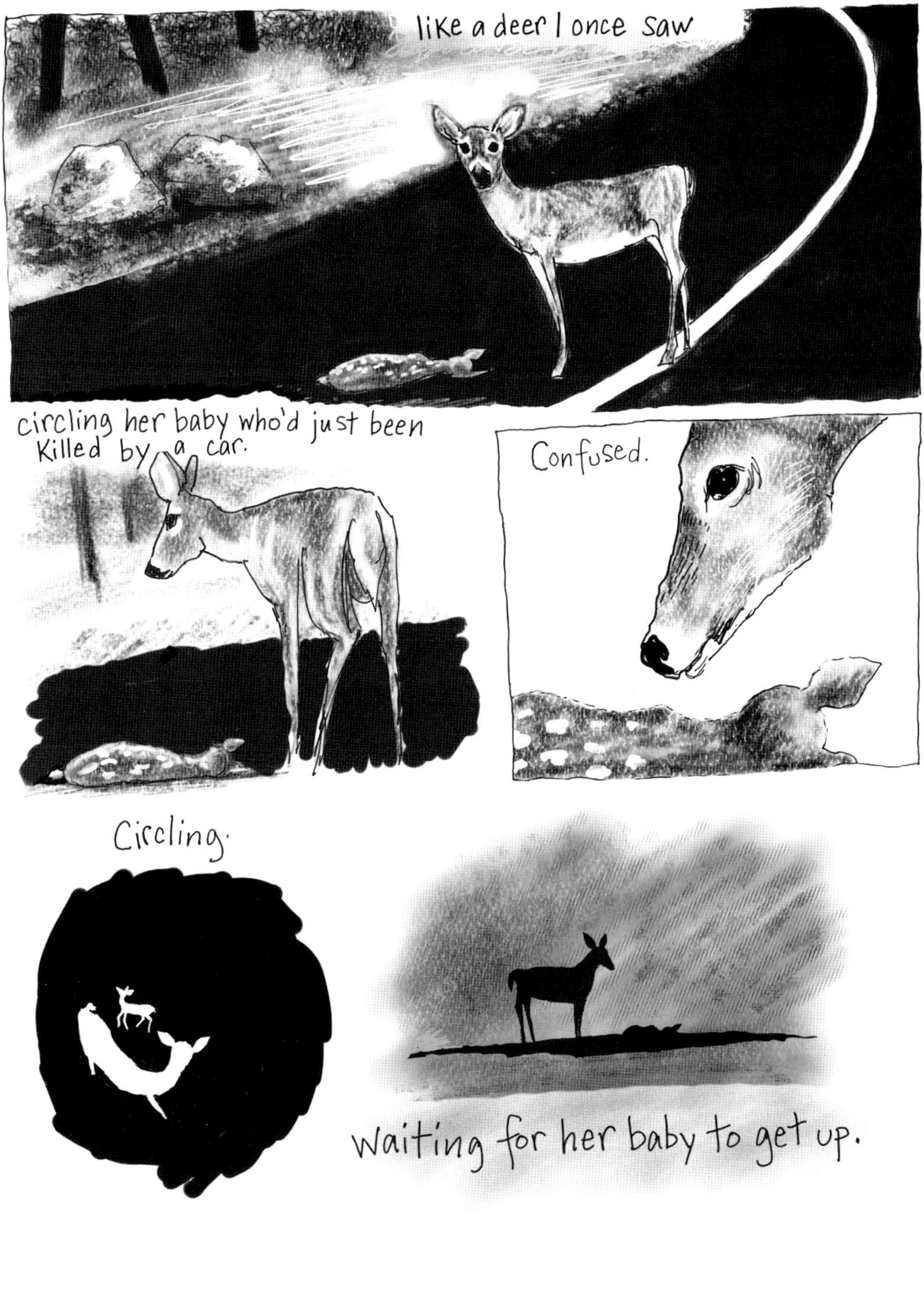
like a deer I once saw
circling her baby who'd just been killed by a car.
Confused.
Circling.
waiting for her baby to get up.

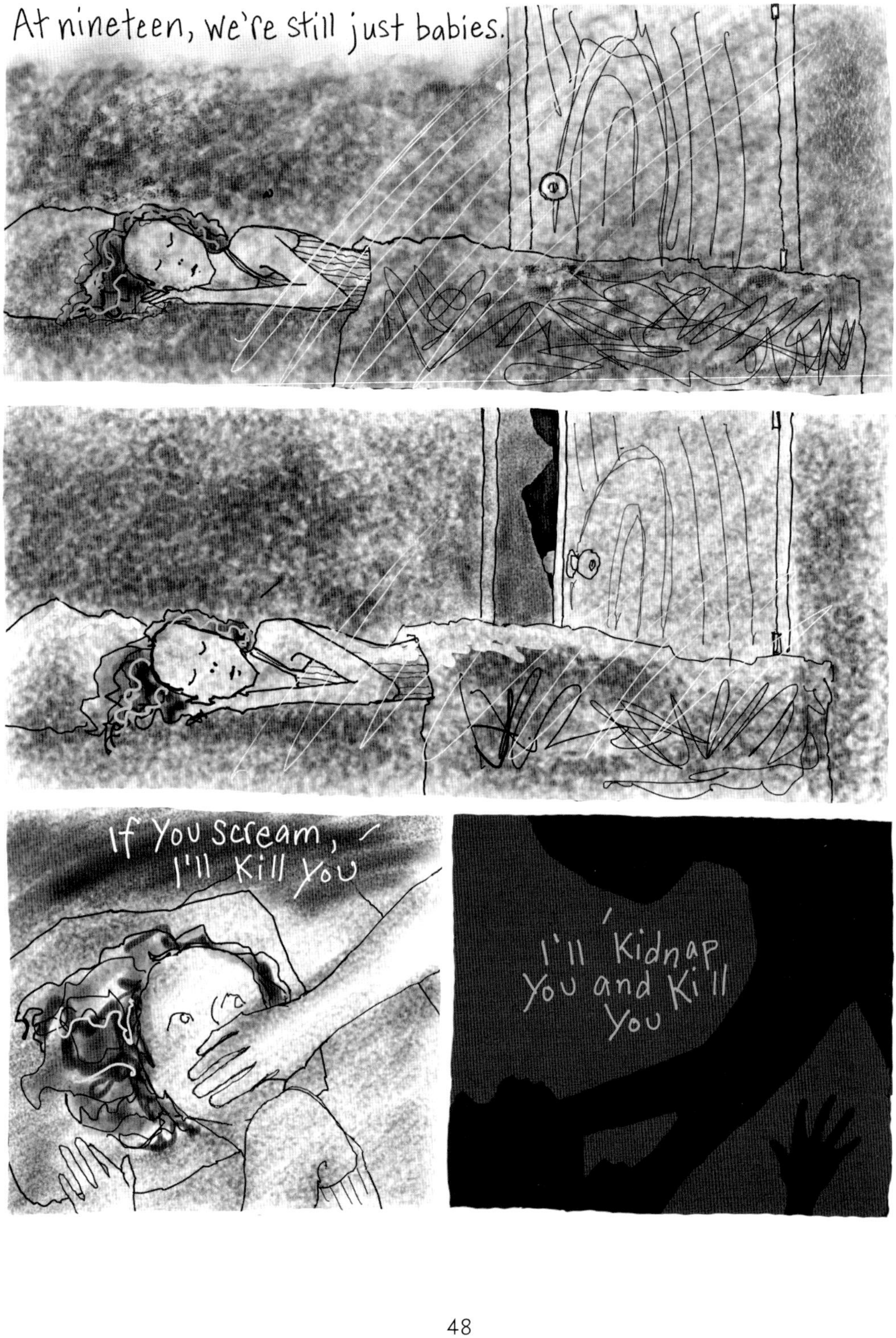
At nineteen, we're still just babies.
If you scream, I'll kill you
I'll kidnap you and kill you

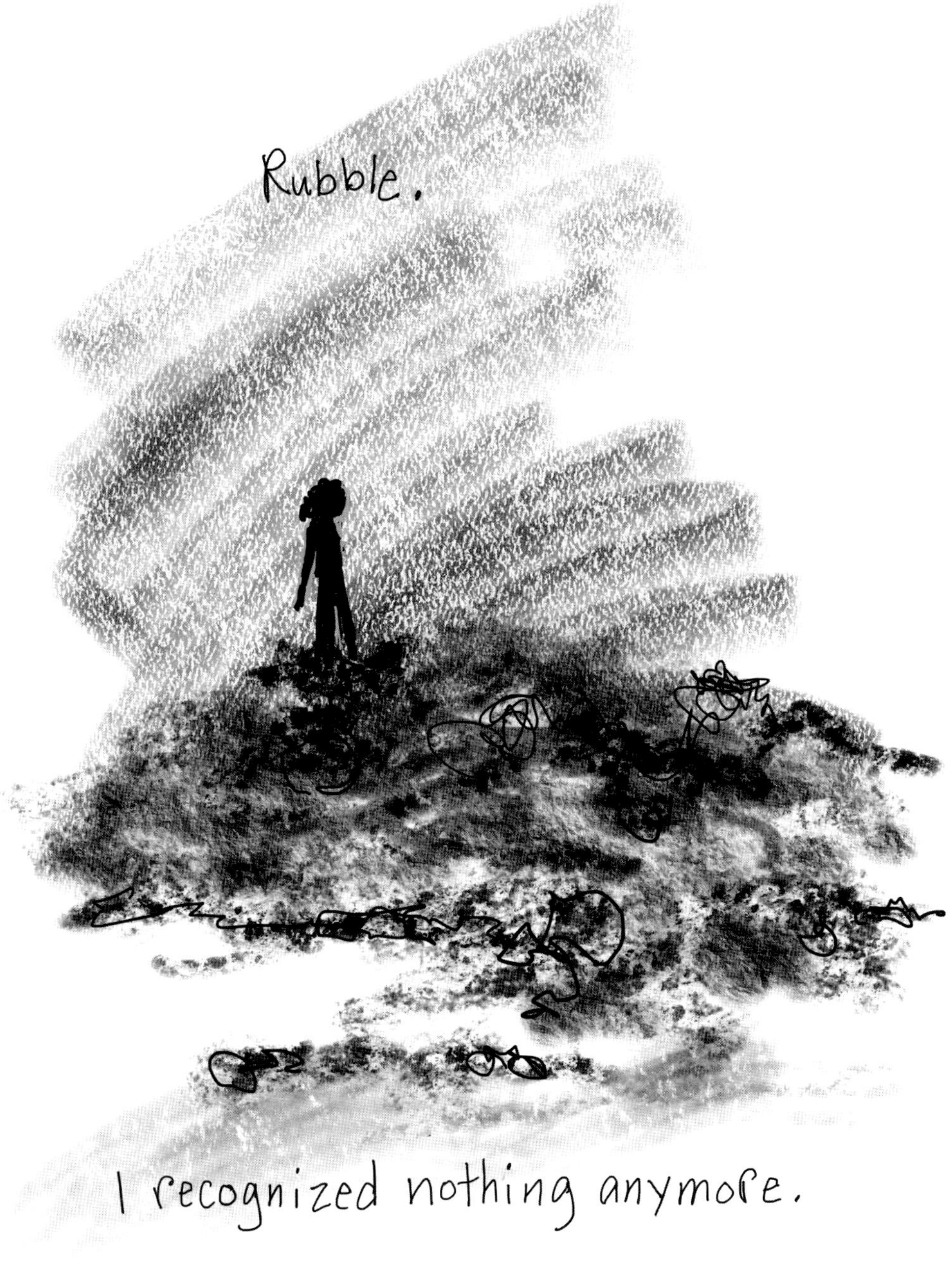
Rubble.
I recognized nothing anymore.

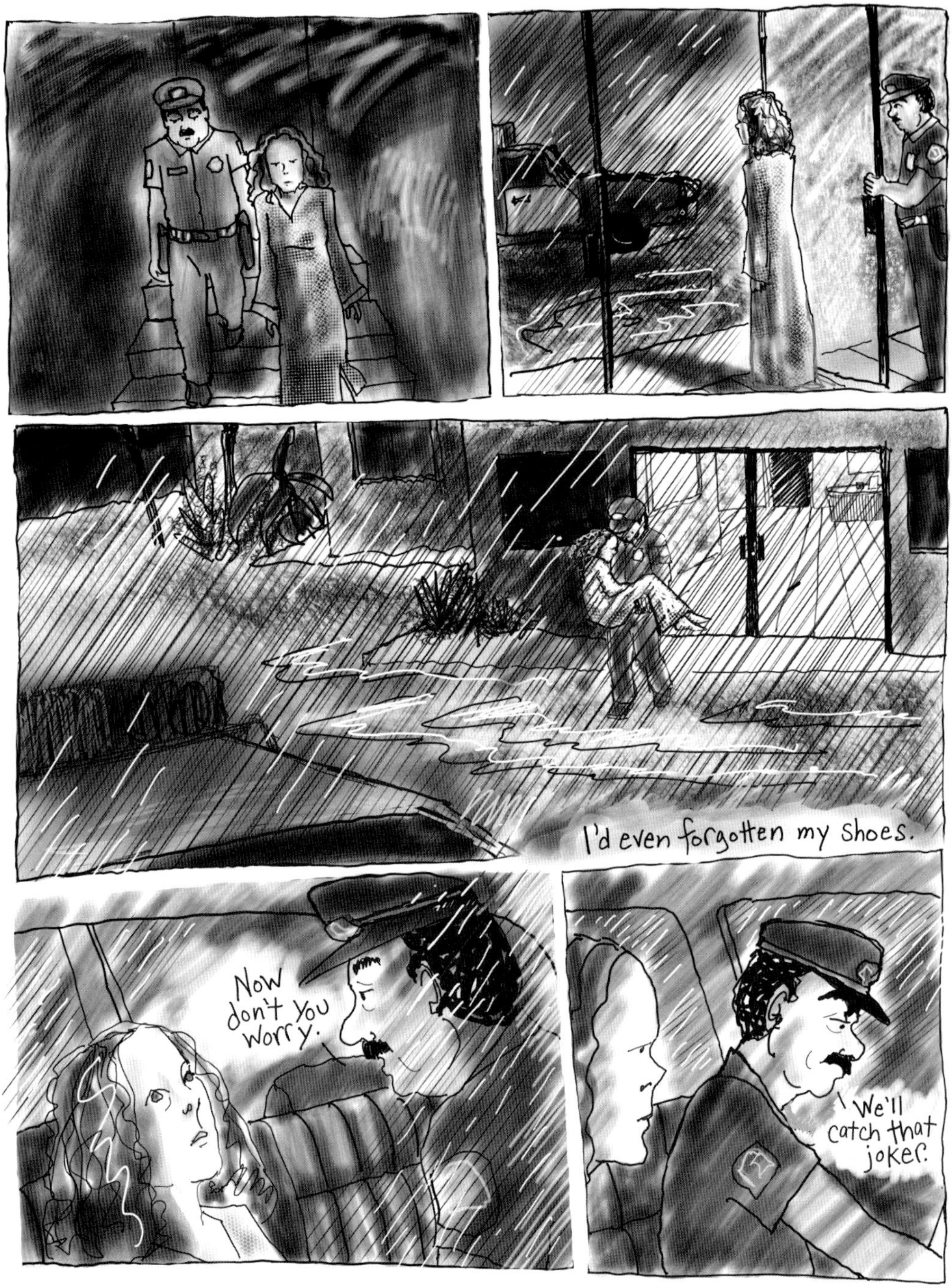
I'd even forgotten my shoes.
Now don't you worry.
We'll catch that joker.

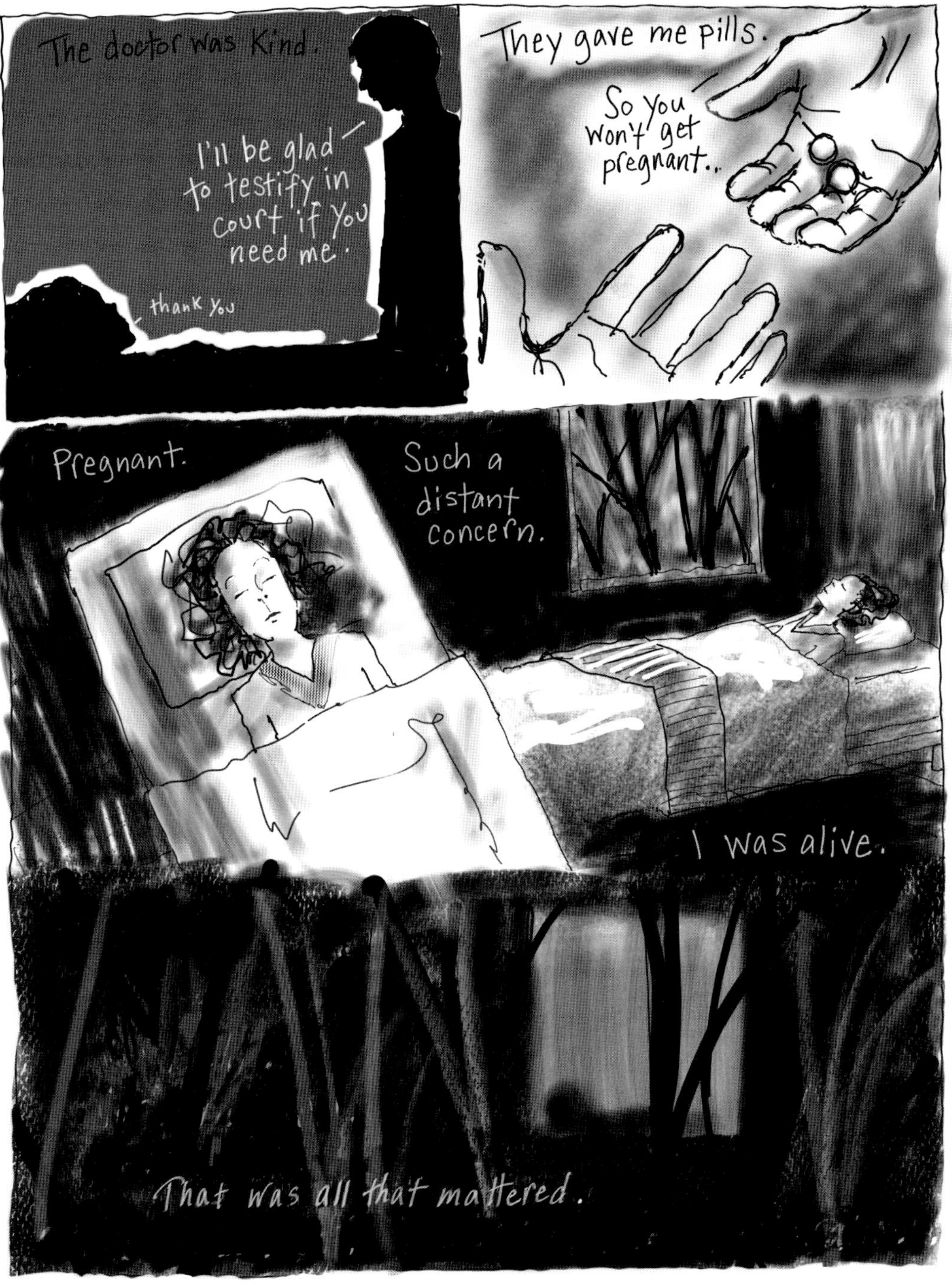

The doctor was kind.
I'll be glad to testify in court if you need me.
thank you
They gave me pills.
So you won't get pregnant..
Pregnant.
Such a distant concern.
I was alive.
That was all that mattered.

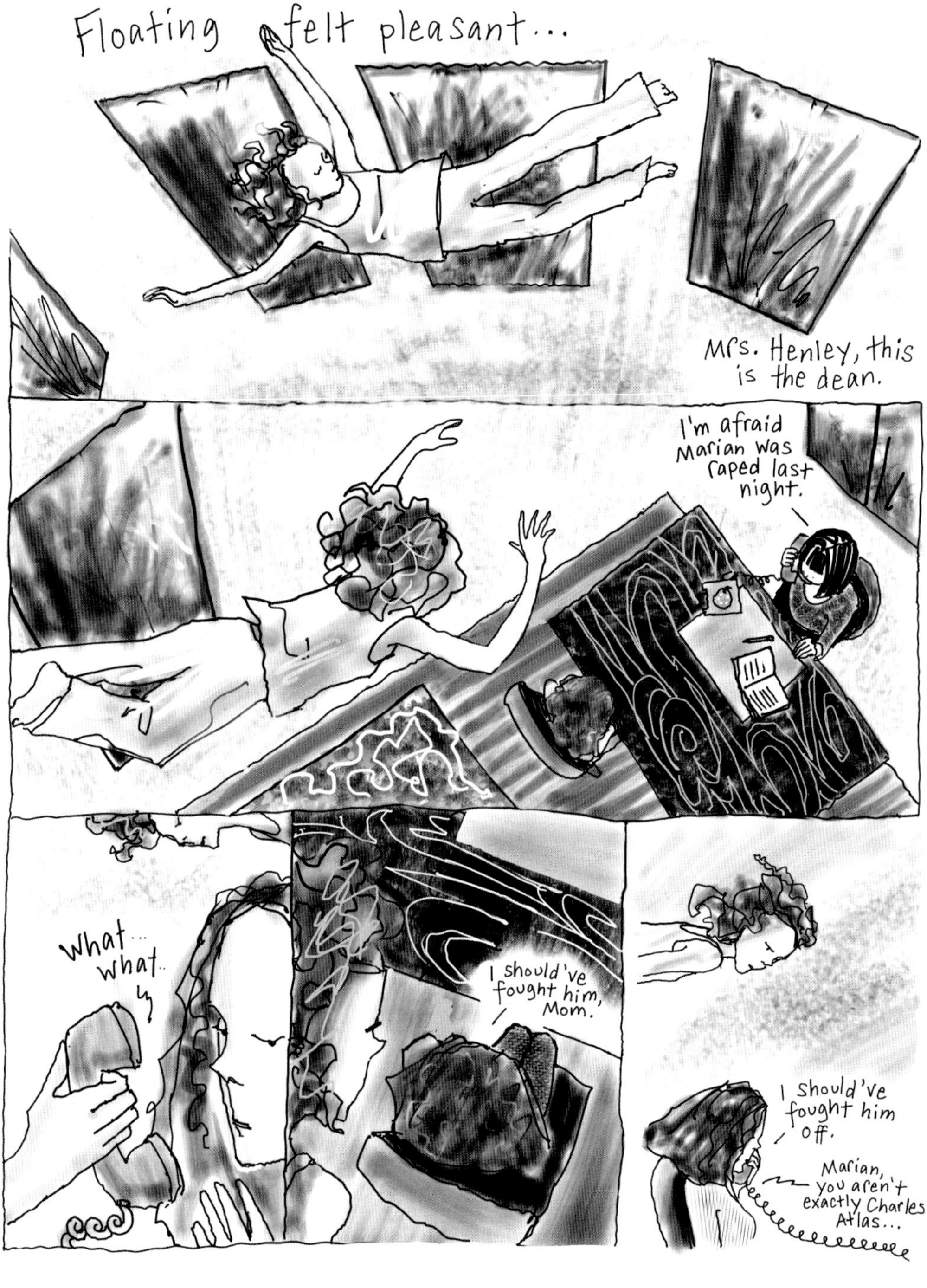
Floating felt pleasant...
Mrs. Henley, this is the dean.
I'm afraid Marian was raped last night.
what... what..
I should've fought him, Mom.
I should've fought him off.
Marian, you aren't exactly Charles Atlas...

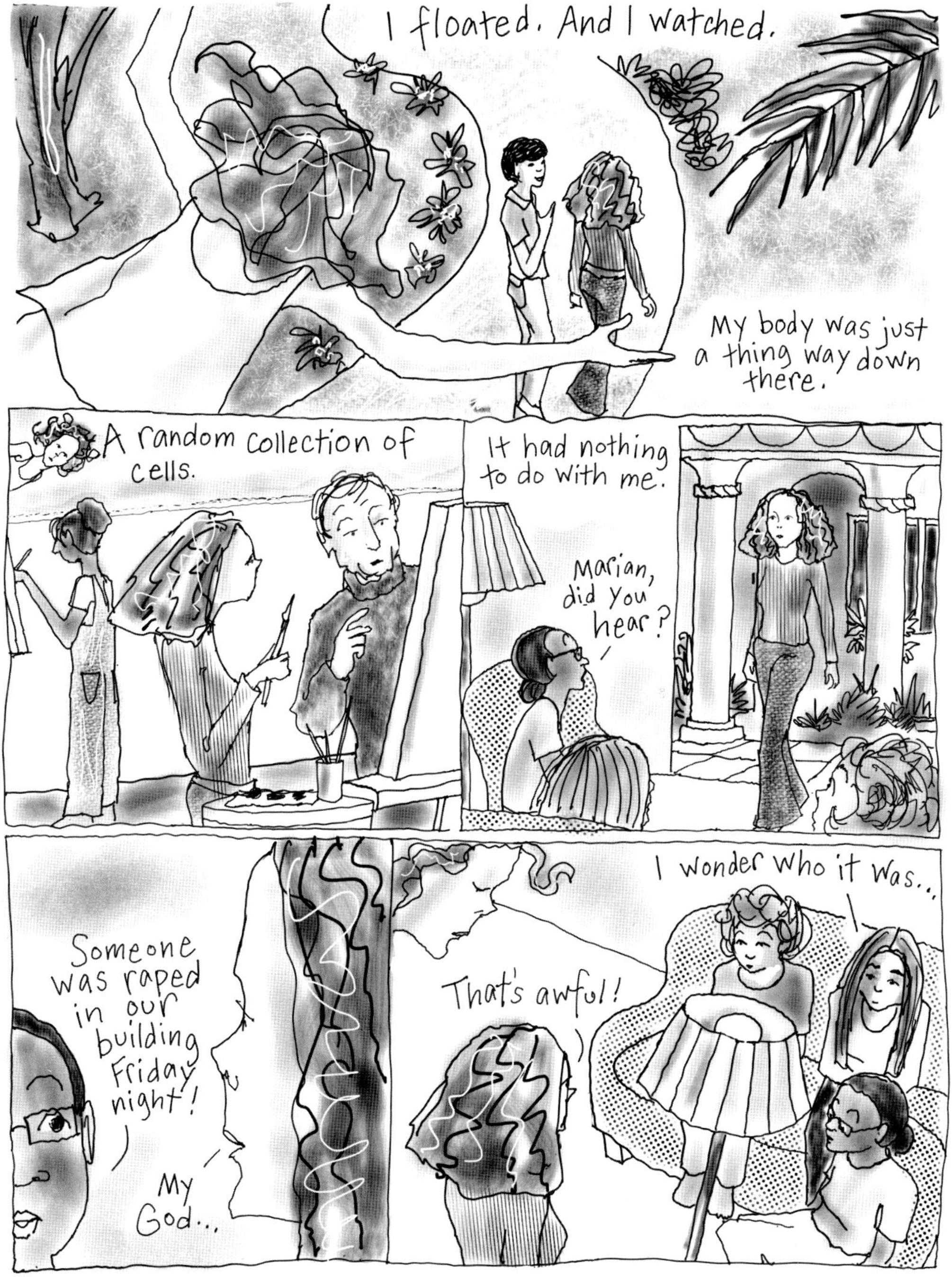
I floated. And I watched.
My body was just a thing way down there.
A random collection of cells.
It had nothing to do with me.
Marian, did you hear?
Someone was raped in our building Friday night!
My God...
That's awful!
I wonder who it was...

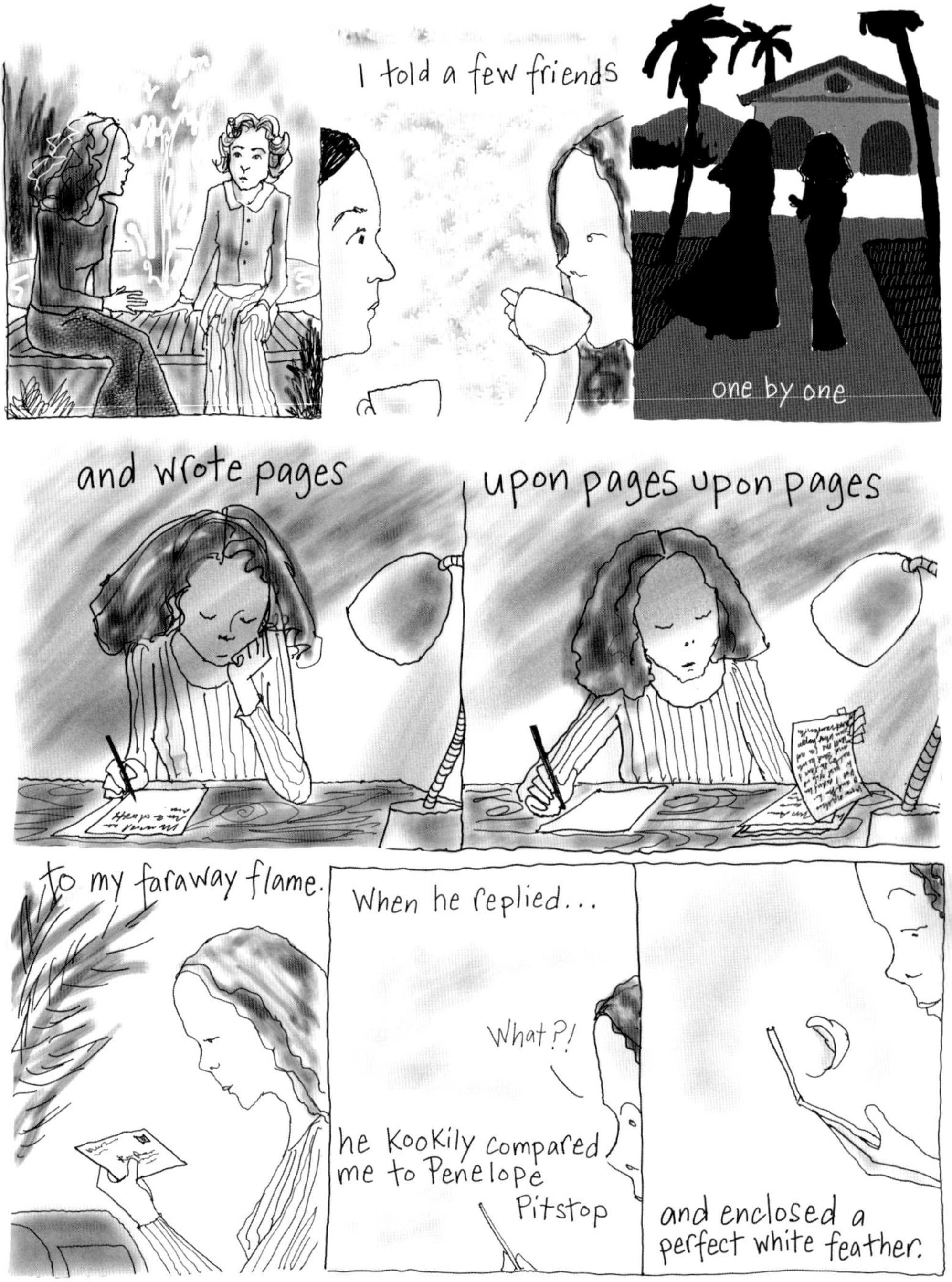
I told a few friends
one by one
and wrote pages
upon pages upon pages
to my faraway flame.
When he replied...
What?!
he KooKily compared me to Penelope Pitstop
and enclosed a perfect white feather.

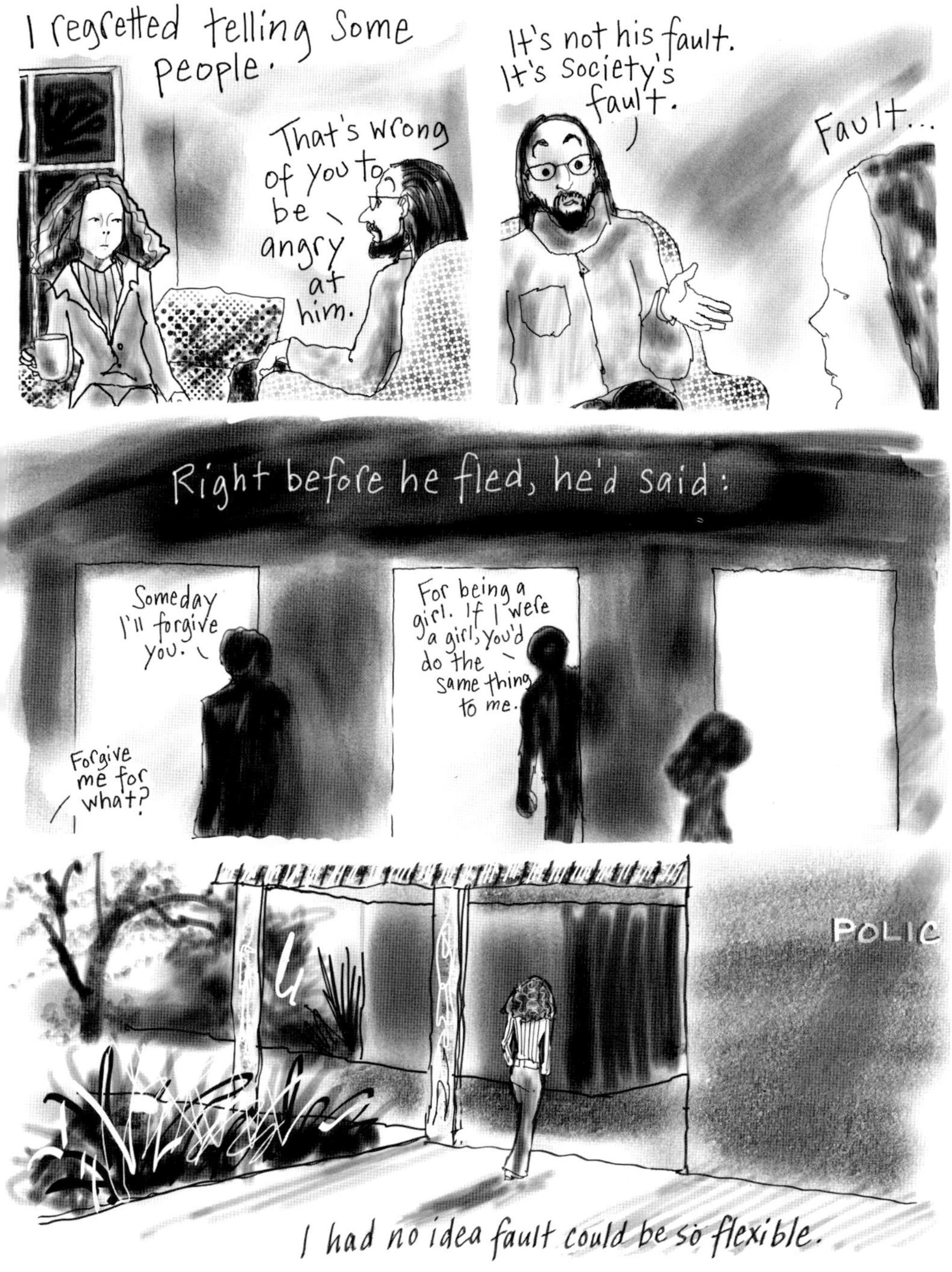
I regretted telling some people.
That's wrong of you to be angry at him.
It's not his fault. It's society's fault.
Fault...
Right before he fled, he'd said:
Someday I'll forgive you.
Forgive me for what?
For being a girl. If I were a girl, you'd do the same thing to me.
POLIC
I had no idea fault could be so flexible.

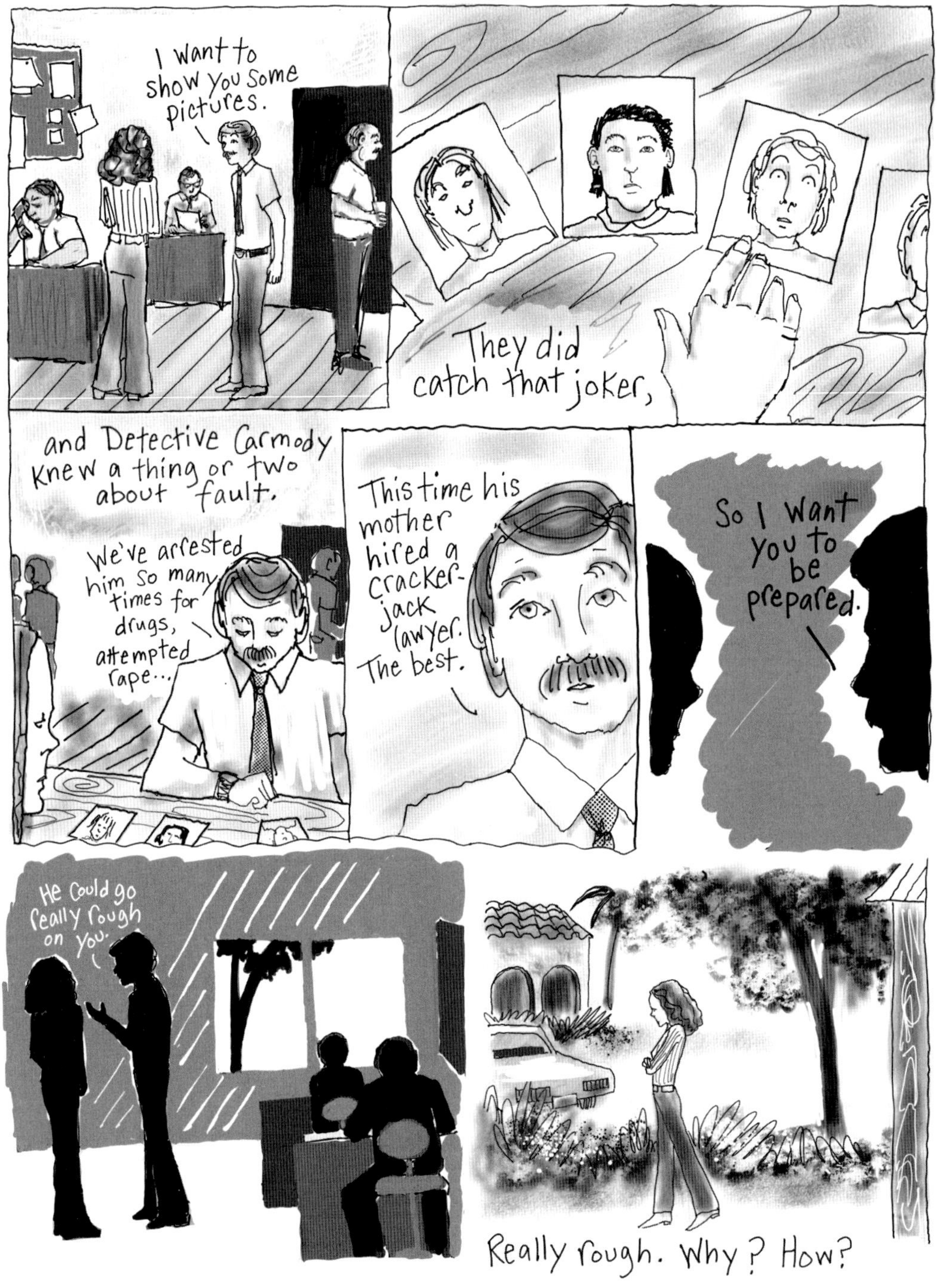
I want to show you some pictures.
They did catch that joker,
and Detective Carmody knew a thing or two about fault.
We've arrested him so many times for drugs, attempted rape...
This time his mother hired a cracker-jack lawyer. The best.
So I want you to be prepared.
He could go really rough on you.
Really rough. Why? How?

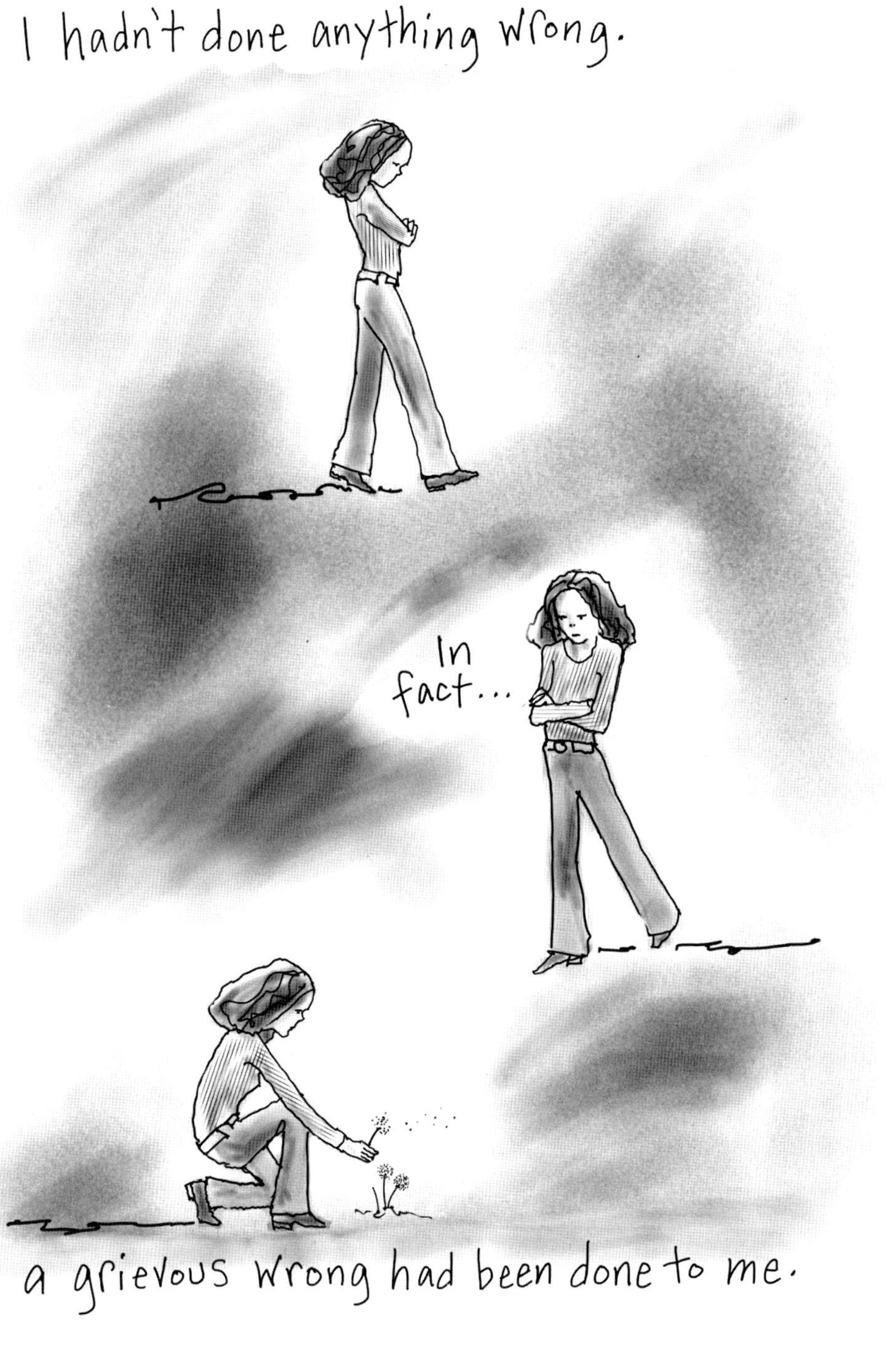
I hadn't done anything wrong.
In fact...
a grievous wrong had been done to me.

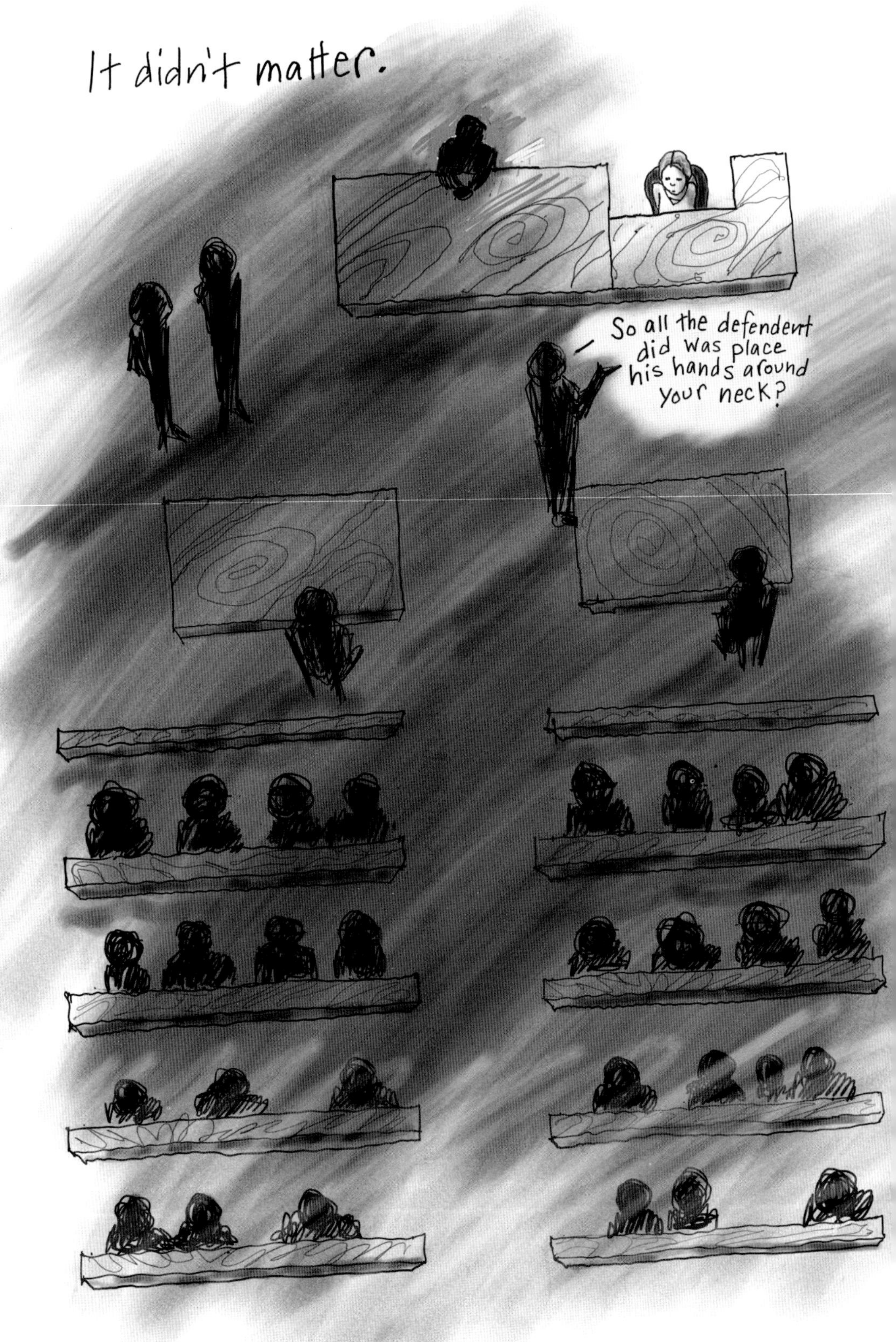
It didn't matter.
So all the defendent did was place his hands around your neck?

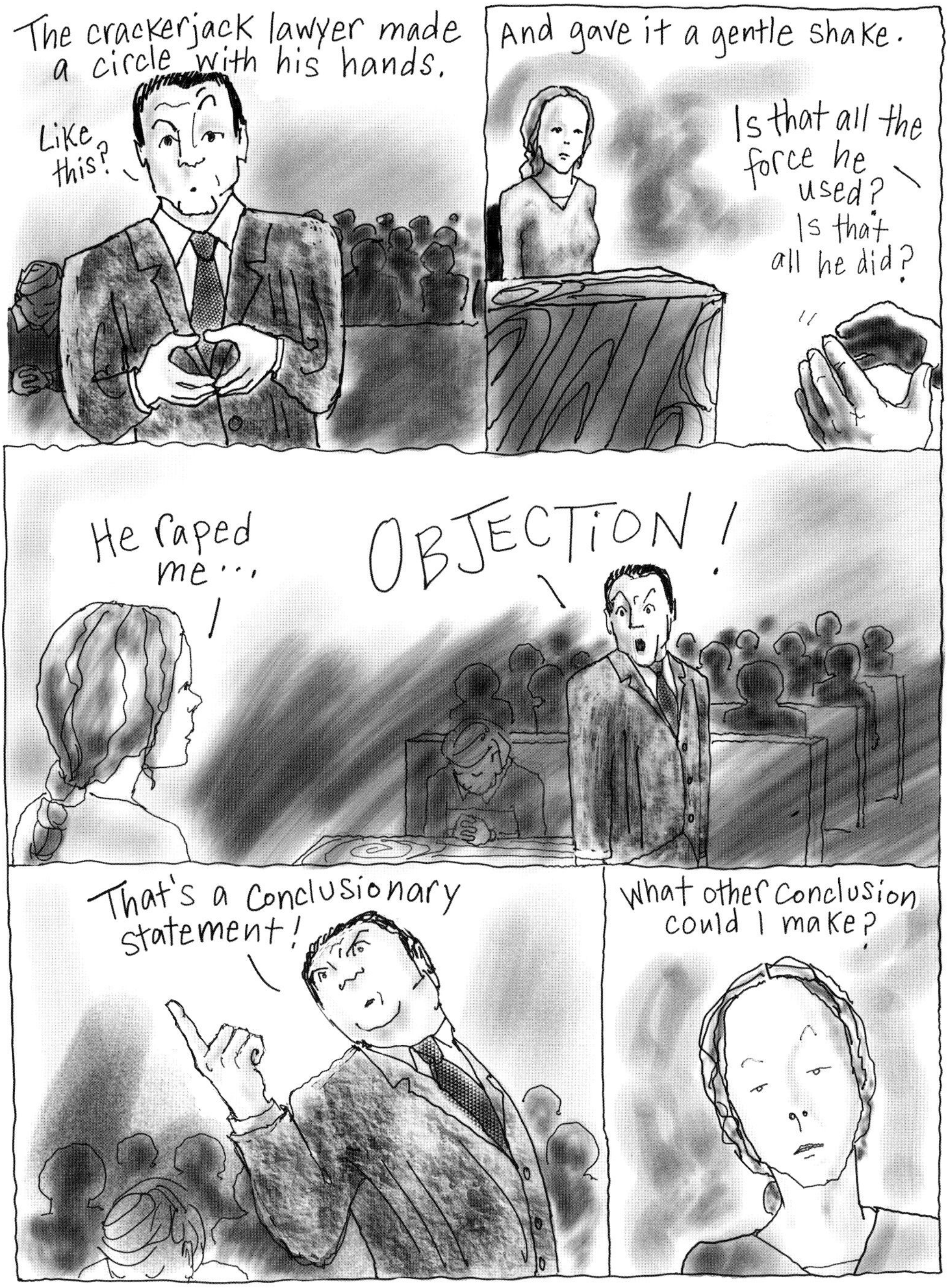

The crackerjack lawyer made a circle with his hands.
Like this?
And gave it a gentle shake.
Is that all the force he used? Is that all he did?
He raped me...
OBJECTION!
That's a conclusionary statement!
What other conclusion could I make?

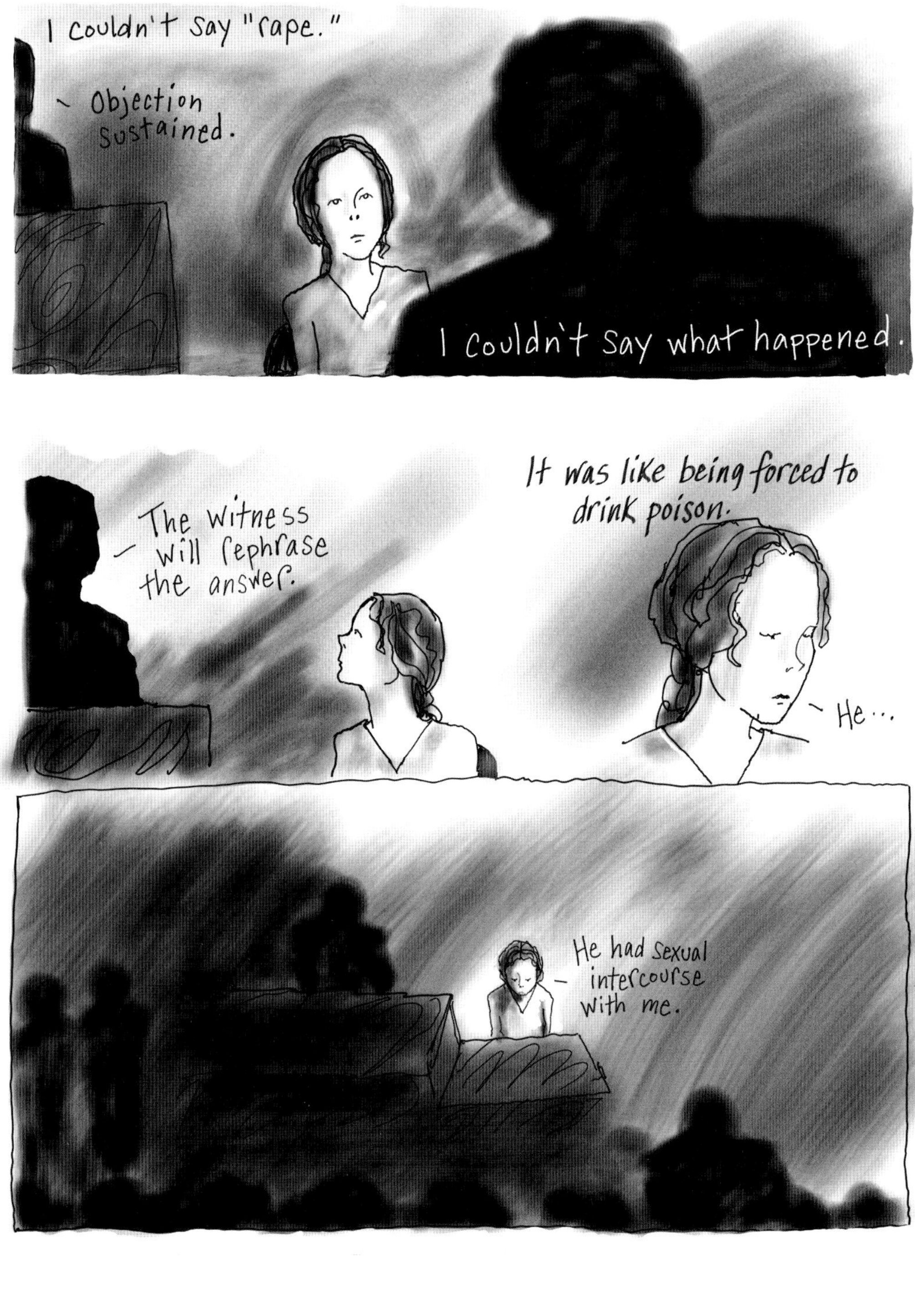
I couldn't say "rape."
Objection sustained.
I couldn't say what happened.
The witness will rephrase the answer.
It was like being forced to drink poison.
He...
He had sexual intercourse with me.

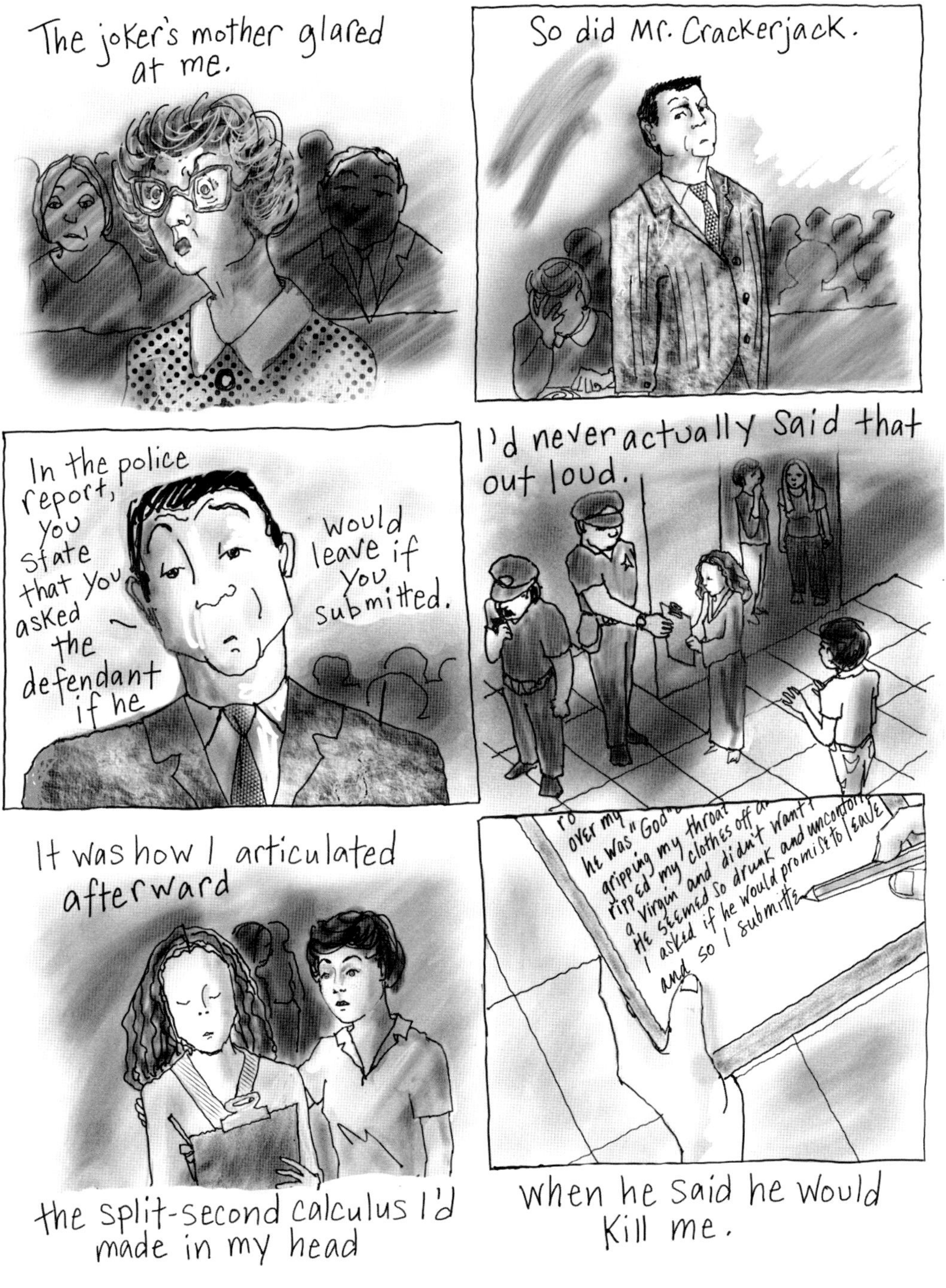
The joker's mother glared at me.
So did Mr. Crackerjack.
In the police report, you state that you asked the defendant if he would leave if you submitted.
I'd never actually said that out loud.
It was how I articulated afterward
over my
he was "God"
gripping my throat
ripped my clothes off
a virgin and didn't want
He seemed so drunk and uncontro
I asked if he would promise to leave
and so I submitte
the split-second calculus I'd made in my head
when he said he would kill me.

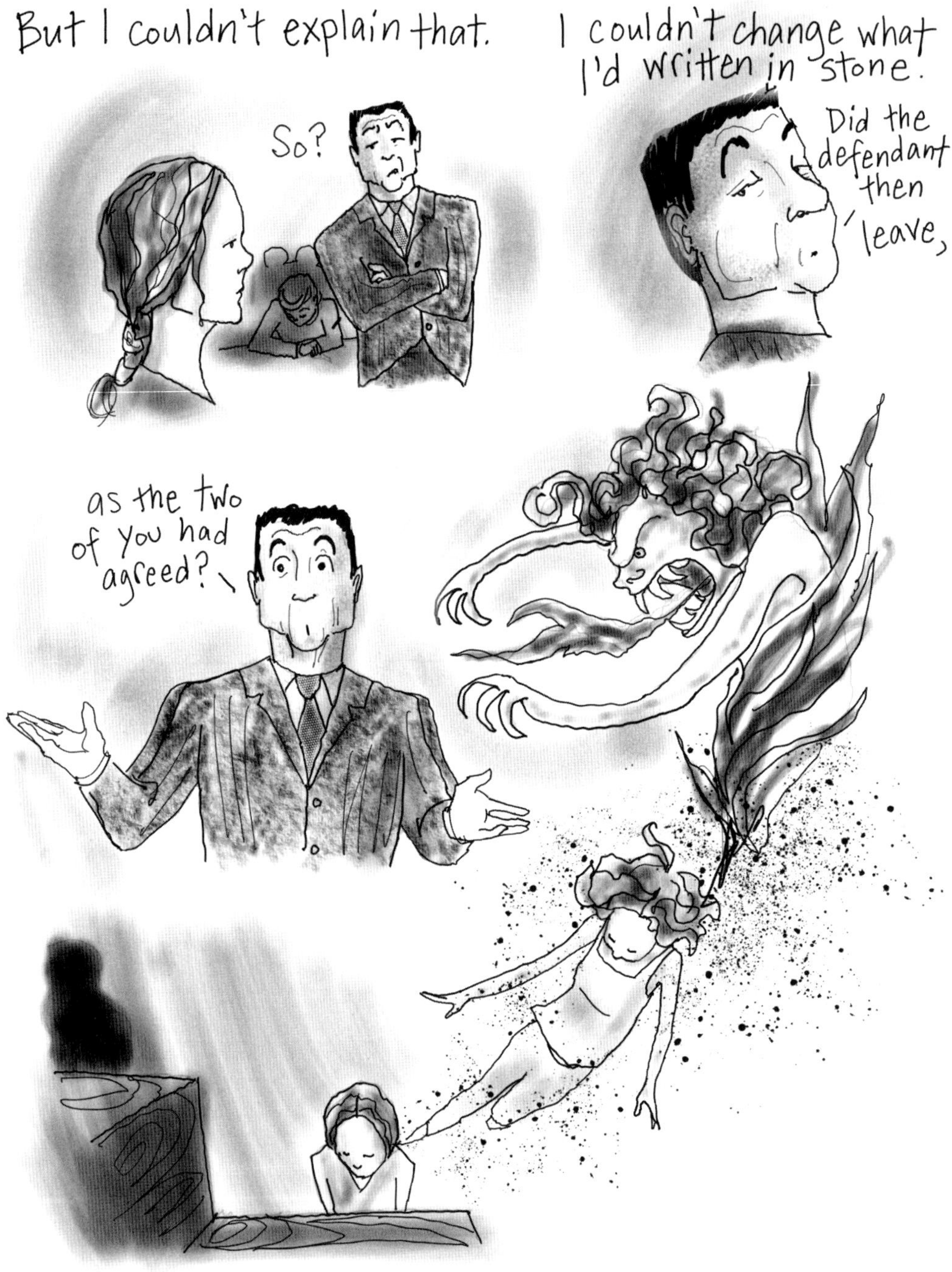

But I couldn't explain that.
So?
I couldn't change what I'd written in stone.
Did the defendant then leave,
as the two of you had agreed?

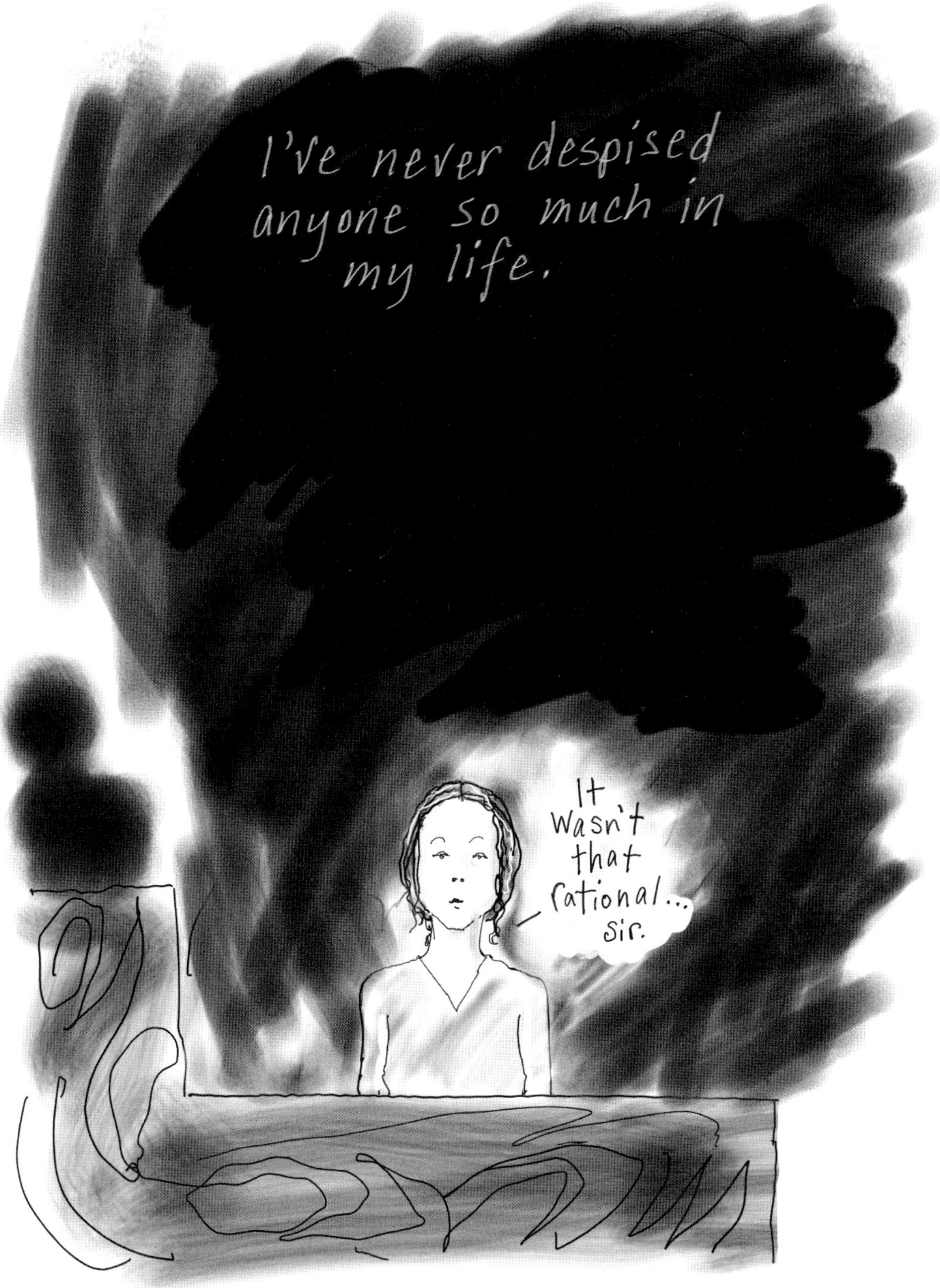
I've never despised anyone so much in my life.
It wasn't that rational... sir.

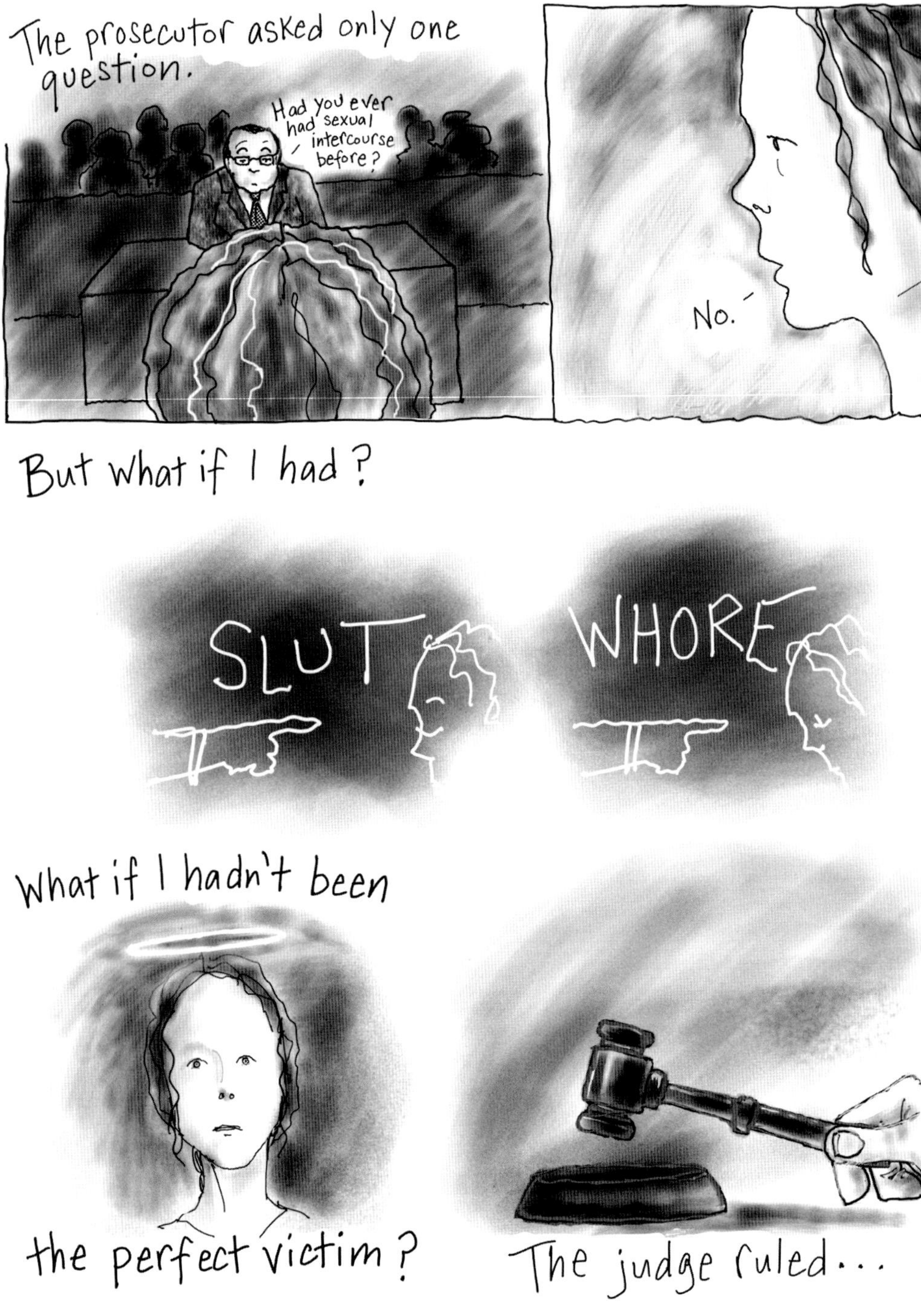
The prosecutor asked only one question.
Had you ever had sexual intercourse before?
No.
But what if I had?
SLUT
WHORE
What if I hadn't been
the perfect victim?
The judge ruled...

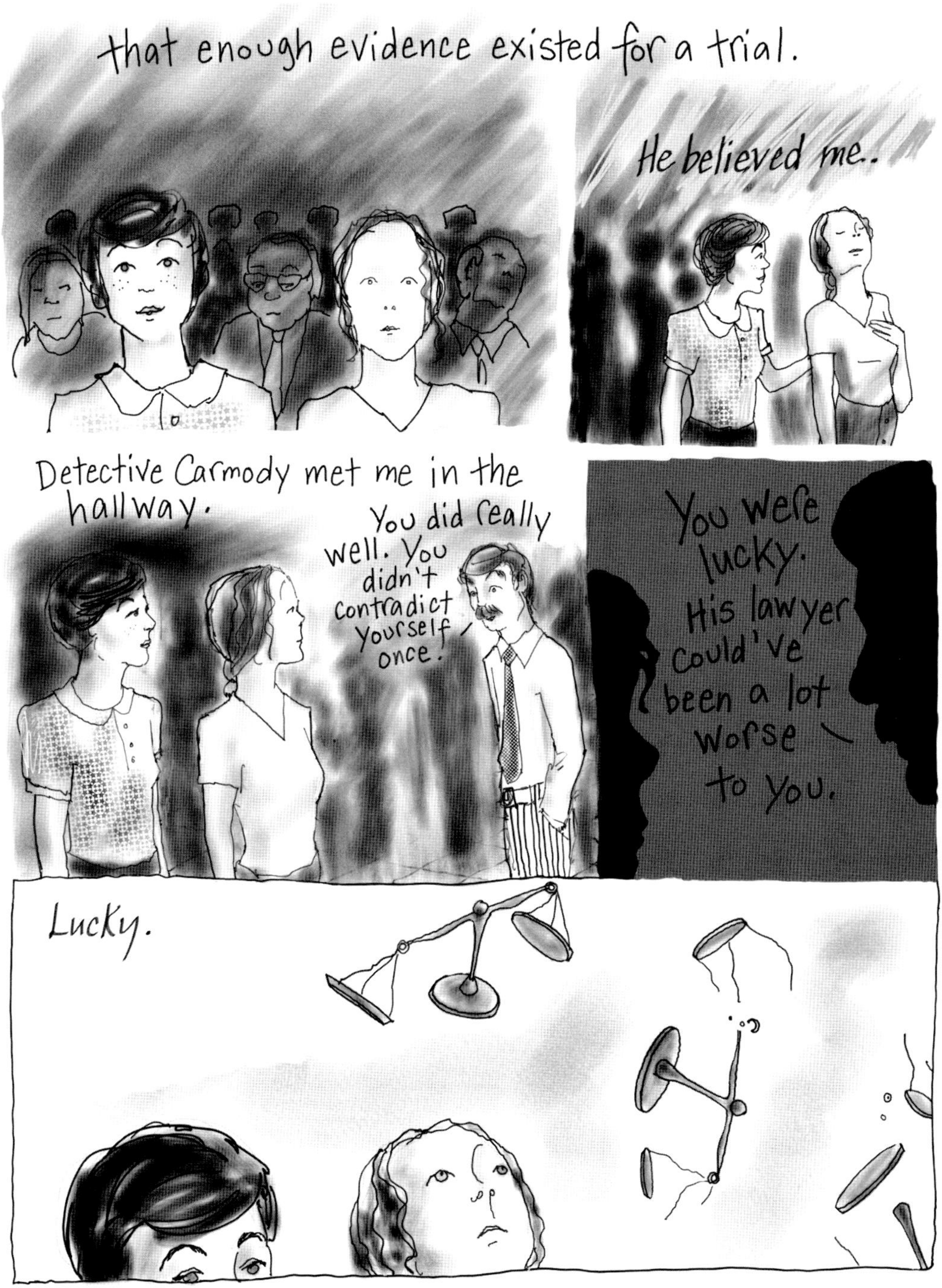
that enough evidence existed for a trial.
He believed me..
Detective Carmody met me in the hallway.
You did really well. You didn't contradict yourself once!
You were lucky. His lawyer could've been a lot worse to you.
Lucky.

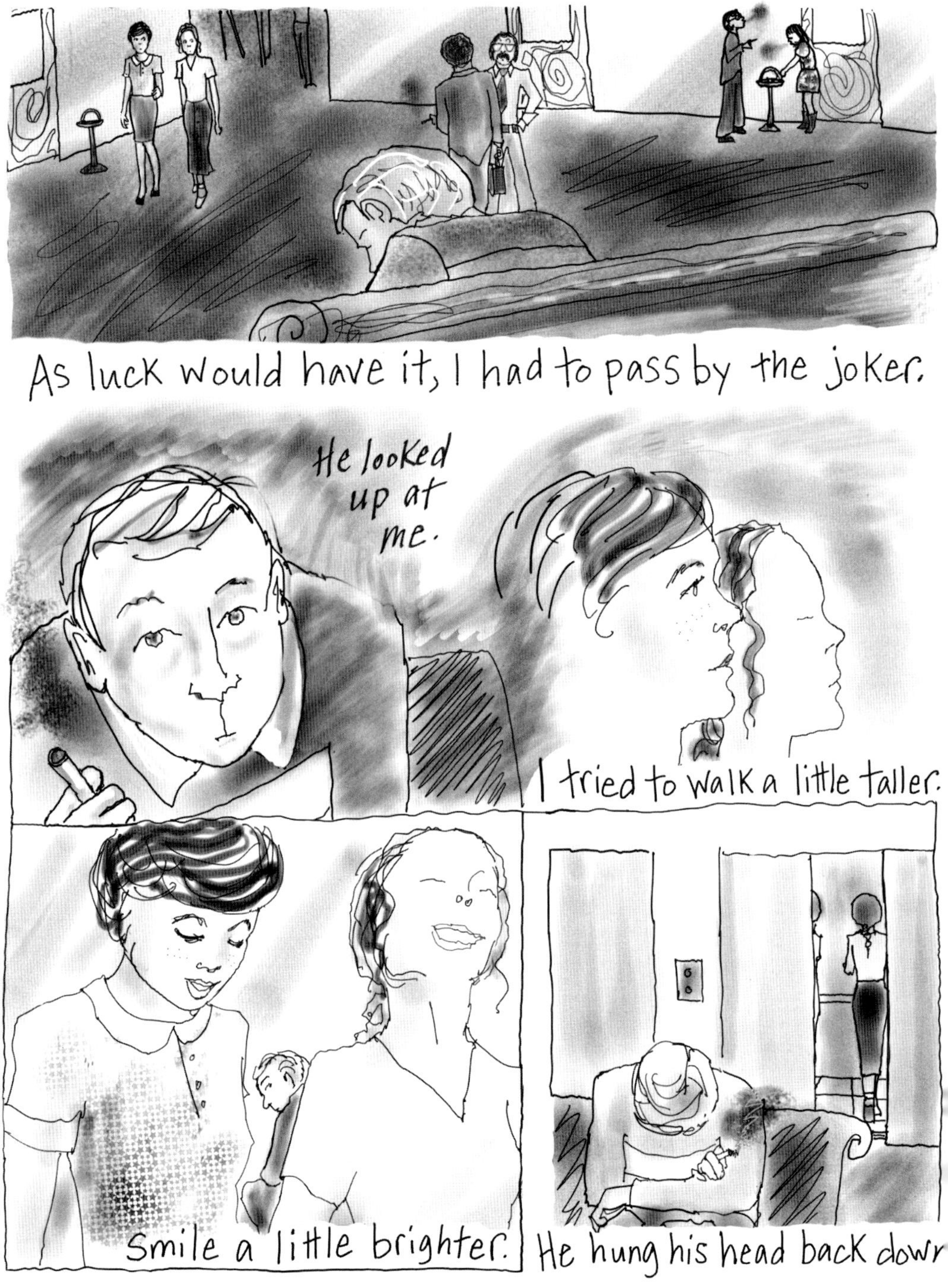
As luck would have it, I had to pass by the joker.
He looked up at me.
I tried to walk a little taller.
Smile a little brighter.
He hung his head back down

Two

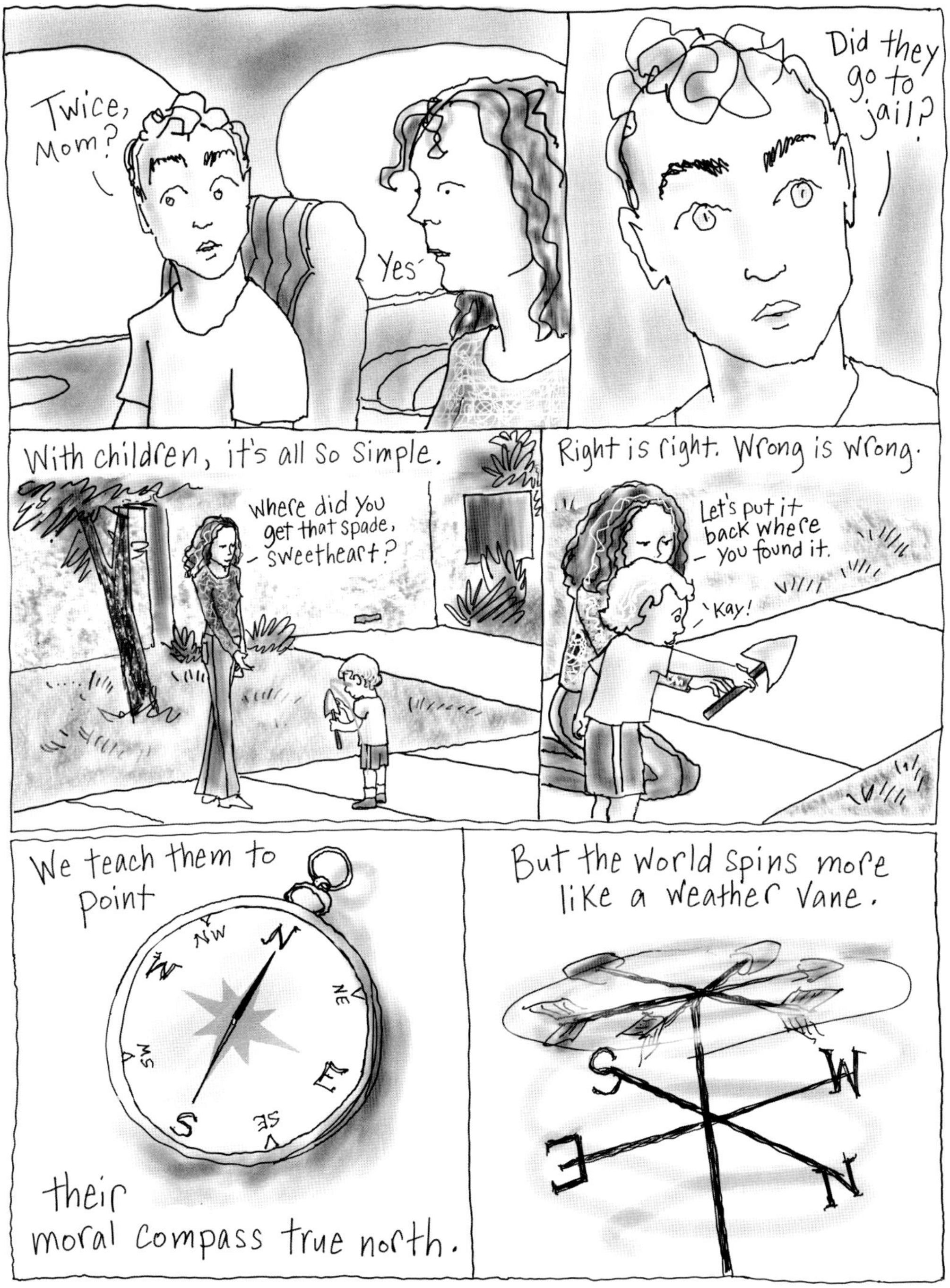
Twice, Mom?
Yes
Did they go to jail?
With children, it's all so simple.
Where did you get that spade, sweetheart?
Right is right. Wrong is wrong.
Let's put it back where you found it.
'Kay!
We teach them to point
NW
N
NE
E
SE
S
SW
W
their moral compass true north.
But the world spins more like a weather vane.
S
W
E
N

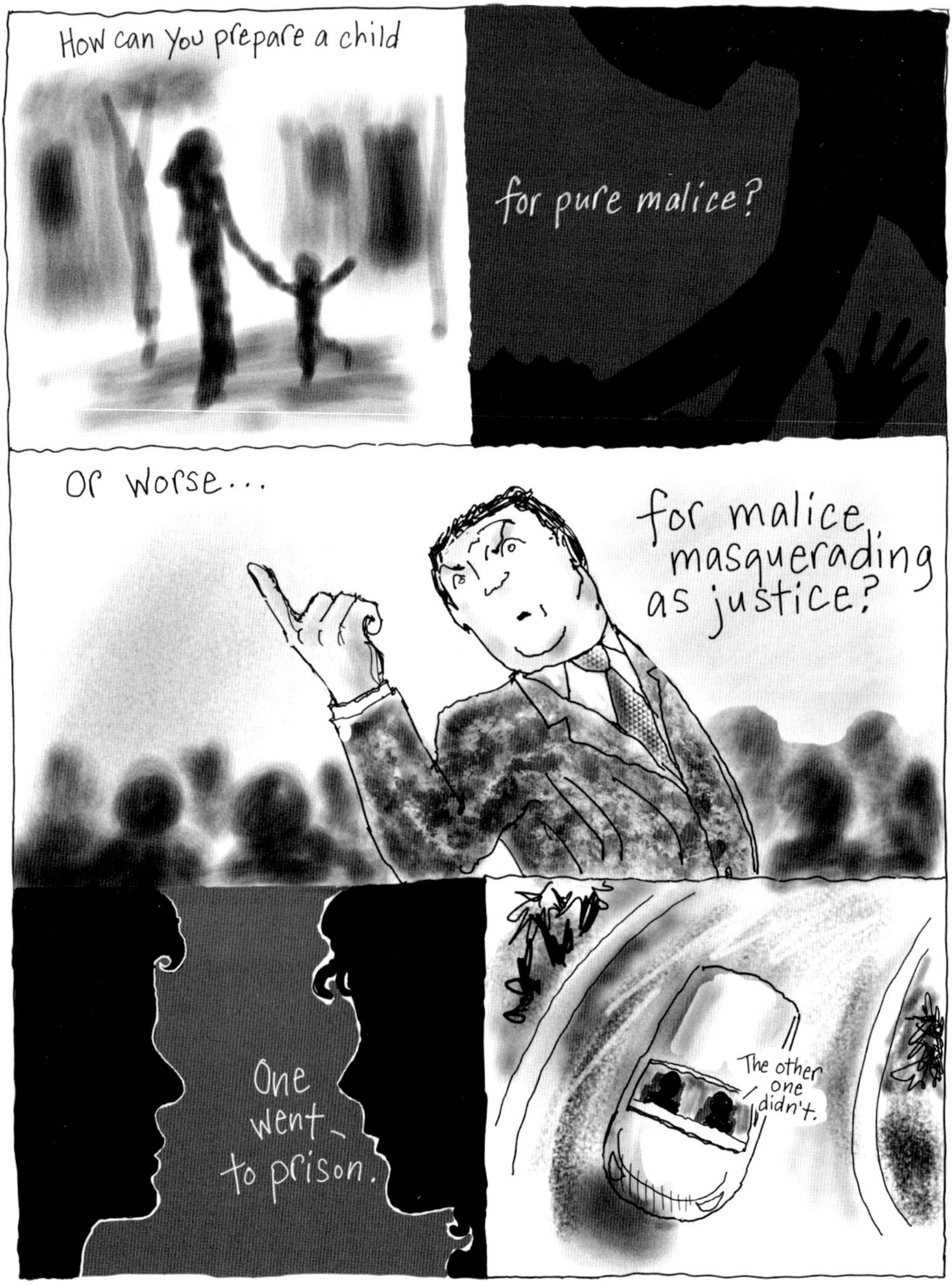
How can you prepare a child
for pure malice?
Or worse...
for malice masquerading as justice?
One went to prison.
The other one didn't.

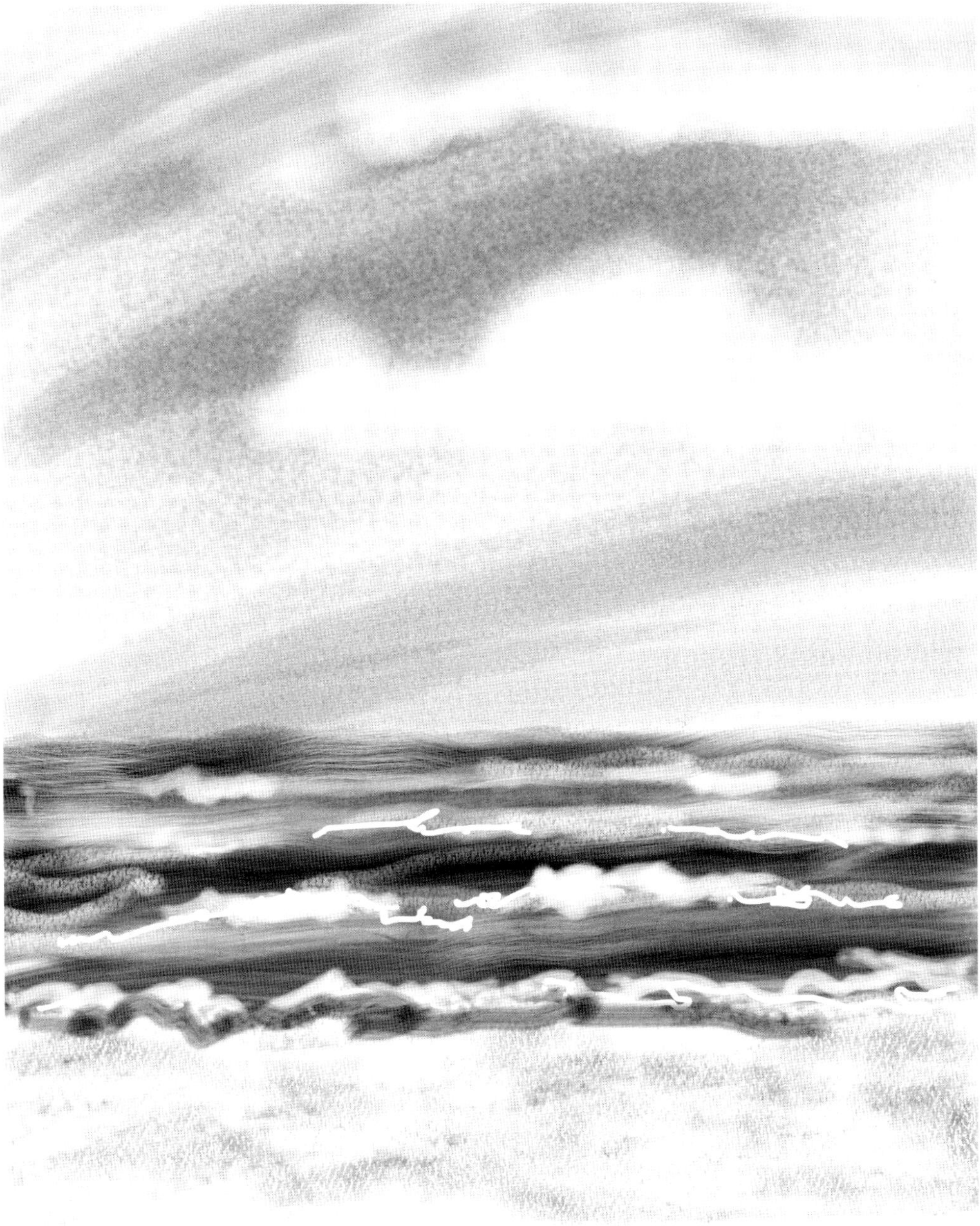

After the pretrial, we took a family trip to the beach.

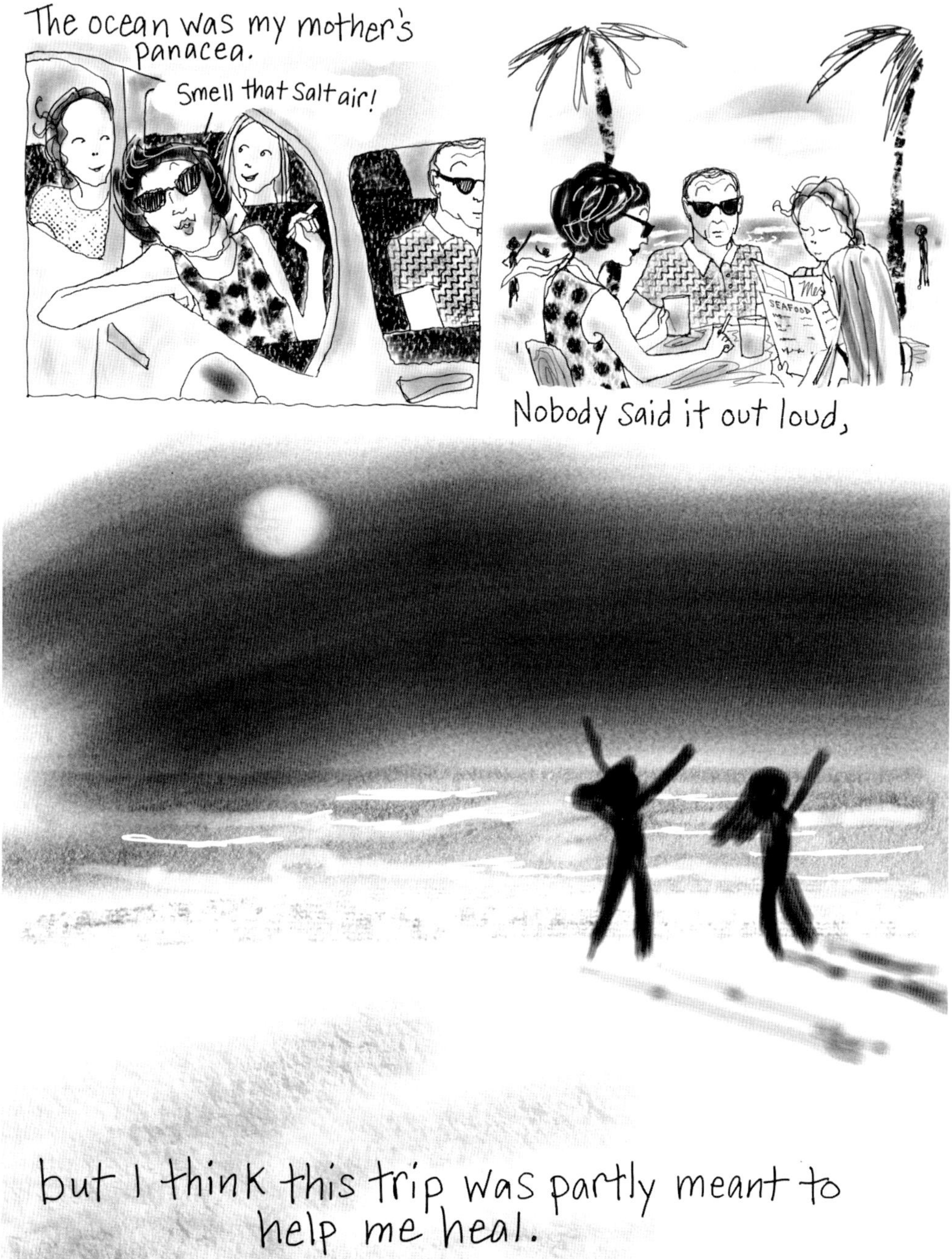
The ocean was my mother's panacea.
Smell that salt air!
SEAFOOD
Nobody said it out loud,
but I think this trip was partly meant to help me heal.

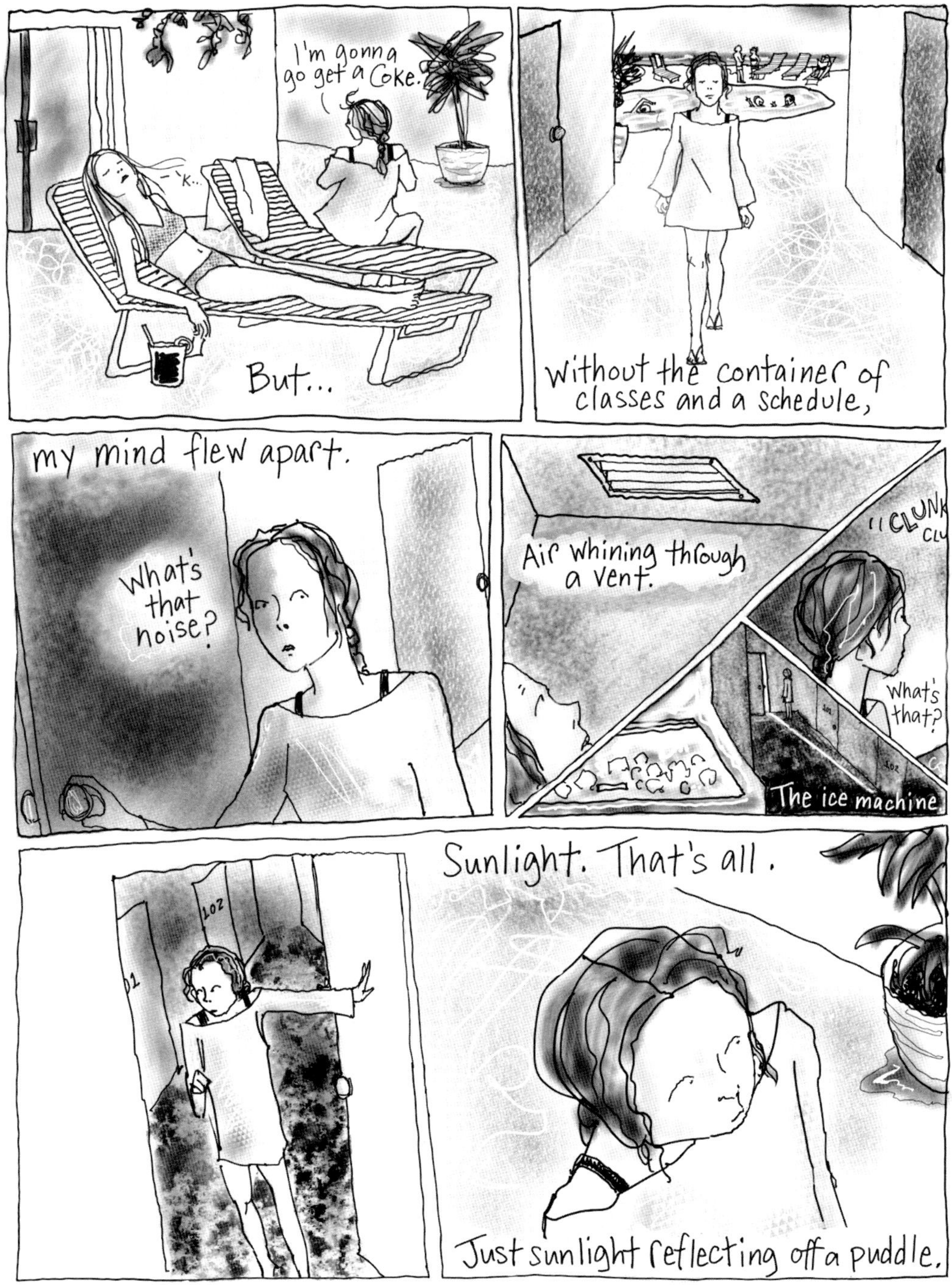
I'm gonna go get a Coke.
K...
But...
Without the container of classes and a schedule,
my mind flew apart.
What's that noise?
Air whining through a vent.
CLUNK
What's that?
The ice machine.
Sunlight. That's all.
Just sunlight reflecting off a puddle.

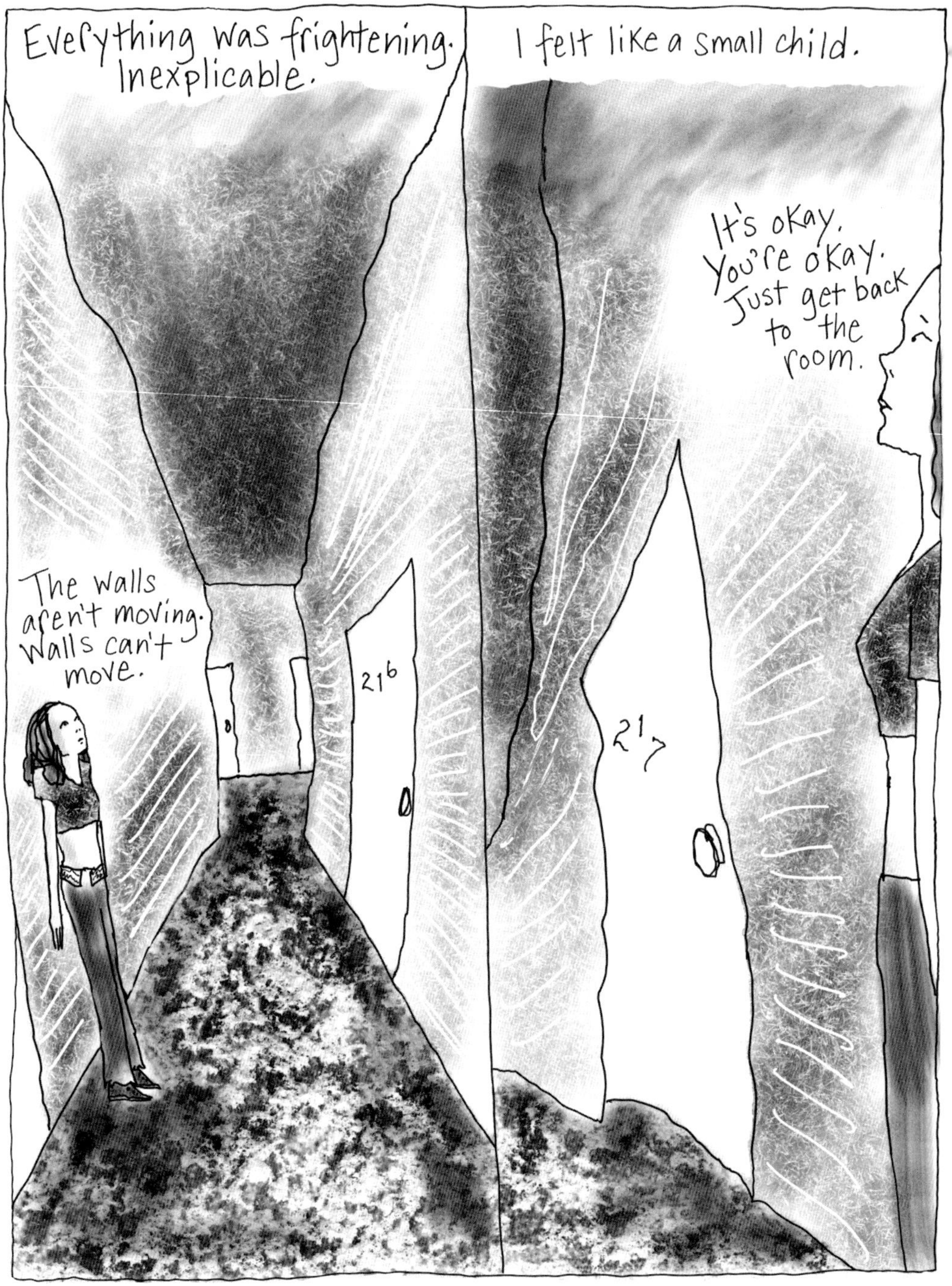
Everything was frightening. Inexplicable.
The walls aren't moving. Walls can't move.
216
I felt like a small child.
It's okay. You're okay. Just get back to the room.
217

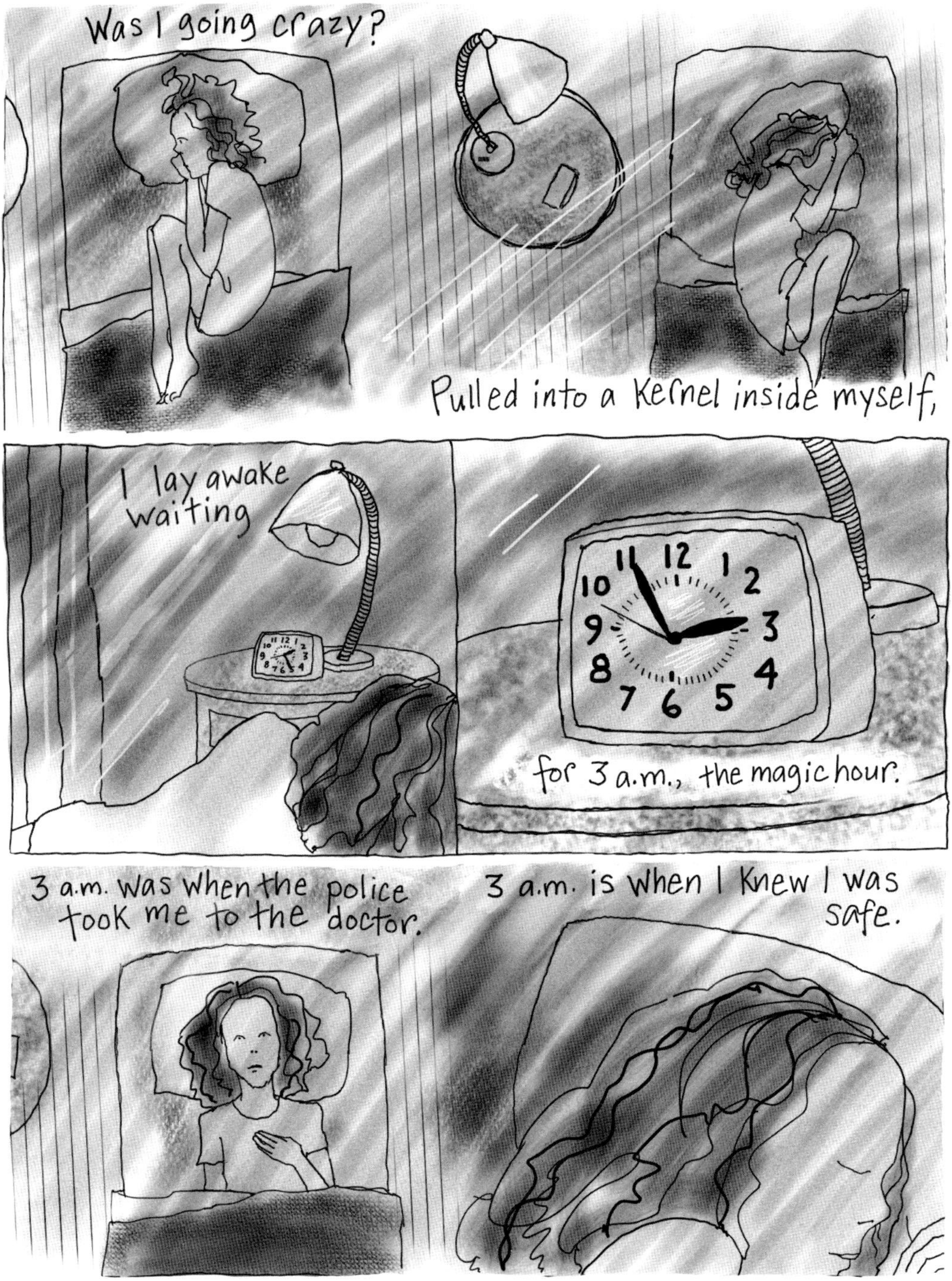
Was I going crazy?
Pulled into a Kernel inside myself,
I lay awake waiting
10 11 12 1 2 3 4 5 6 7 8 9
for 3 a.m., the magic hour.
3 a.m. was when the police took me to the doctor.
3 a.m. is when I Knew I was safe.

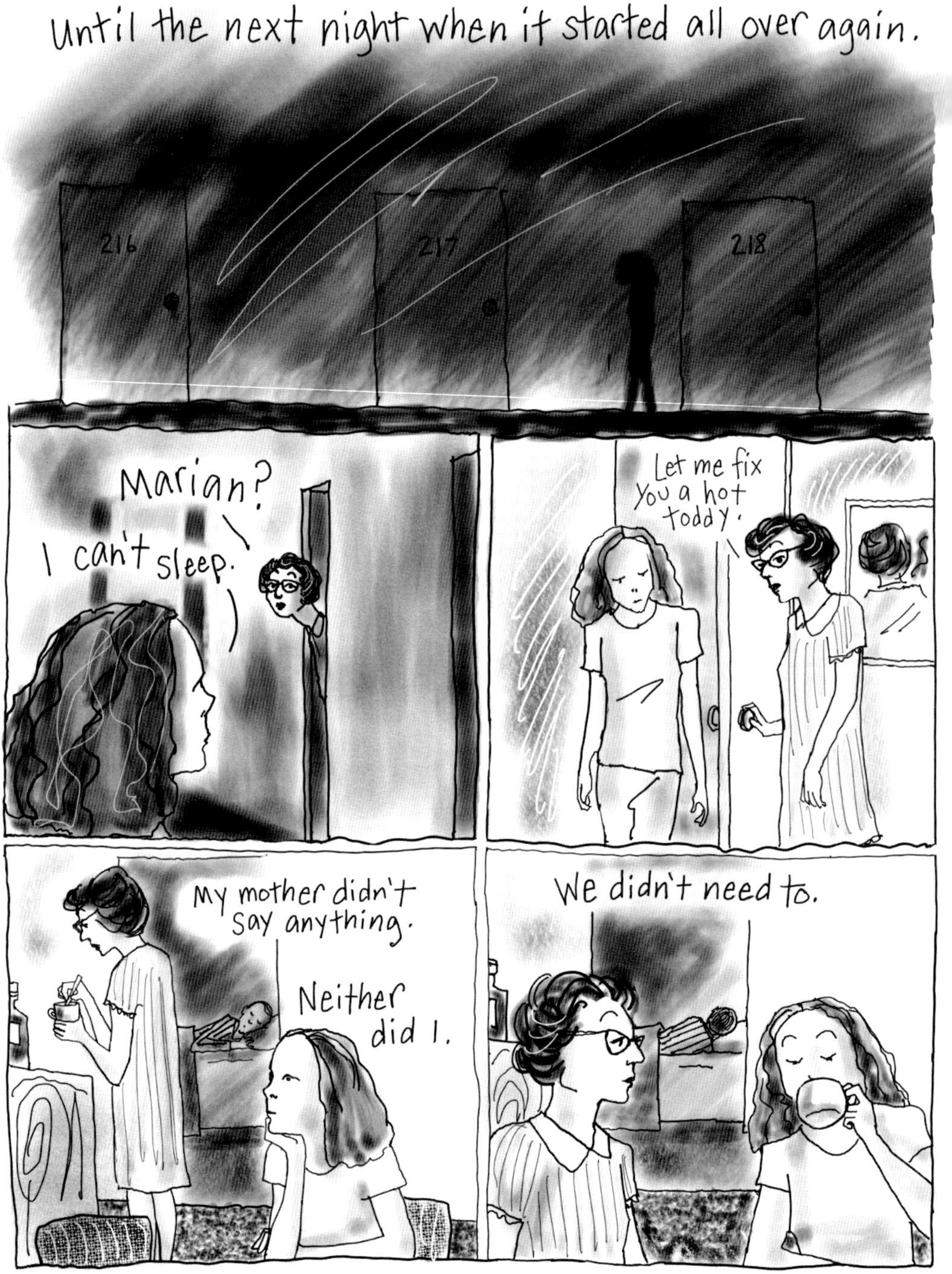
Until the next night when it started all over again.
216
217
218
Marian?
I can't sleep.
Let me fix you a hot toddy.
My mother didn't say anything.
Neither did I.
We didn't need to.

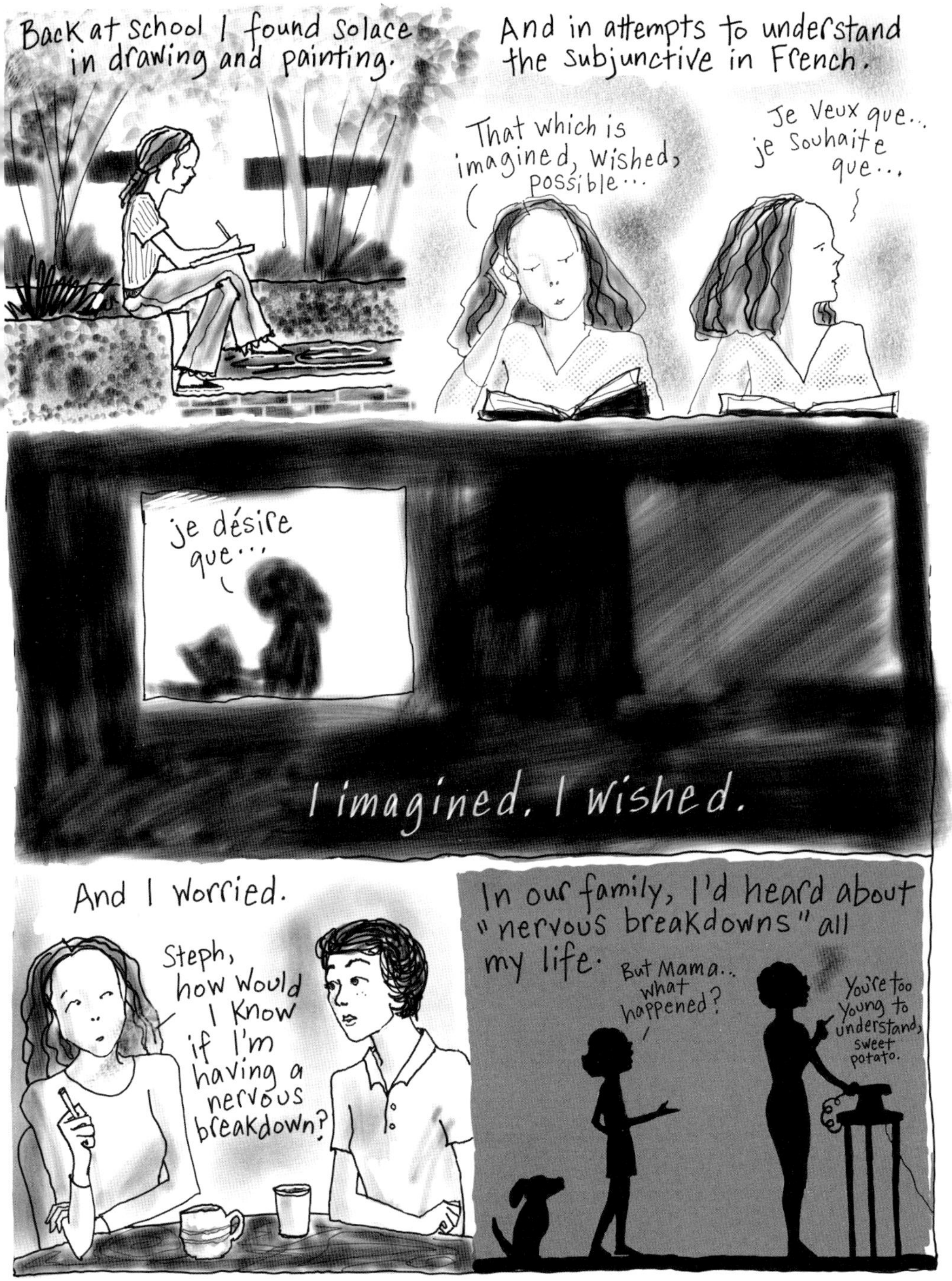
Back at school I found solace in drawing and painting.
And in attempts to understand the subjunctive in French.
That which is imagined, wished, possible...
Je veux que... je souhaite que...
je désire que...
I imagined. I wished.
And I worried.
Steph, how would I know if I'm having a nervous breakdown?
In our family, I'd heard about "nervous breakdowns" all my life.
But Mama... what happened?
You're too young to understand, sweet potato.

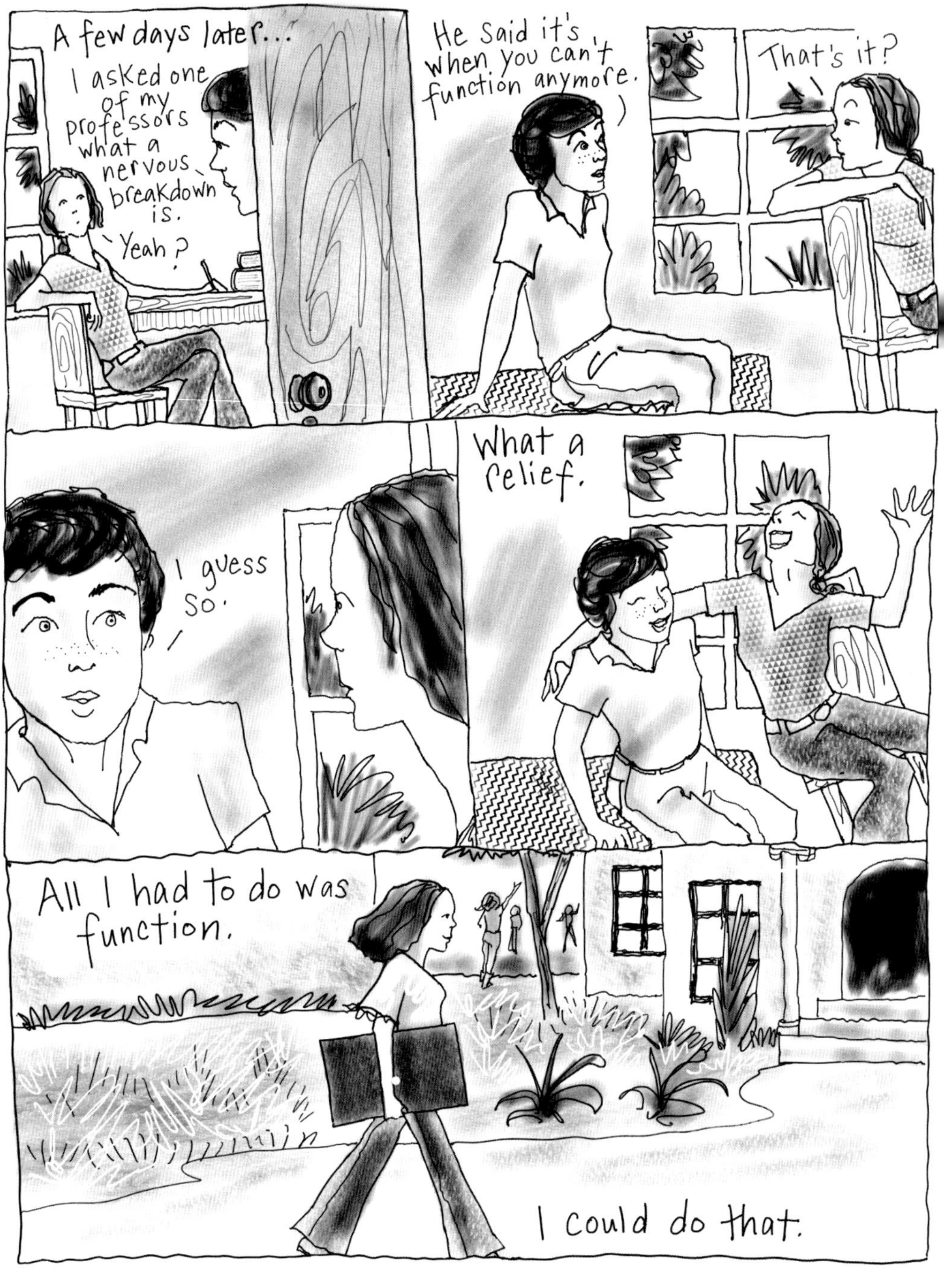
A few days later...
I asked one of my professors what a nervous breakdown is.
Yeah?
He said it's when you can't function anymore.
That's it?
I guess so.
What a relief.
All I had to do was function.
I could do that.

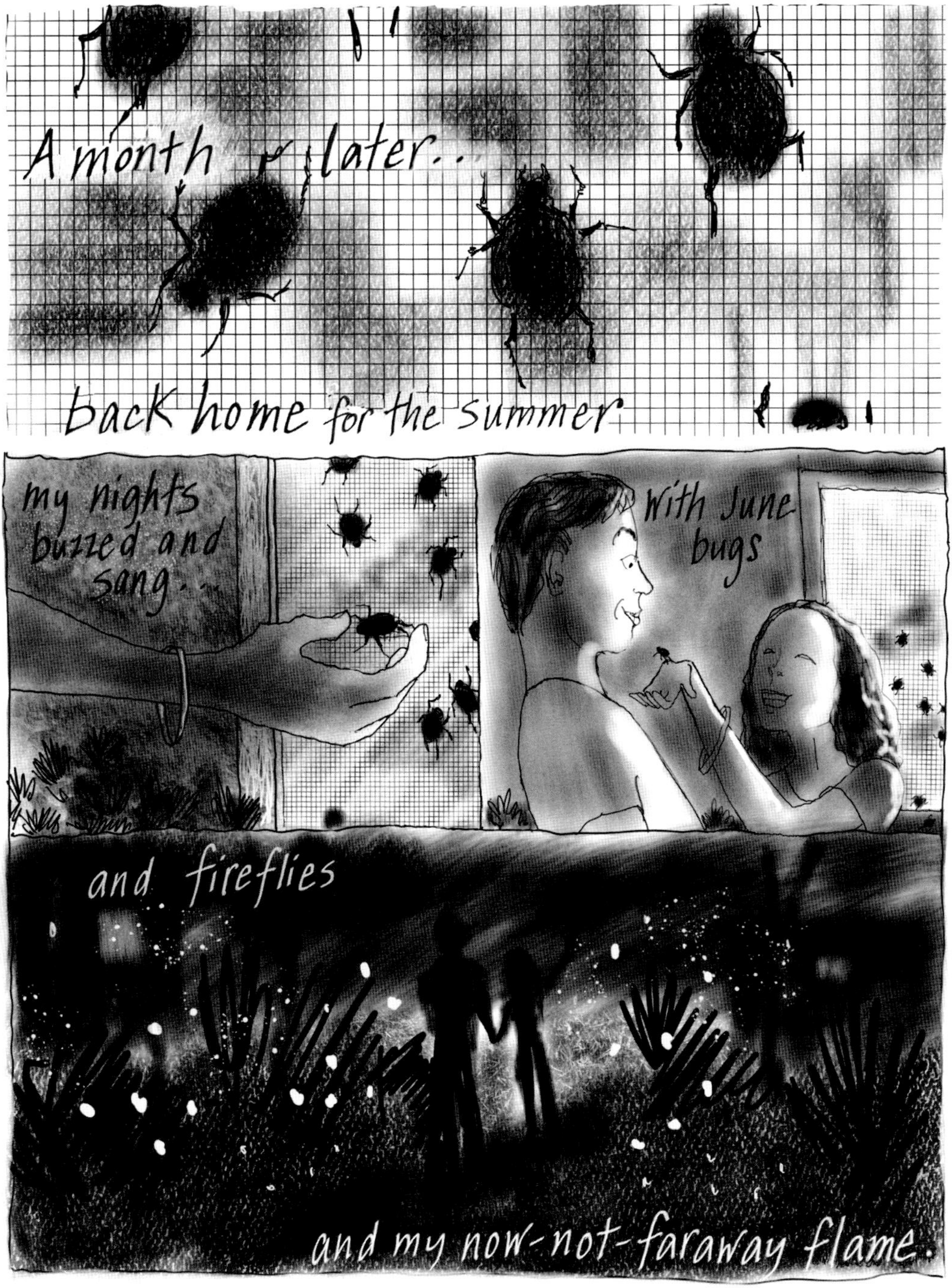
A month later...
back home for the summer
my nights buzzed and sang...
with June bugs
and fireflies
and my now-not-faraway flame.

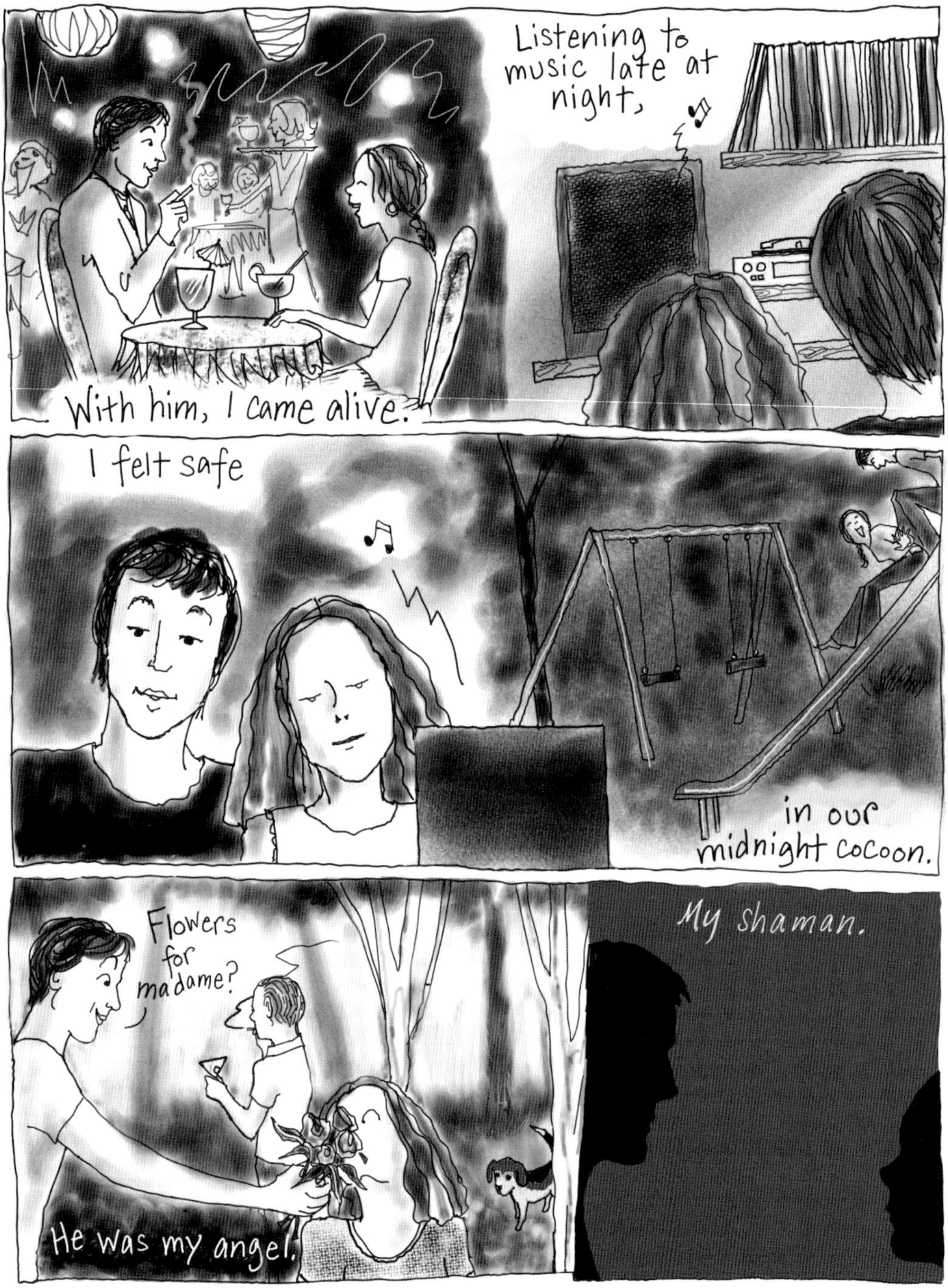

Listening to music late at night,
With him, I came alive.
I felt safe
in our midnight cocoon.
Flowers for madame?
He was my angel.
My shaman.

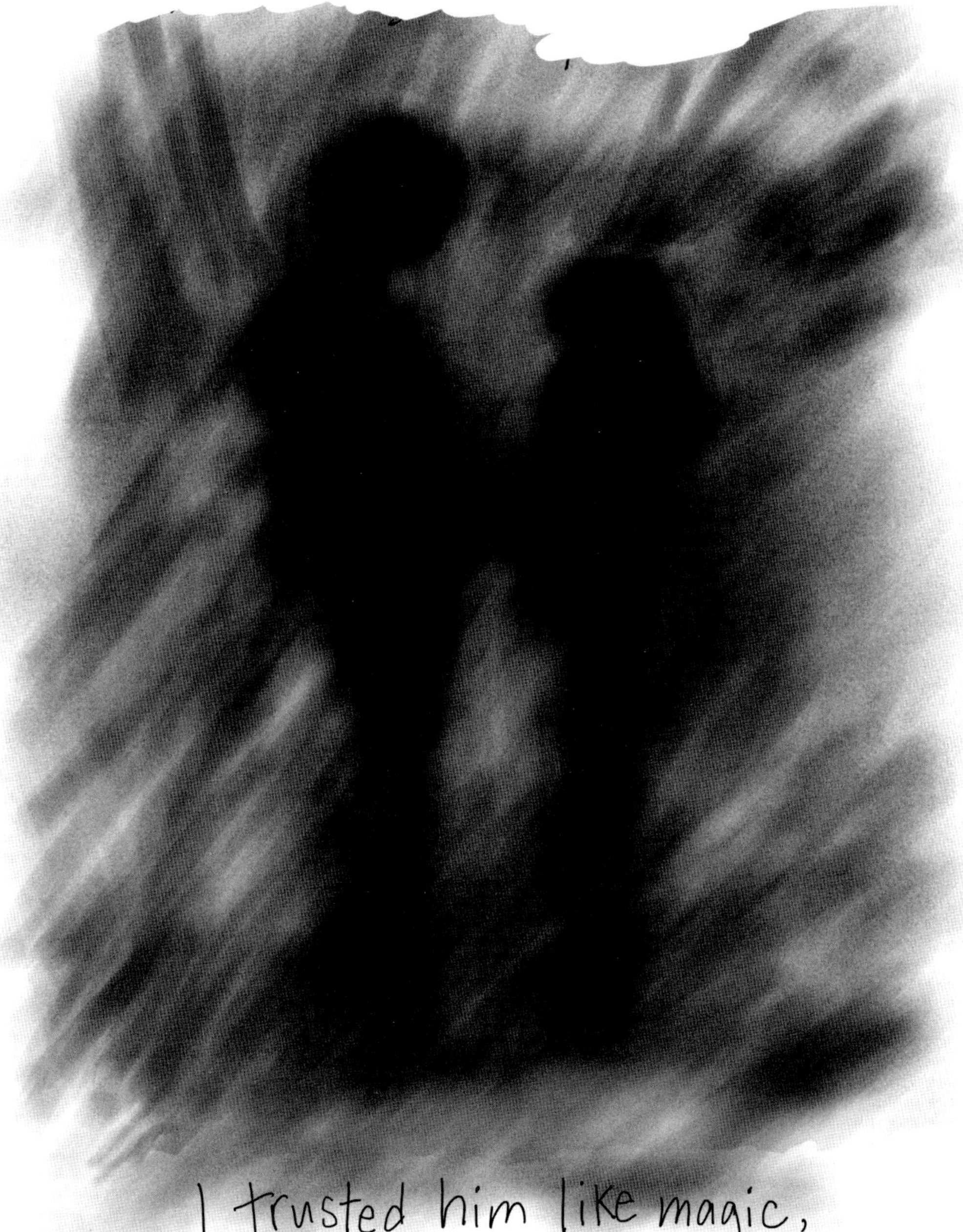

I trusted him like magic,

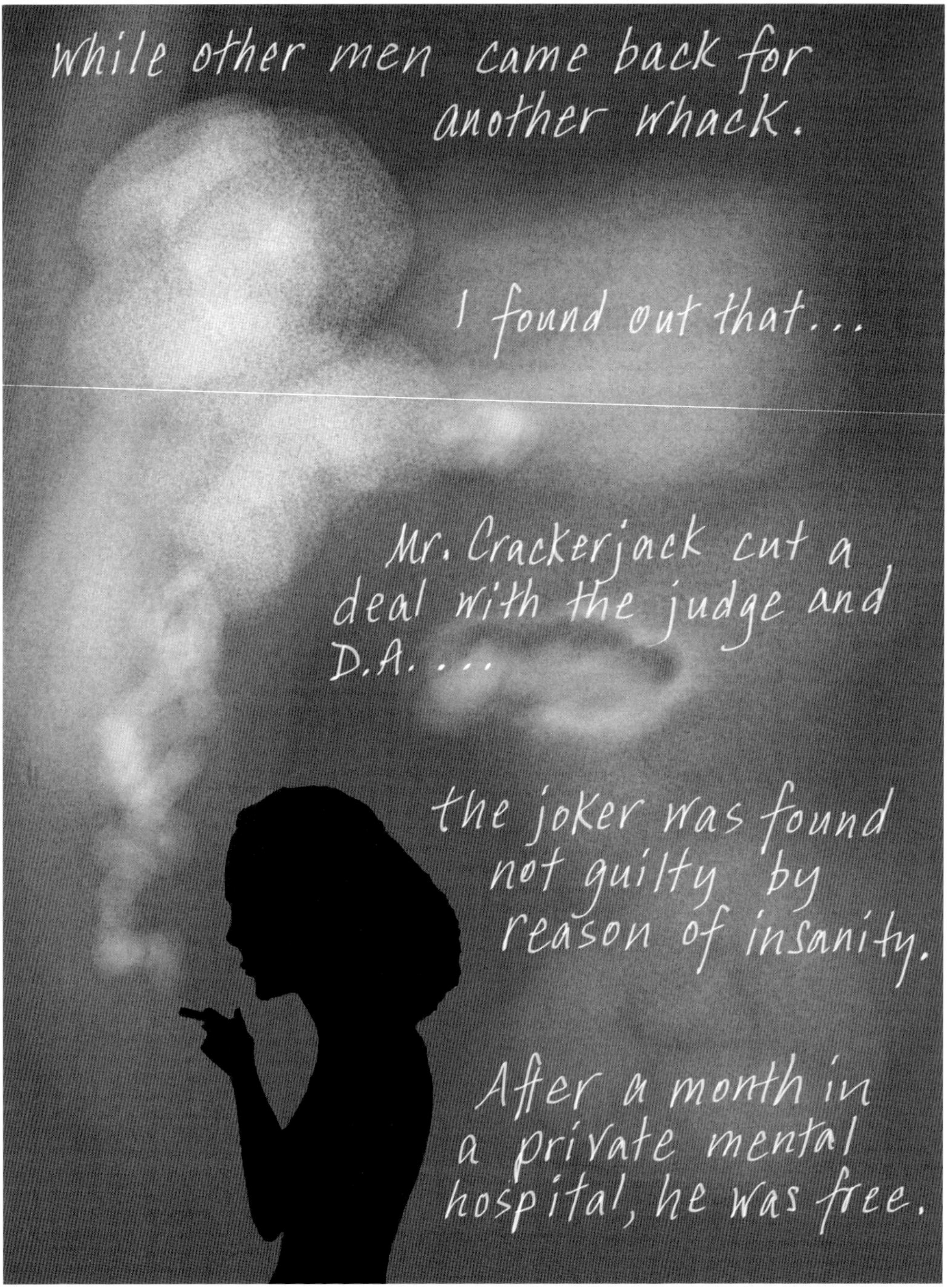
While other men came back for another whack.
I found out that...
Mr. Crackerjack cut a deal with the judge and D.A. ...
the joker was found not guilty by reason of insanity.
After a month in a private mental hospital, he was free.

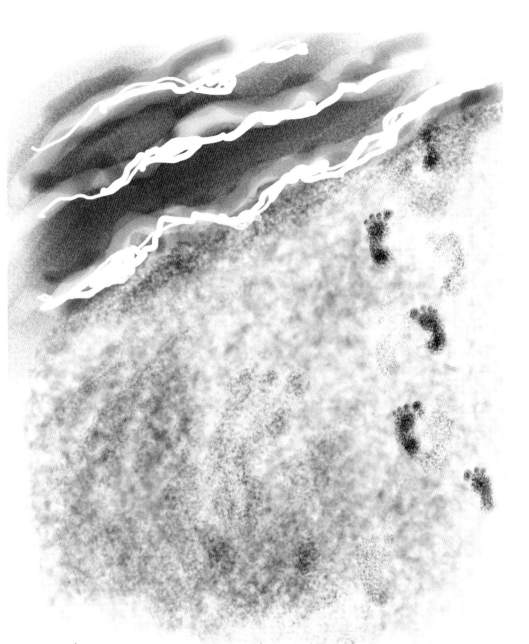

Nobody had even bothered to tell me.

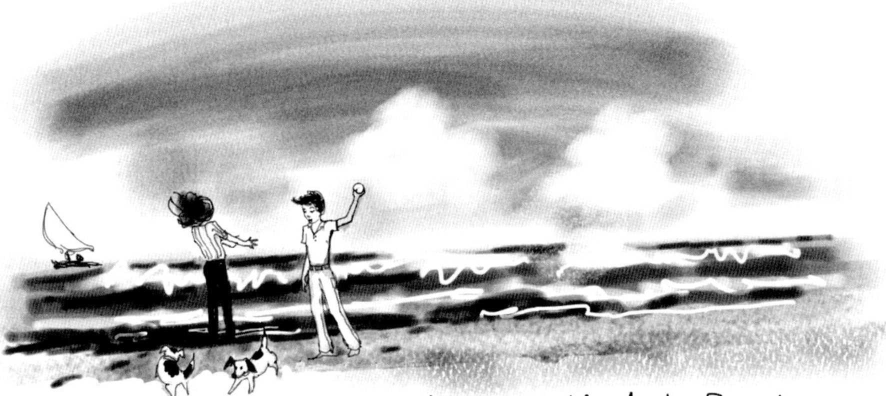

In late July, I spent a week with Steph,

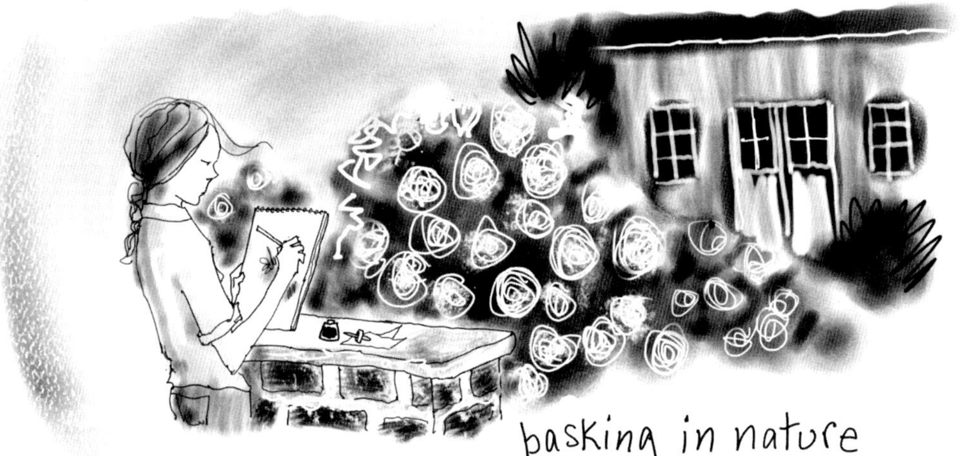

basking in nature

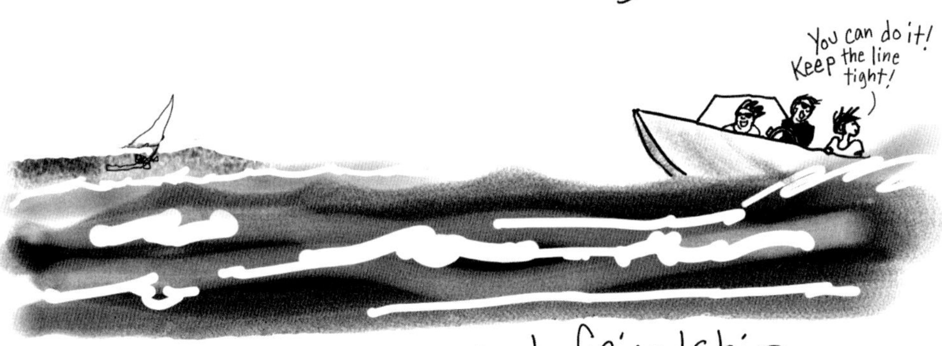
You can do it!
Keep the line tight!

and friendship.

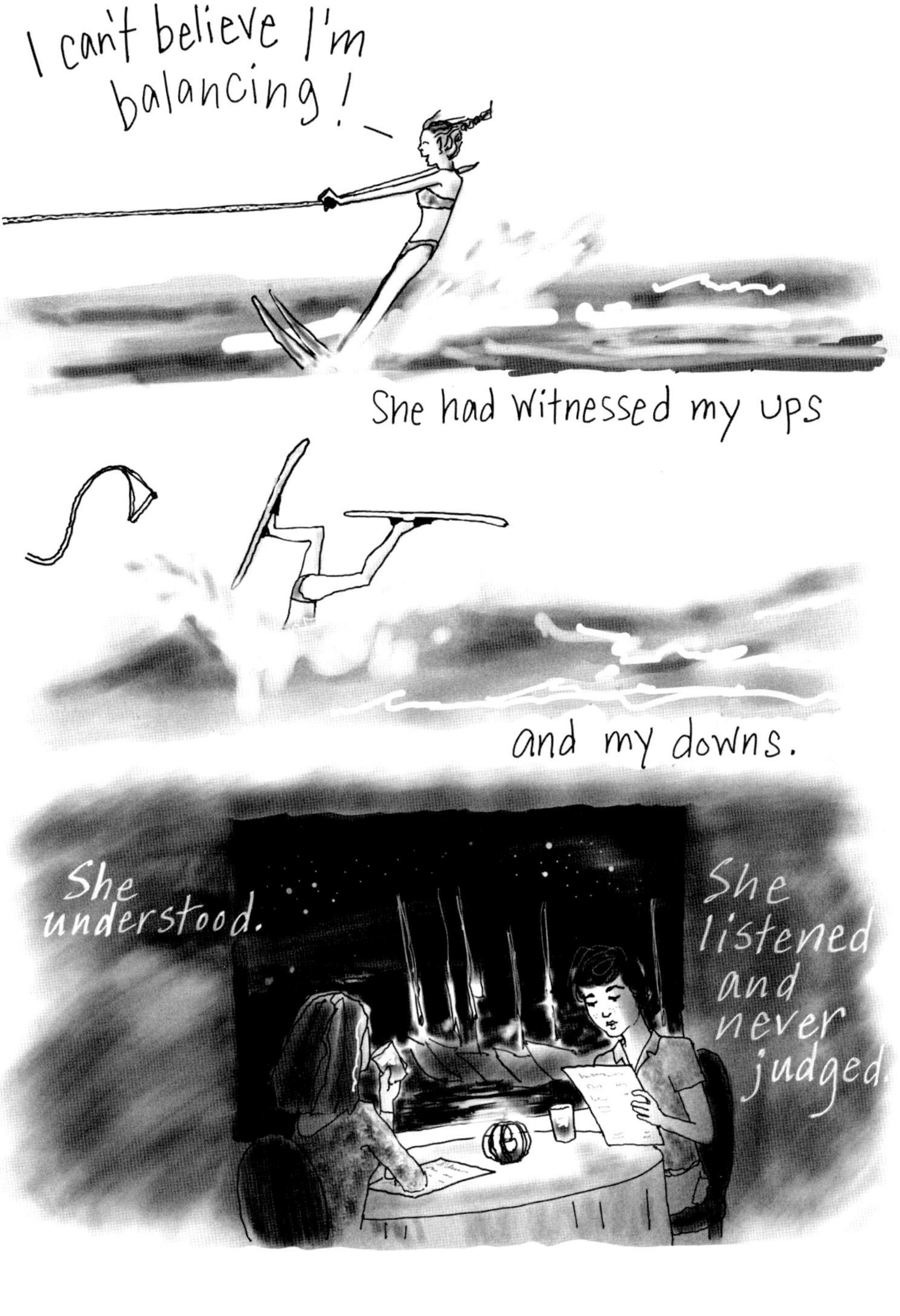
I can't believe I'm balancing!
She had witnessed my ups
and my downs.
She understood.
She listened and never judged.

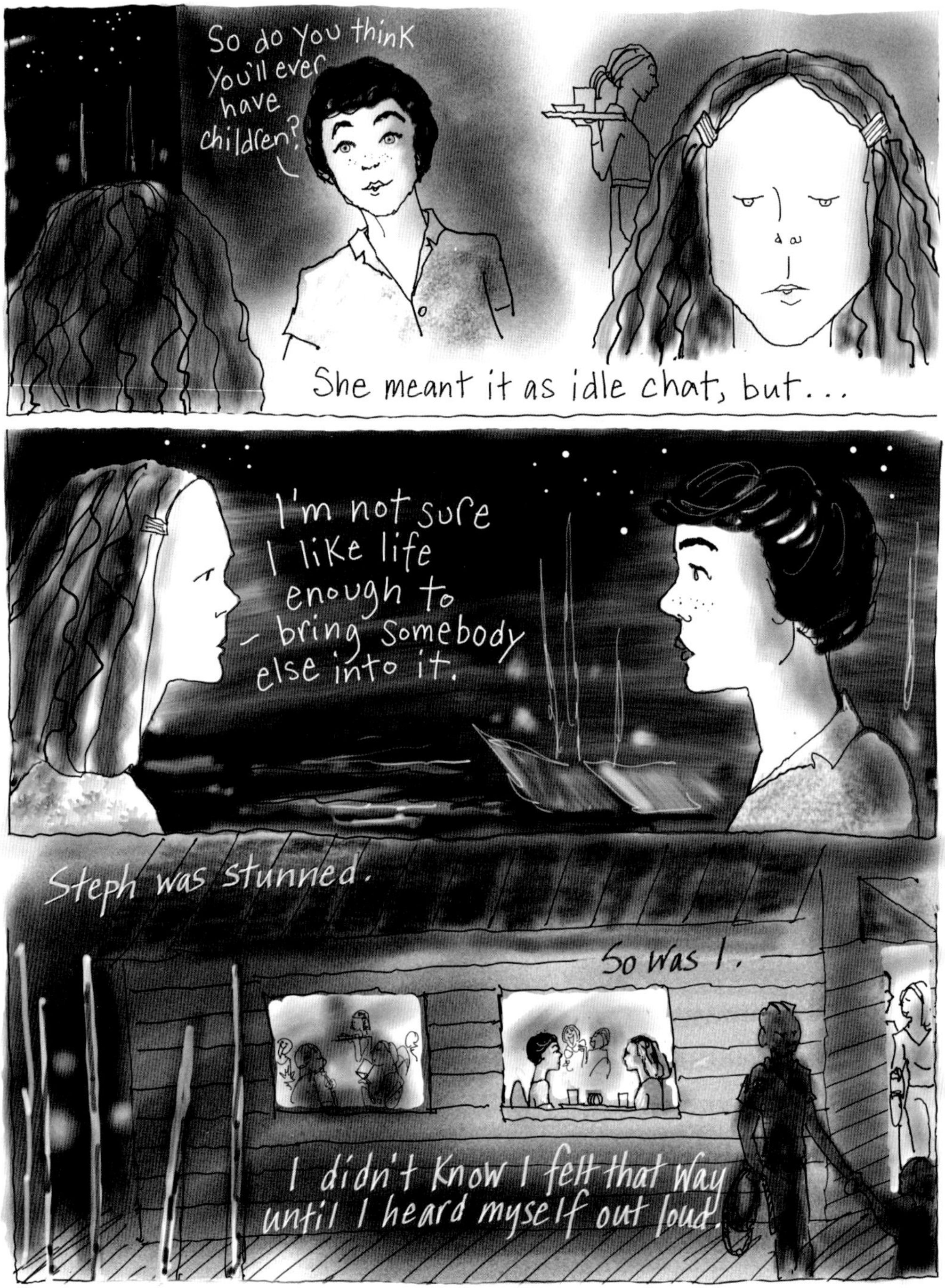
So do you think you'll ever have children?
She meant it as idle chat, but...
I'm not sure I like life enough to bring somebody else into it.
Steph was stunned.
So was I.
I didn't know I felt that way until I heard myself out loud.

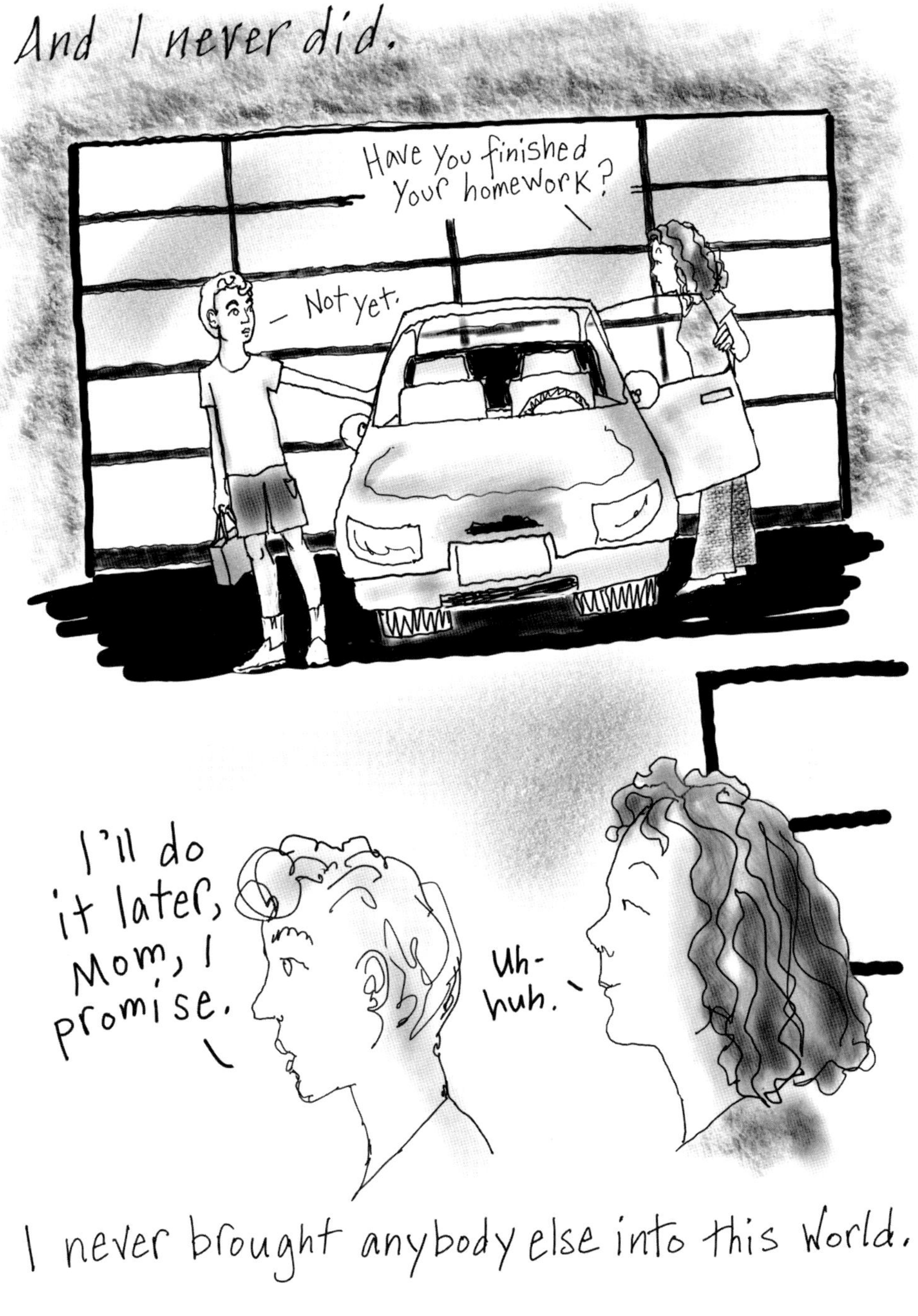
And I never did.
Have you finished your homework?
Not yet.
I'll do it later, Mom, I promise.
Uh-huh.
I never brought anybody else into this World.

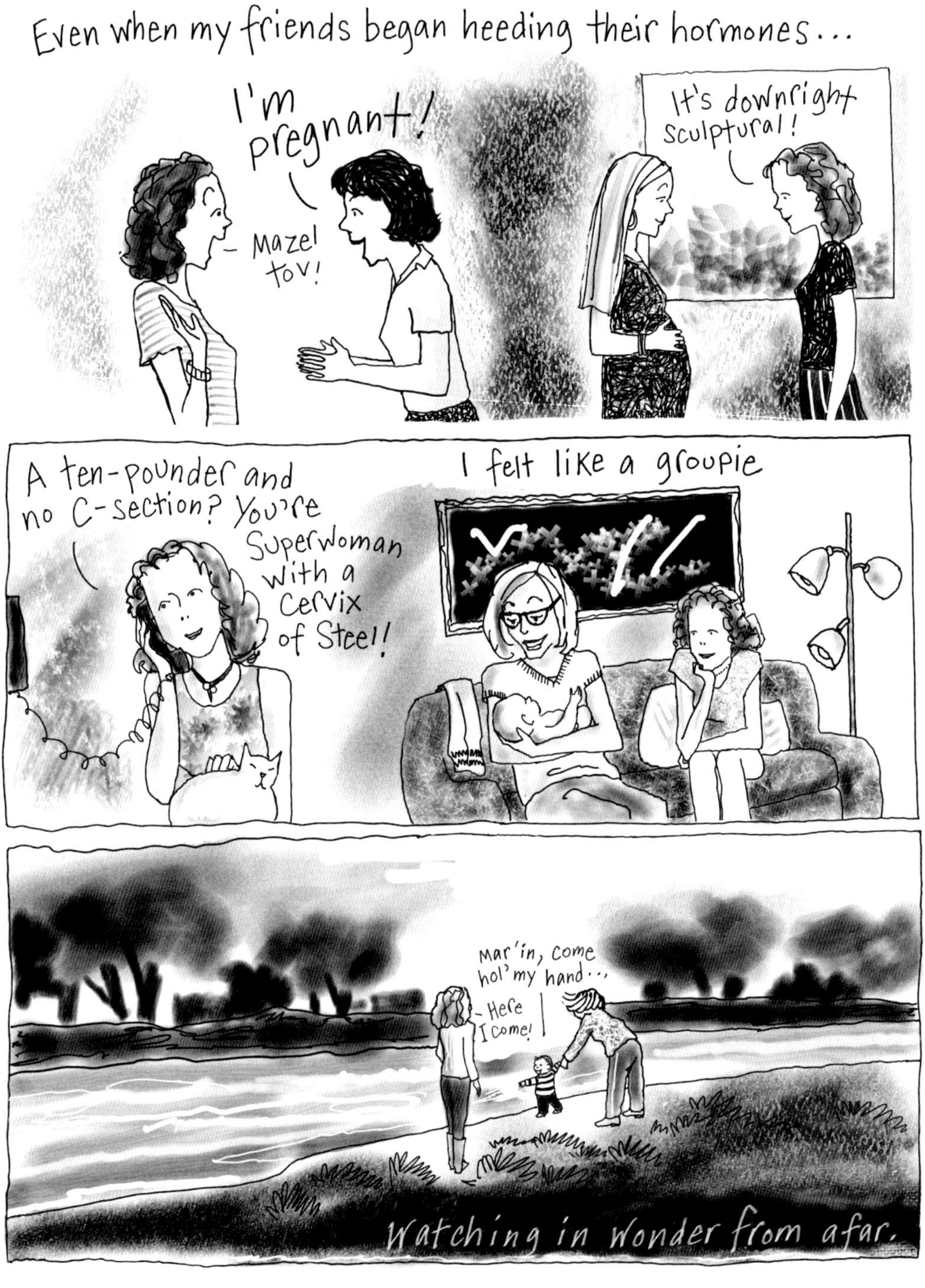
Even when my friends began heeding their hormones...
I'm pregnant!
Mazel tov!
It's downright sculptural!
A ten-pounder and no C-section? You're Superwoman with a Cervix of Steel!
I felt like a groupie
Mar'in, come hol' my hand...
Here I come!
watching in wonder from afar.

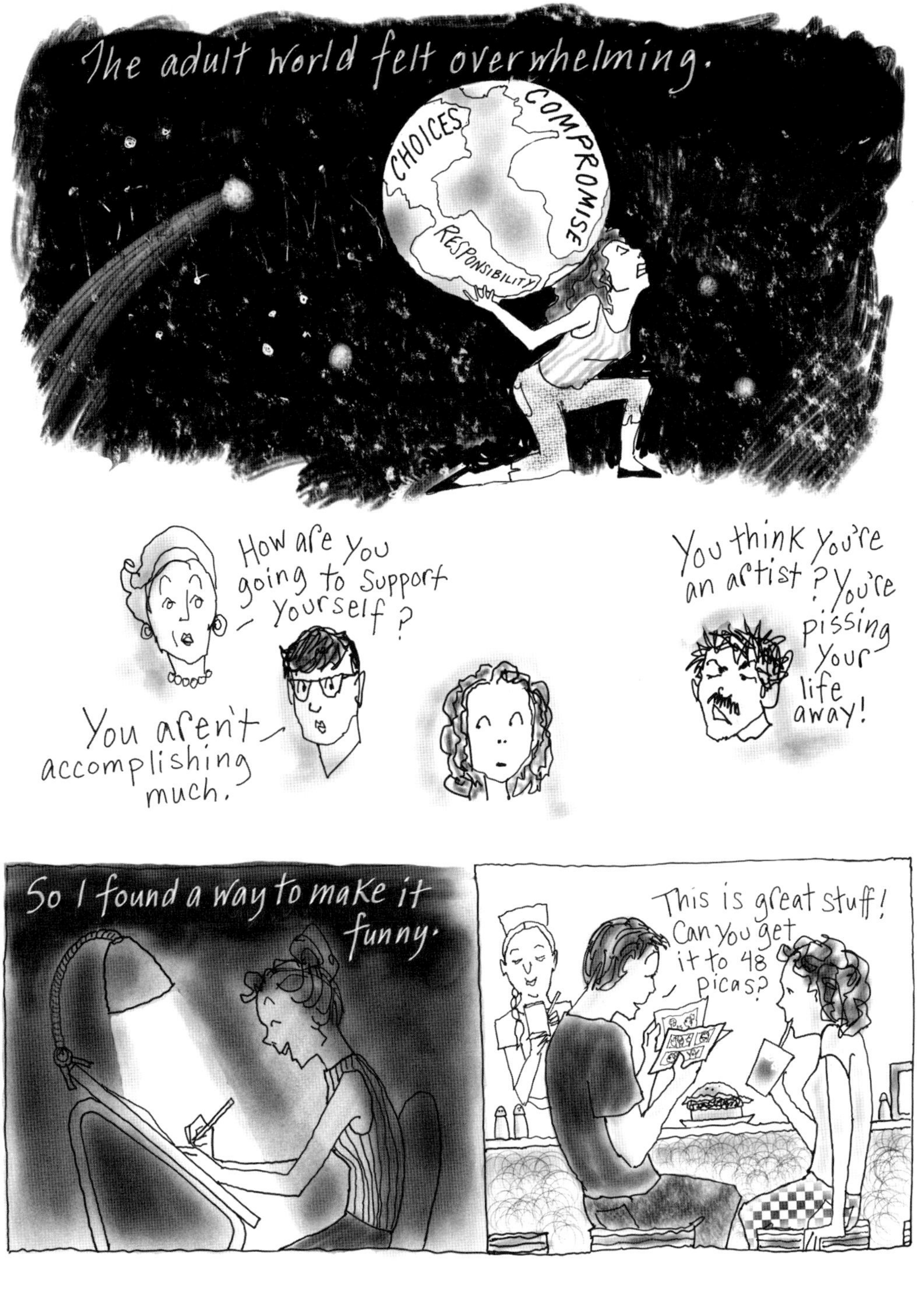
The adult world felt overwhelming.
CHOICES
COMPROMISE
RESPONSIBILITY
How are you going to support yourself?
You aren't accomplishing much.
You think you're an artist? You're pissing your life away!
So I found a way to make it funny.
This is great stuff! Can you get it to 48 picas?

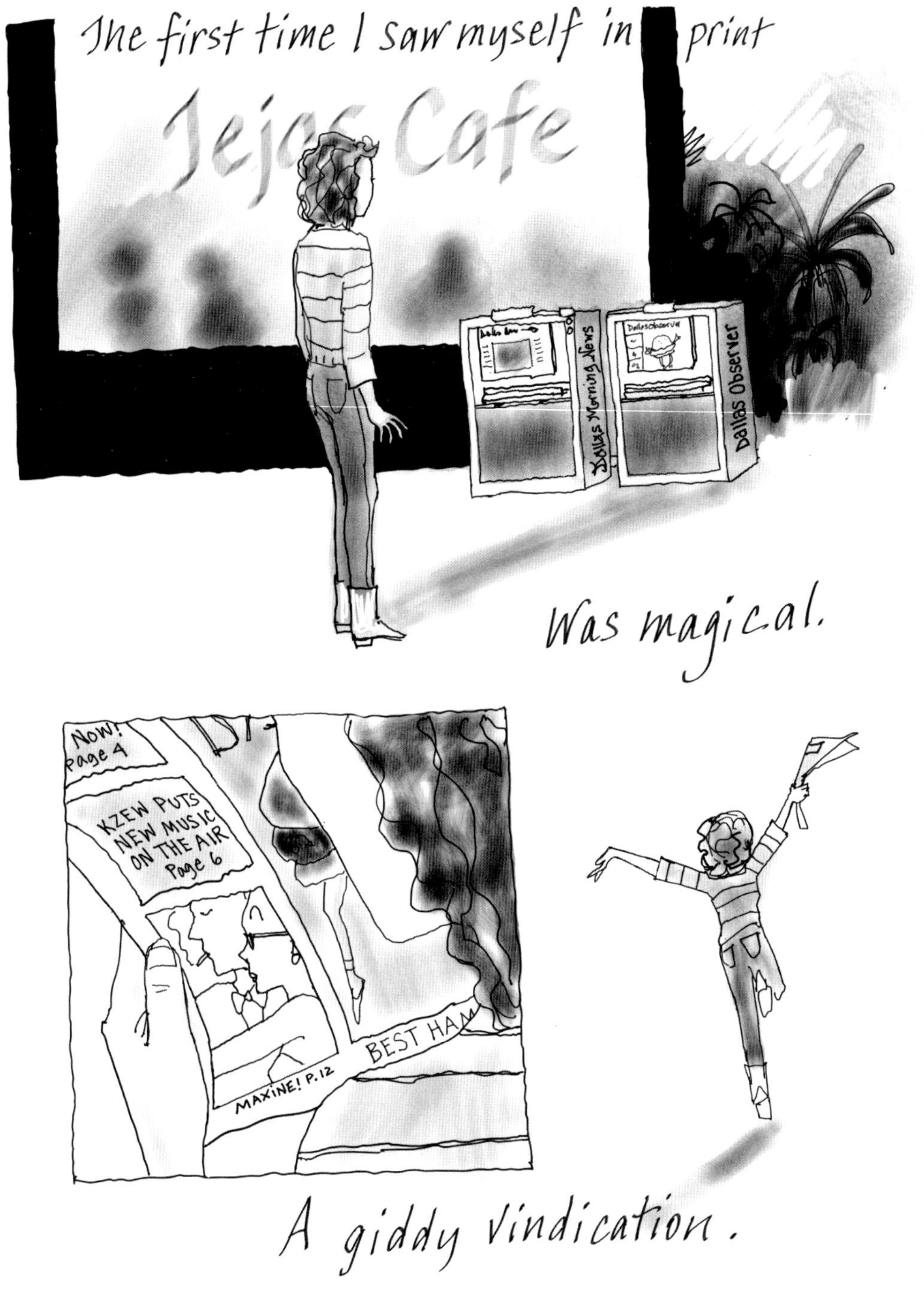
The first time I saw myself in print
Dallas Morning News
Dallas Observer
Was magical.
Now! Page 4
KZEW PUTS NEW MUSIC ON THE AIR Page 6
BEST HAM
MAXINE! P.12
A giddy vindication.

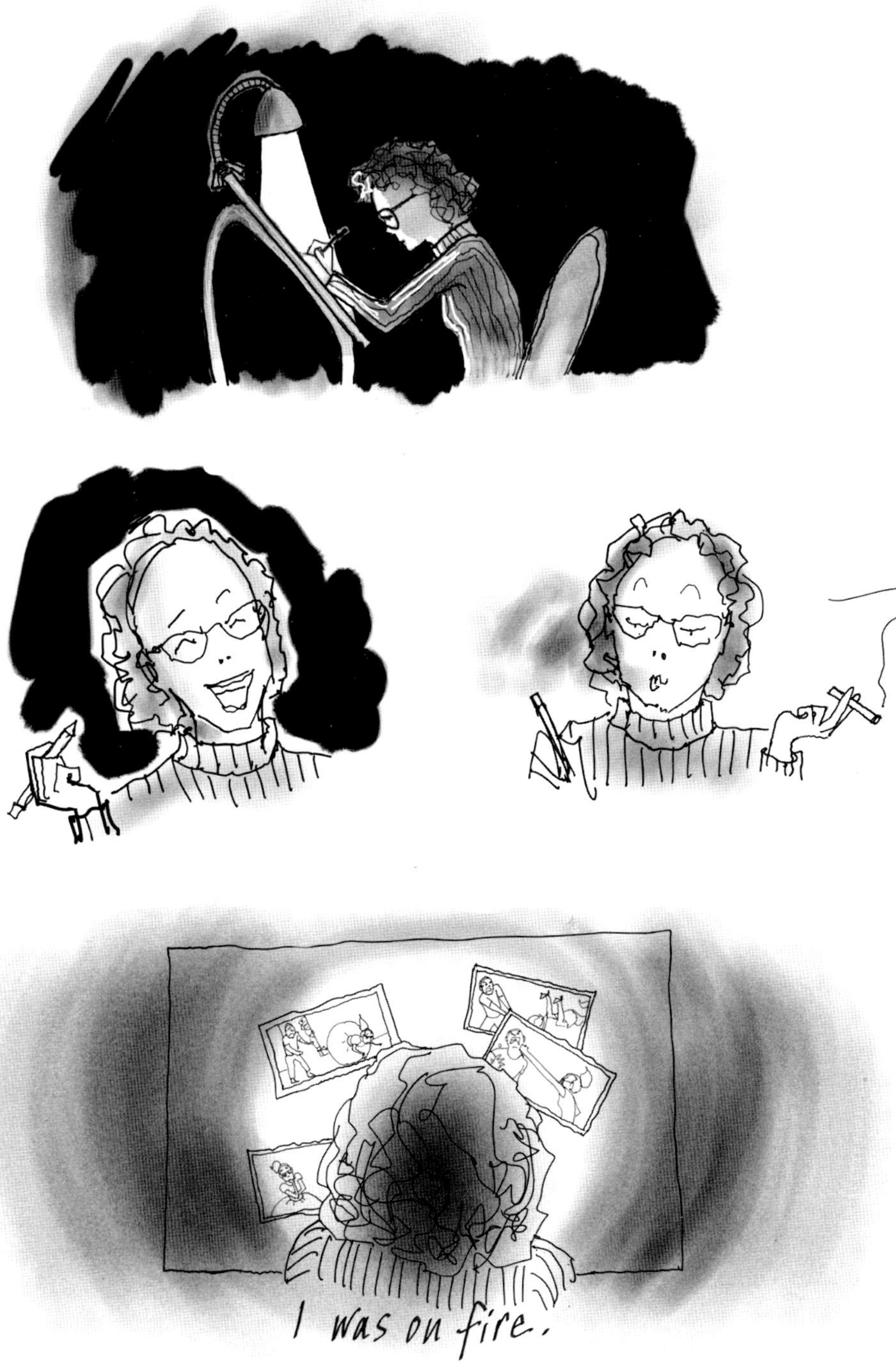
I was on fire.

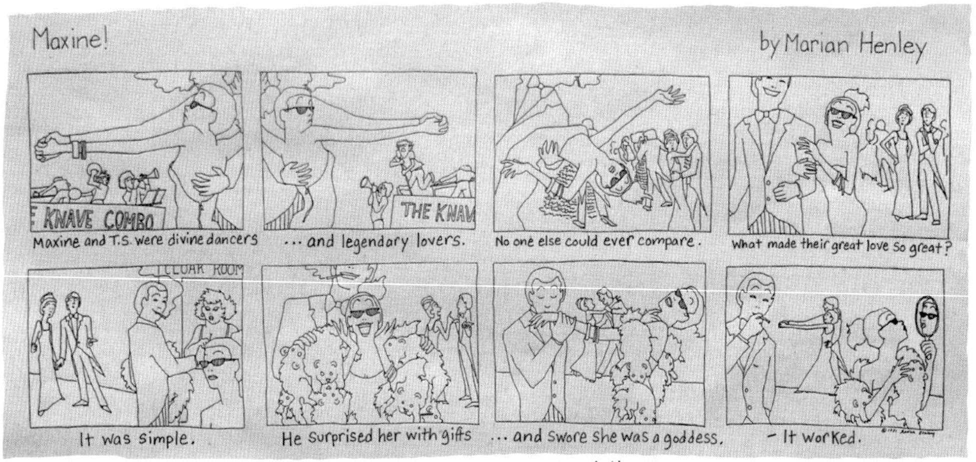
Maxine!
by Marian Henley
THE KNAVE COMBO
Maxine and T.S. were divine dancers
THE KNAVE
... and legendary lovers.
No one else could ever compare.
What made their great love so great?
It was simple.
He surprised her with gifts
... and swore she was a goddess.
- It worked.

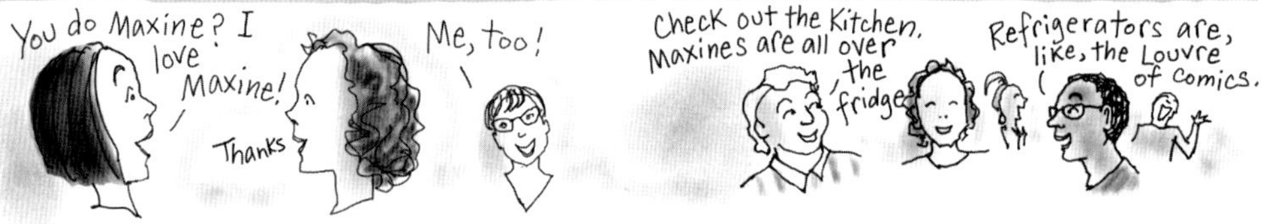
You do Maxine? I love Maxine!
Thanks
Me, too!
Check out the Kitchen. Maxines are all over the fridge.
Refrigerators are, like, the Louvre of comics.

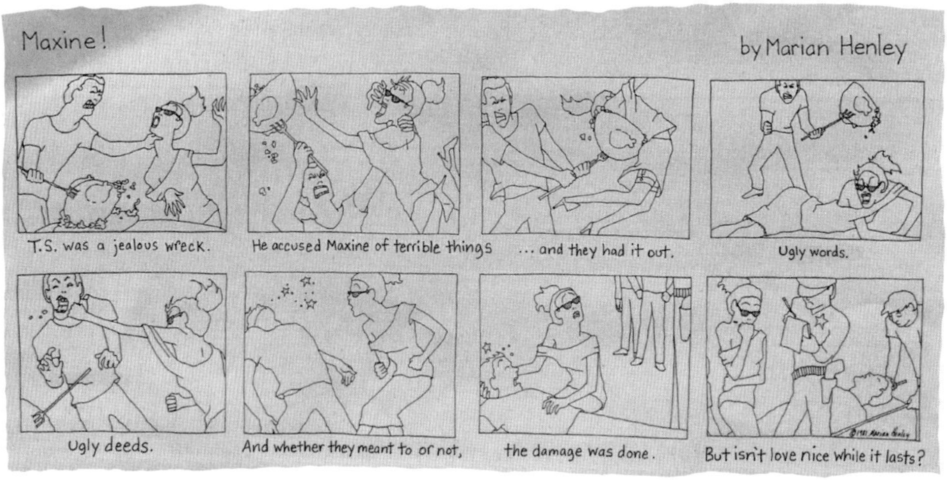
Maxine!
by Marian Henley
T.S. was a jealous wreck.
He accused Maxine of terrible things
... and they had it out.
Ugly words.
Ugly deeds.
And whether they meant to or not,
the damage was done.
But isn't love nice while it lasts?

In my own way, I'd struck a vein of the zeitgeist.

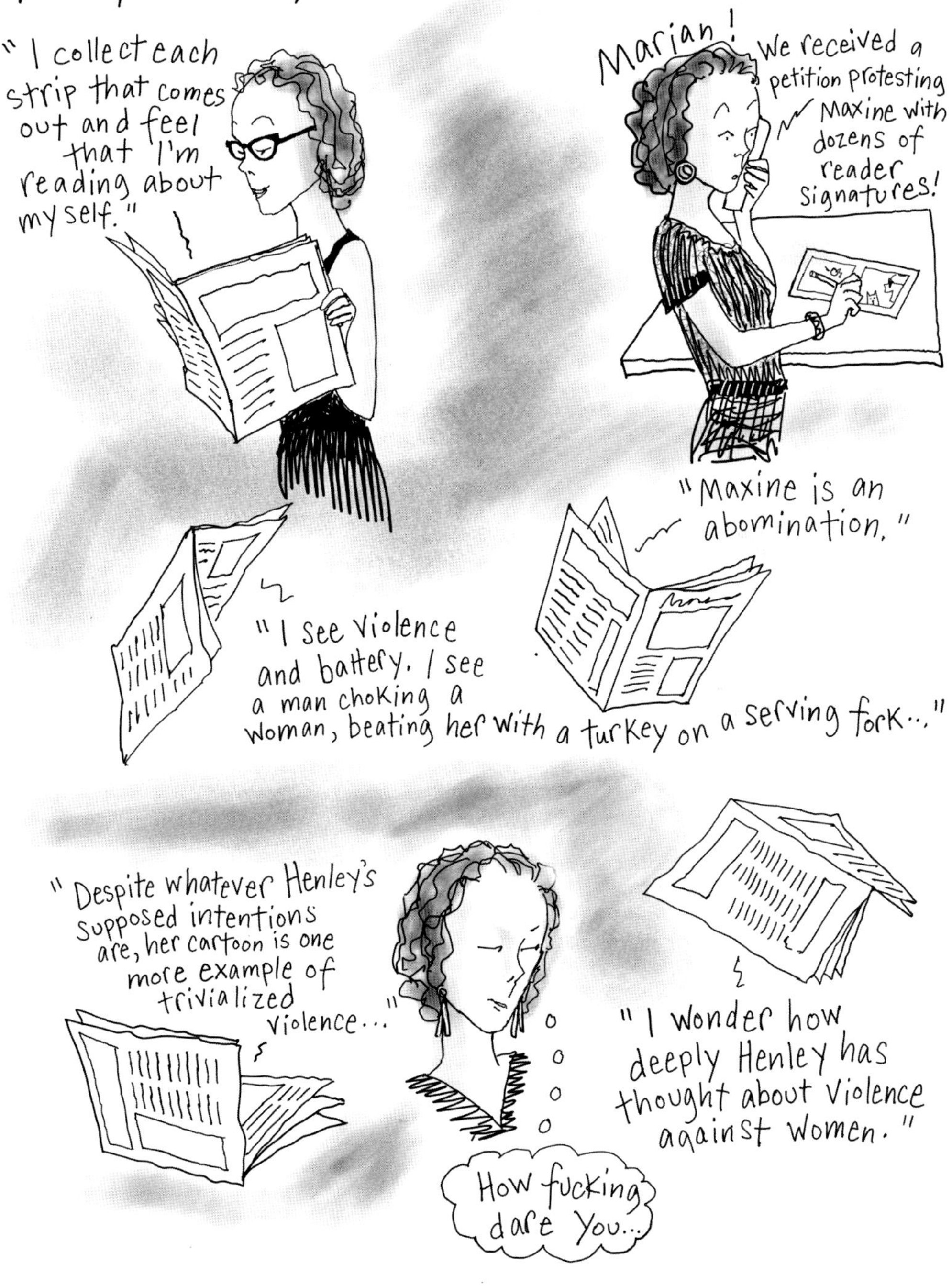
"I collect each strip that comes out and feel that I'm reading about myself."
Marian! We received a petition protesting Maxine with dozens of reader signatures!
"Maxine is an abomination."
"I see violence and battery. I see a man choking a woman, beating her with a turkey on a serving fork..."
"Despite whatever Henley's supposed intentions are, her cartoon is one more example of trivialized violence..."
"I wonder how deeply Henley has thought about violence against women."
How fucking dare you...

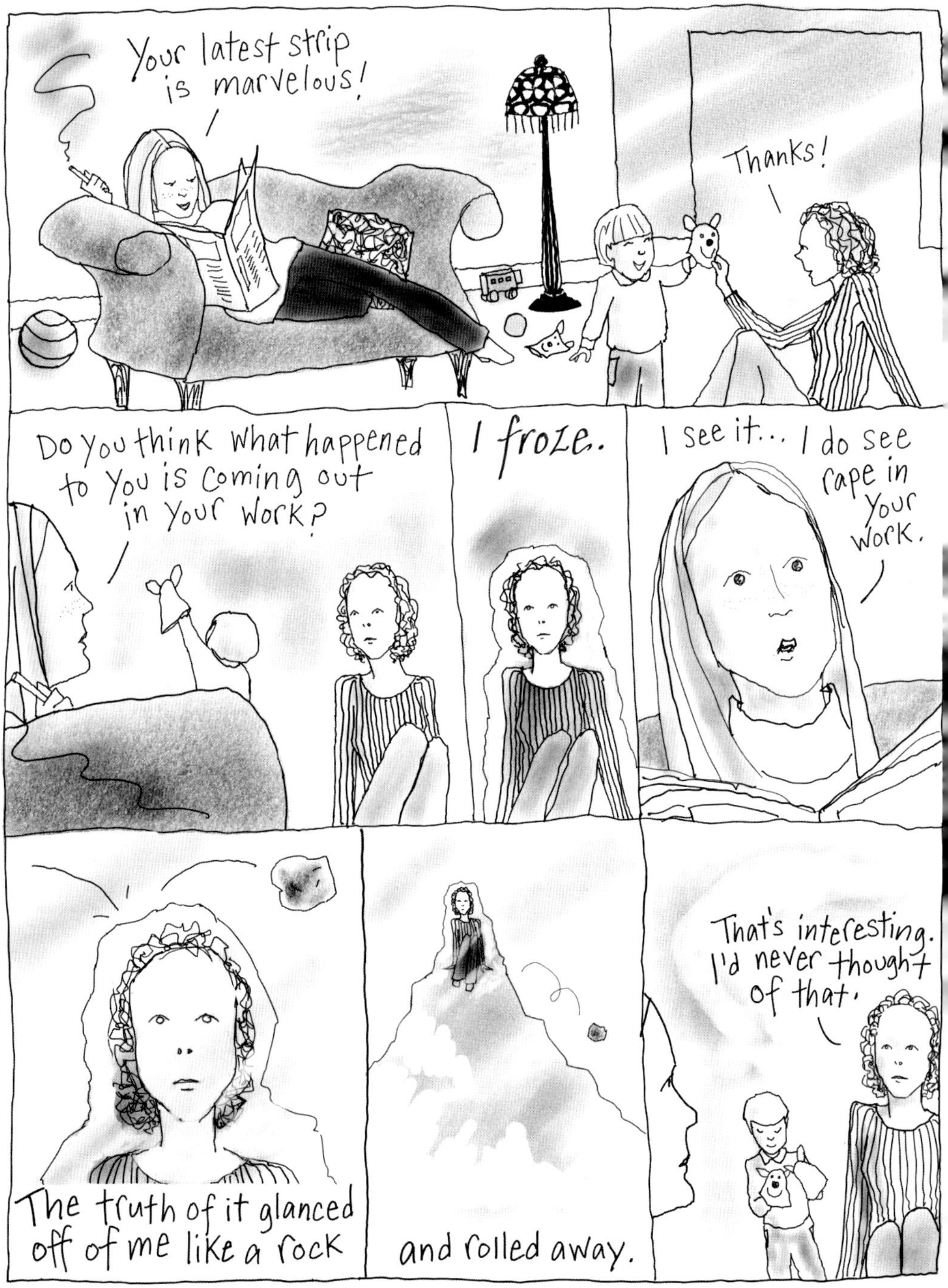
Your latest strip is marvelous!
Thanks!
Do you think what happened to you is coming out in your work?
I froze.
I see it... I do see rape in your work.
The truth of it glanced off of me like a rock
and rolled away.
That's interesting. I'd never thought of that.

But I was my own self.

 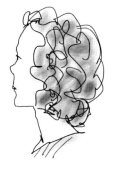

Not the joker's.

Not Mr. Crackerjack's.

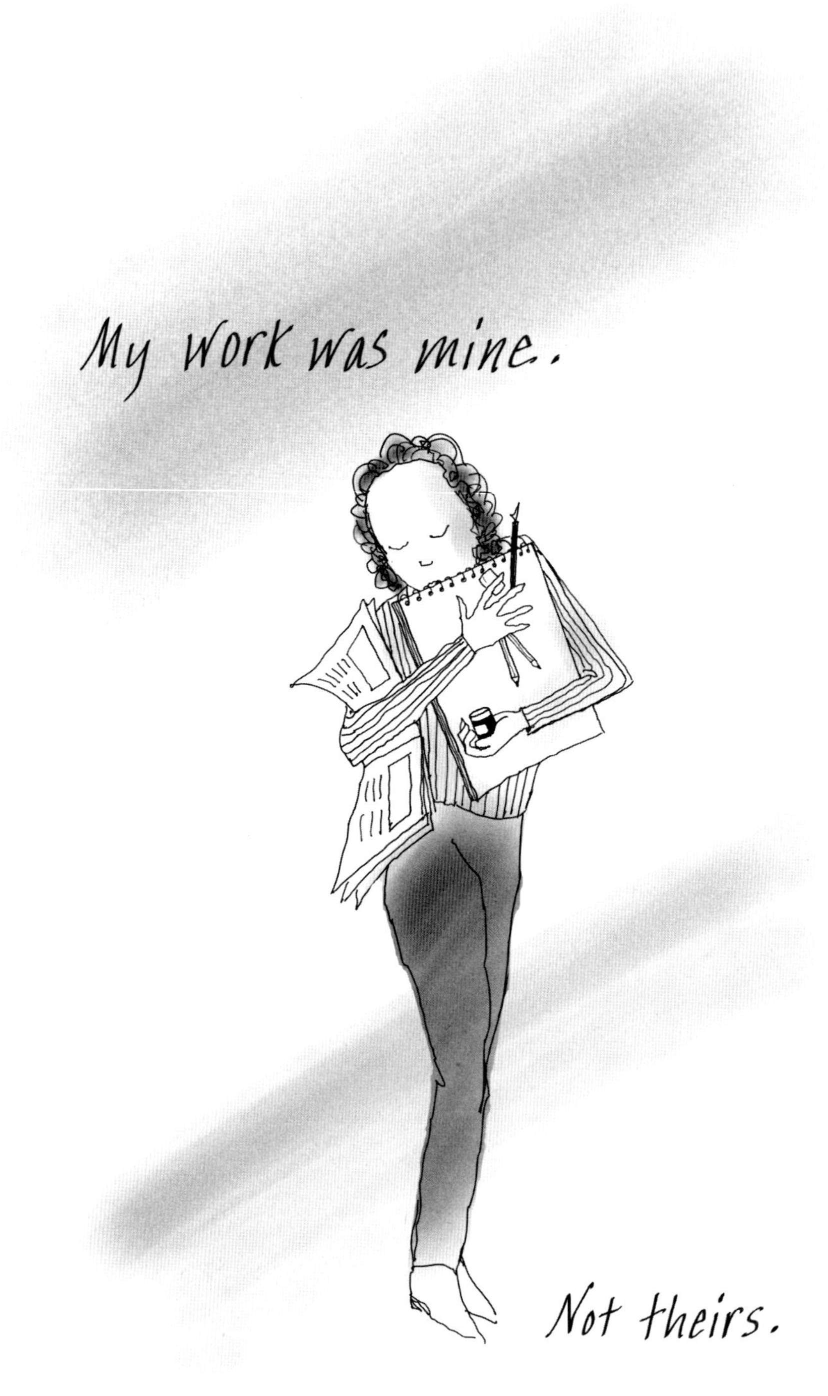
My work was mine.
Not theirs.

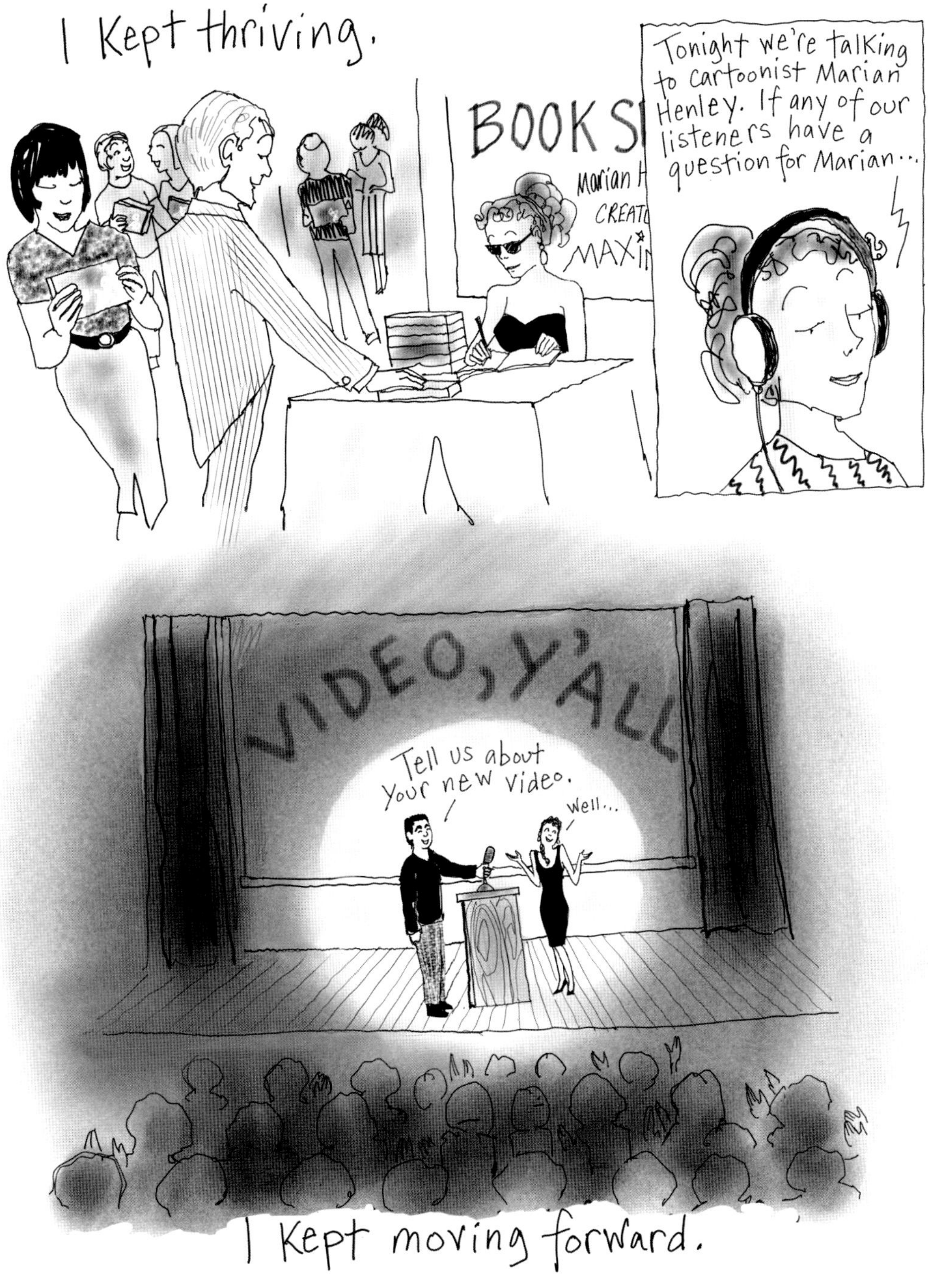
I kept thriving.
Tonight we're talking to cartoonist Marian Henley. If any of our listeners have a question for Marian...
VIDEO, Y'ALL
Tell us about your new video.
Well...
I kept moving forward.

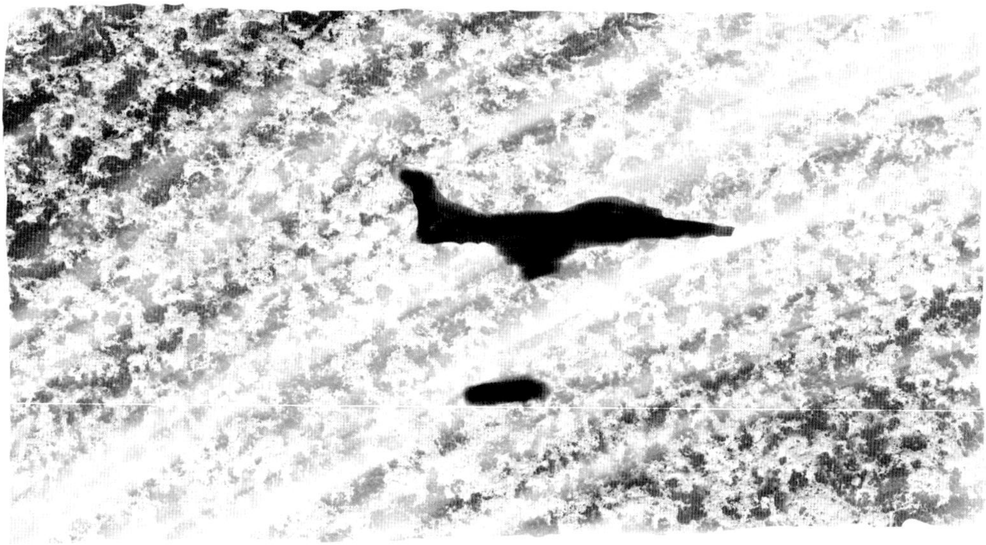

But rape is like a bomb

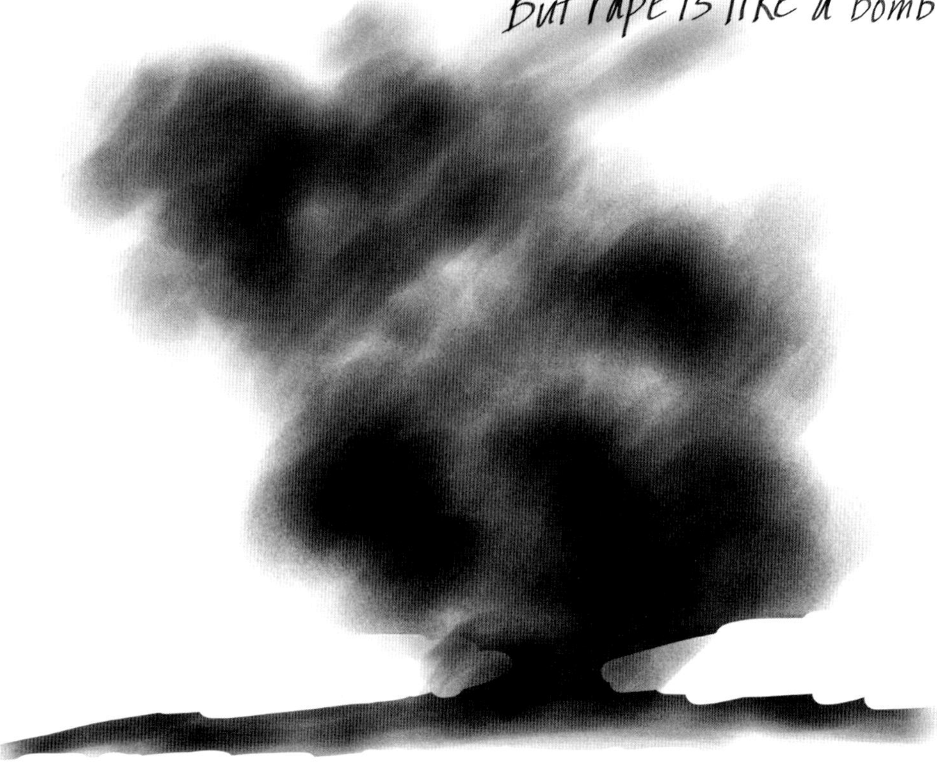

leaving part of you destroyed

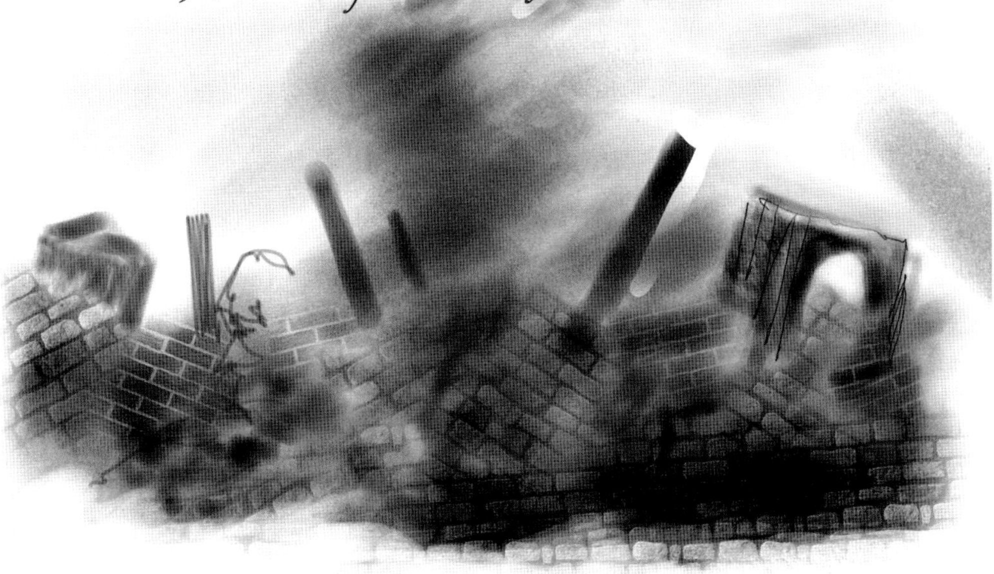

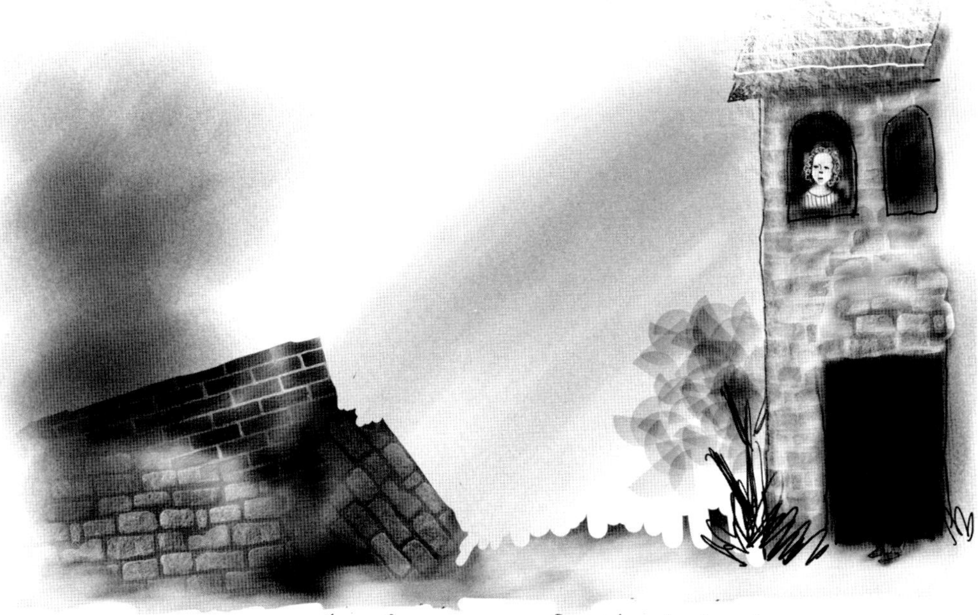

and part of you perfectly intact.

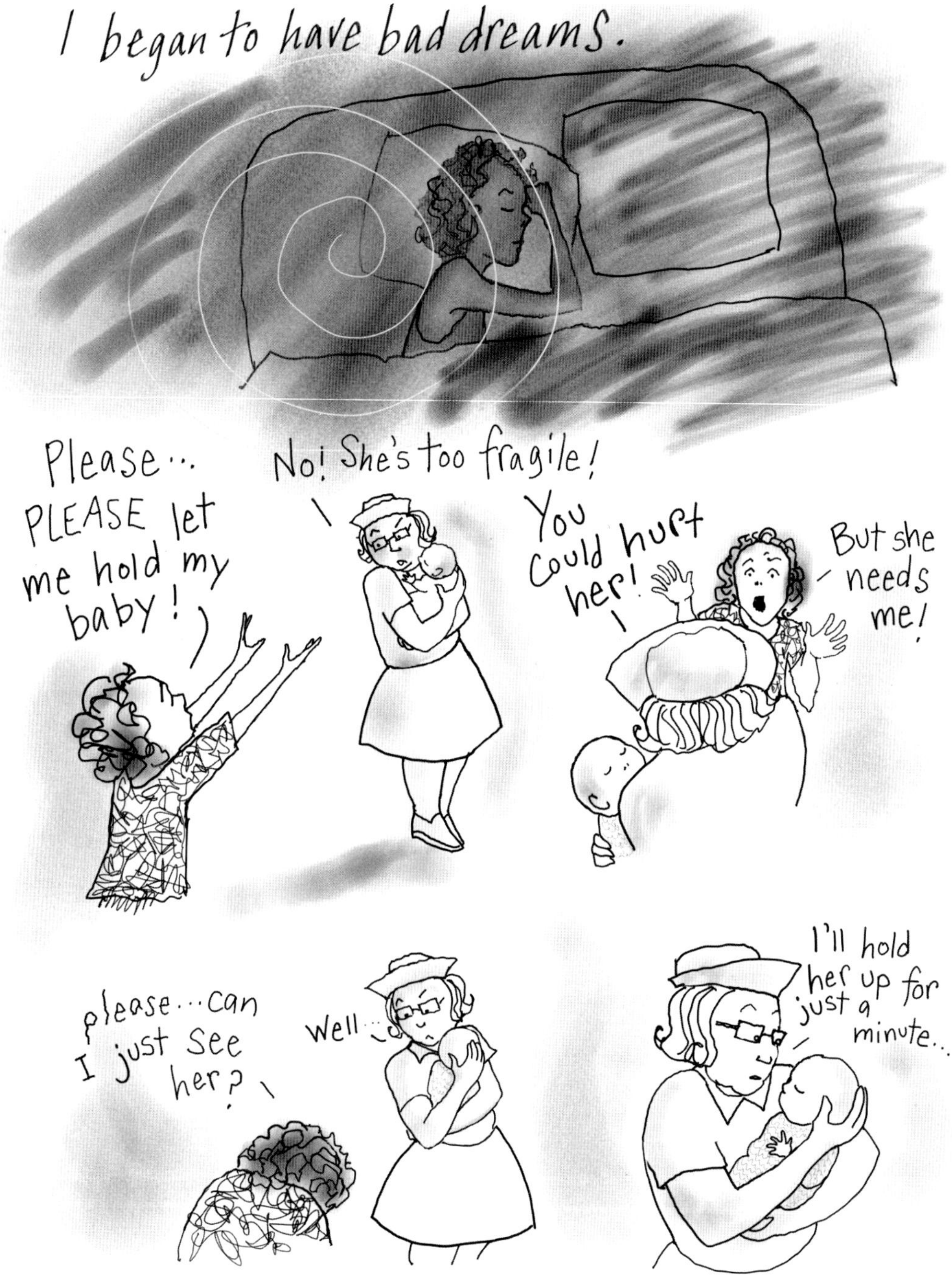
I began to have bad dreams.
Please... PLEASE let me hold my baby!
No! She's too fragile!
You could hurt her!
But she needs me!
please...can I just see her?
Well...
I'll hold her up for just a minute...

The baby was weak.

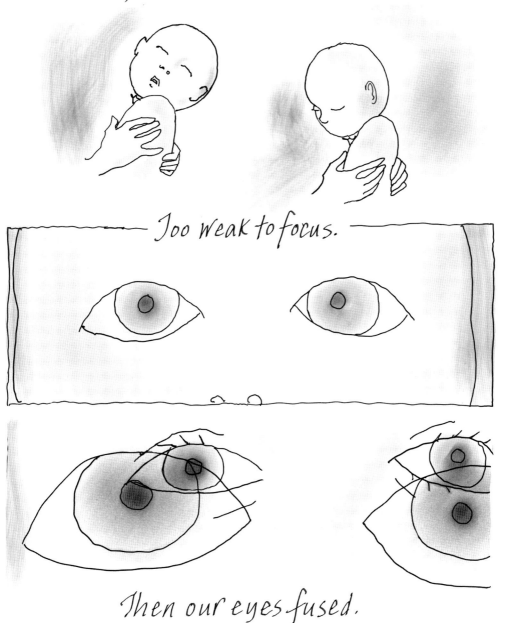

Too weak to focus.

Then our eyes fused.

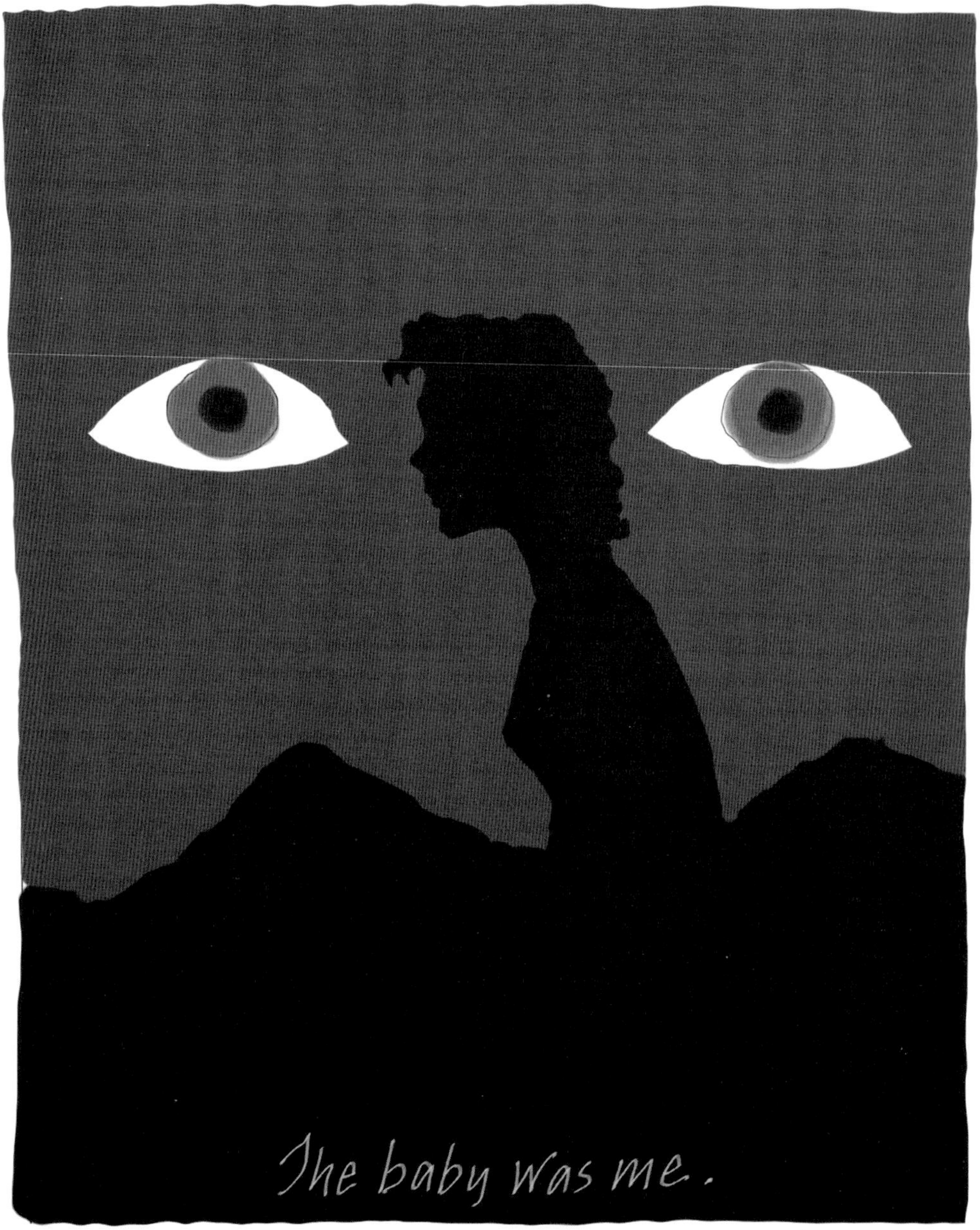
The baby was me.

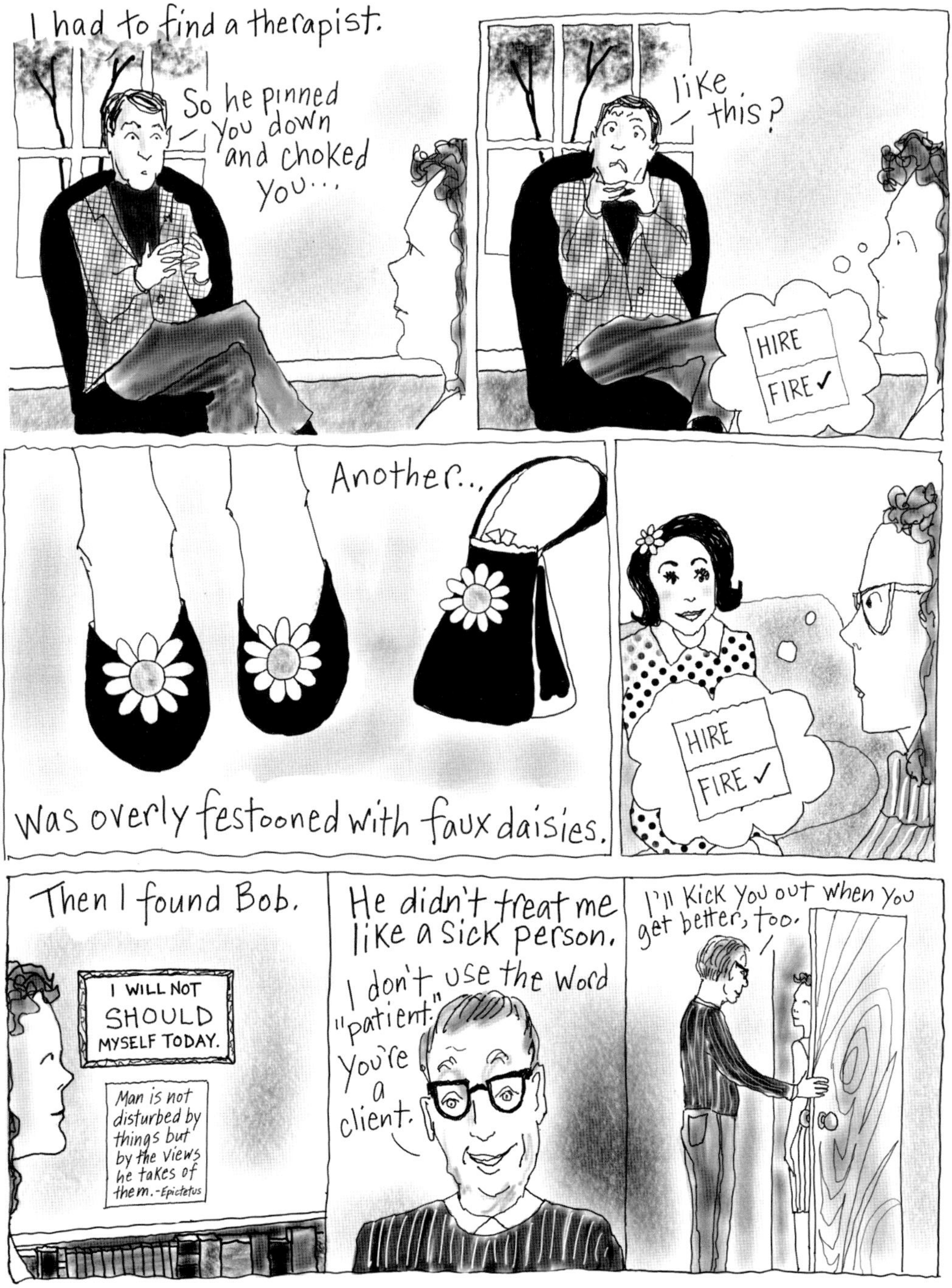
I had to find a therapist.
So he pinned you down and choked you...
like this?
HIRE
FIRE ✓
Another...
was overly festooned with faux daisies.
HIRE
FIRE ✓
Then I found Bob.
I WILL NOT SHOULD MYSELF TODAY.
Man is not disturbed by things but by the views he takes of them. -Epictetus
He didn't treat me like a sick person.
I don't use the word "patient." You're a client.
I'll kick you out when you get better, too.

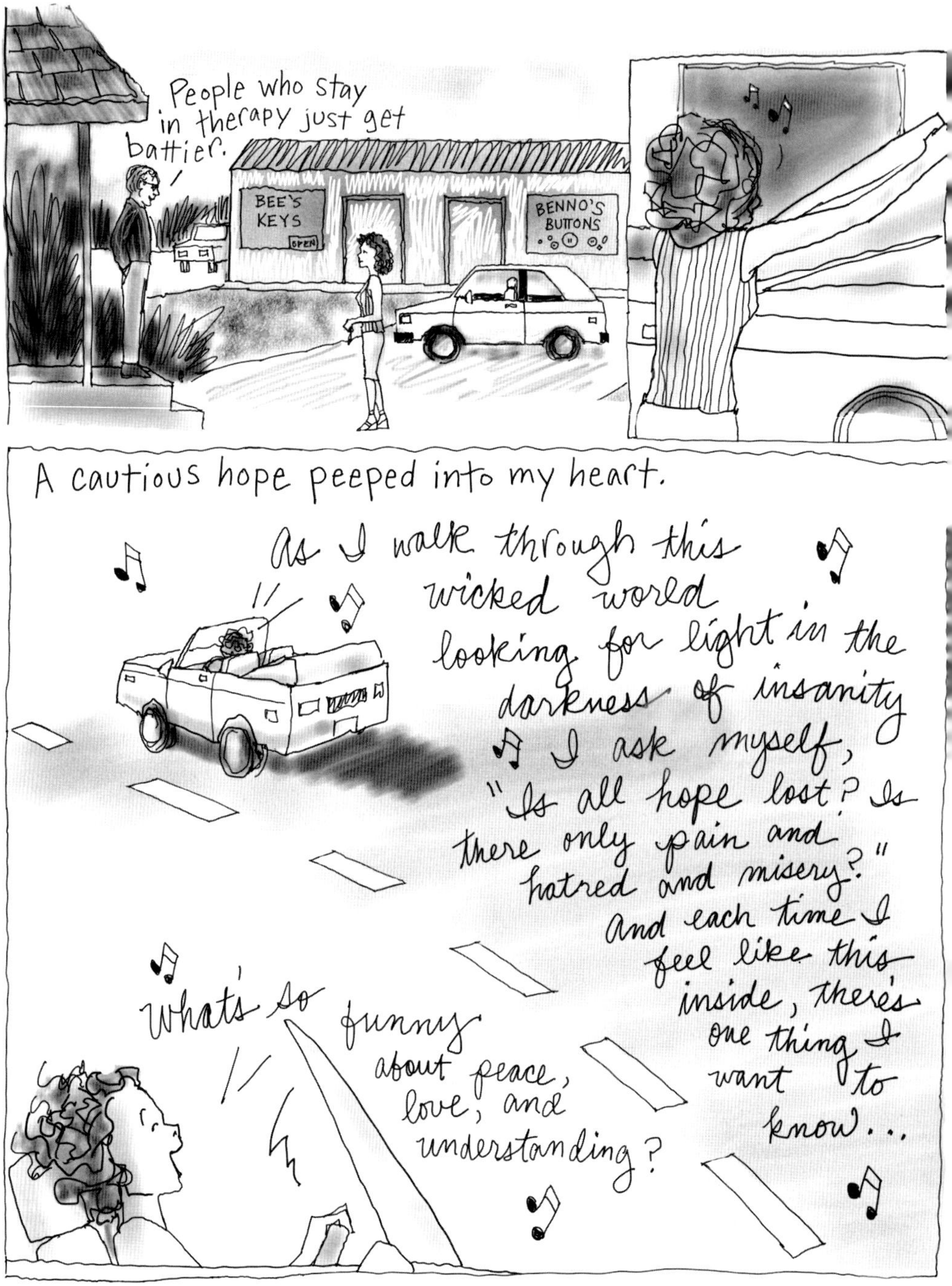
People who stay in therapy just get battier.
BEE'S KEYS
OPEN
BENNO'S BUTTONS
A cautious hope peeped into my heart.
As I walk through this wicked world looking for light in the darkness of insanity I ask myself, "Is all hope lost? Is there only pain and hatred and misery?" And each time I feel like this inside, there's one thing I want to know...
What's so funny about peace, love, and understanding?

I tried other kinds of therapy, too.

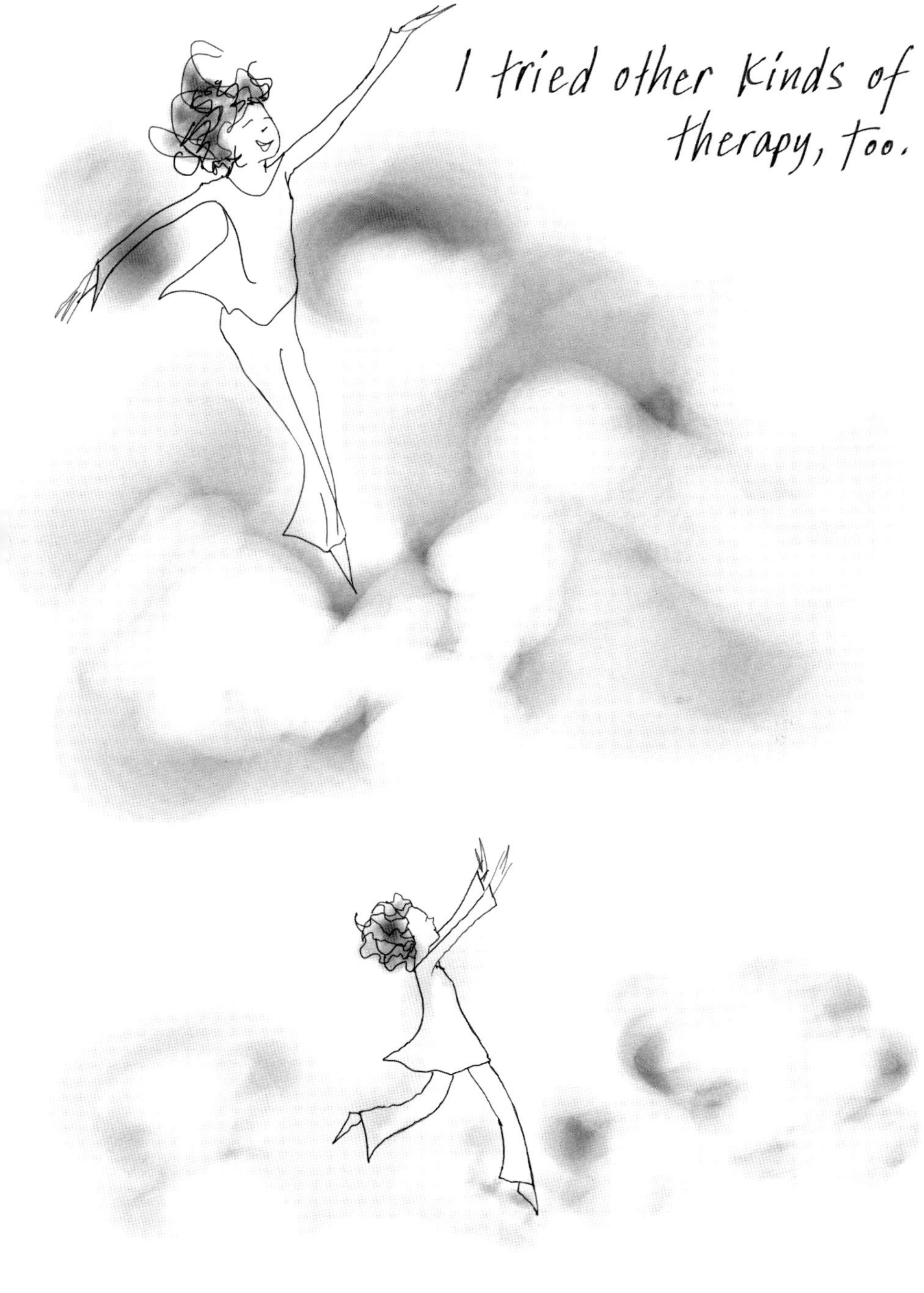

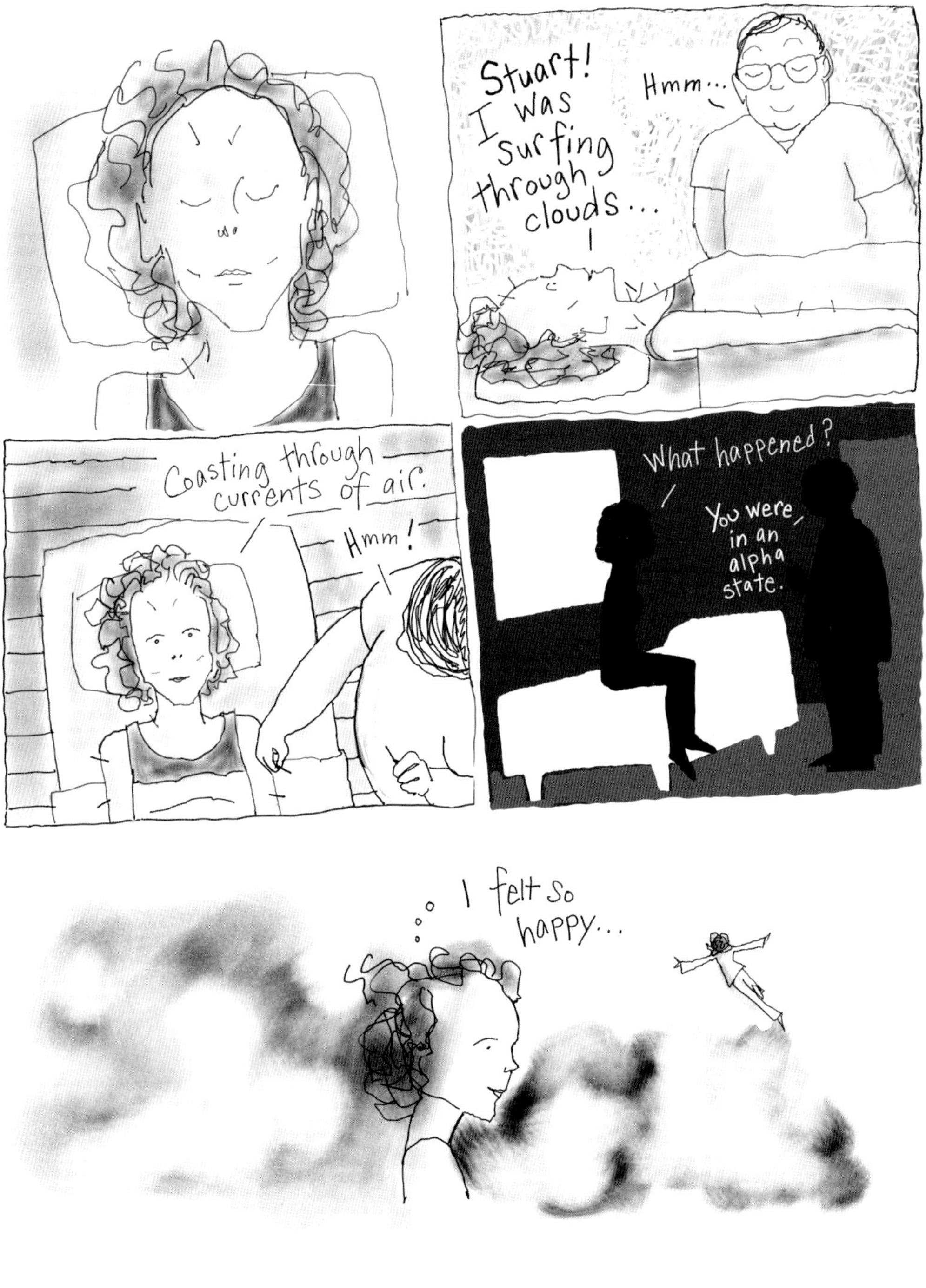
Stuart! I was surfing through clouds...
Hmm...
Coasting through currents of air.
Hmm!
What happened?
You were in an alpha state.
I felt so happy...

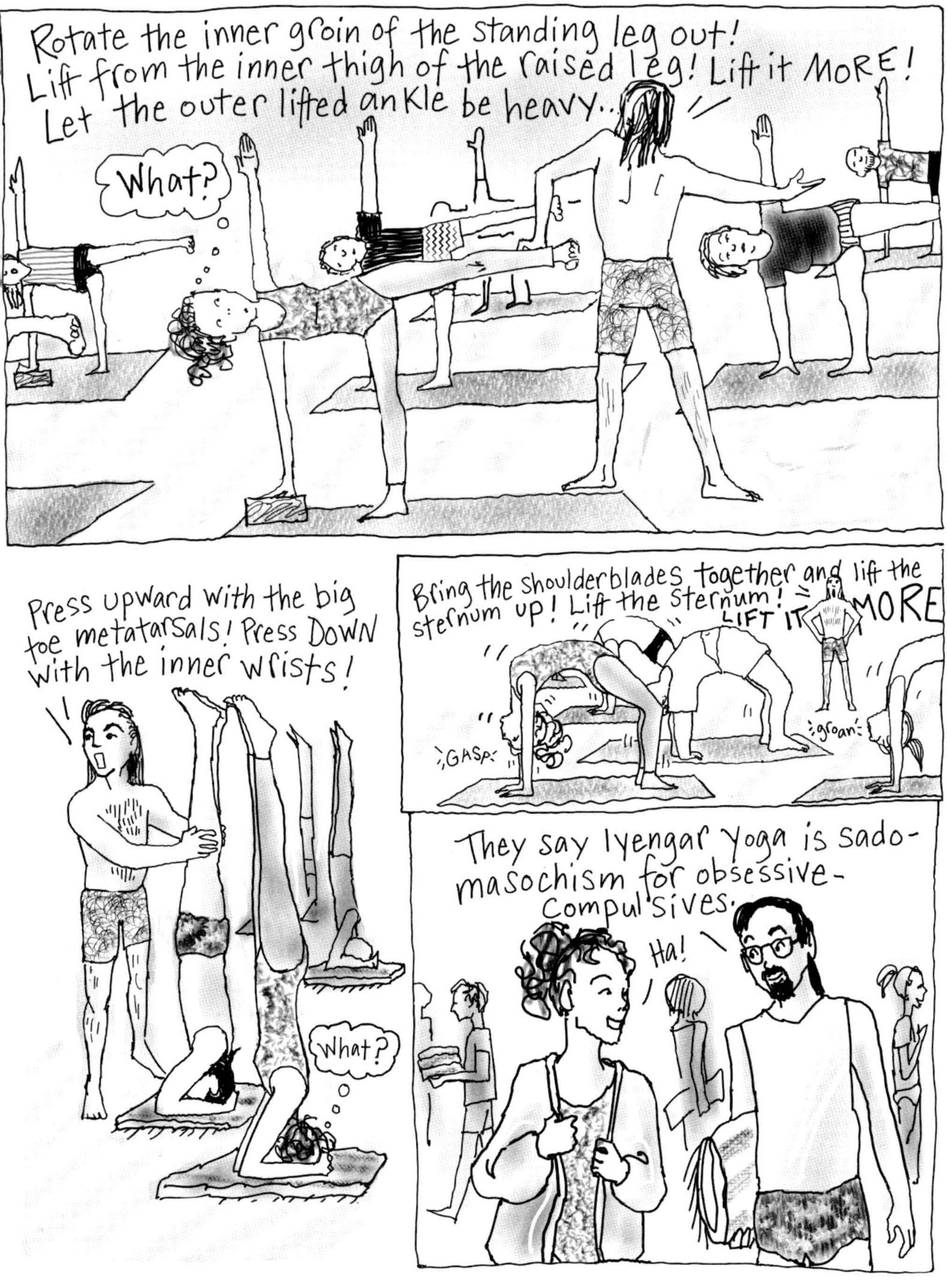
Rotate the inner groin of the standing leg out!
Lift from the inner thigh of the raised leg! Lift it MORE!
Let the outer lifted ankle be heavy...
What?
Press upward with the big toe metatarsals! Press DOWN with the inner wrists!
What?
Bring the shoulderblades together and lift the sternum up! Lift the sternum!
LIFT IT MORE
GASP
groan
They say Iyengar Yoga is sado-masochism for obsessive-compulsives.
Ha!

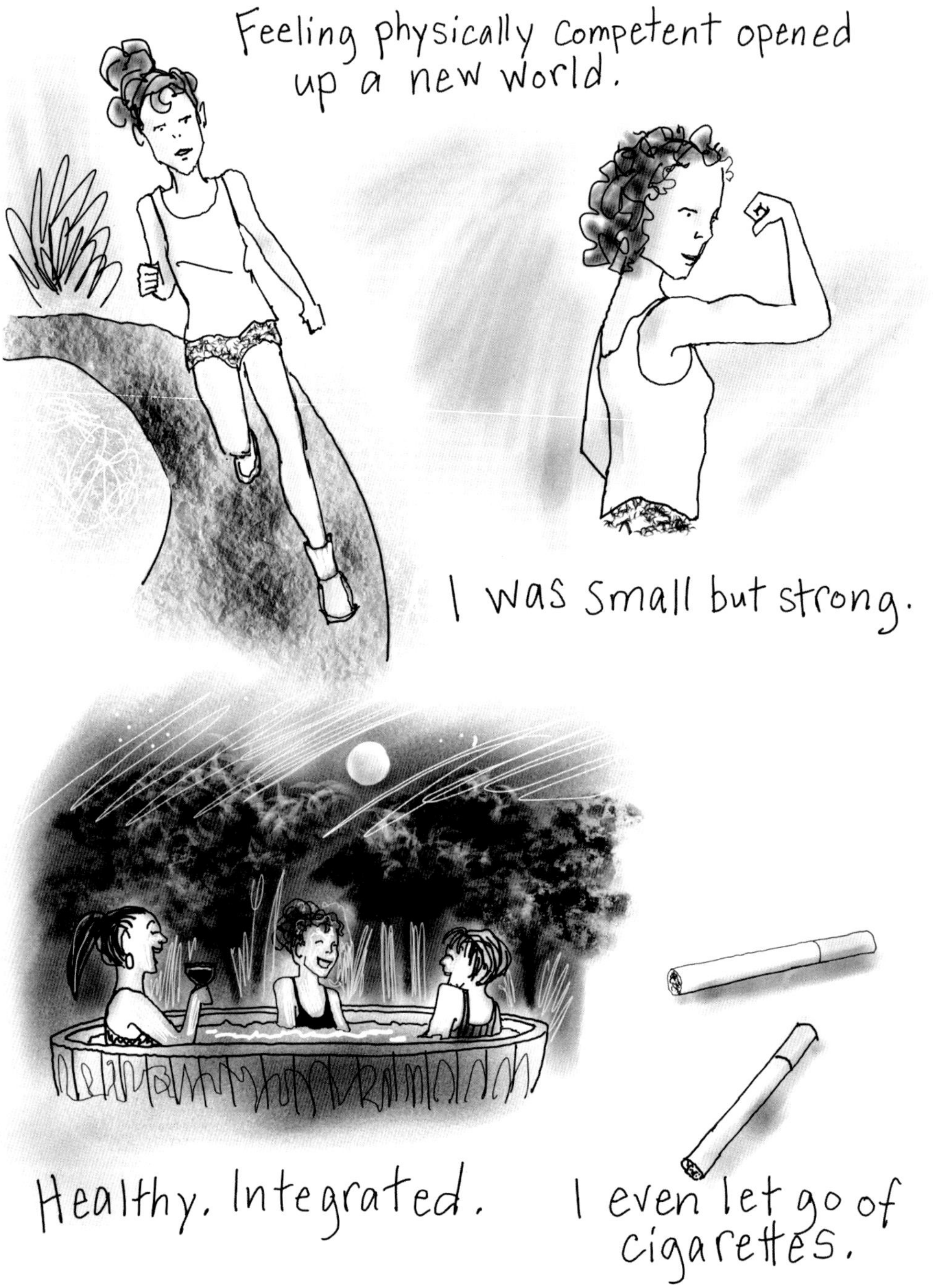
Feeling physically competent opened up a new world.
I was small but strong.
Healthy. Integrated.
I even let go of cigarettes.

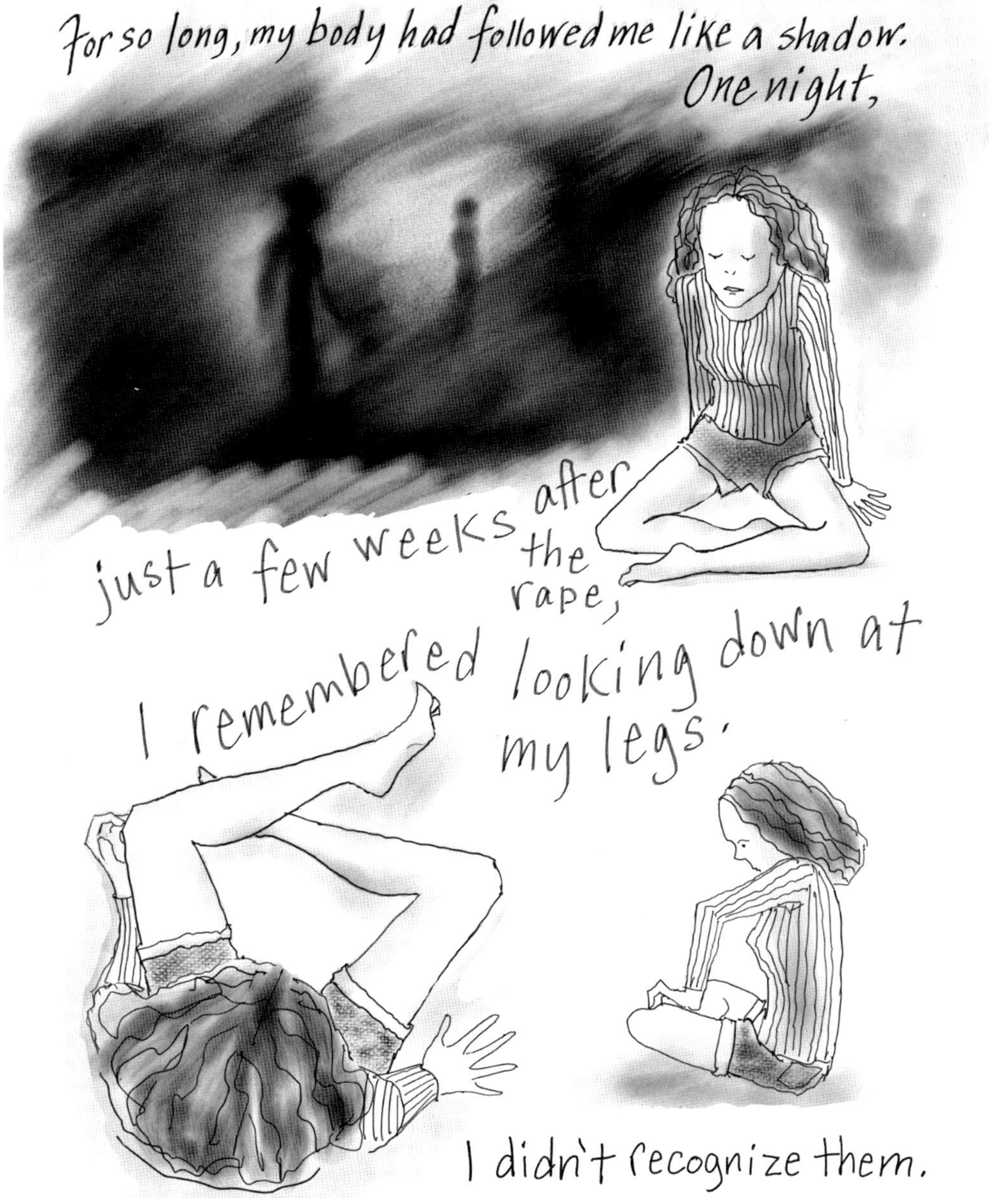
For so long, my body had followed me like a shadow.
One night,
just a few weeks after the rape,
I remembered looking down at my legs.
I didn't recognize them.

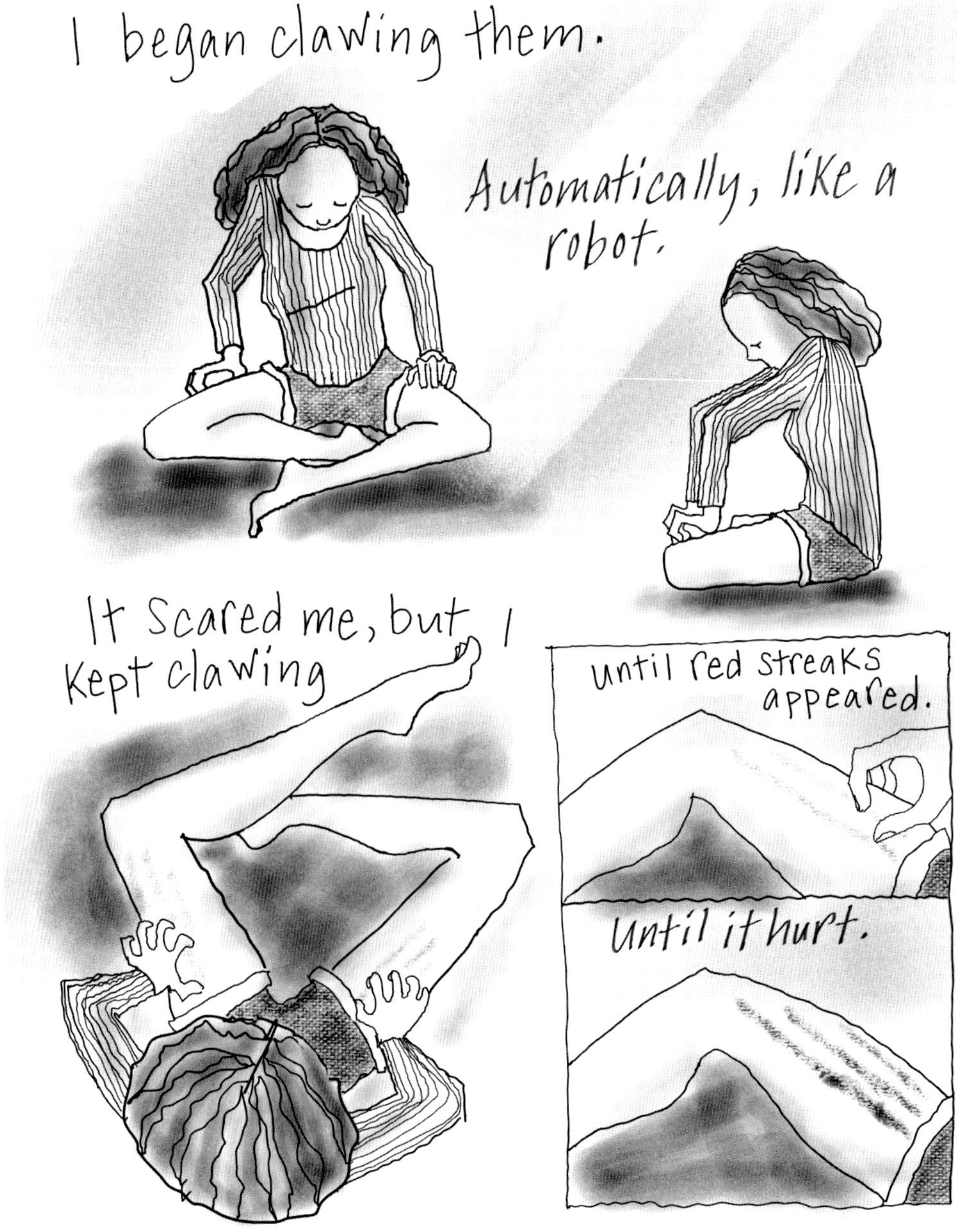
I began clawing them.
Automatically, like a robot.
It Scared me, but I Kept clawing
until red streaks appeared.
Until it hurt.

Pain forced a connection between self and flesh.

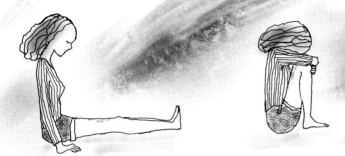

It proved that my body was me.

Now my body and I were one. At last.

We could do all kinds of things.

Together.

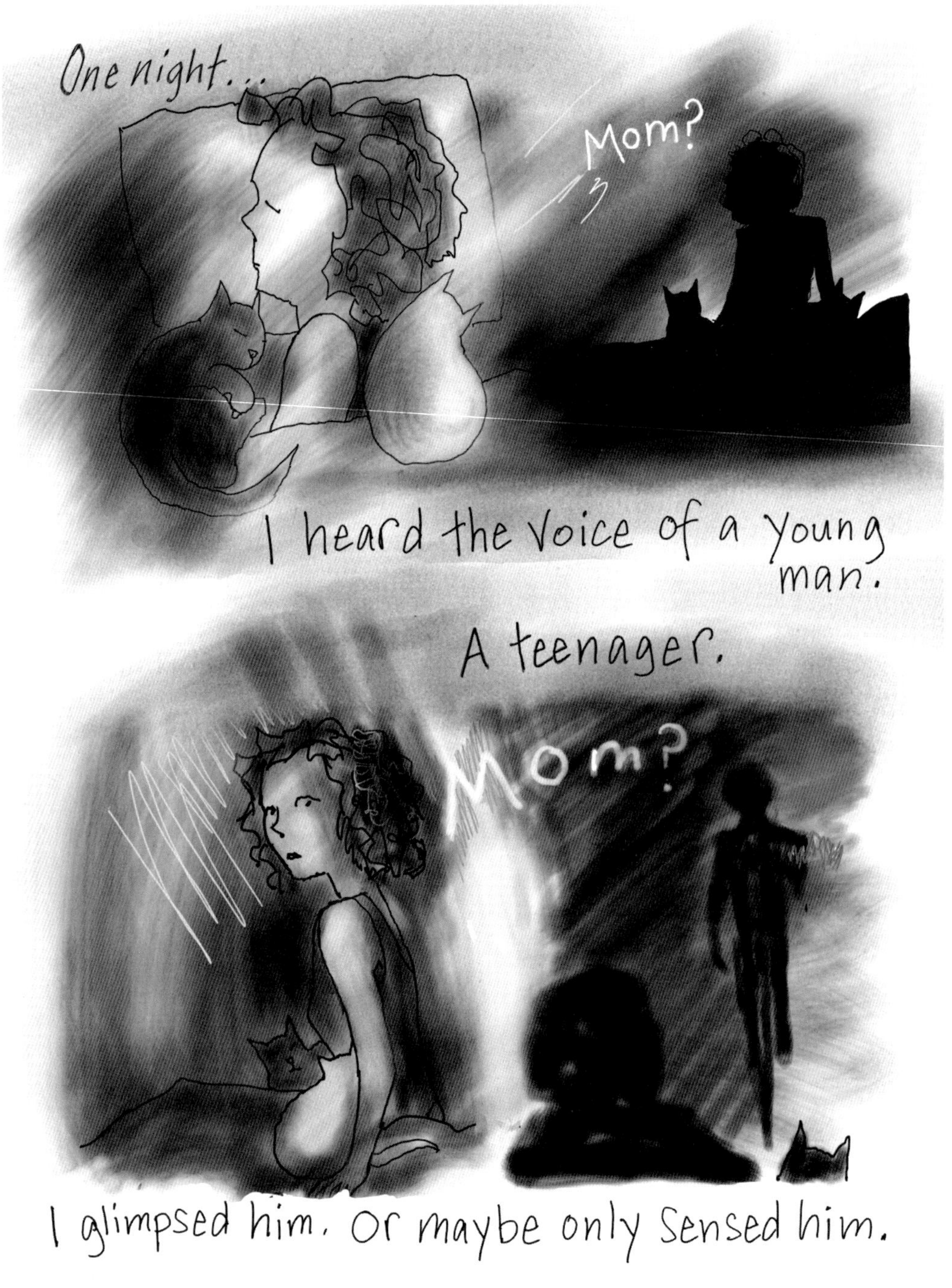

One night...
Mom?
I heard the voice of a young man.
A teenager.
Mom?
I glimpsed him. Or maybe only sensed him.

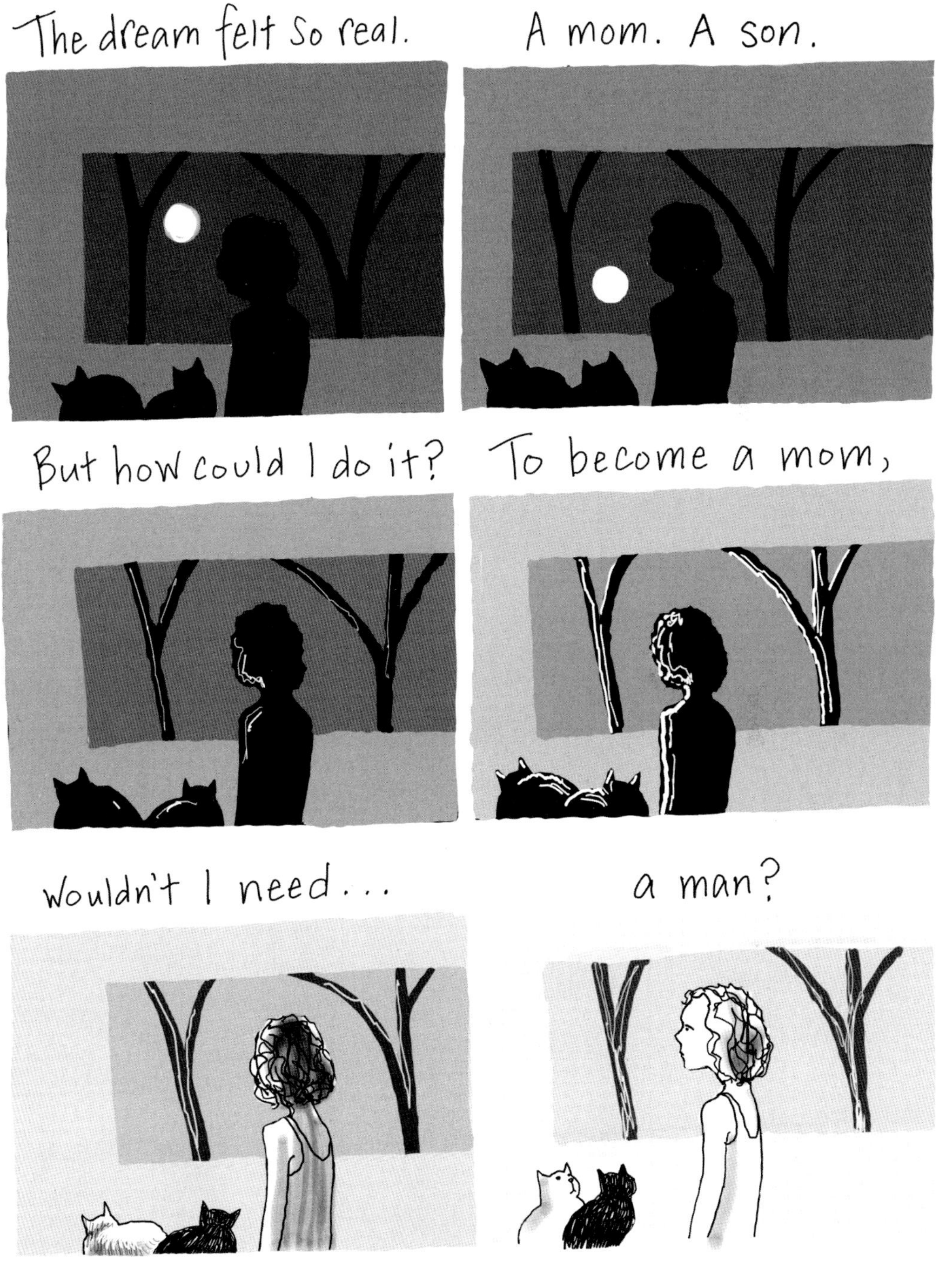
The dream felt so real.
A mom. A son.
But how could I do it?
To become a mom,
Wouldn't I need...
a man?

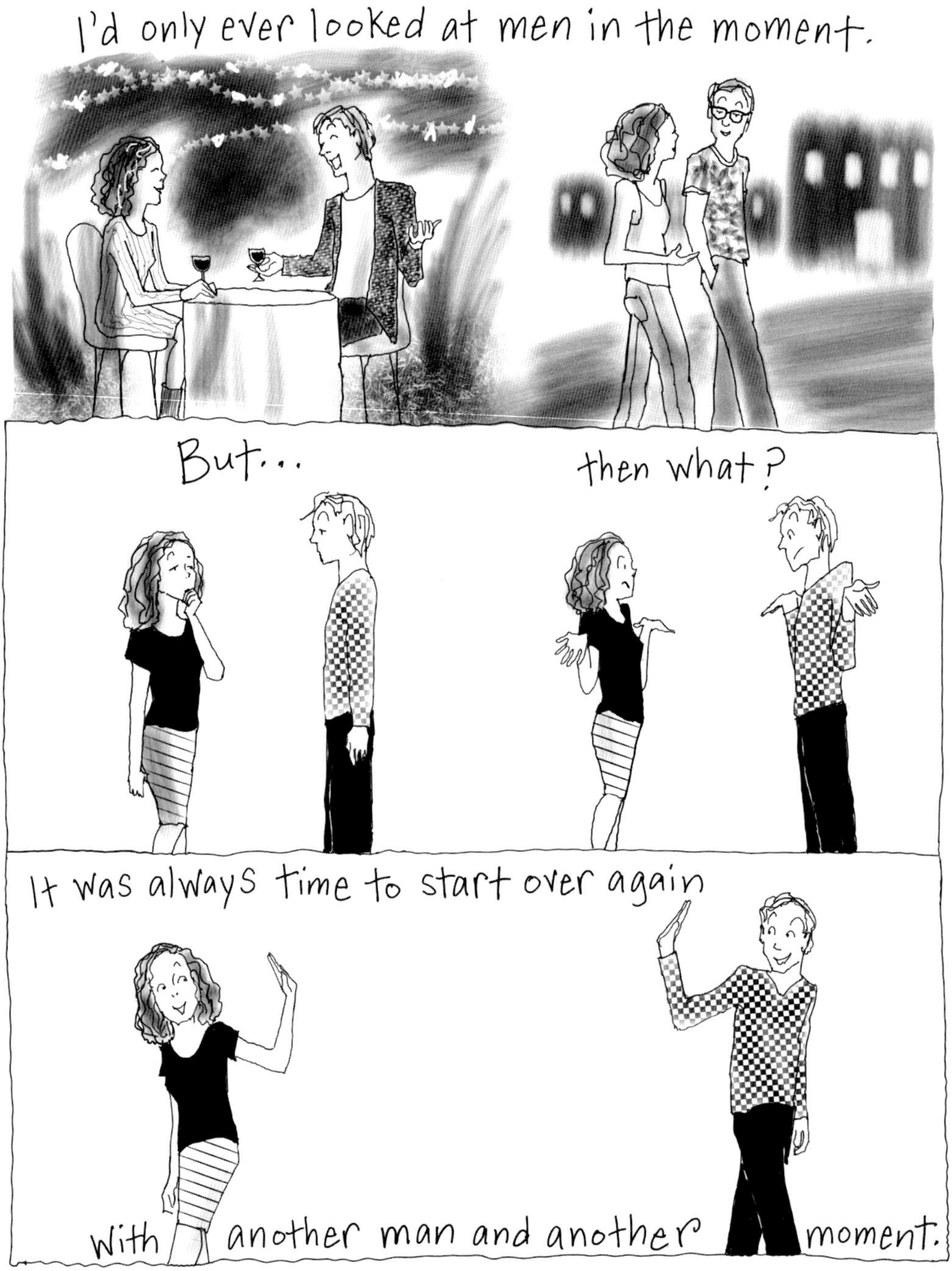
I'd only ever looked at men in the moment.
But...
then what?
It was always time to start over again
with another man and another moment.

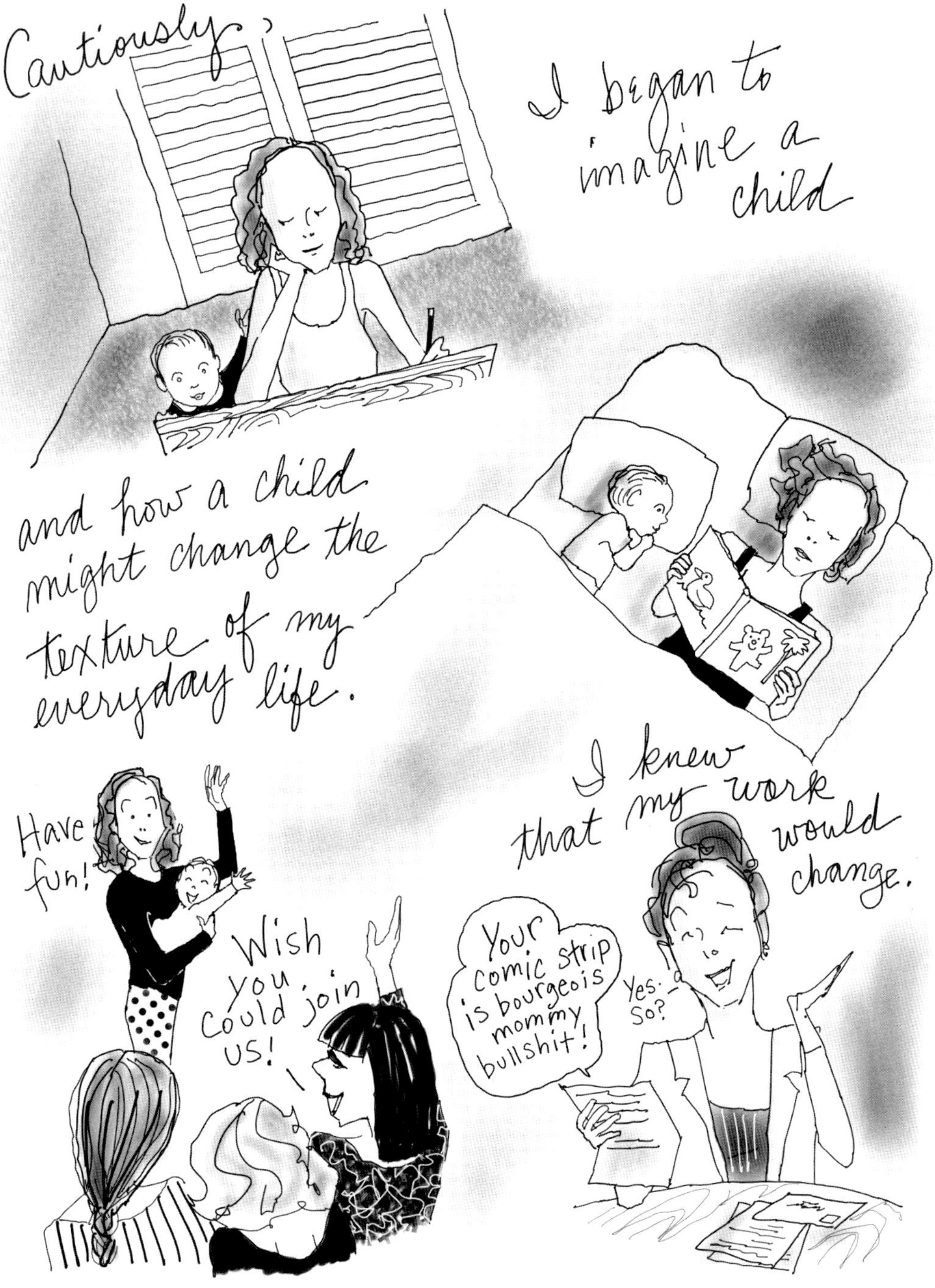
Cautiously,
I began to imagine a child
and how a child might change the texture of my everyday life.
I knew that my work would change.
Have fun!
Wish you could join US!
Your comic strip is bourgeois mommy bullshit!
Yes. So?

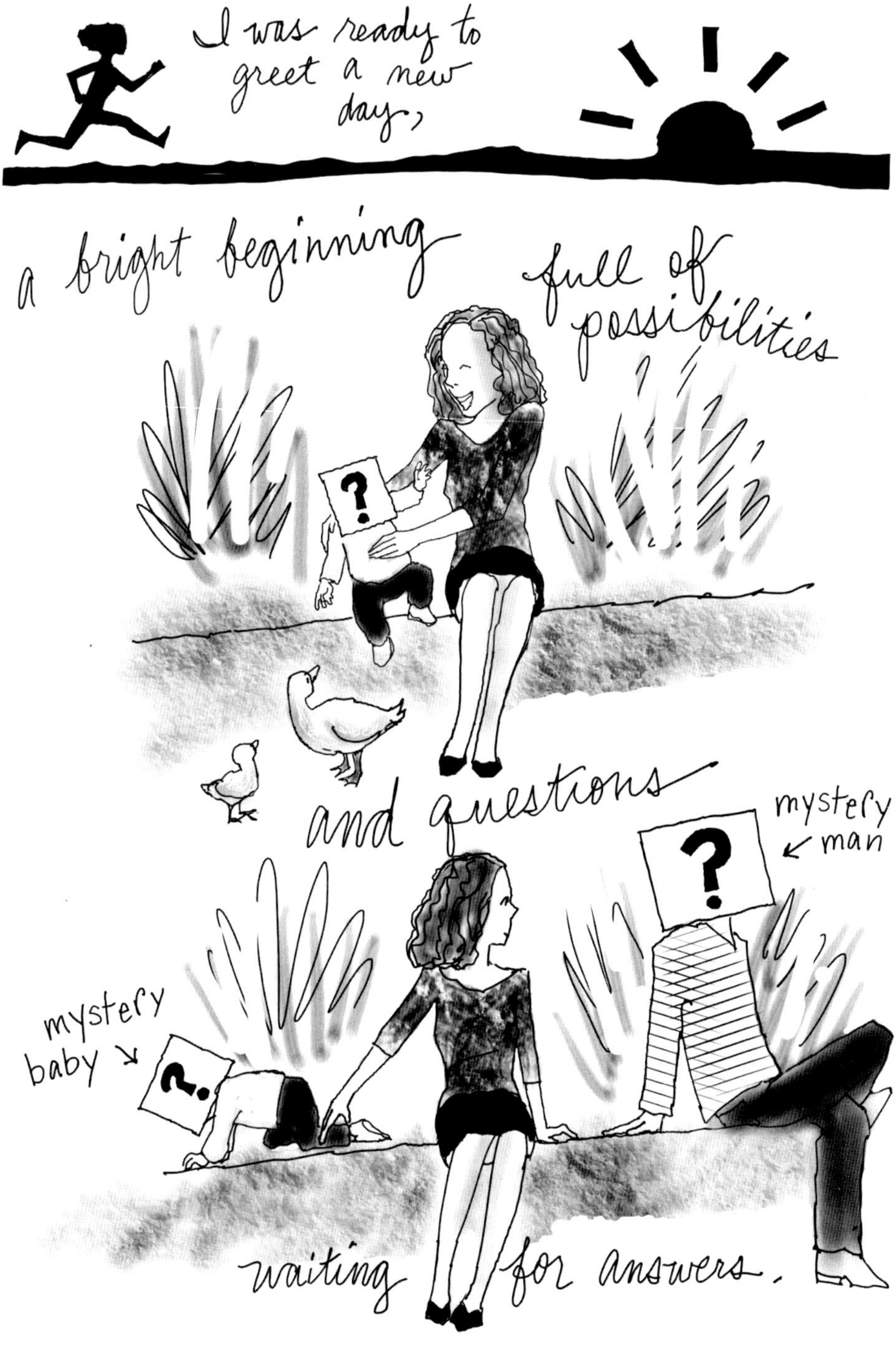
I was ready to greet a new day,
a bright beginning
full of possibilities
and questions
mystery man
mystery baby
waiting for answers.

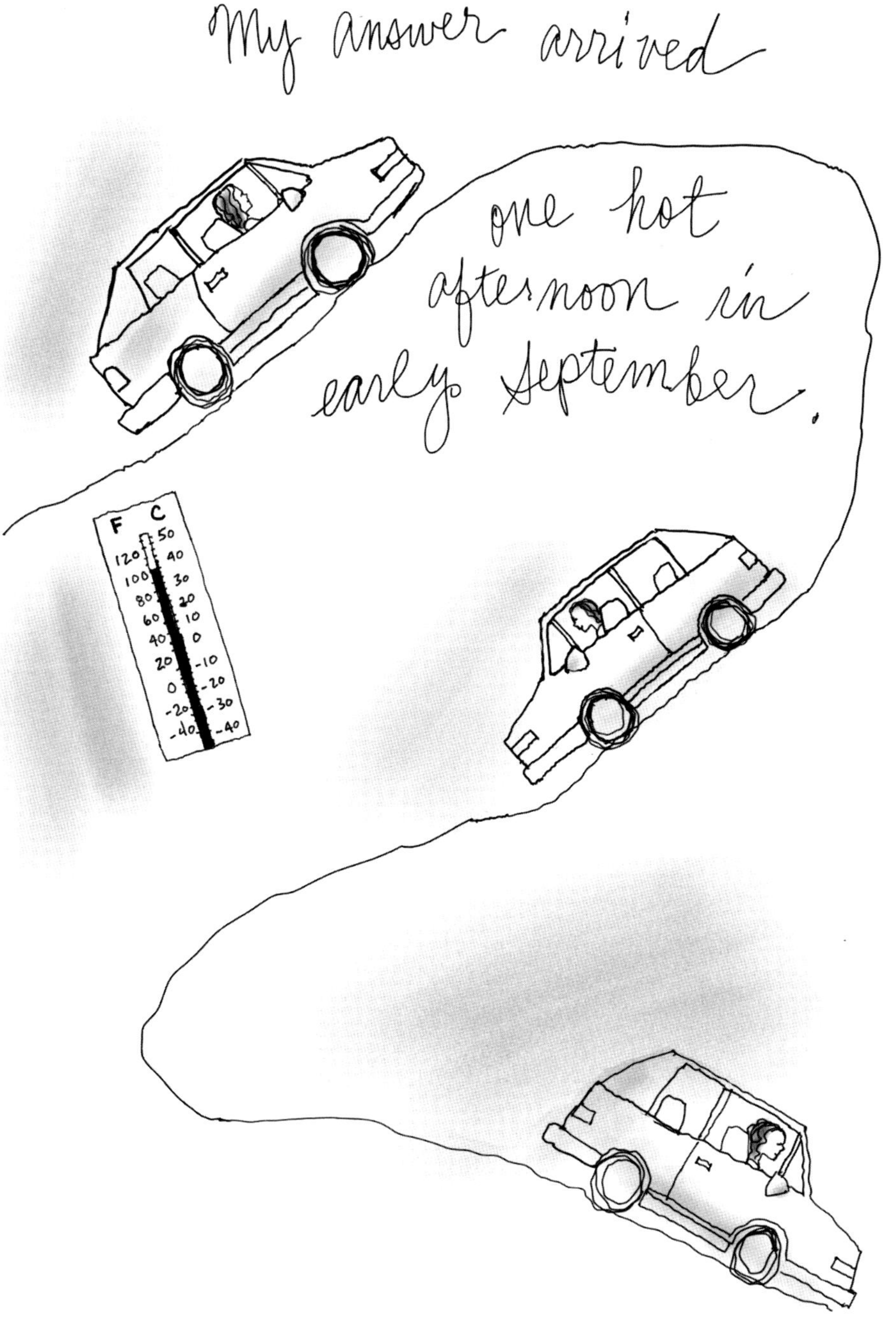
My answer arrived
one hot afternoon in early September.
F C
120 50
100 40
80 30
60 20
40 10
20 0
0 -10
-20 -20
-40 -30
-40

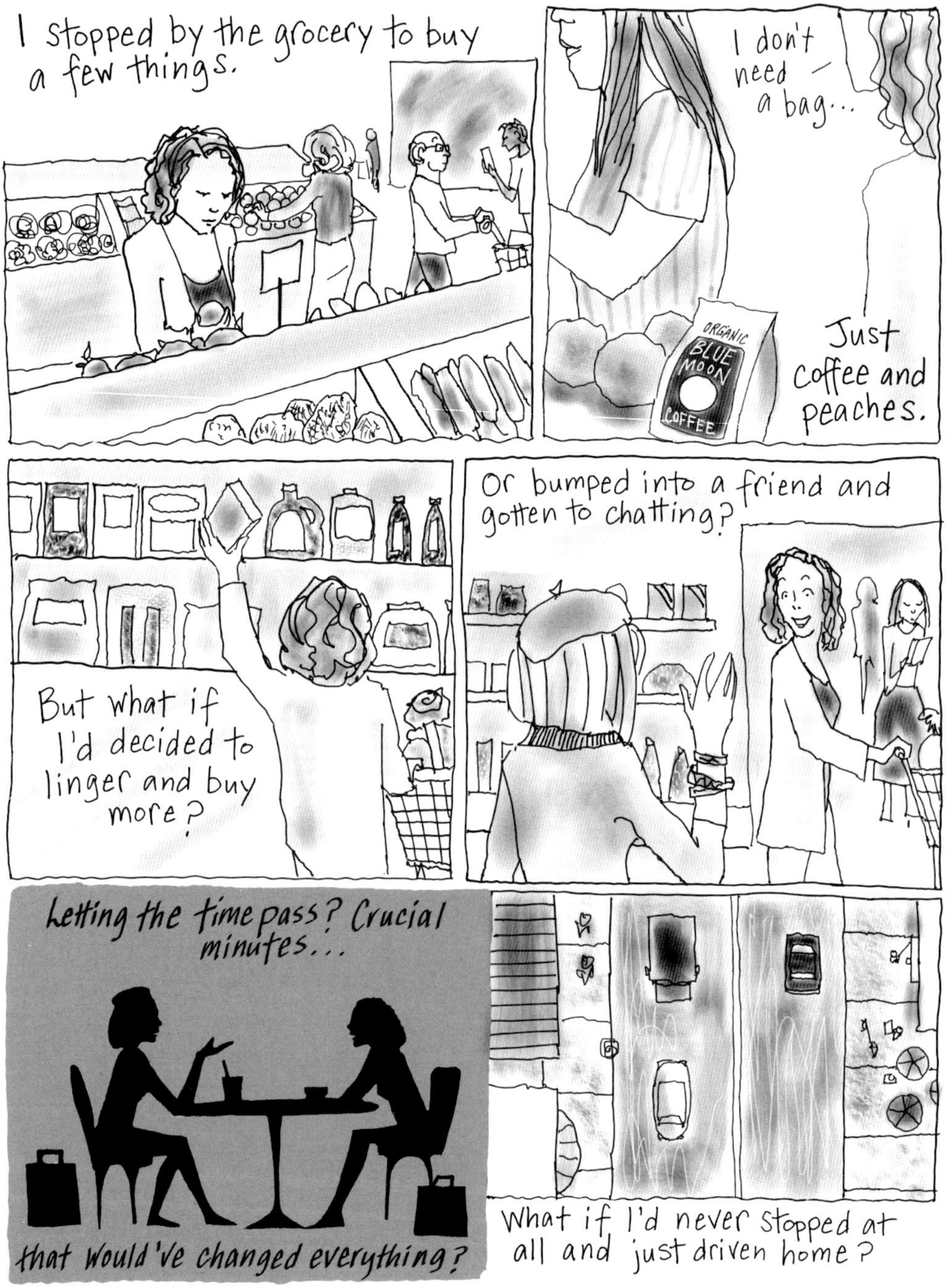
I stopped by the grocery to buy a few things.
I don't need a bag...
Just coffee and peaches.
ORGANIC BLUE MOON COFFEE
But what if I'd decided to linger and buy more?
Or bumped into a friend and gotten to chatting?
Letting the time pass? Crucial minutes...
that would've changed everything?
What if I'd never stopped at all and just driven home?

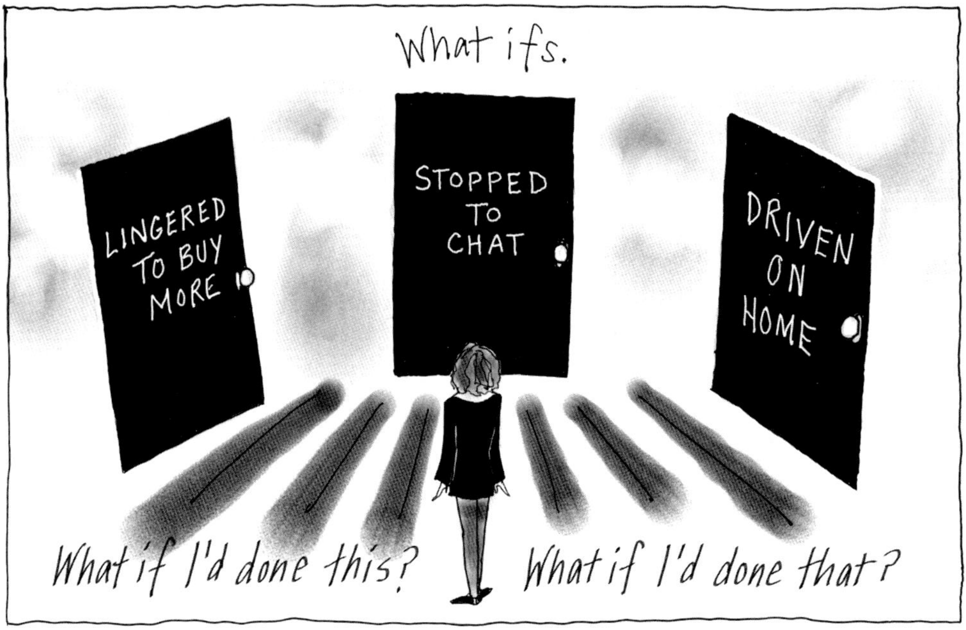
What ifs.
LINGERED TO BUY MORE
STOPPED TO CHAT
DRIVEN ON HOME
What if I'd done this?
What if I'd done that?

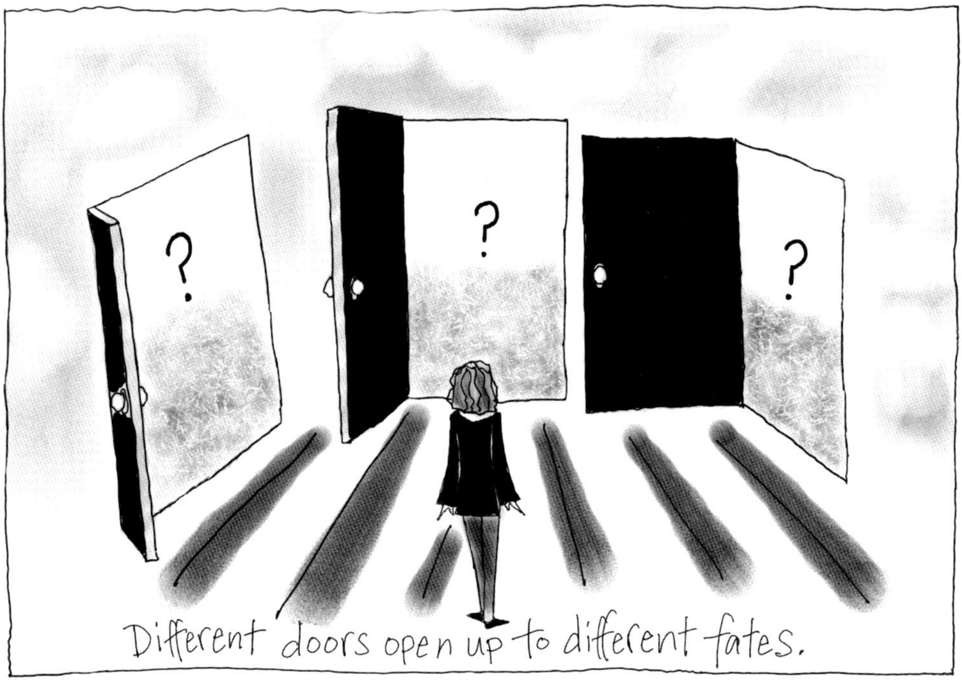
?
?
?
Different doors open up to different fates.

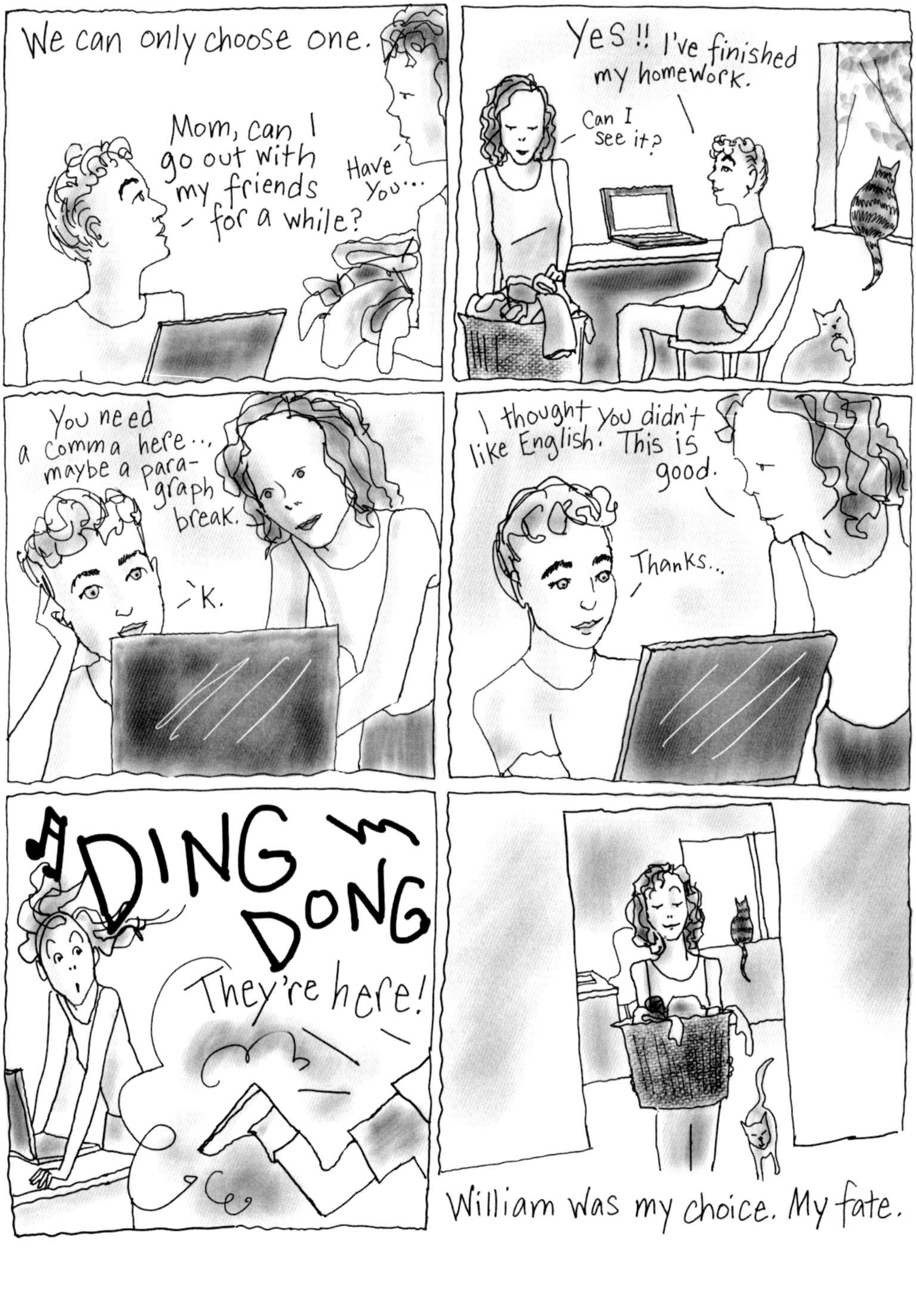
We can only choose one.
Mom, can I go out with my friends for a while?
Have you...
Yes!! I've finished my homework.
Can I see it?
You need a comma here... maybe a paragraph break.
'K.
I thought you didn't like English. This is good.
Thanks...
DING DONG
They're here!
William was my choice. My fate.

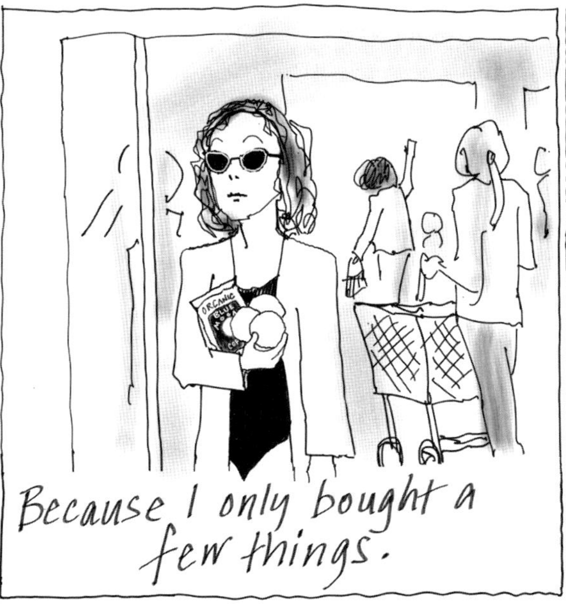
Because I only bought a few things.

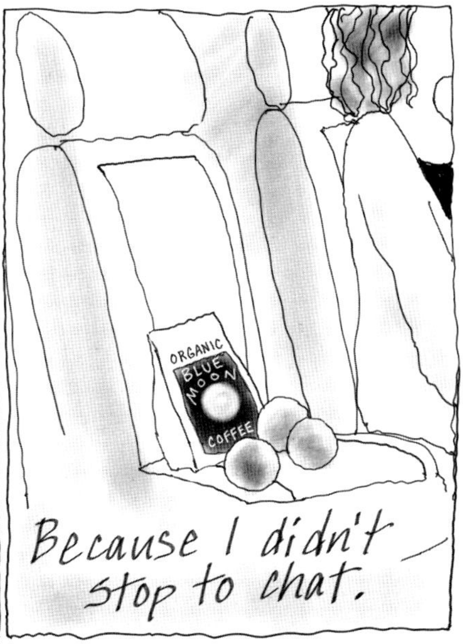
ORGANIC
BLUE MOON
COFFEE
Because I didn't stop to chat.

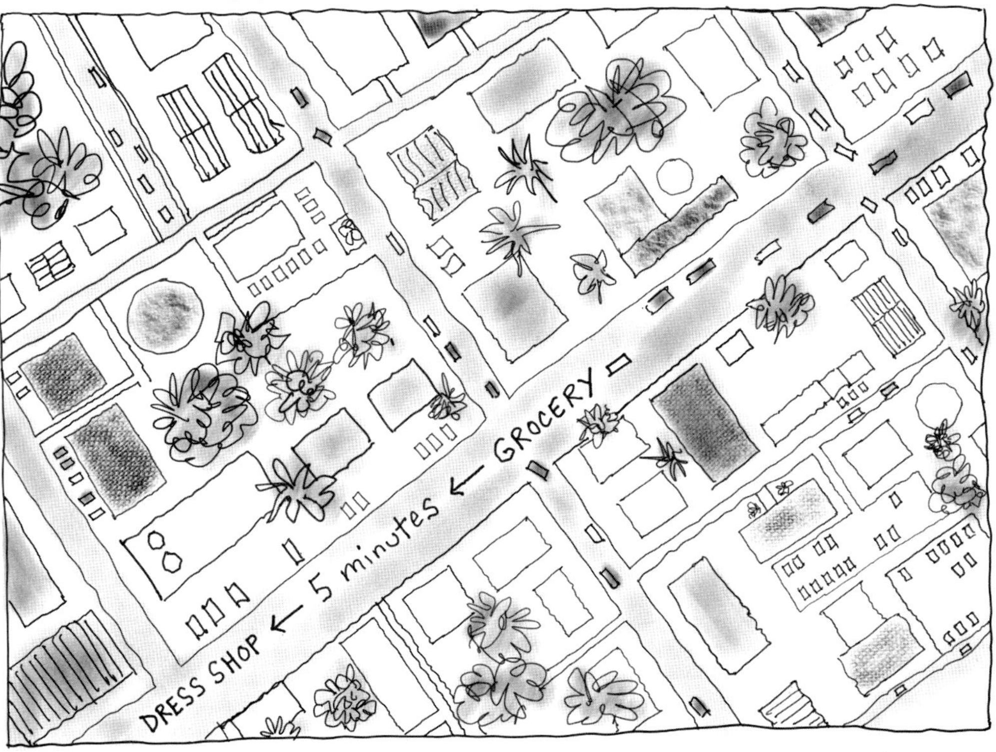
DRESS SHOP ← 5 minutes ← GROCERY

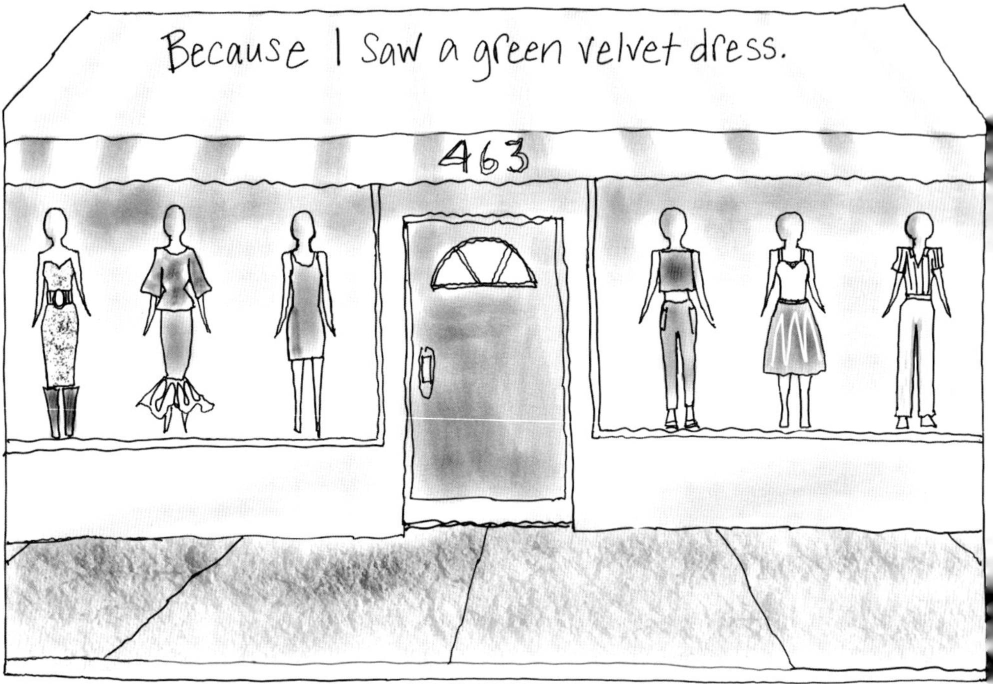
Because I saw a green velvet dress.
463

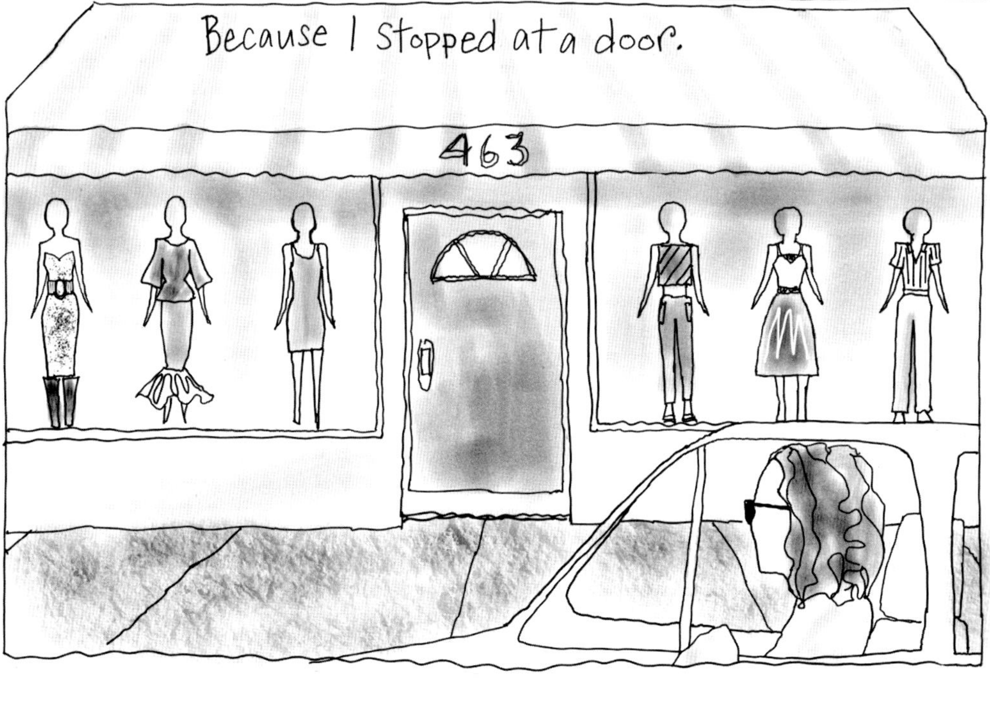
Because I stopped at a door.
463

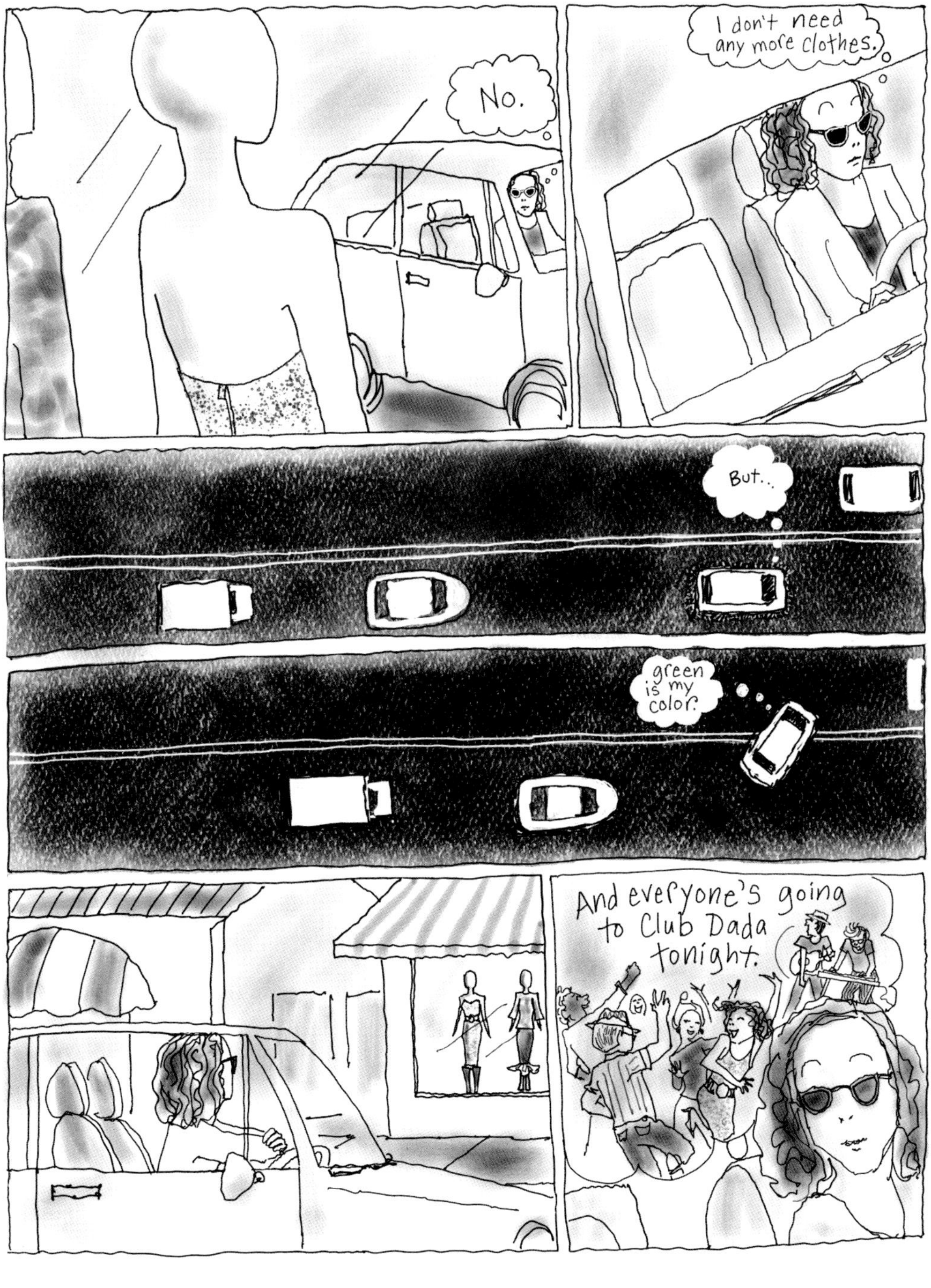
No.
I don't need any more clothes.
But...
green is my color.
And everyone's going to Club Dada tonight.

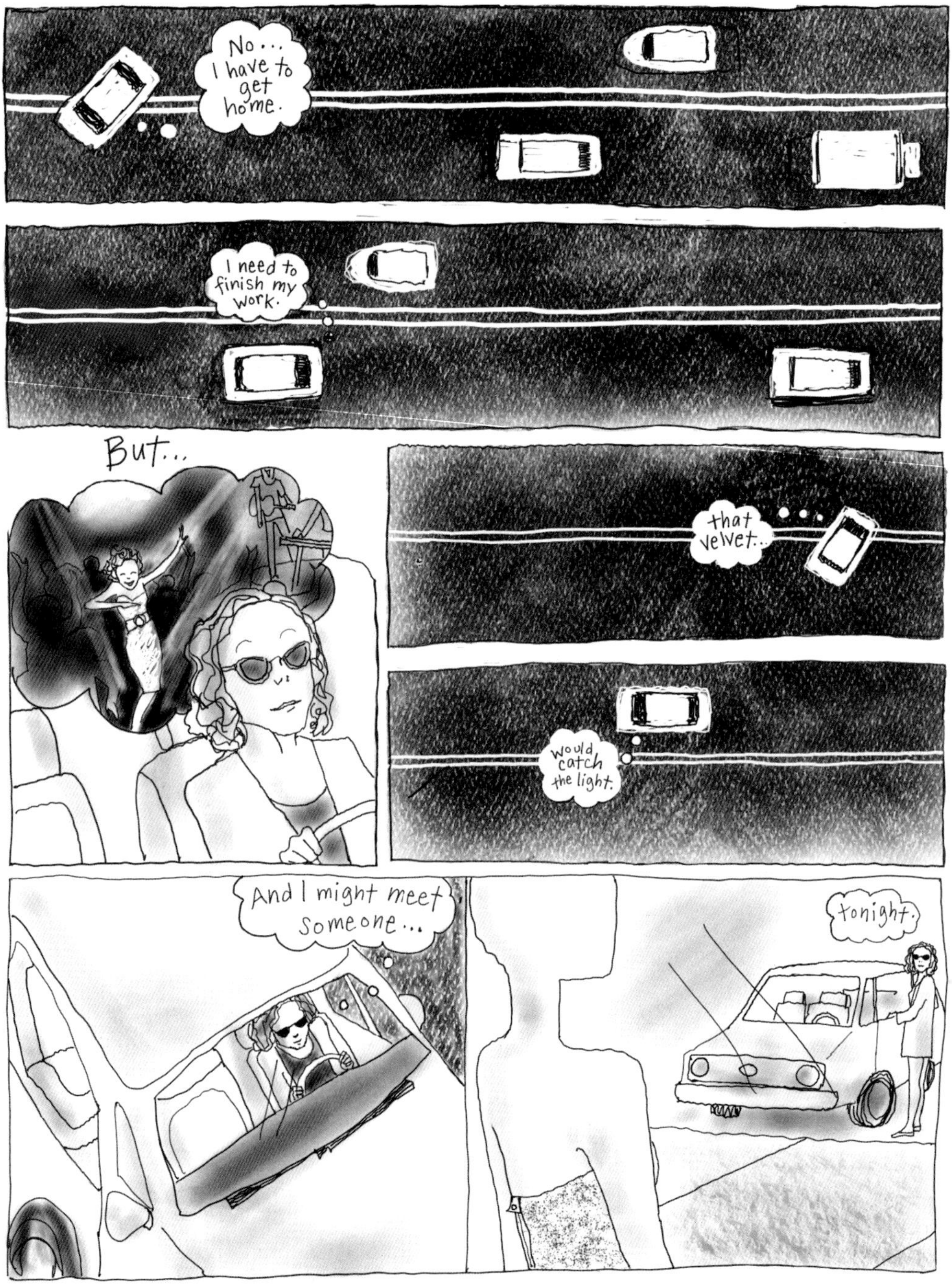
No... I have to get home.
I need to finish my work.
But...
that velvet...
would catch the light.
And I might meet someone...
tonight.

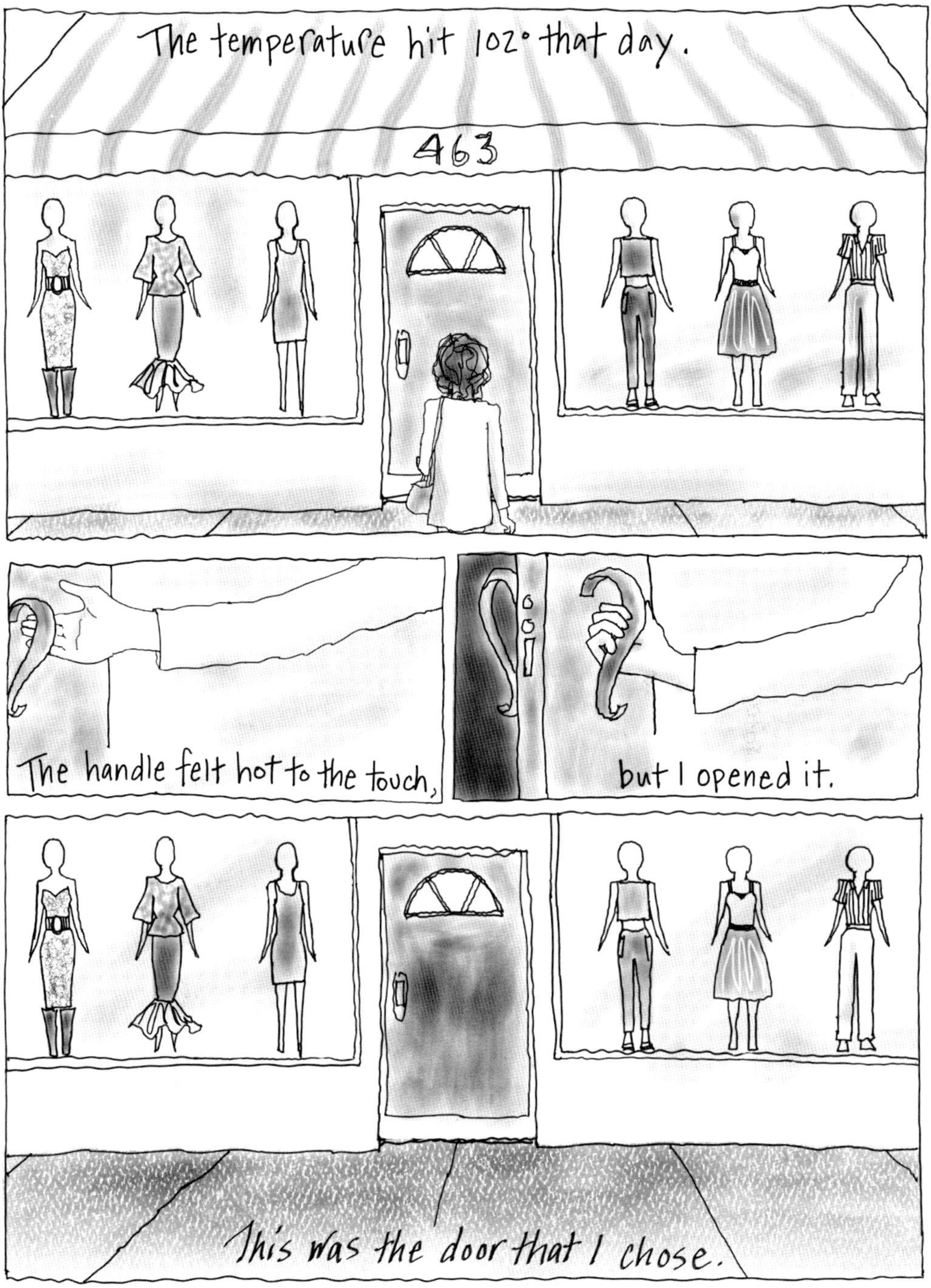
The temperature hit 102° that day.
463
The handle felt hot to the touch,
but I opened it.
This was the door that I chose.

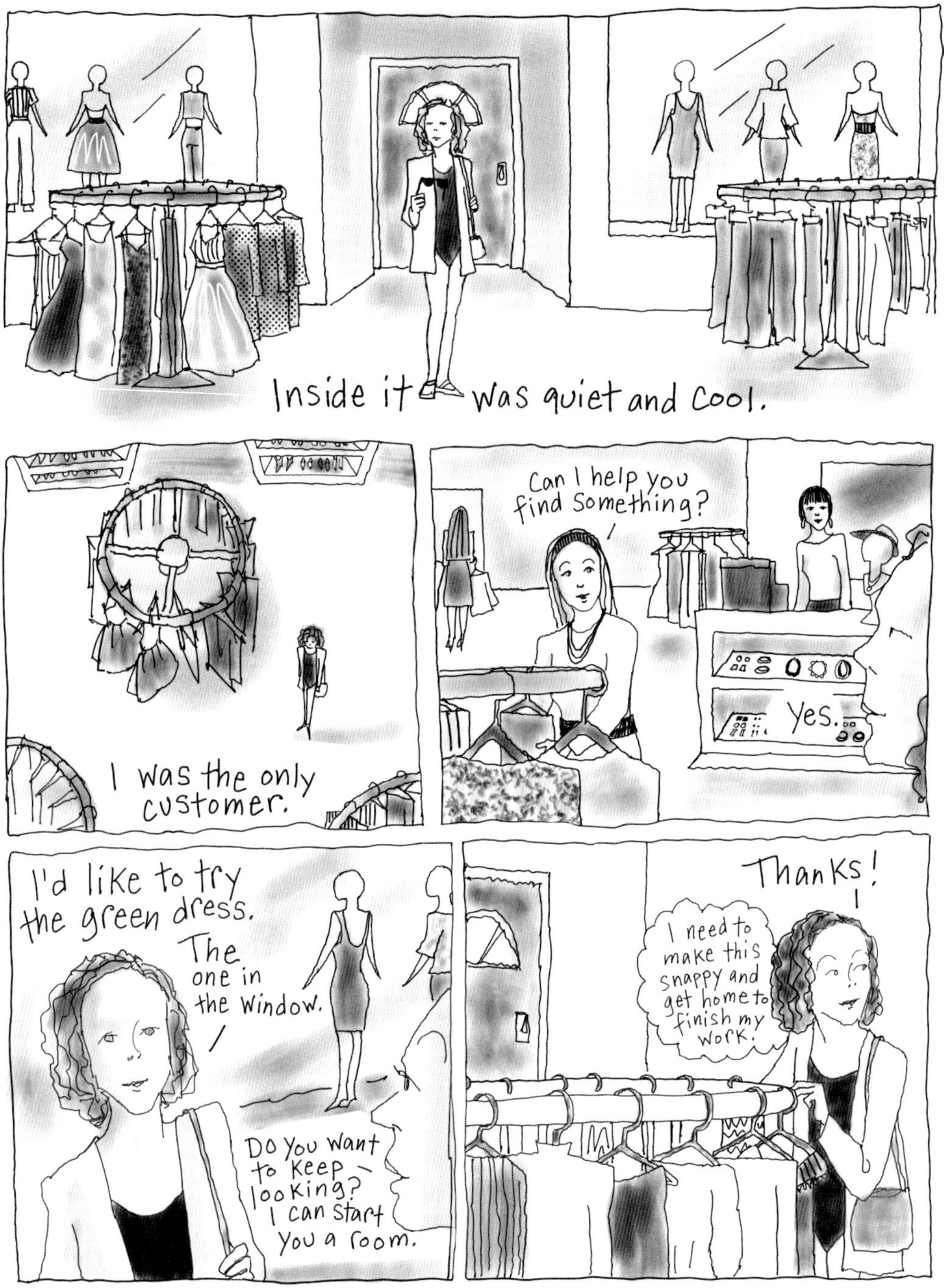
Inside it was quiet and cool.
I was the only customer.
Can I help you find something?
Yes.
I'd like to try the green dress.
The one in the window.
Do you want to keep looking? I can start you a room.
I need to make this snappy and get home to finish my work.
Thanks!

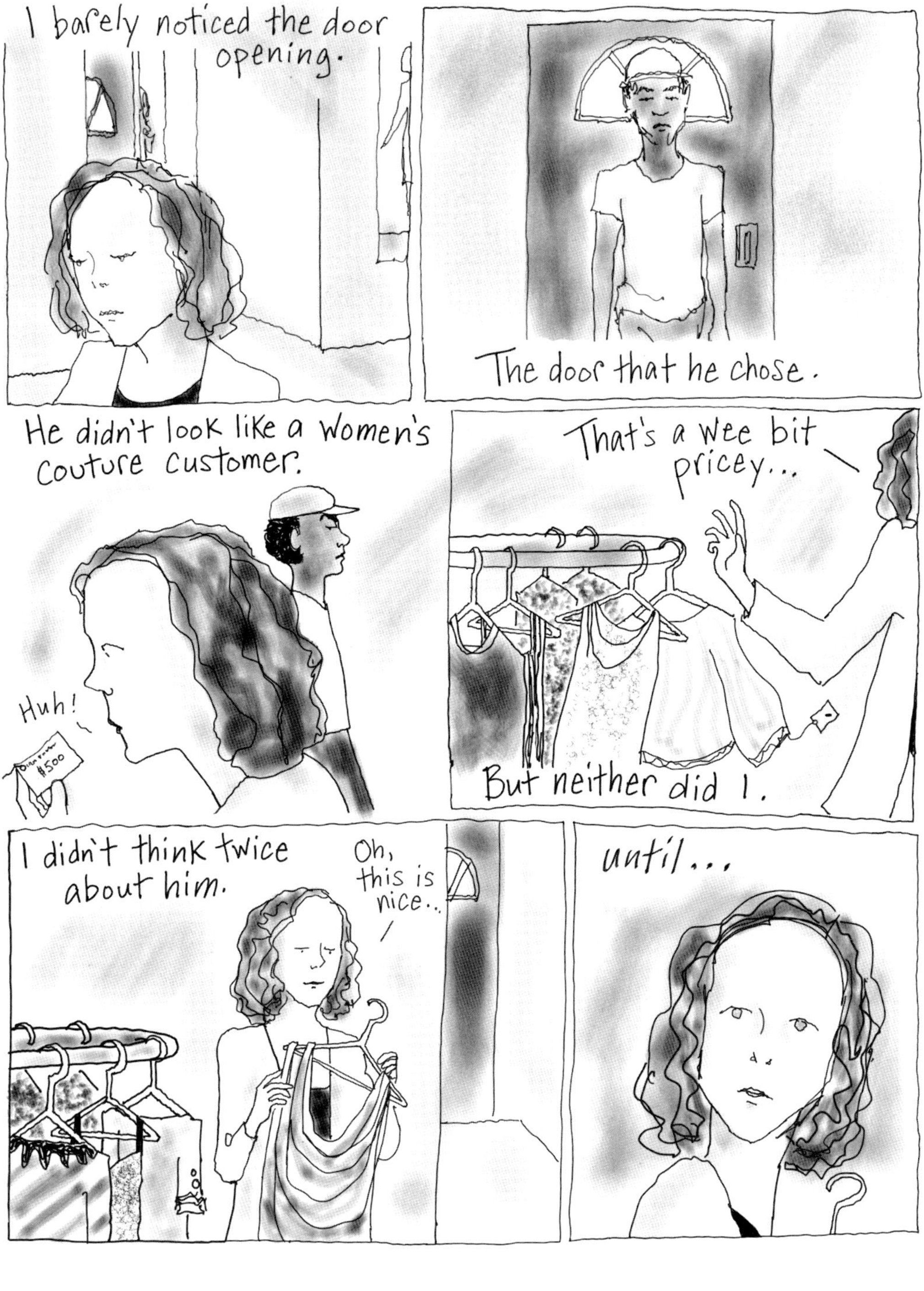

I barely noticed the door opening.
The door that he chose.
He didn't look like a women's couture customer.
Huh!
$500
That's a wee bit pricey...
But neither did I.
I didn't think twice about him.
Oh, this is nice...
until...

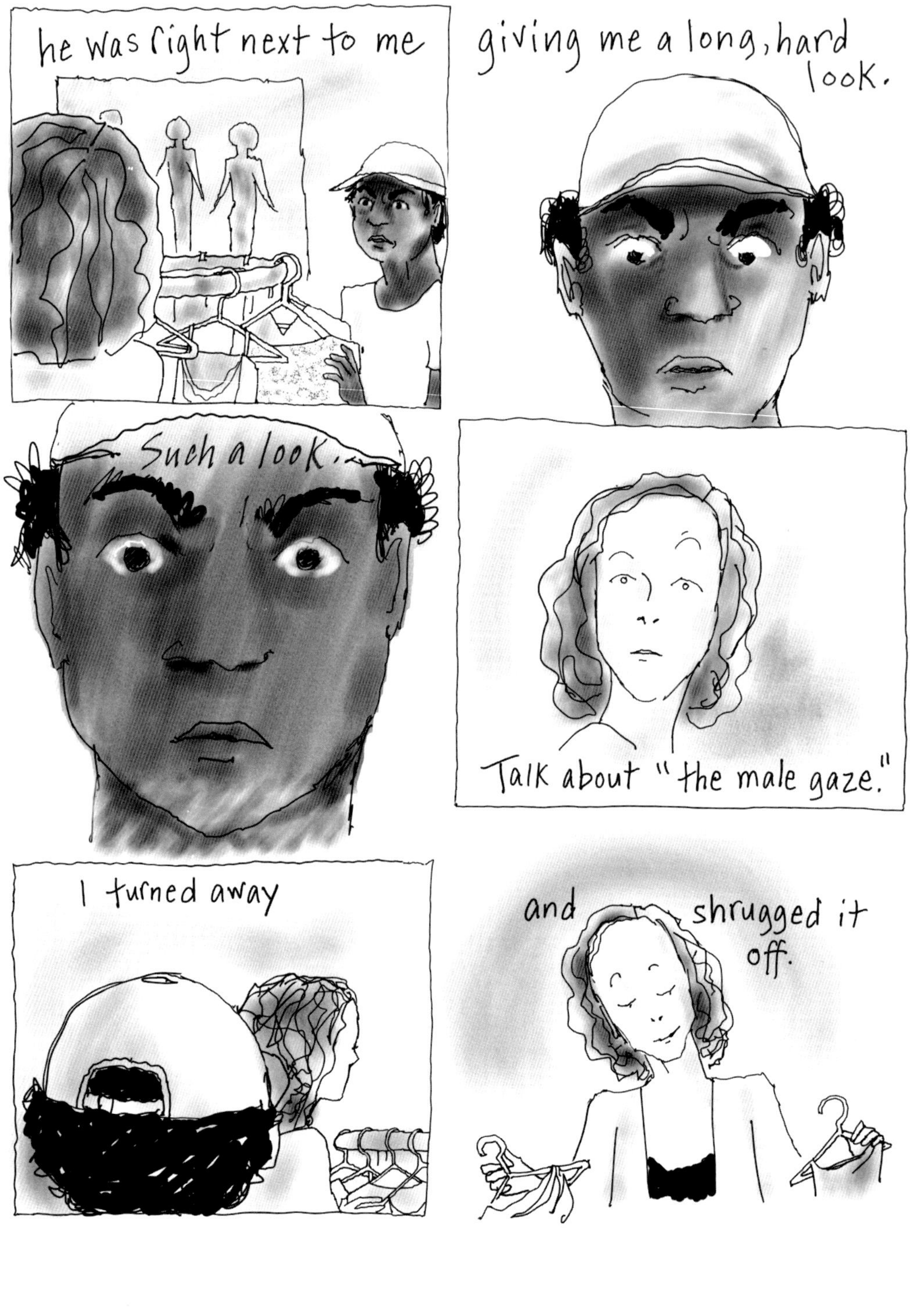
he was right next to me
giving me a long, hard look.
Such a look.
Talk about "the male gaze."
I turned away
and shrugged it off.

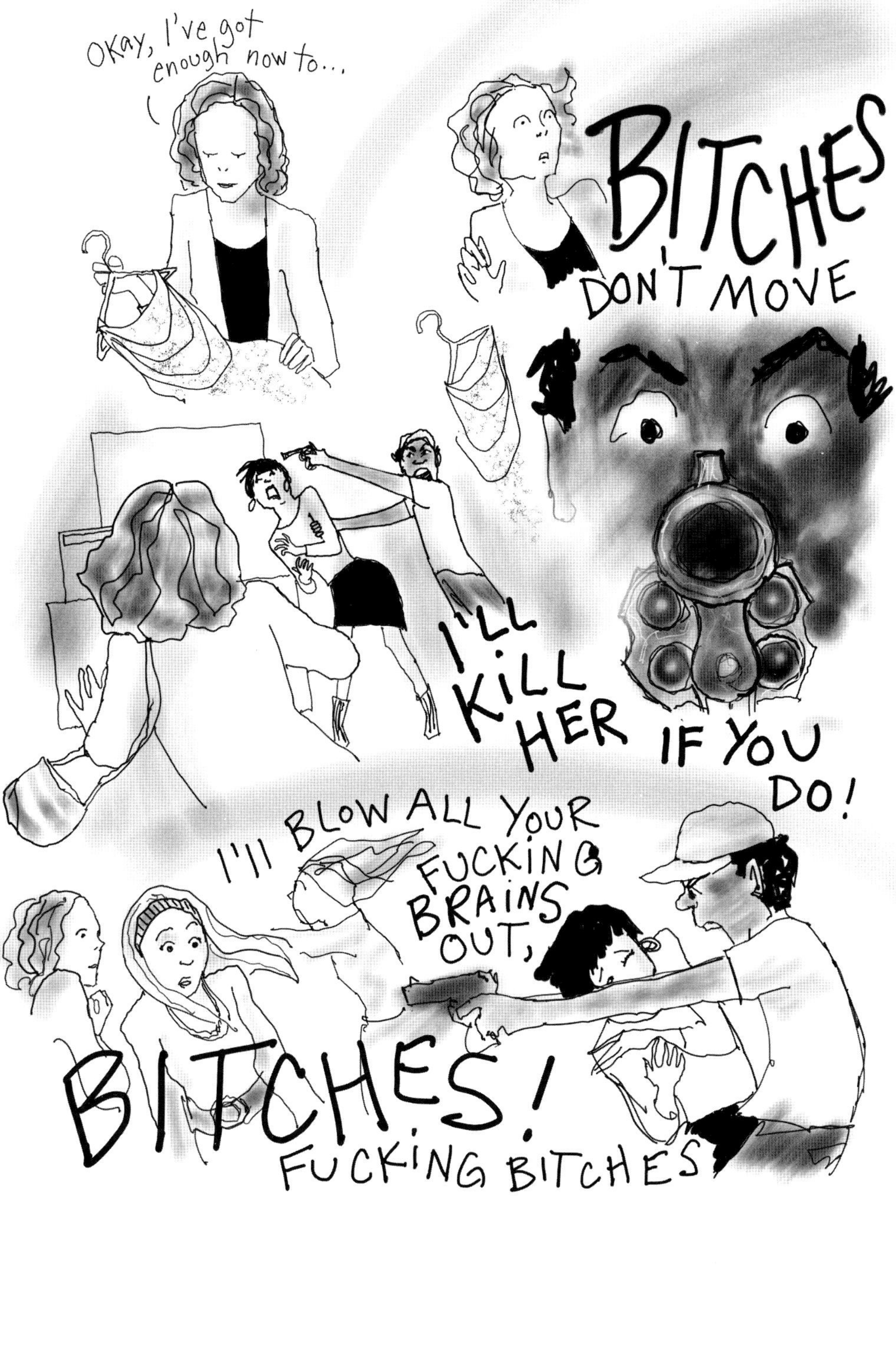
Okay, I've got enough now to...
BITCHES DON'T MOVE
I'LL KILL HER IF YOU DO!
I'll BLOW ALL YOUR FUCKING BRAINS OUT,
BITCHES!
FUCKING BITCHES

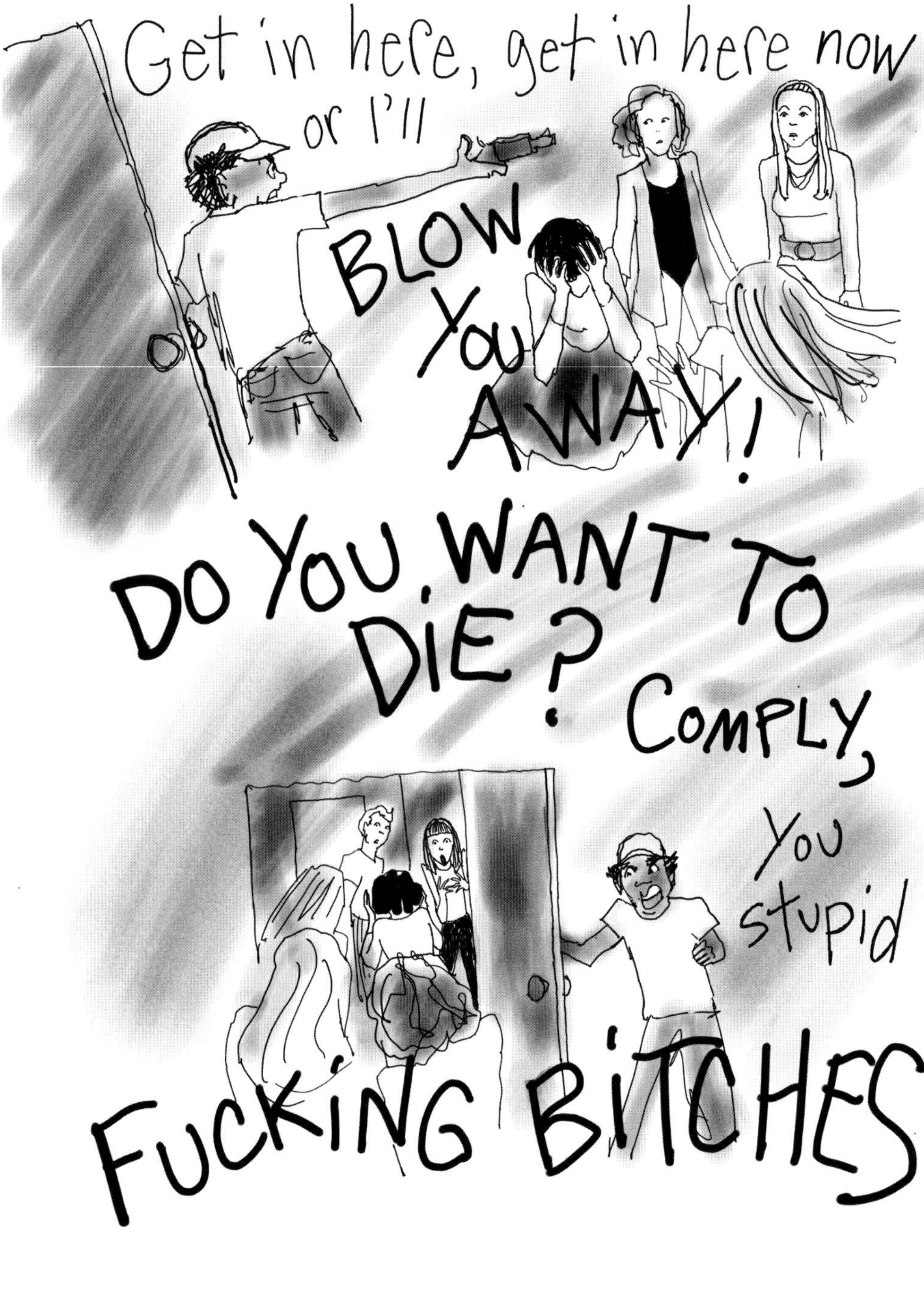
Get in here, get in here now or I'll
BLOW YOU AWAY!
DO YOU WANT TO DIE?
COMPLY, YOU stupid
FUCKING BITCHES

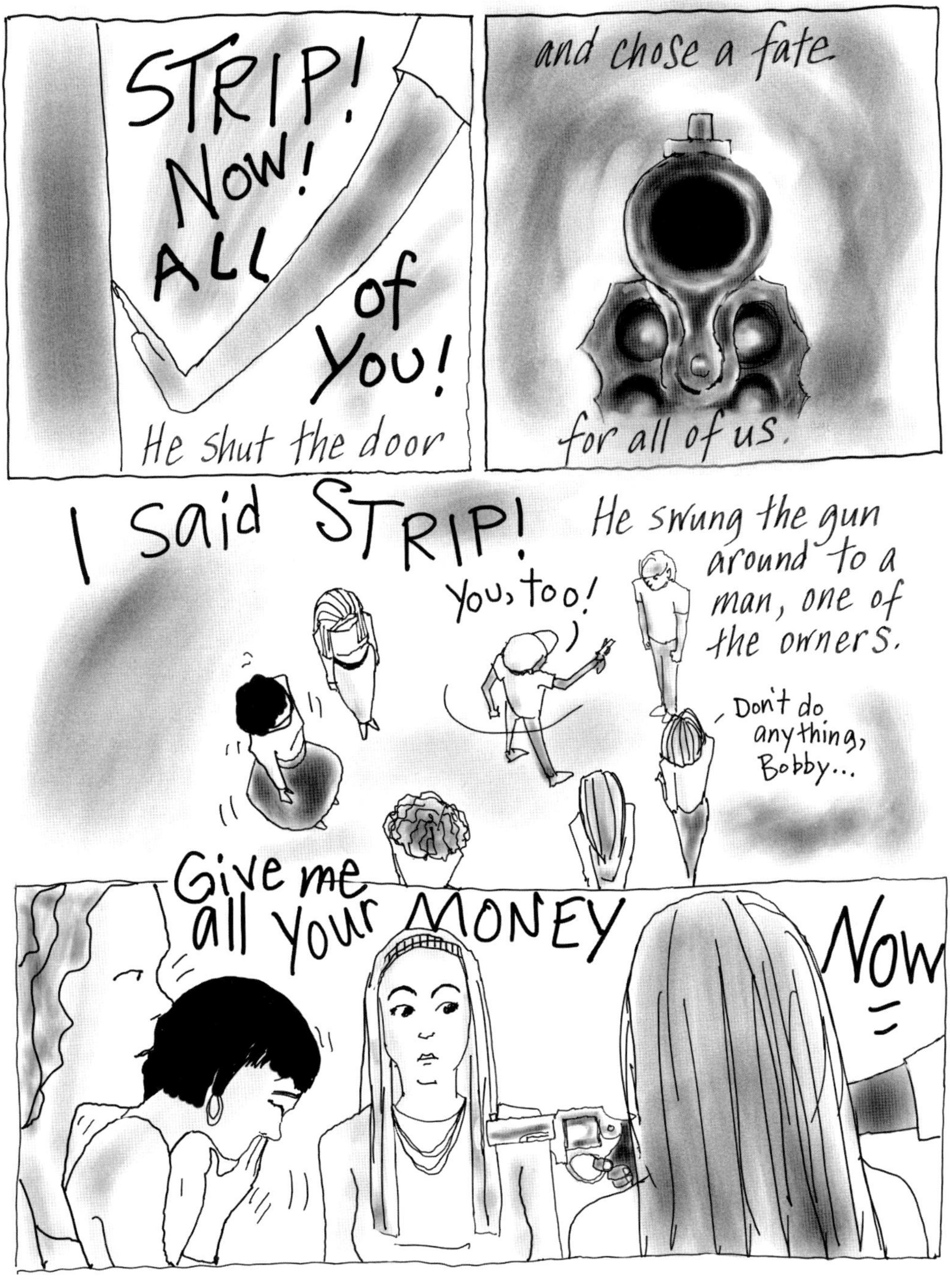
STRIP! Now! ALL of You!
He shut the door
and chose a fate
for all of us.
I said STRIP!
He swung the gun around to a man, one of the owners.
You, too!
Don't do anything, Bobby...
Give me all your MONEY
Now

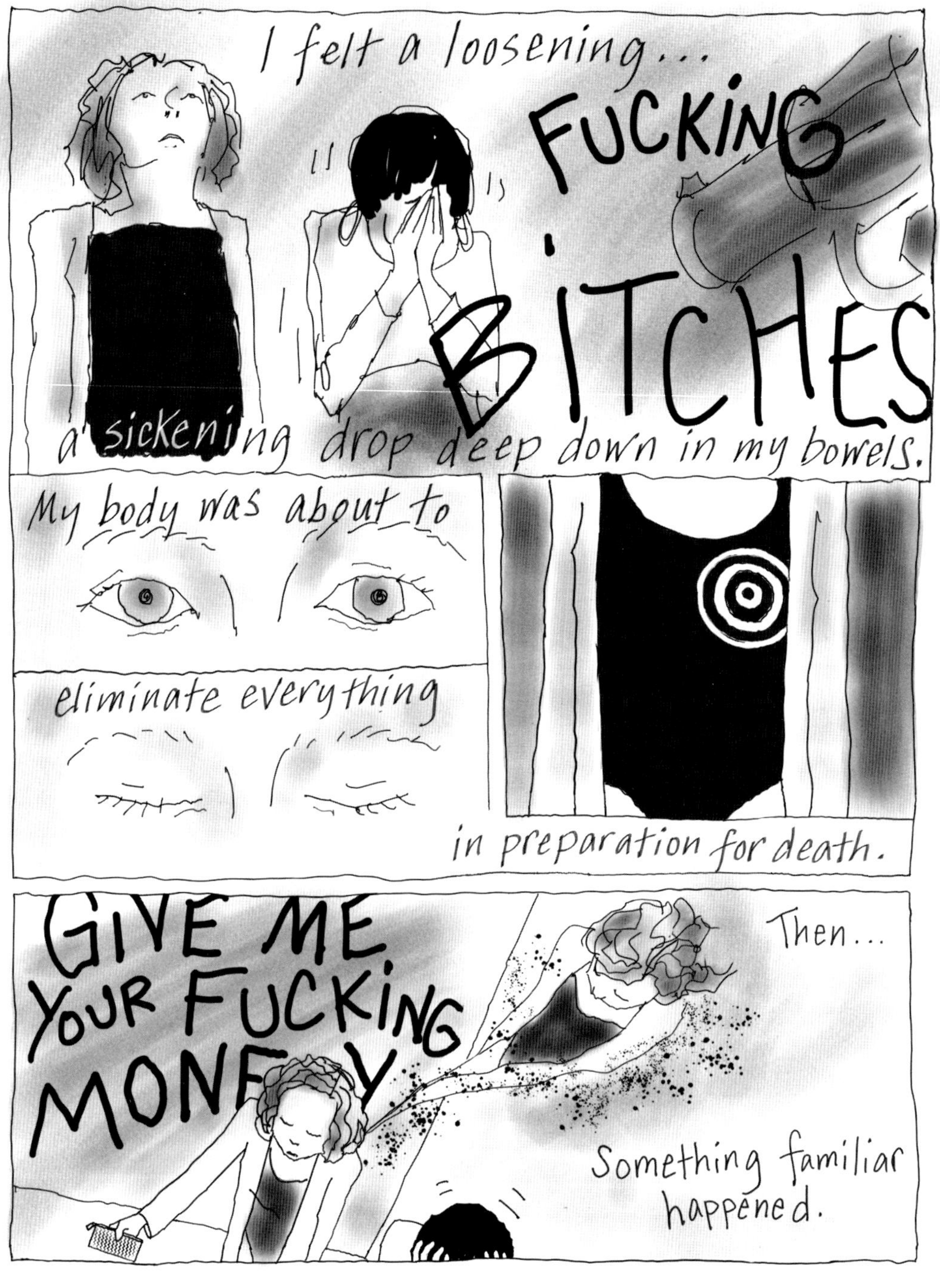
I felt a loosening...
FUCKING BITCHES
a sickening drop deep down in my bowels.
My body was about to
eliminate everything
in preparation for death.
GIVE ME YOUR FUCKING MONEY
Then...
Something familiar happened.

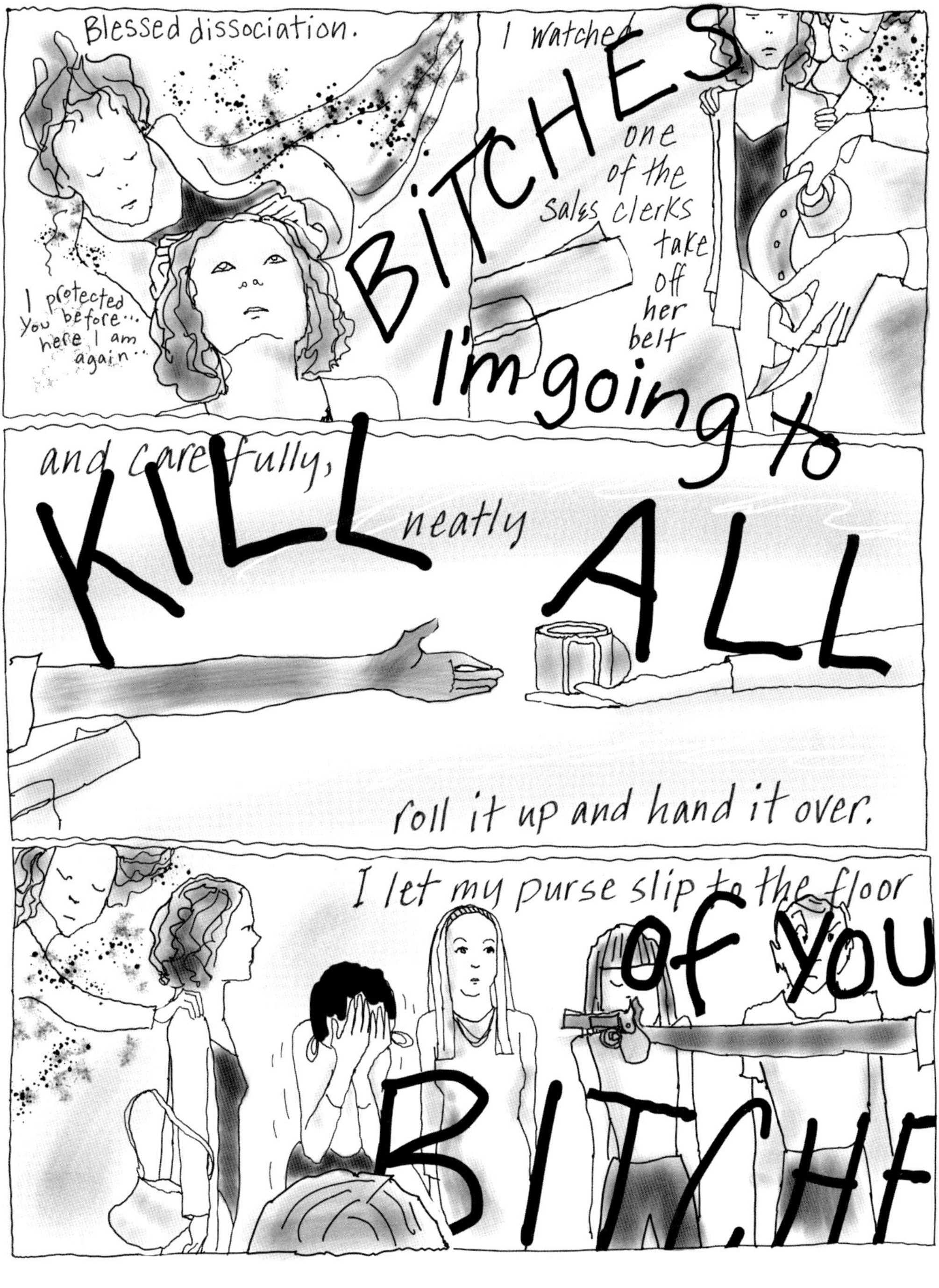
Blessed dissociation.
I protected you before... here I am again...
I watched one of the sales clerks take off her belt
BITCHES I'm going to KILL ALL
and carefully, neatly
roll it up and hand it over.
I let my purse slip to the floor
of you
BITCHE

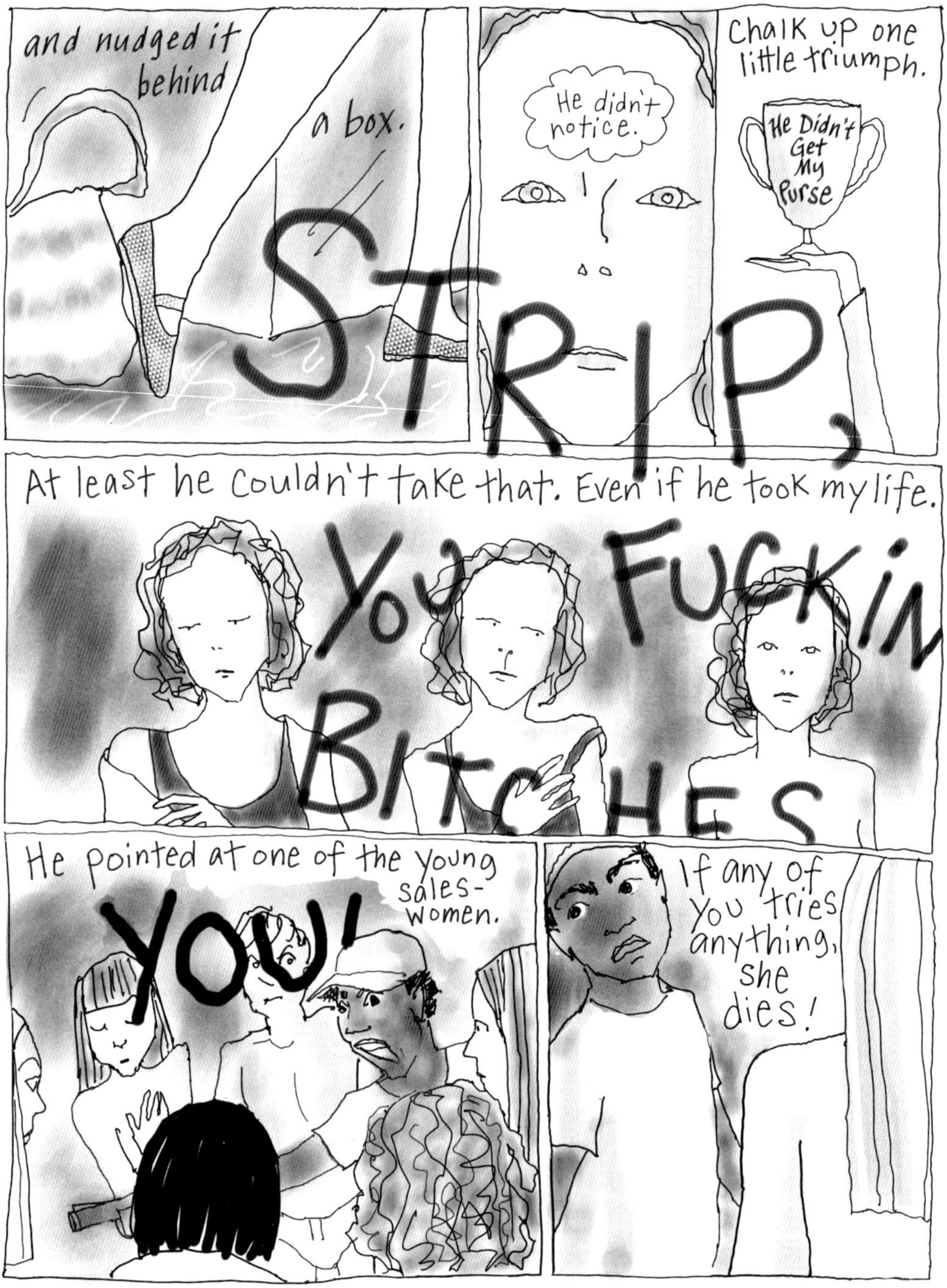
and nudged it behind
a box.
He didn't notice.
Chalk up one little triumph.
He Didn't Get My Purse
STRIP,
At least he couldn't take that. Even if he took my life.
YOU FUCKIN BITCHES
He pointed at one of the young sales-women.
YOU!
If any of you tries anything, she dies!

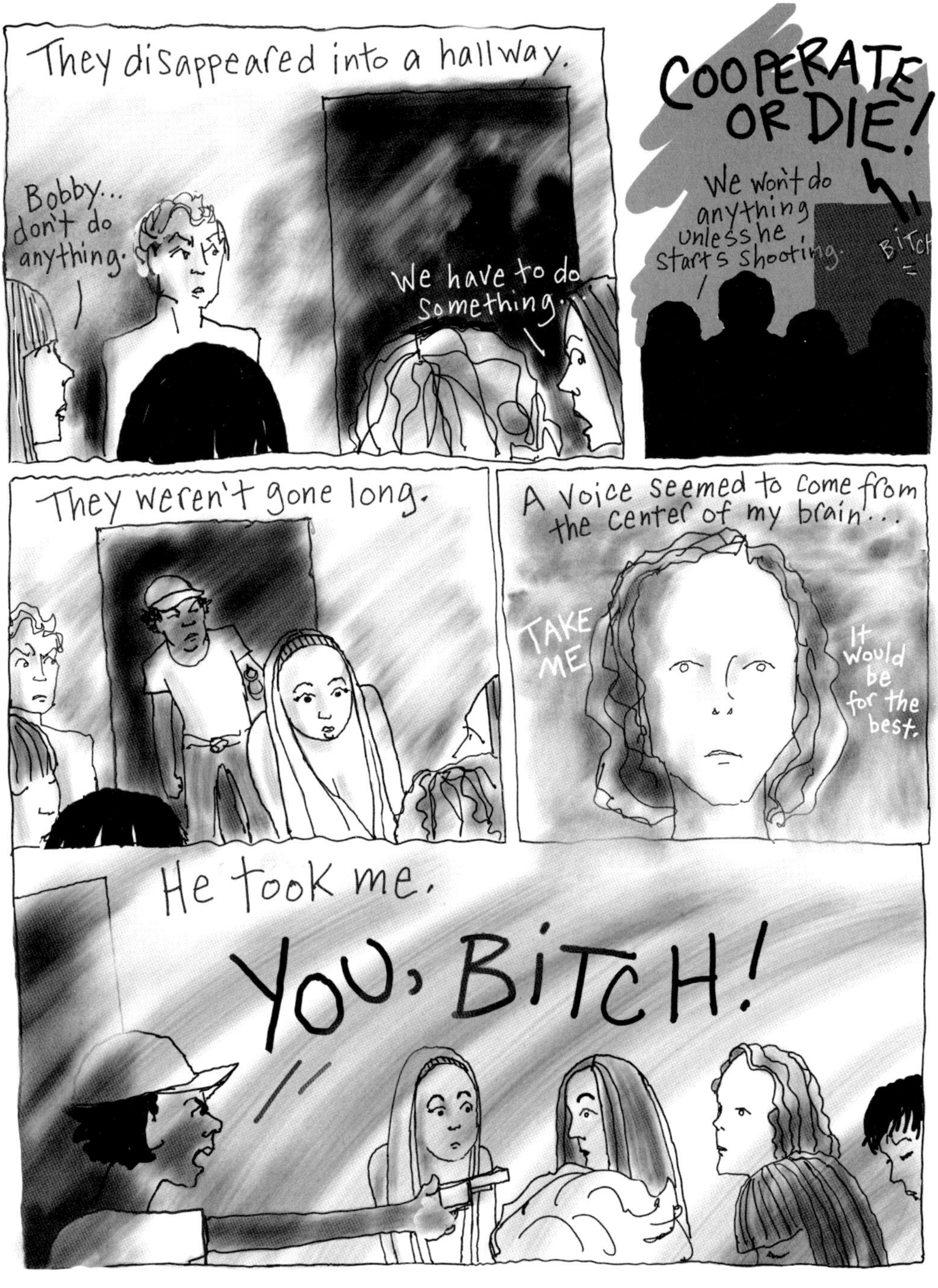
They disappeared into a hallway.
Bobby... don't do anything.
We have to do something...
COOPERATE OR DIE!
We won't do anything unless he starts shooting.
BITCH
They weren't gone long.
A voice seemed to come from the center of my brain...
TAKE ME
It would be for the best.
He took me.
YOU, BITCH!

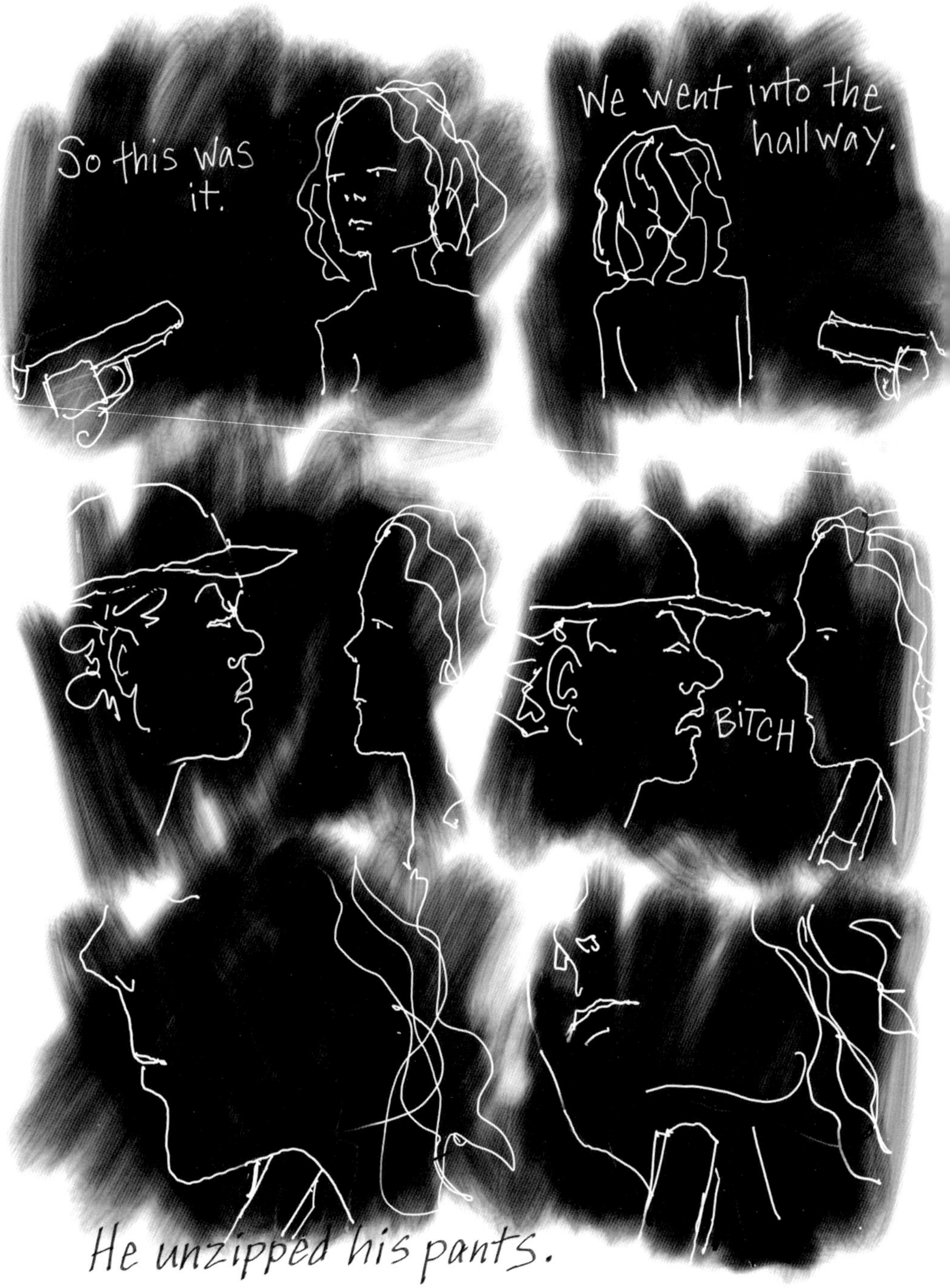

So this was it.
We went into the hallway.
BITCH
He unzipped his pants.

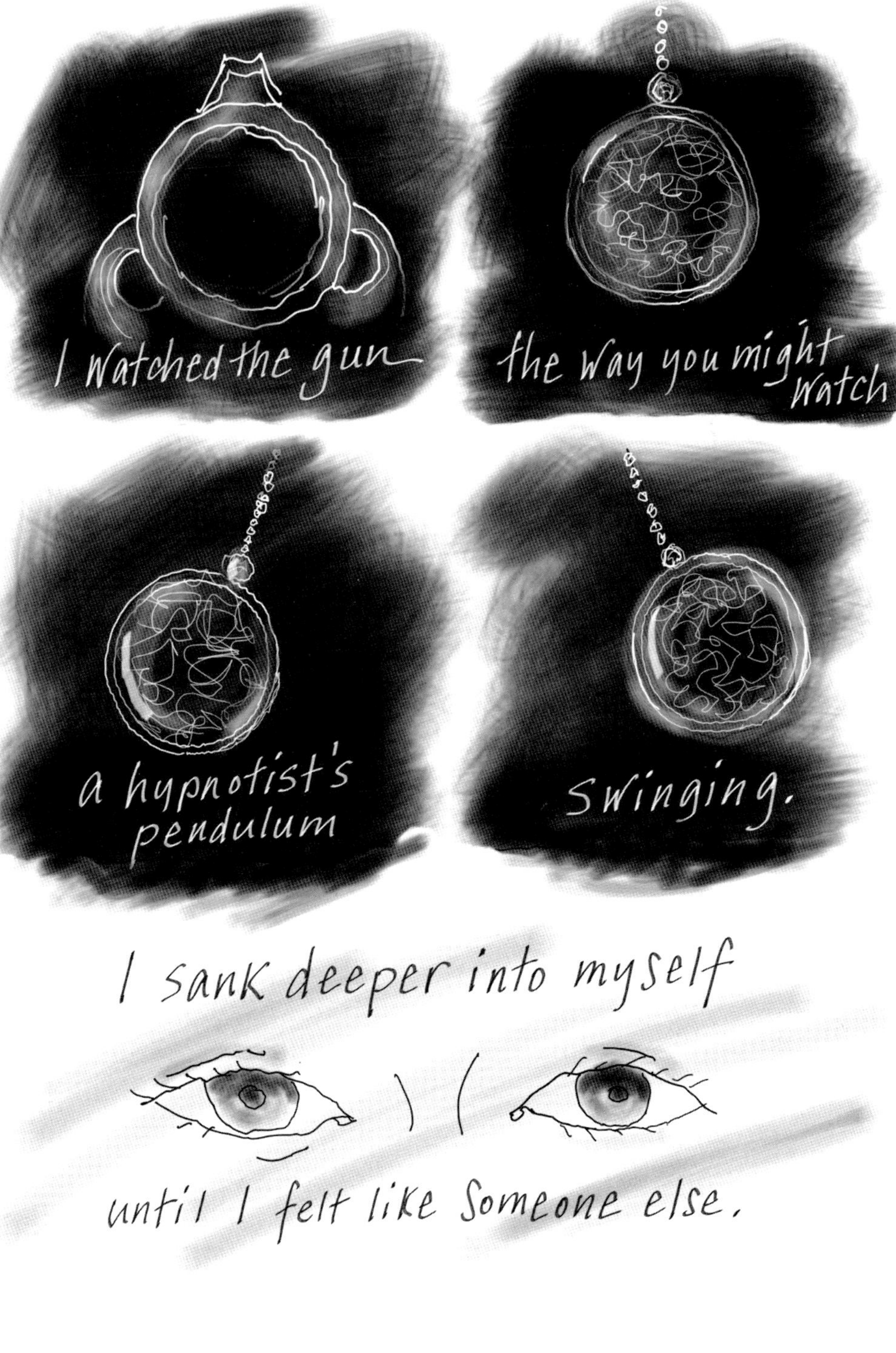
I watched the gun
the way you might watch
a hypnotist's pendulum
swinging.
I sank deeper into myself
until I felt like Someone else.

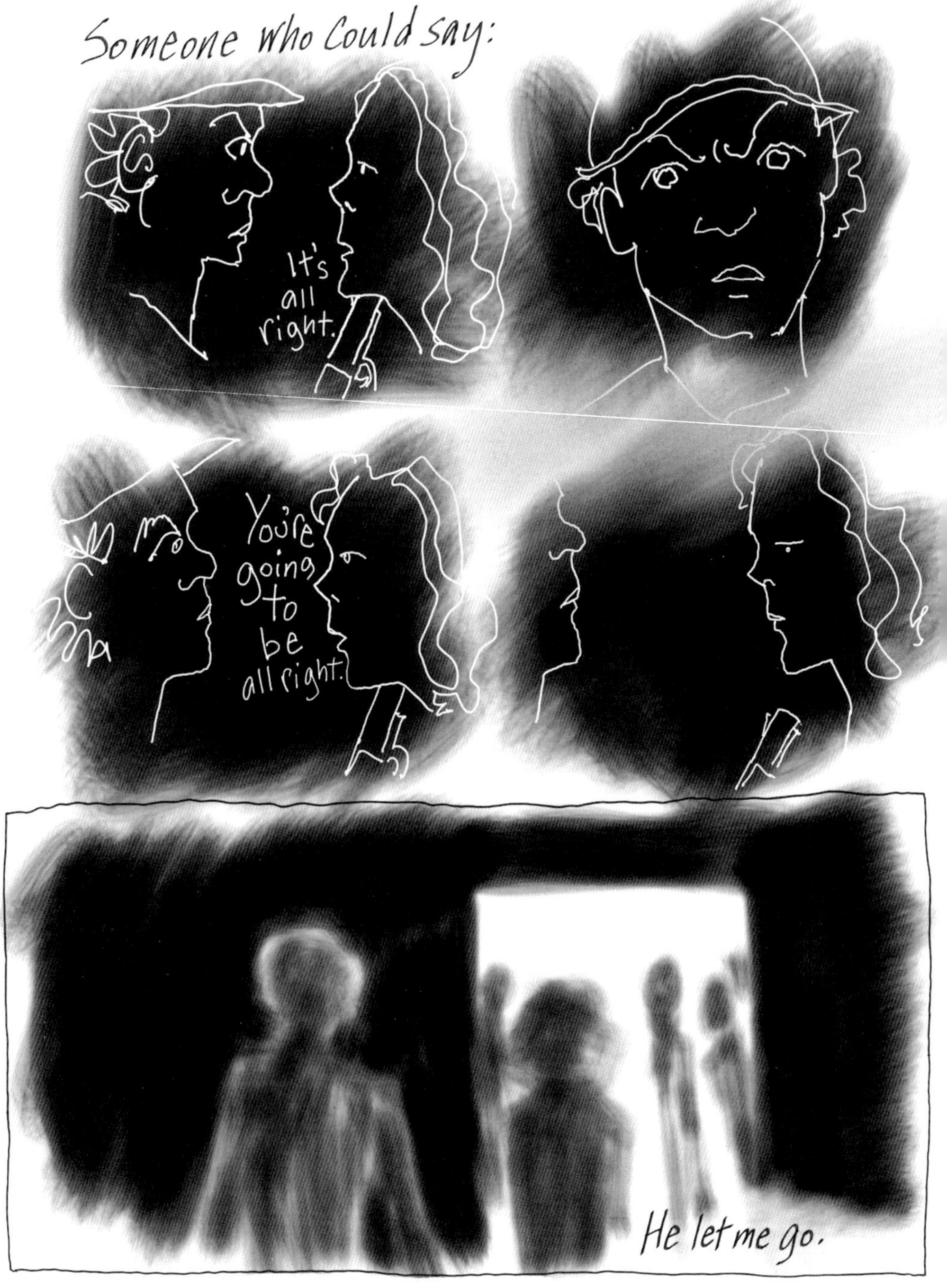
Someone who could say:
It's all right.
You're going to be all right.
He let me go.

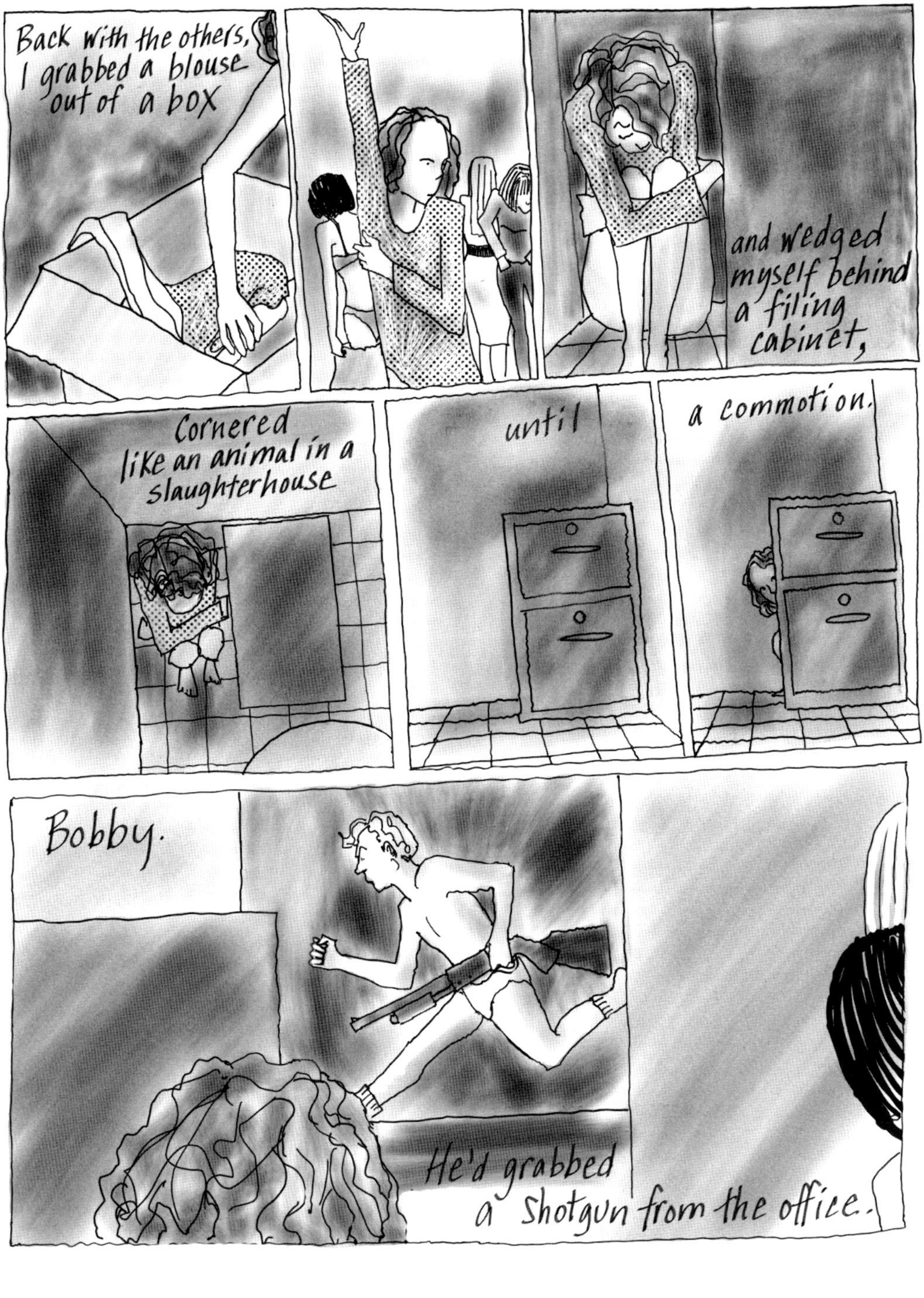
Back with the others, I grabbed a blouse out of a box
and wedged myself behind a filing cabinet,
Cornered like an animal in a slaughterhouse
until
a commotion.
Bobby.
He'd grabbed a shotgun from the office.

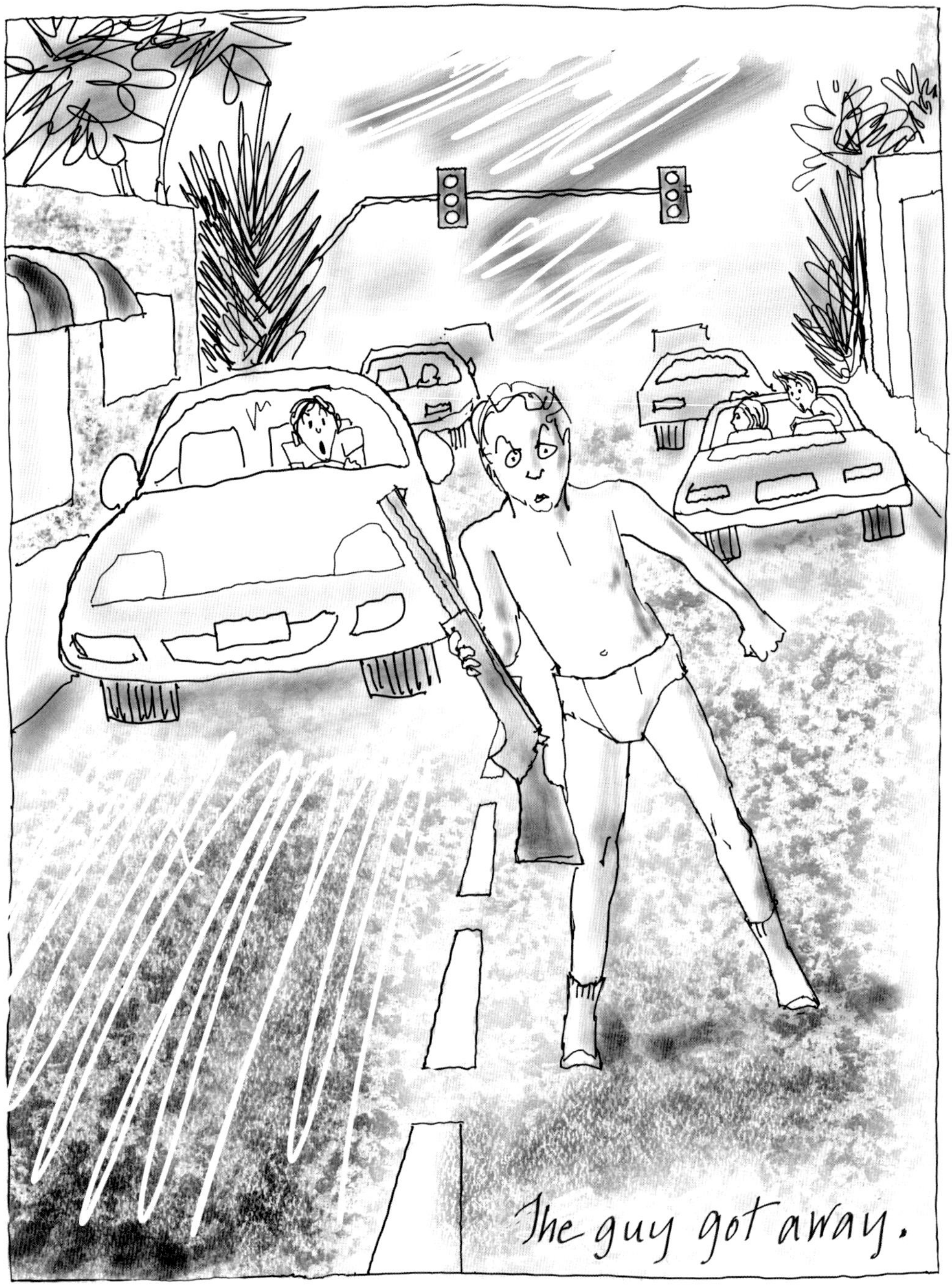
The guy got away.

Three

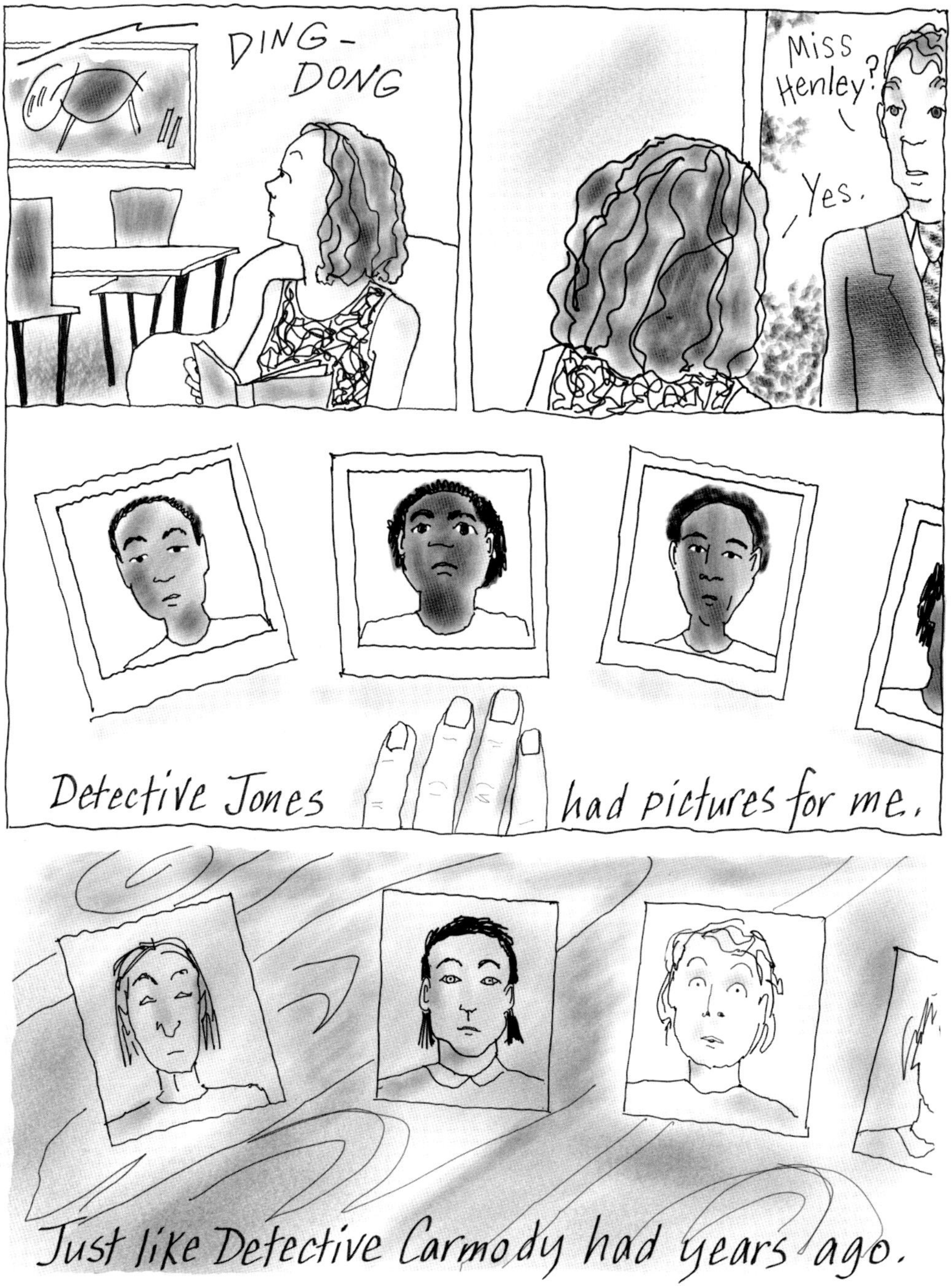
DING-DONG
Miss Henley?
Yes.
Detective Jones had pictures for me.
Just like Detective Carmody had years ago.

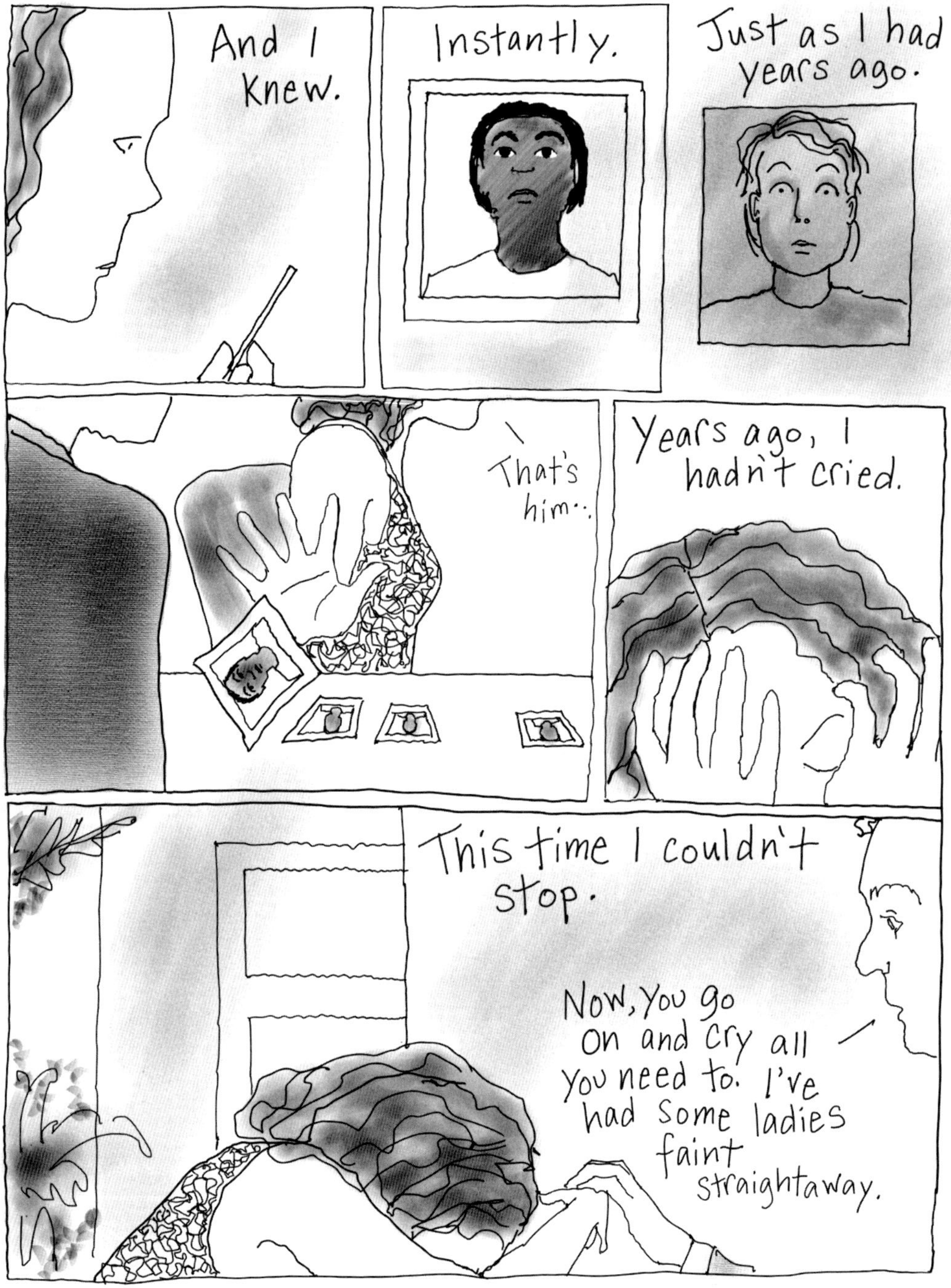
And I knew.
Instantly.
Just as I had years ago.
That's him...
Years ago, I hadn't cried.
This time I couldn't stop.
Now, you go on and cry all you need to. I've had some ladies faint straightaway.

You aren't damaged — goods.

We'll be in touch, Miss Henley.

Thank you.

He was kind and well-meaning,

but this concept of

DAMAGED
DAMAGED
DAMAGED
NOT
DAMAGED
DAMAGED
NOT
DAMAGED
NOT DAMAGED

As if women were toys that some guy could break and no other guy would want.

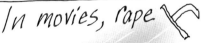

In movies, rape

victims are always showering, scrubbing,

and saying they feel dirty.

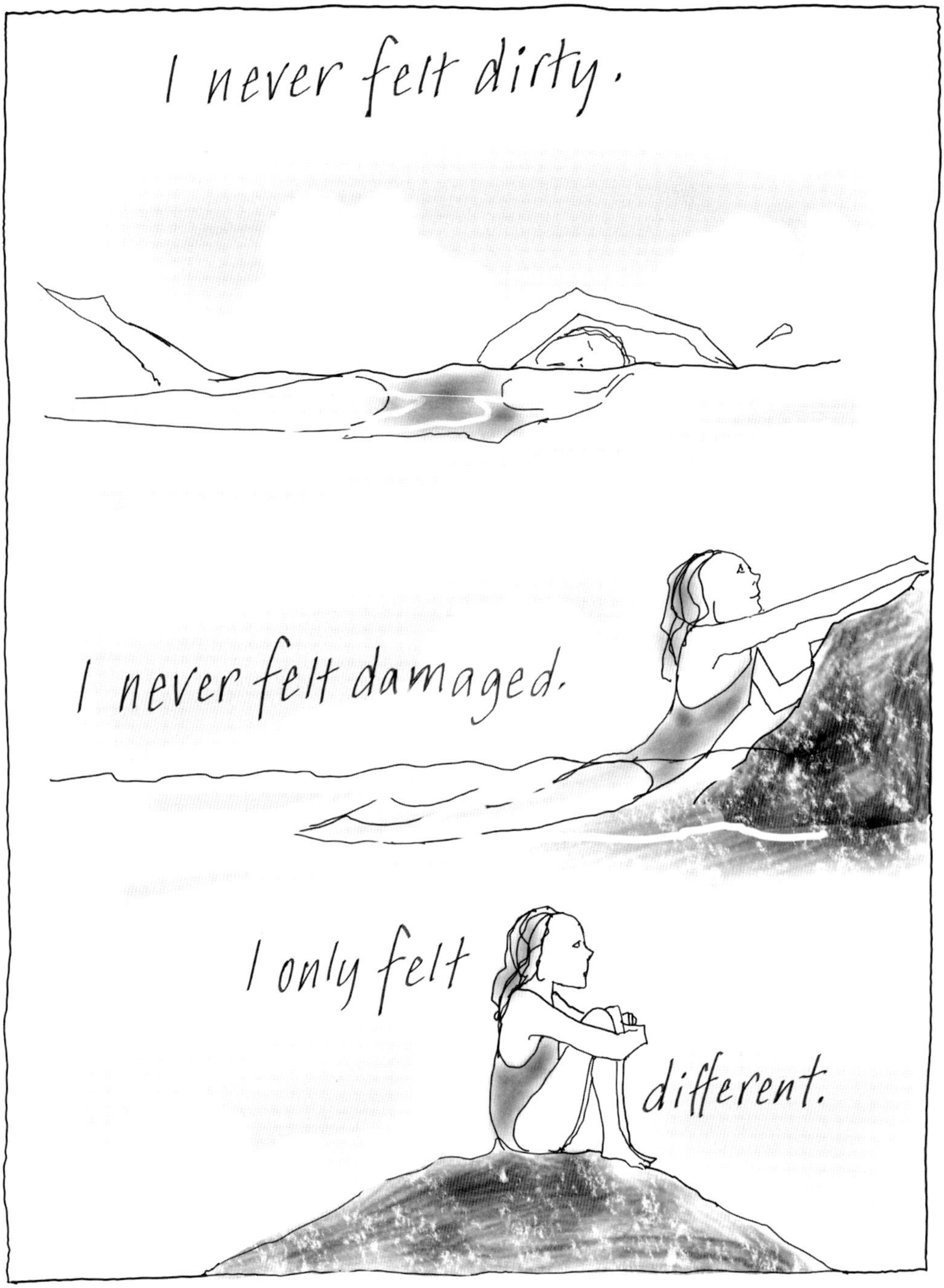

I never felt dirty.
I never felt damaged.
I only felt
different.

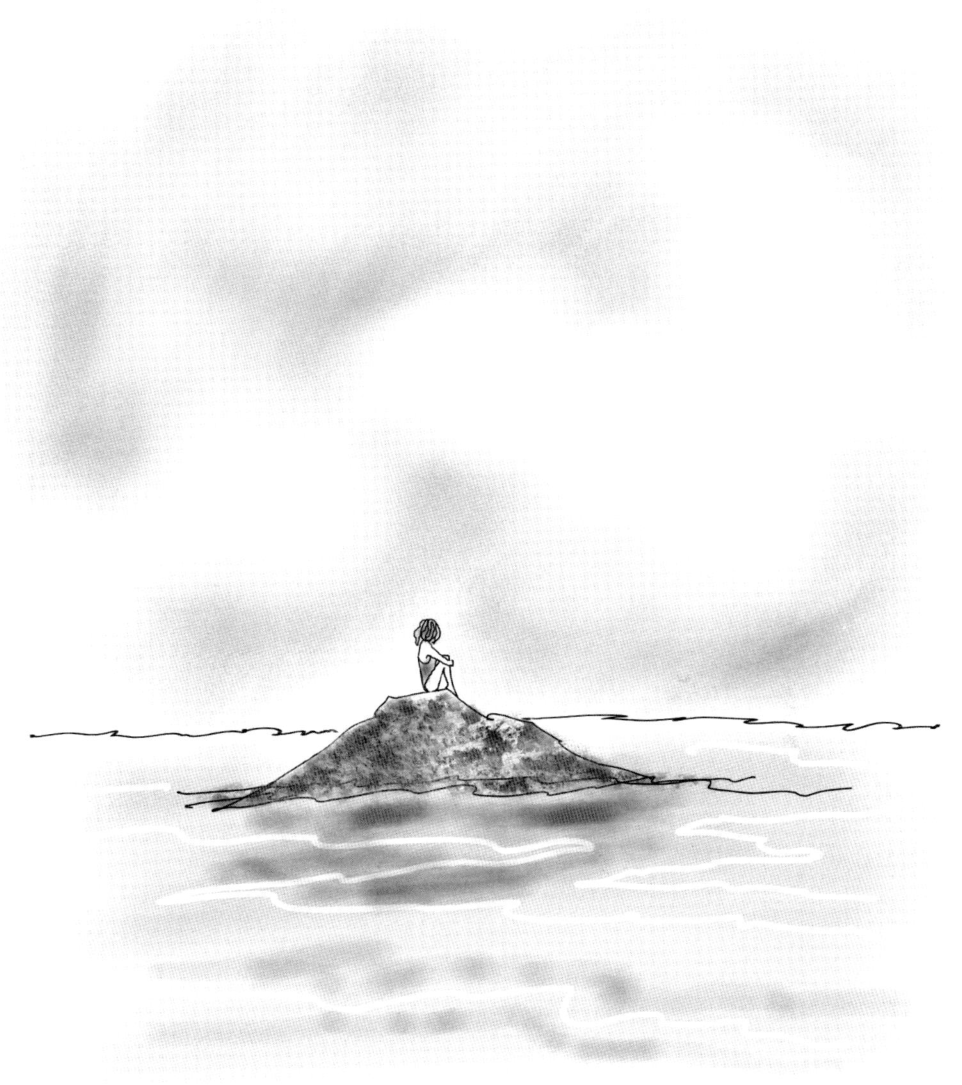

I felt alone.

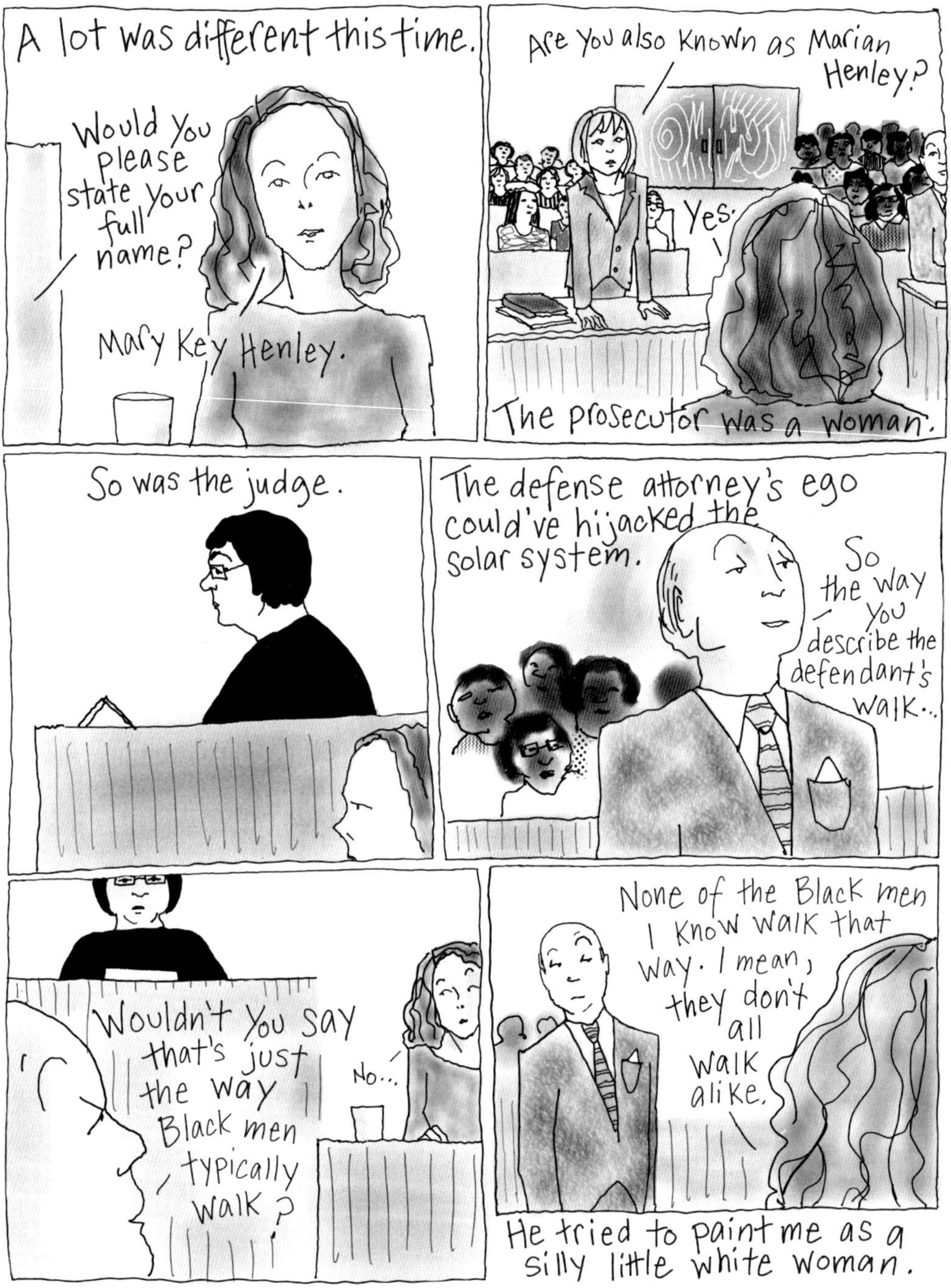

A lot was different this time.
Would you please state your full name?
Mary Key Henley.
Are you also known as Marian Henley?
Yes.
The prosecutor was a woman.
So was the judge.
The defense attorney's ego could've hijacked the solar system.
So the way you describe the defendant's walk...
Wouldn't you say that's just the way Black men typically walk?
No...
None of the Black men I know walk that way. I mean, they don't all walk alike.
He tried to paint me as a silly little white woman.

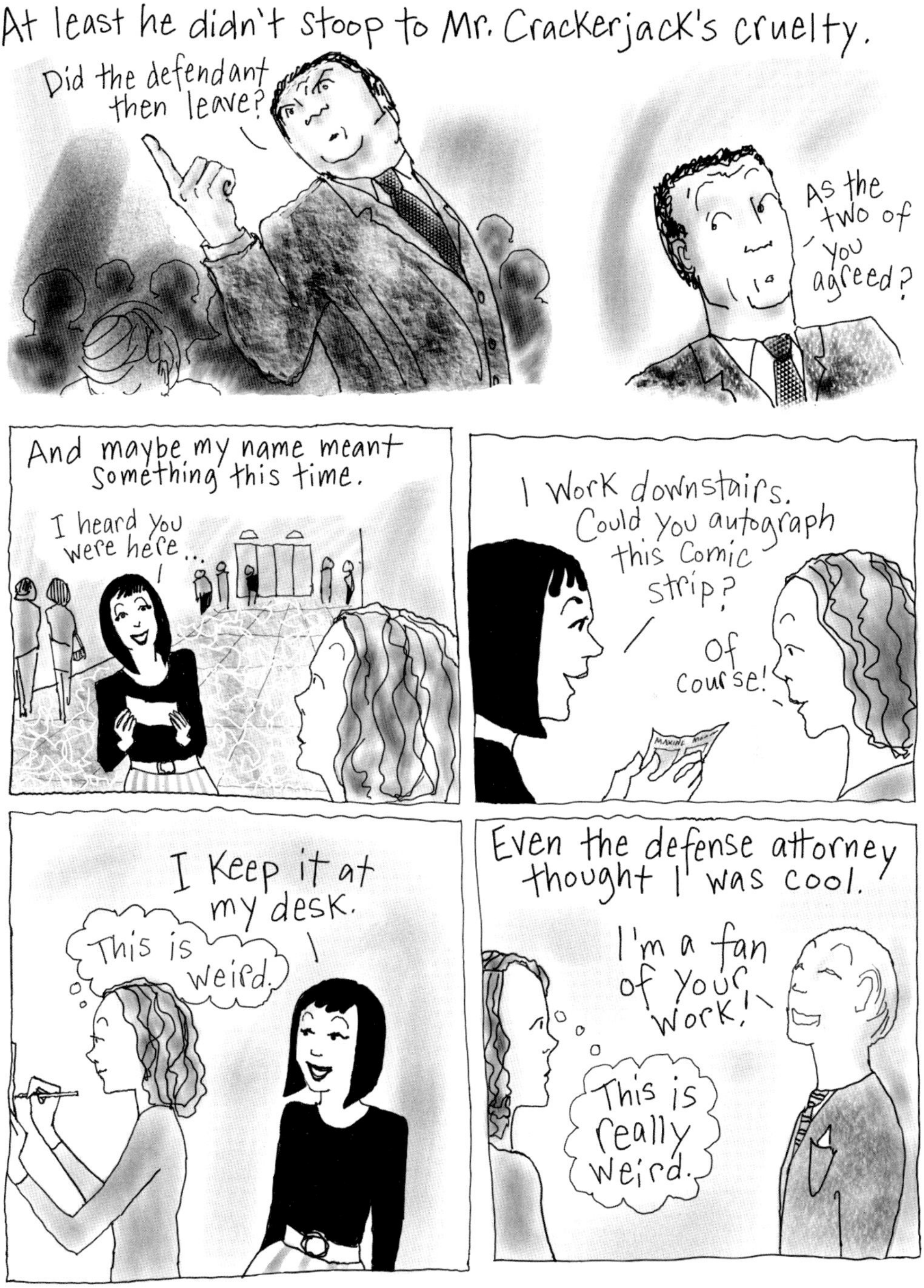
At least he didn't stoop to Mr. Crackerjack's cruelty.
Did the defendant then leave?
As the two of you agreed?
And maybe my name meant something this time.
I heard you were here...
I work downstairs. Could you autograph this comic strip?
Of course!
I keep it at my desk.
This is weird.
Even the defense attorney thought I was cool.
I'm a fan of your work!
This is really weird.

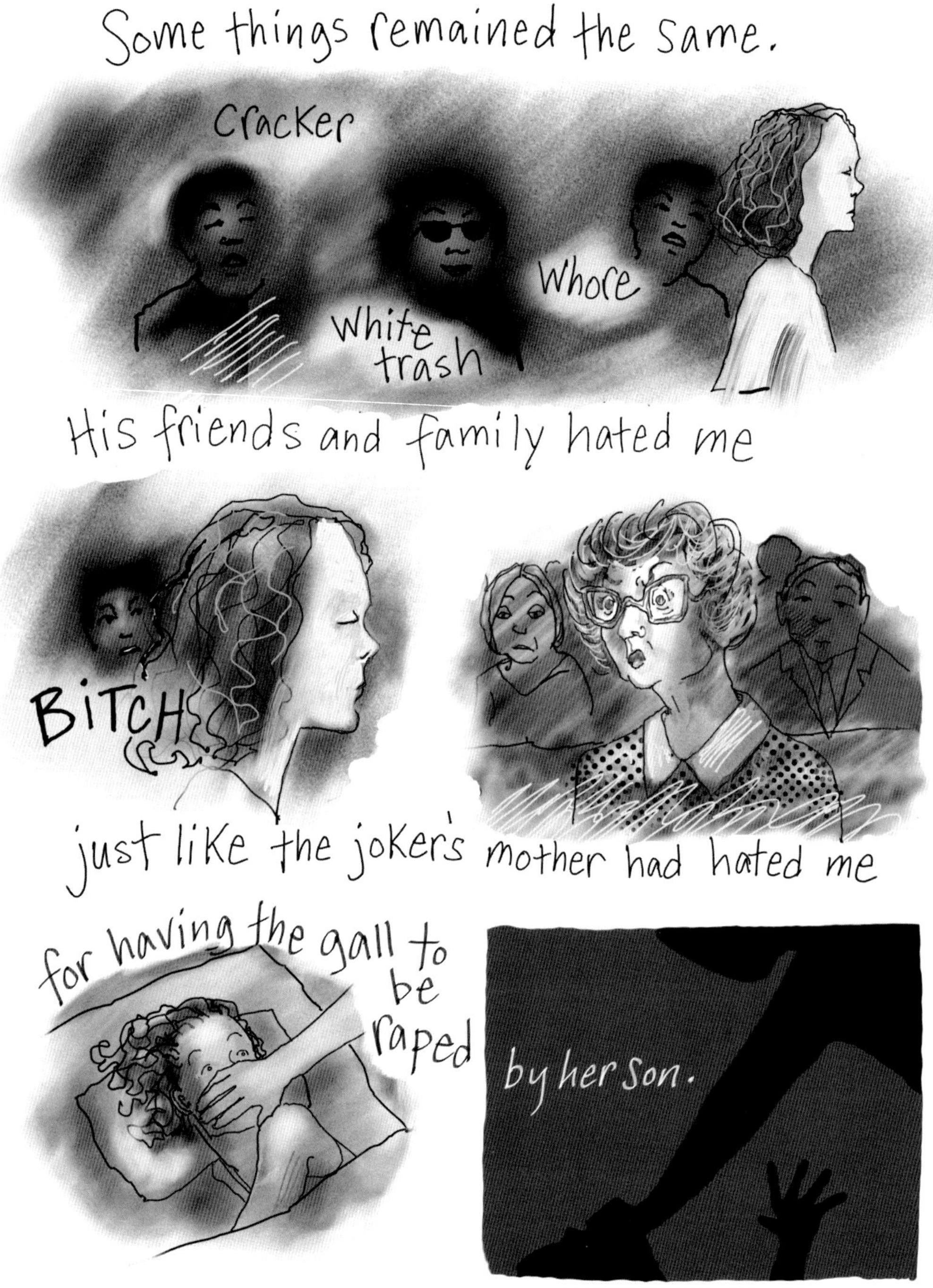
Some things remained the same.
Cracker
Whore
White trash
His friends and family hated me
BITCH
just like the joker's mother had hated me
for having the gall to be raped
by her son.

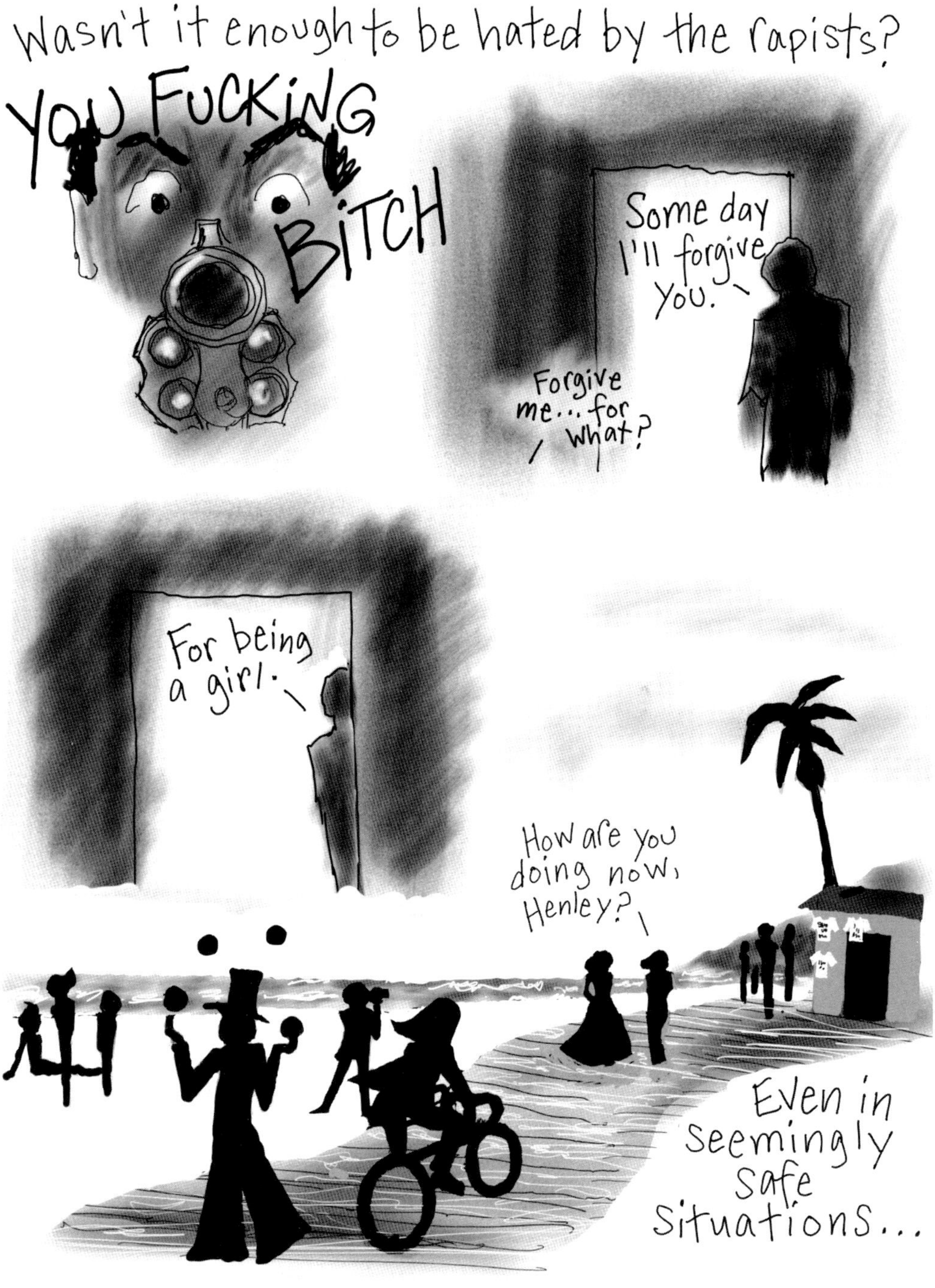
Wasn't it enough to be hated by the rapists?
YOU FUCKING BITCH
Some day I'll forgive you.
Forgive me... for what?
For being a girl.
How are you doing now, Henley?
Even in seemingly safe situations...

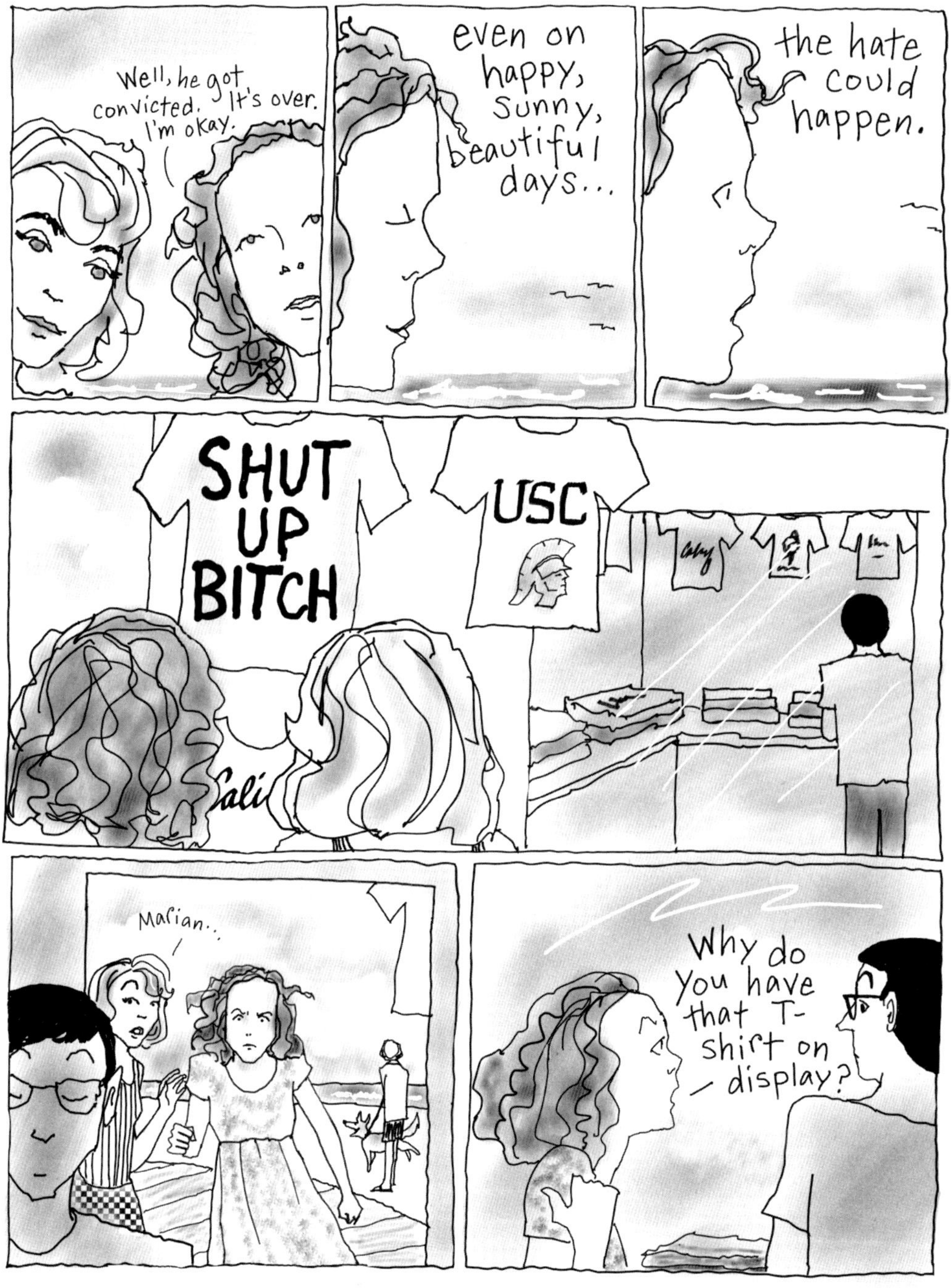
Well, he got convicted. It's over. I'm okay.
even on happy, sunny, beautiful days...
the hate could happen.
SHUT UP BITCH
USC
Marian...
Why do you have that T-shirt on display?

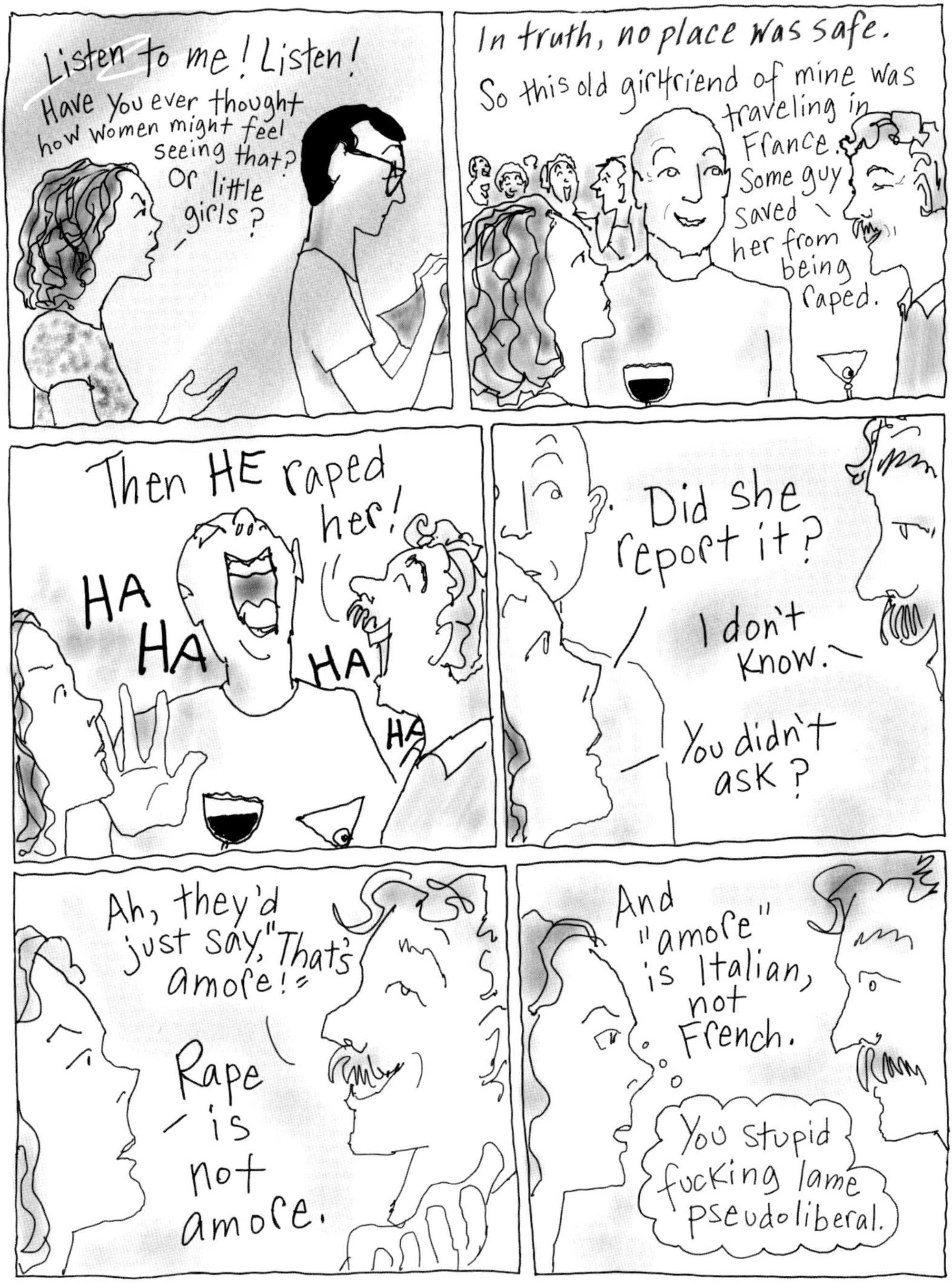
Listen to me! Listen!
Have you ever thought how women might feel seeing that? Or little girls?
In truth, no place was safe.
So this old girlfriend of mine was traveling in France. Some guy saved her from being raped.
Then HE raped her!
HA HA HA HA
Did she report it?
I don't know.
You didn't ask?
Ah, they'd just say, "That's amore!"
Rape is not amore.
And "amore" is Italian, not French.
You stupid fucking lame pseudoliberal.

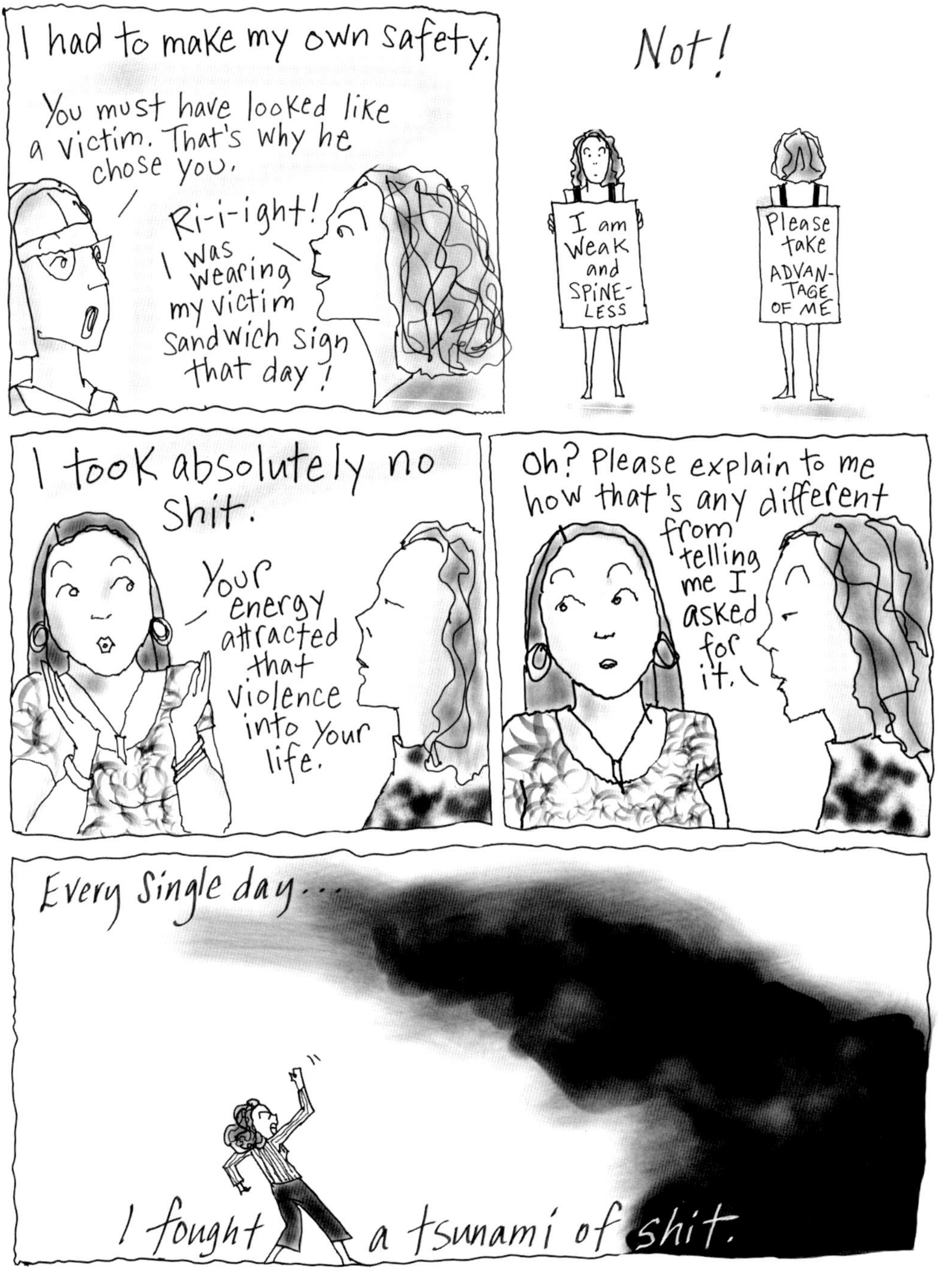
I had to make my own safety.
You must have looked like a victim. That's why he chose you.
Ri-i-ight! I was wearing my victim sandwich sign that day!
Not!
I am weak and spineless
Please take advantage of me
I took absolutely no shit.
Your energy attracted that violence into your life.
Oh? Please explain to me how that's any different from telling me I asked for it.
Every single day...
I fought a tsunami of shit.

Survival was moment to moment.

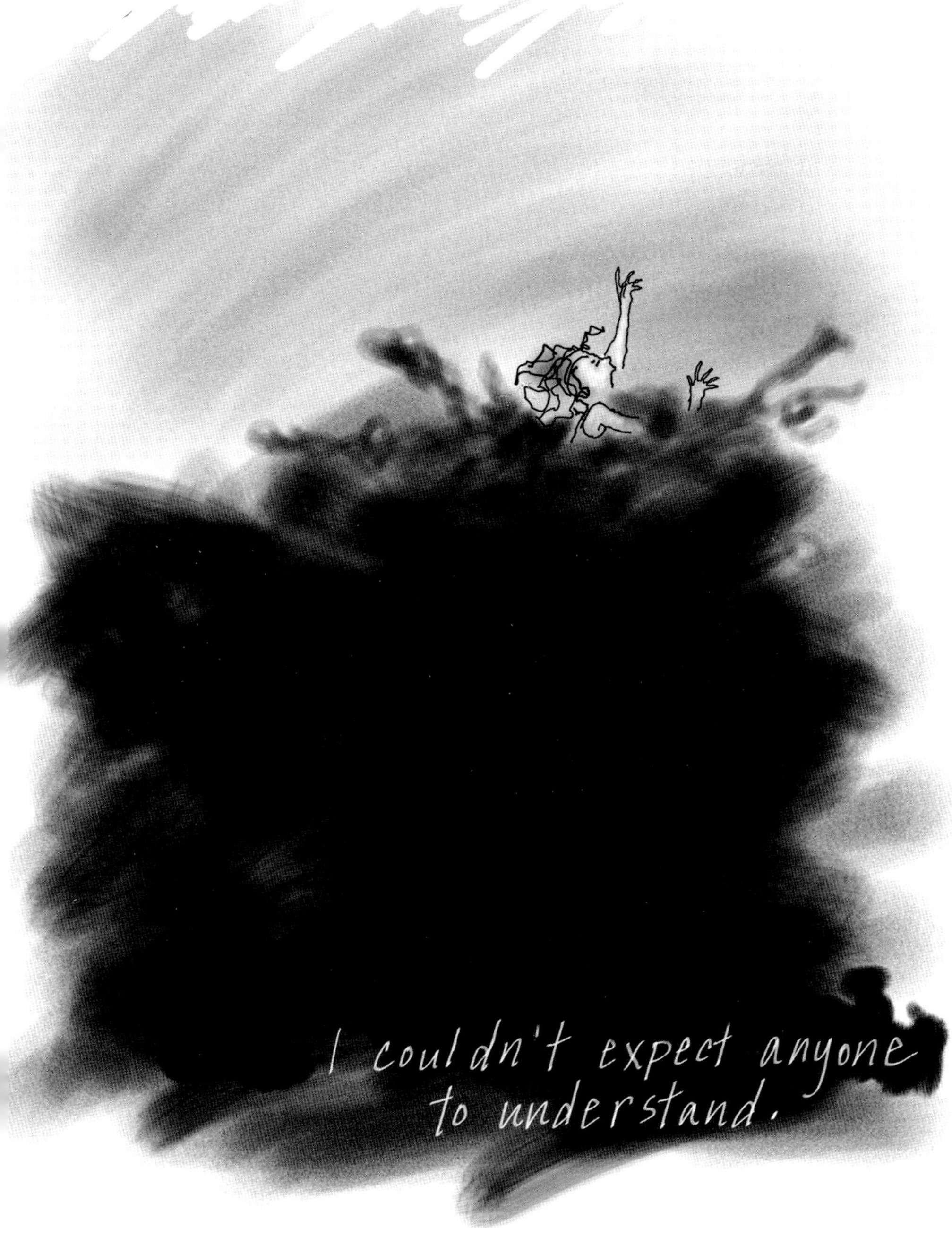
I couldn't expect anyone to understand.

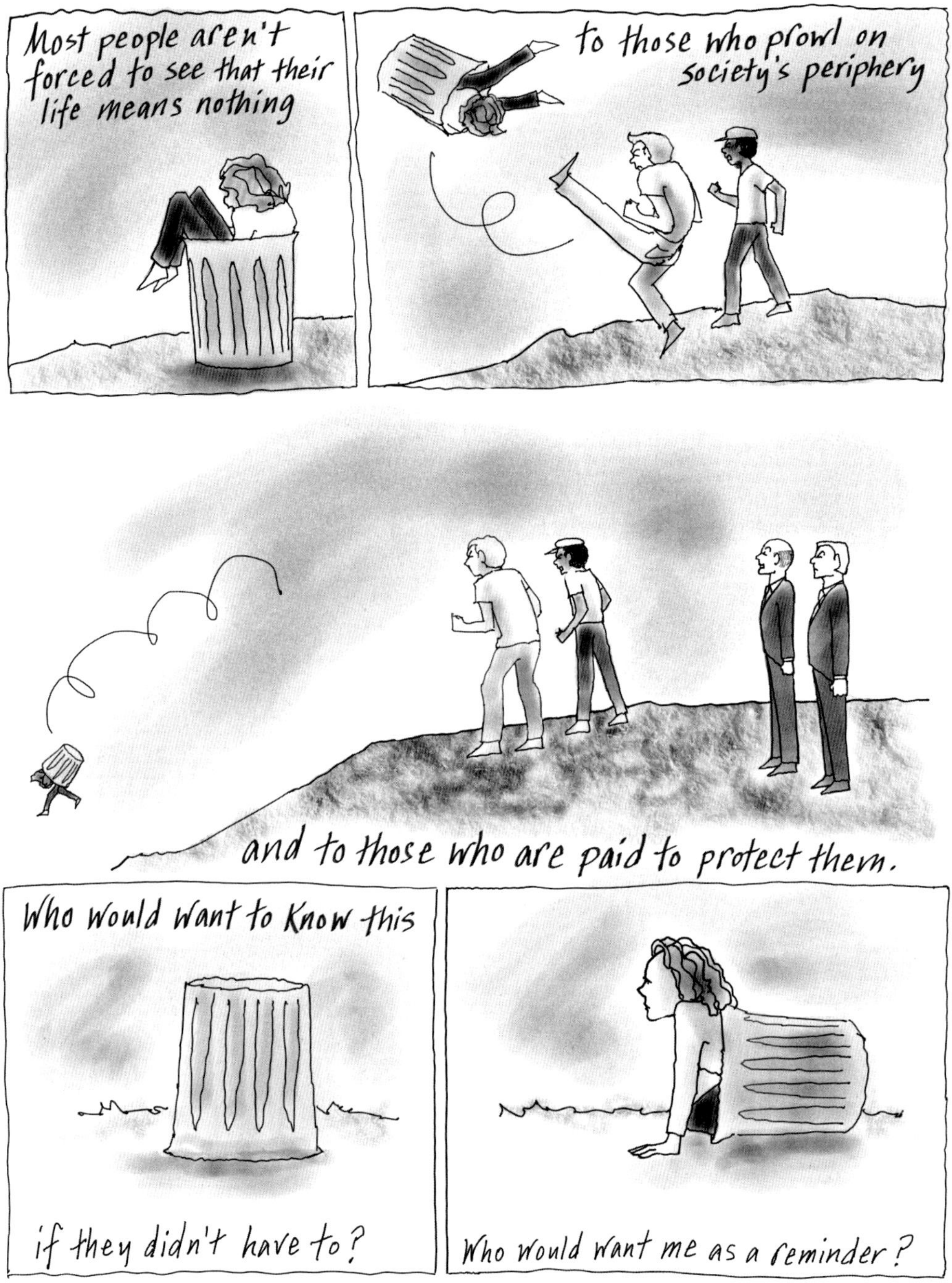
Most people aren't forced to see that their life means nothing
to those who prowl on society's periphery
and to those who are paid to protect them.
Who would want to know this
if they didn't have to?
Who would want me as a reminder?

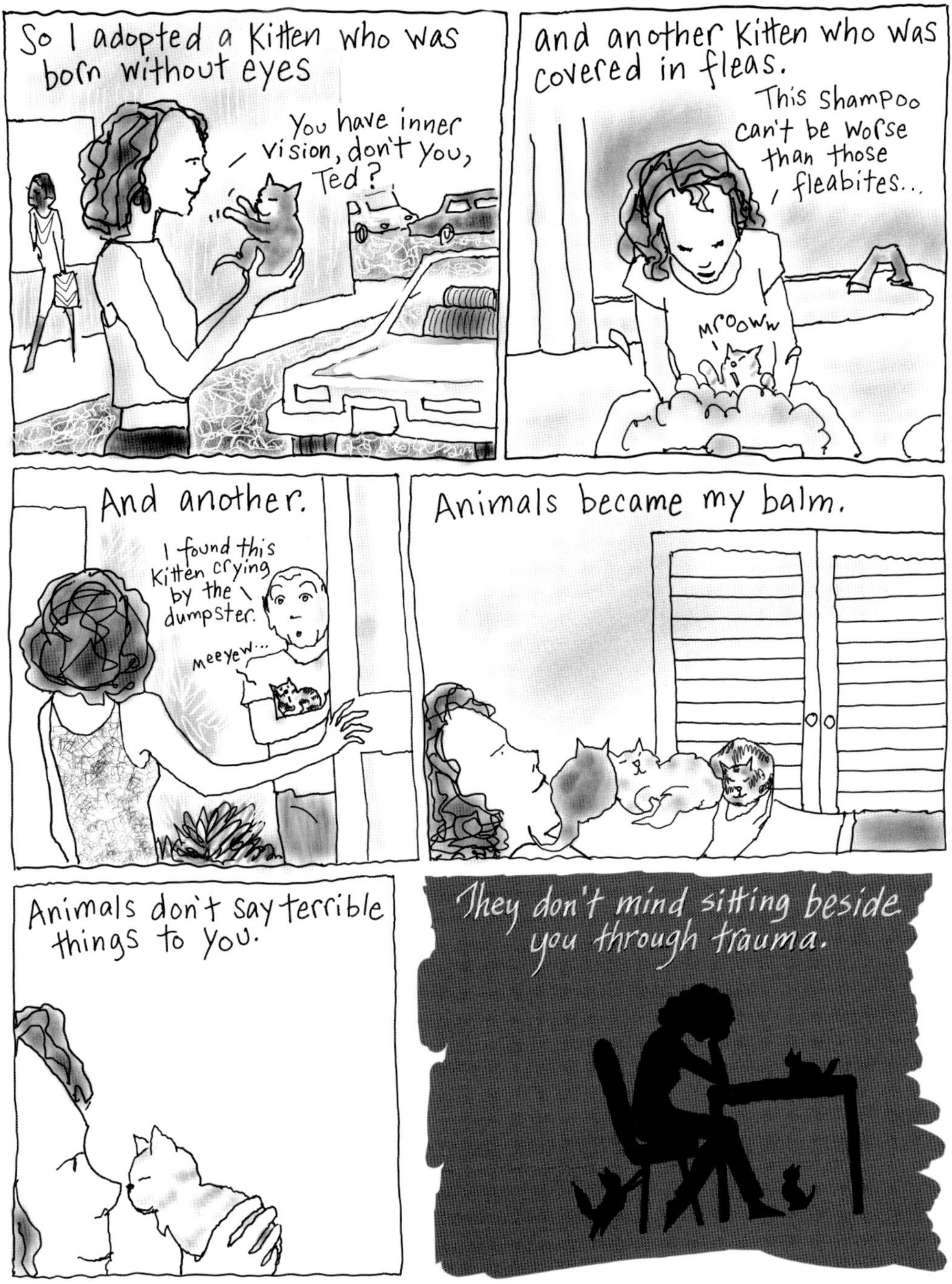
So I adopted a kitten who was born without eyes
You have inner vision, don't you, Ted?
and another kitten who was covered in fleas.
This shampoo can't be worse than those fleabites...
MROOWW
And another.
I found this kitten crying by the dumpster.
meeyew...
Animals became my balm.
Animals don't say terrible things to you.
They don't mind sitting beside you through trauma.

I would need their simple devotion more than I knew.

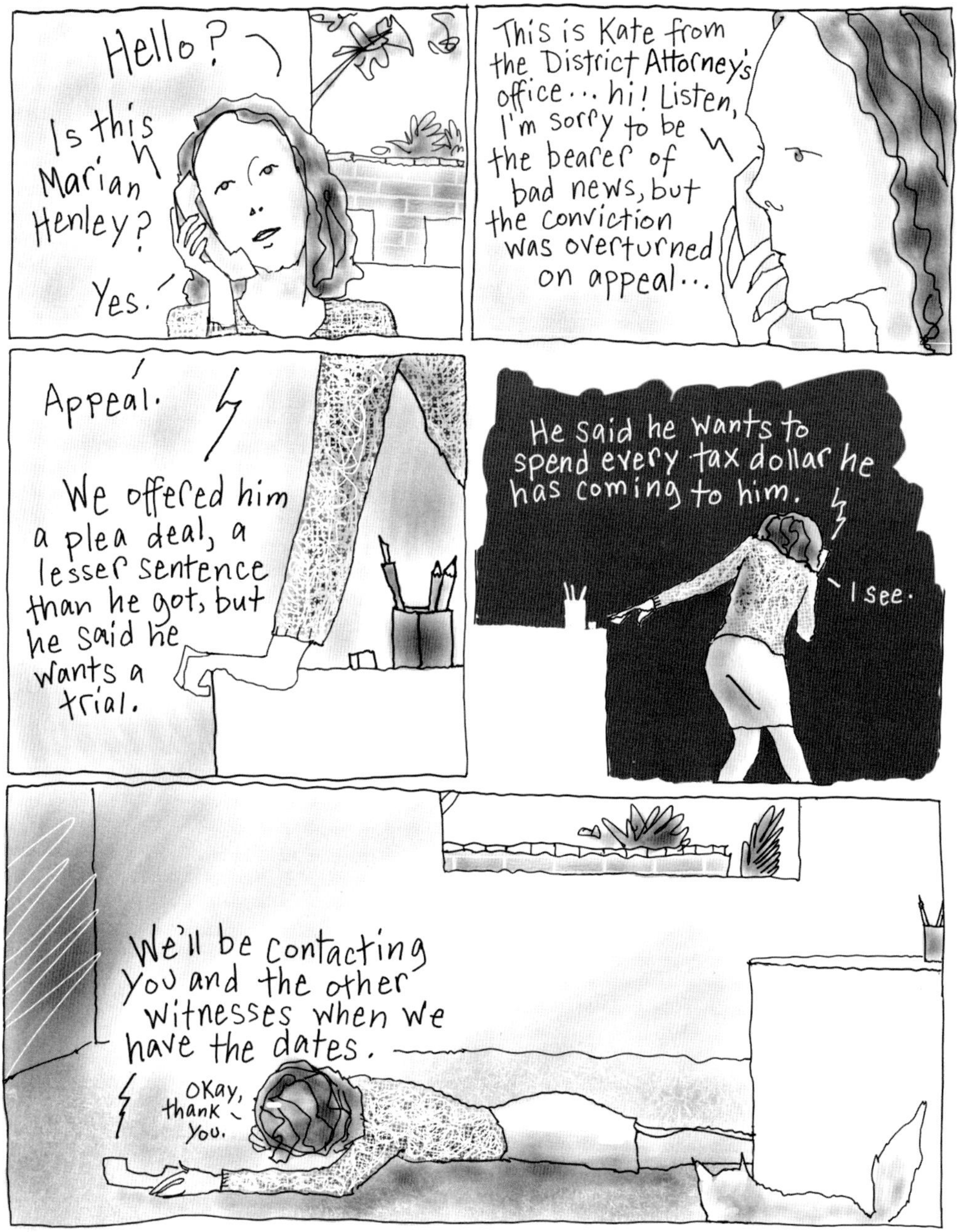
Hello?
Is this Marian Henley?
Yes.
This is Kate from the District Attorney's office... hi! Listen, I'm sorry to be the bearer of bad news, but the conviction was overturned on appeal...
Appeal.
We offered him a plea deal, a lesser sentence than he got, but he said he wants a trial.
He said he wants to spend every tax dollar he has coming to him.
I see.
We'll be contacting you and the other witnesses when we have the dates.
Okay, thank you.

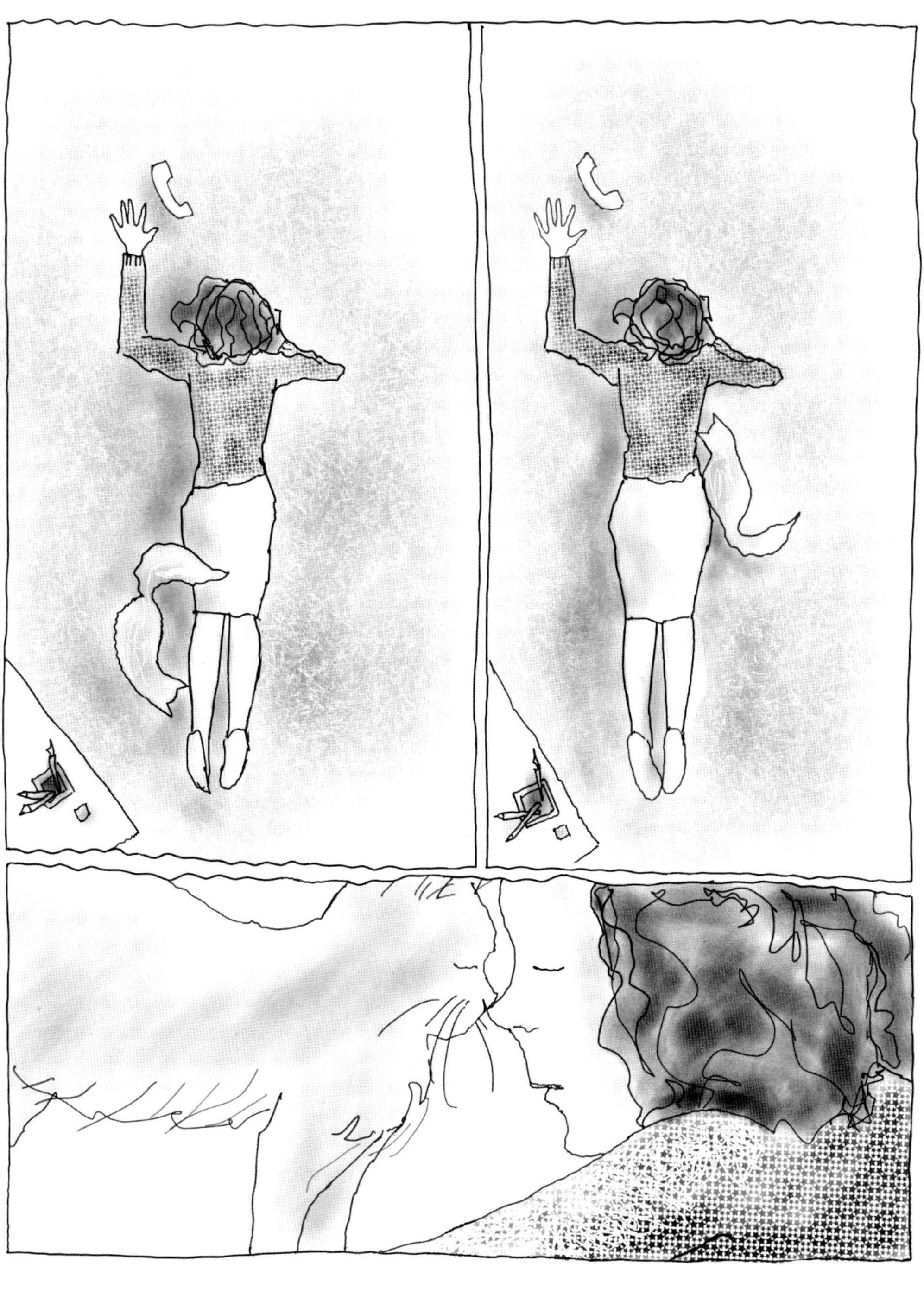

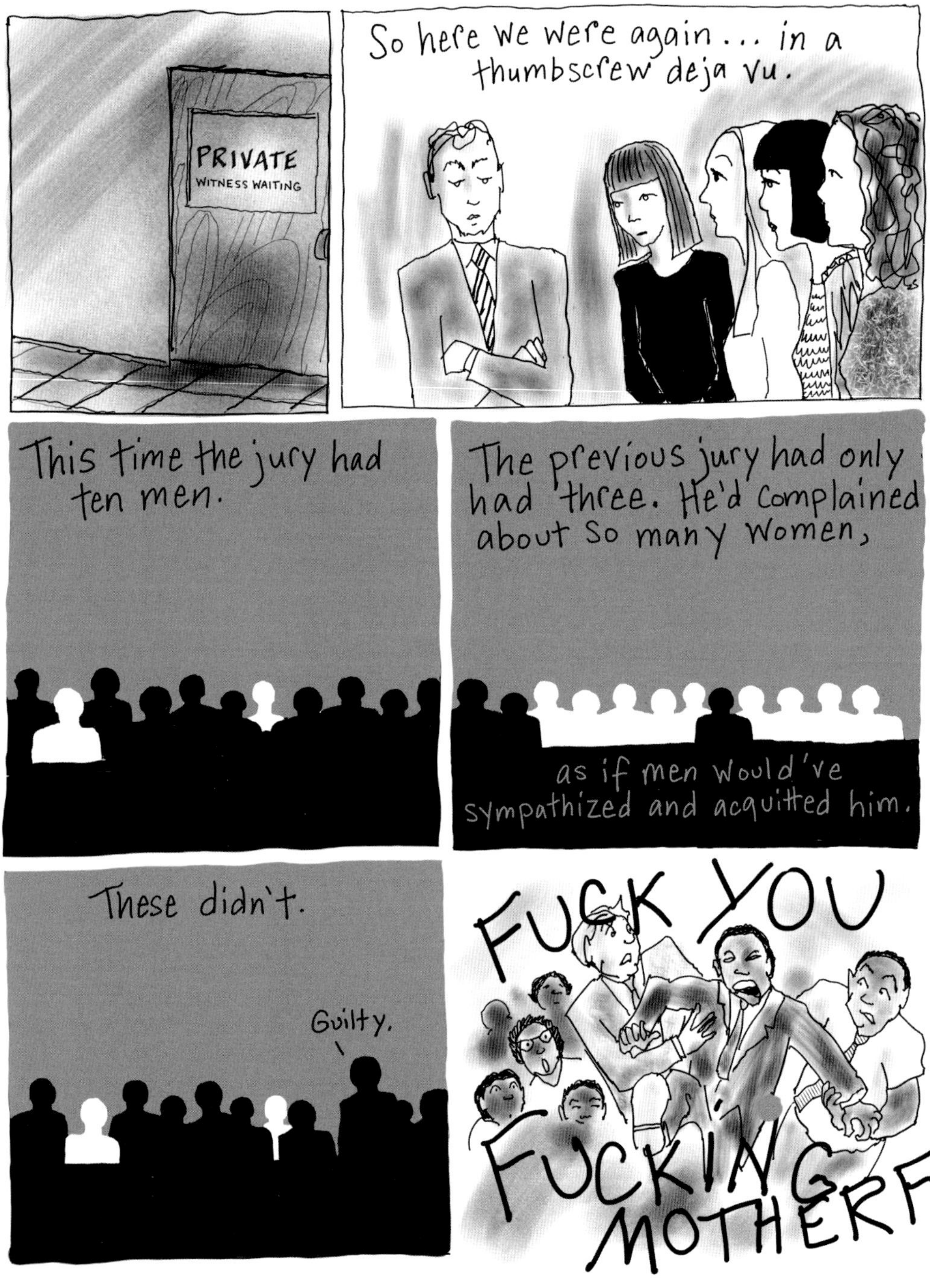
PRIVATE
WITNESS WAITING
So here we were again... in a thumbscrew deja vu.
This time the jury had ten men.
The previous jury had only had three. He'd complained about so many women,
as if men would've sympathized and acquitted him.
These didn't.
Guilty.
FUCK YOU
FUCKING MOTHERF

The courtroom got to see...
FUCKING COCKSUCKERS FUCKING BITCHES

the person we had seen that day in the store,

I was too nauseous to move.

My friend Catherine gave me half an Ativan.

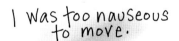

It was all over now.

Can you walk?

Yes.

Maybe.

As for having a family,

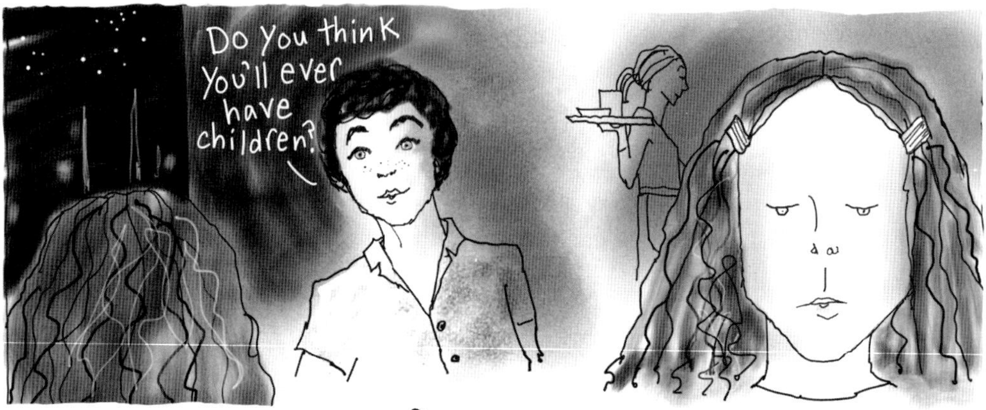
Do you think you'll ever have children?

I'd told Steph years ago...

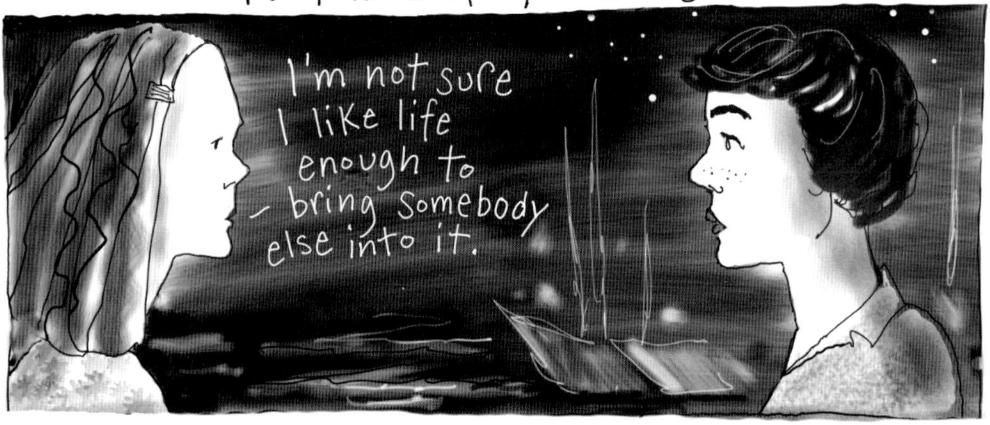
I'm not sure I like life enough to bring somebody else into it.

How could I have a child

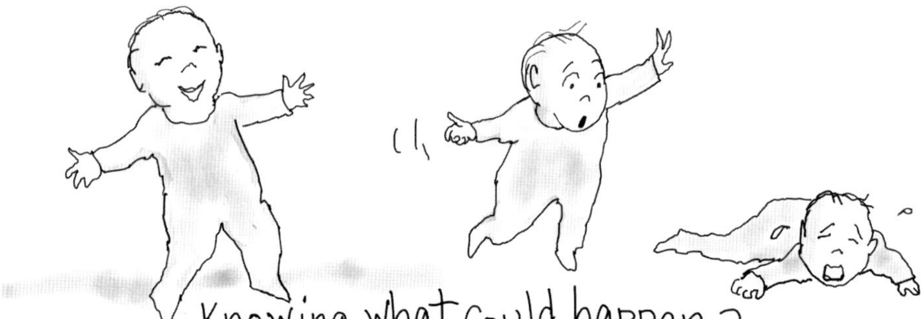

Knowing what could happen?

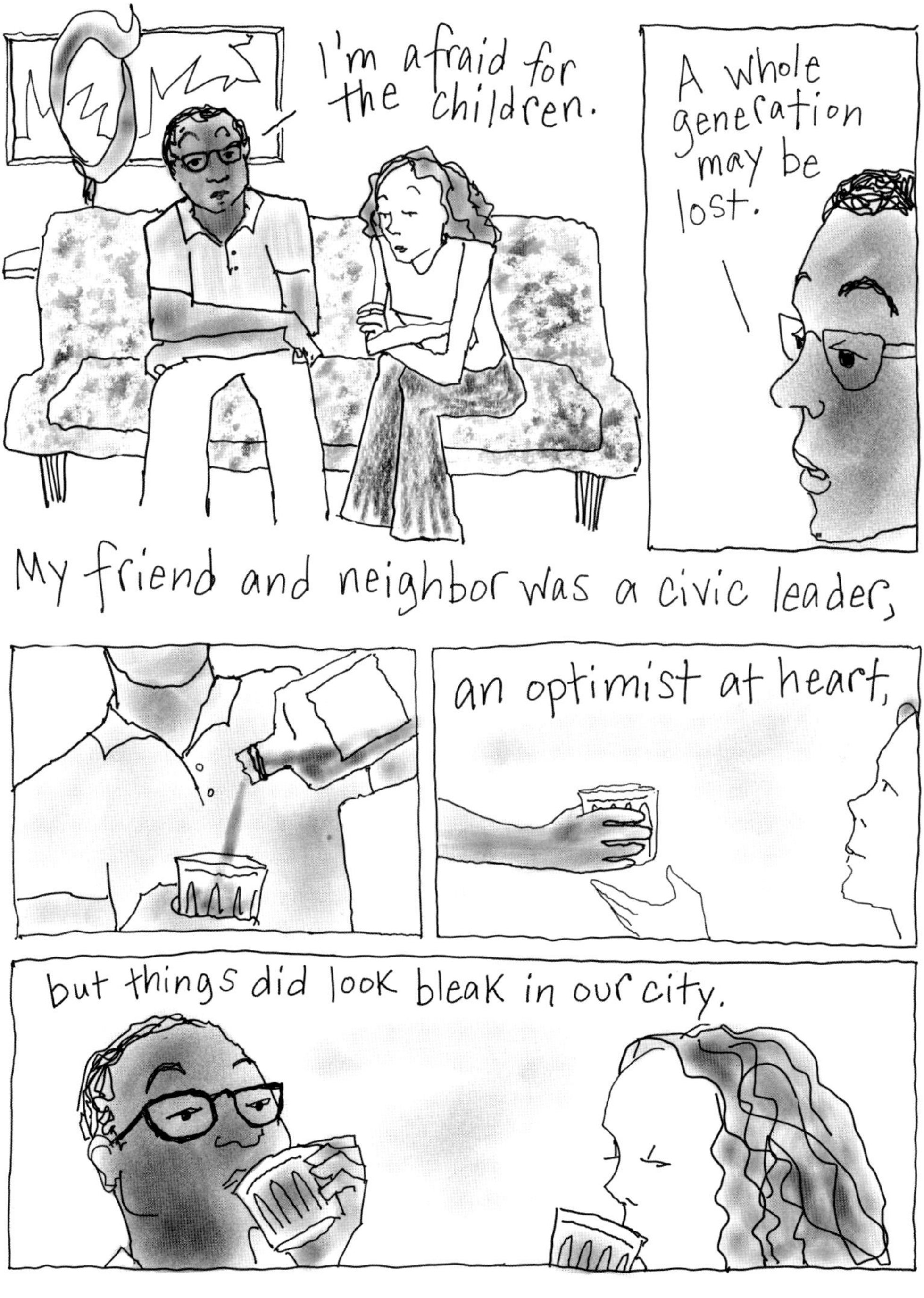
I'm afraid for the children.
A whole generation may be lost.
My friend and neighbor was a civic leader,
an optimist at heart,
but things did look bleak in our city.

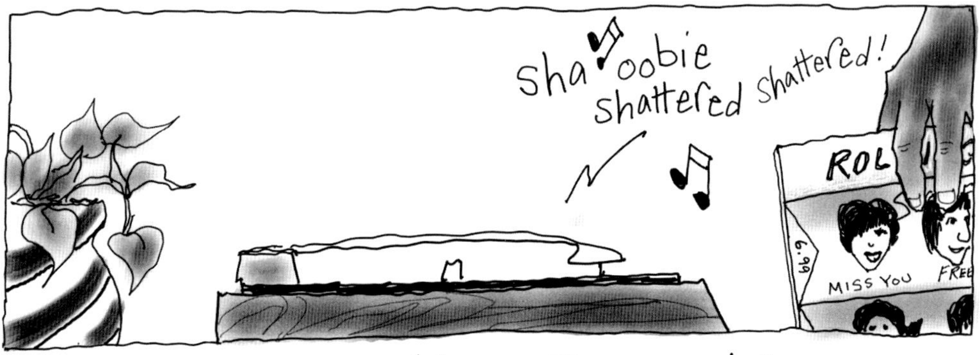
Sha oobie
shattered shattered!
ROL
MISS YOU
FREE
6.99

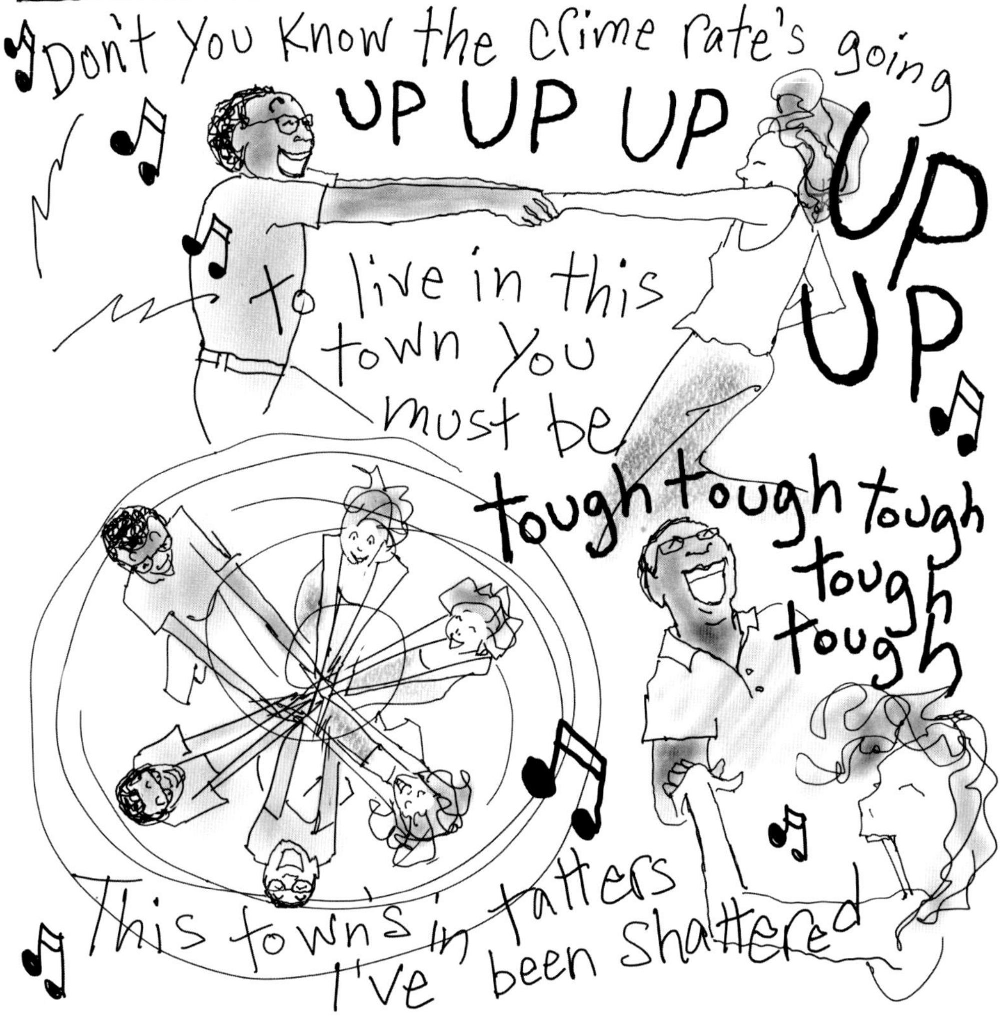
Don't you know the crime rate's going
UP UP UP
UP
UP
to live in this
town you
must be
tough tough tough
tough
tough
This town's in tatters
I've been shattered

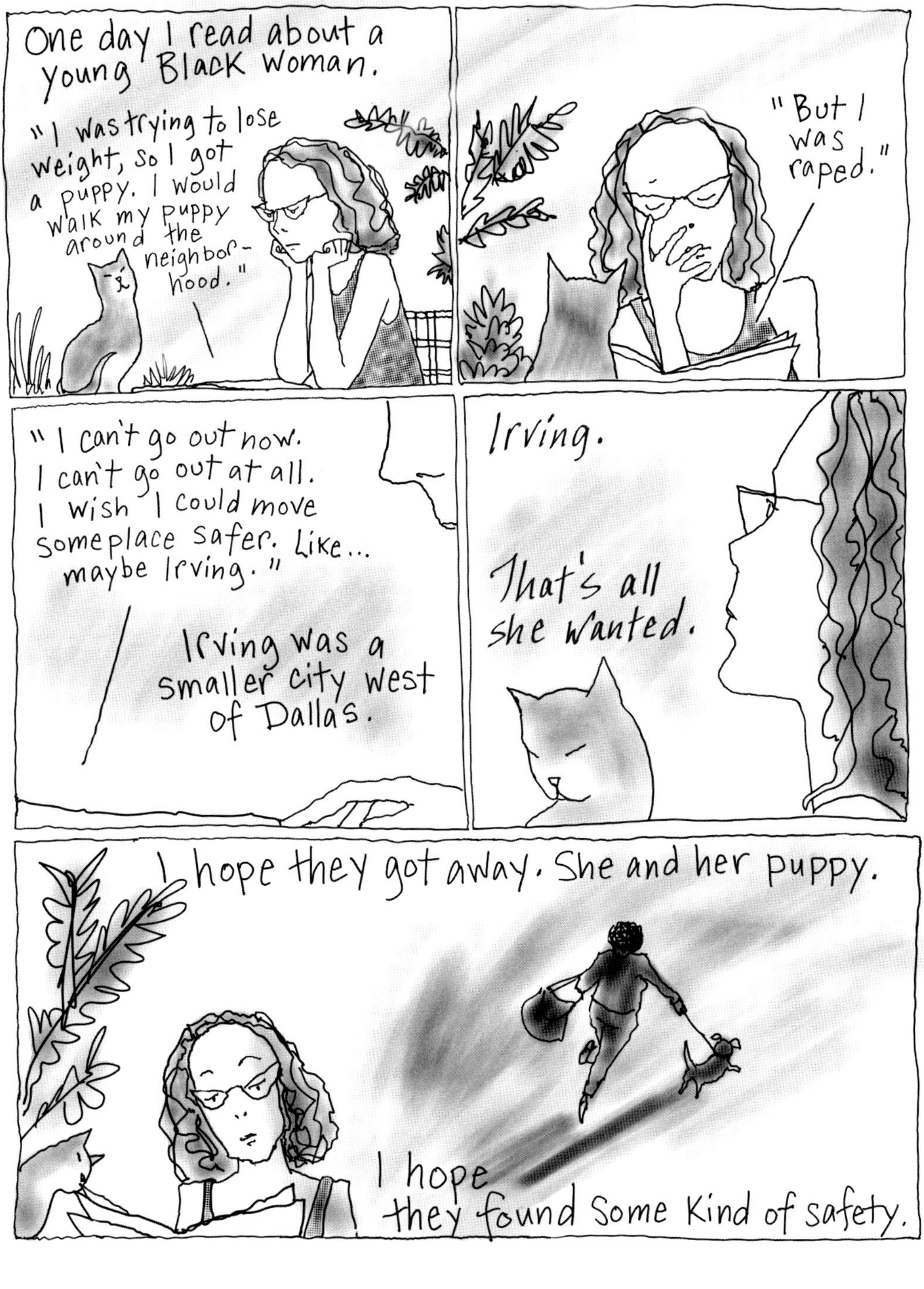
One day I read about a young Black woman.
"I was trying to lose weight, so I got a puppy. I would walk my puppy around the neighborhood."
"But I was raped."
"I can't go out now. I can't go out at all. I wish I could move someplace safer. Like... maybe Irving."
Irving was a smaller city west of Dallas.
Irving.
That's all she wanted.
I hope they got away. She and her puppy.
I hope they found some kind of safety.

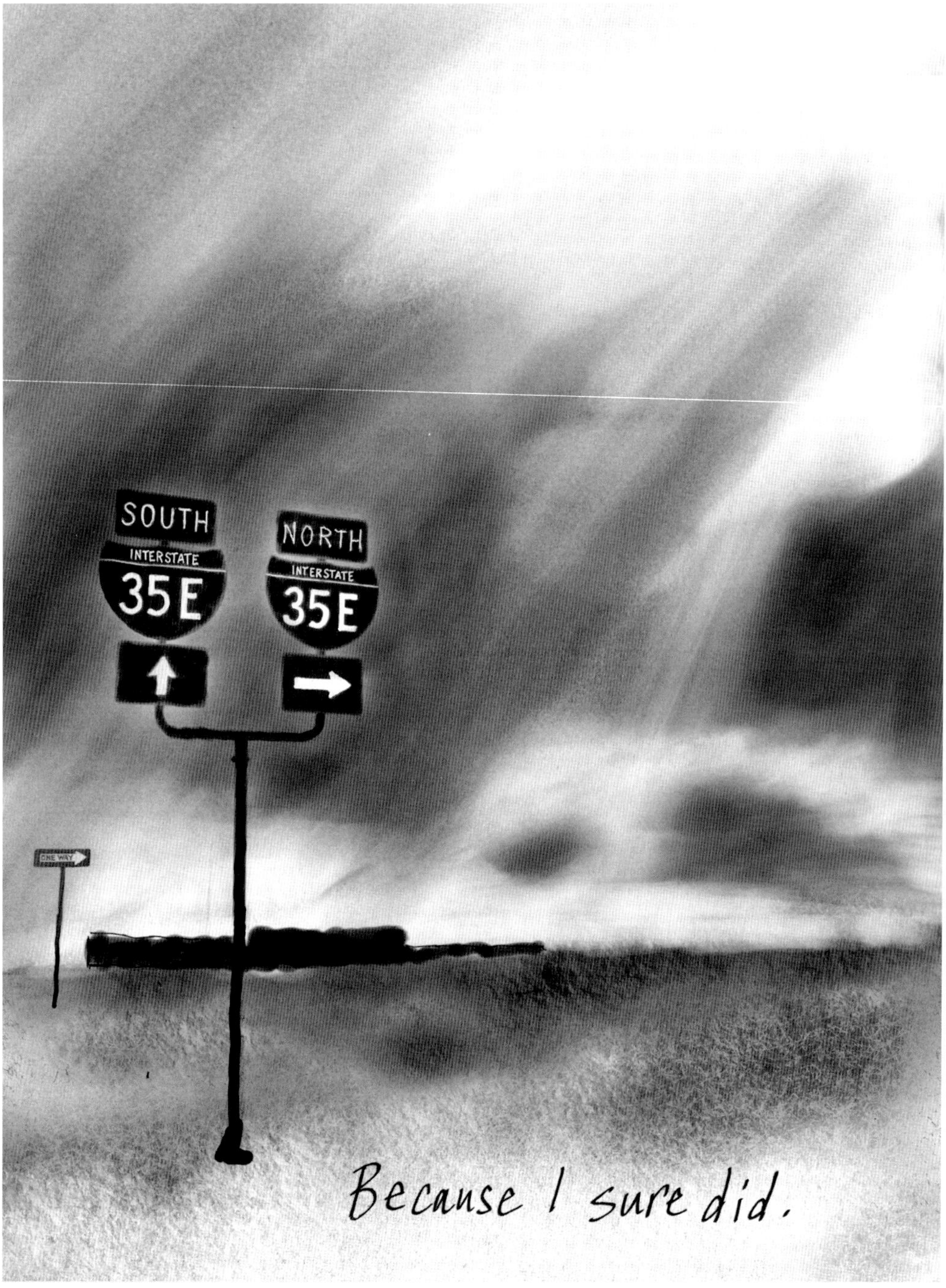
SOUTH
INTERSTATE
35E
NORTH
INTERSTATE
35E
ONE WAY
Because I sure did.

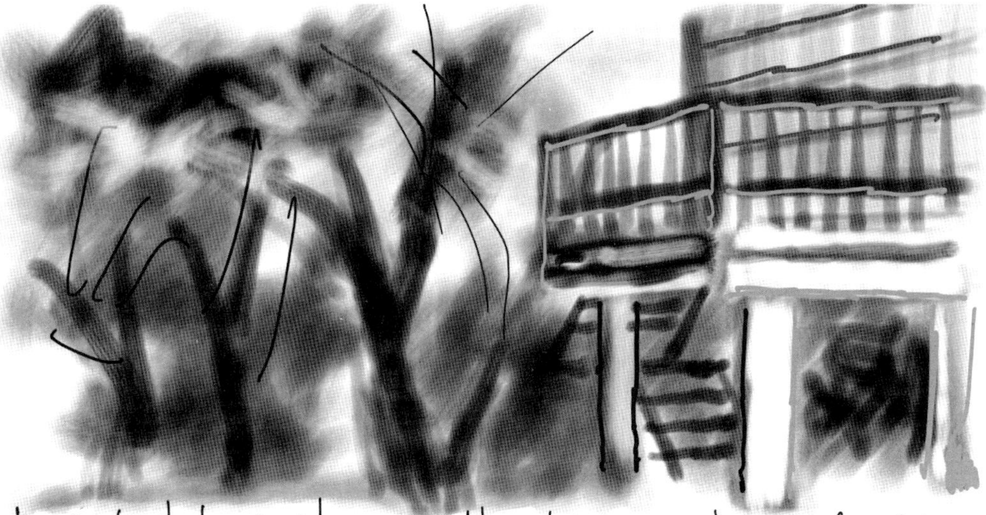

I moved to a place in the hills outside Austin,

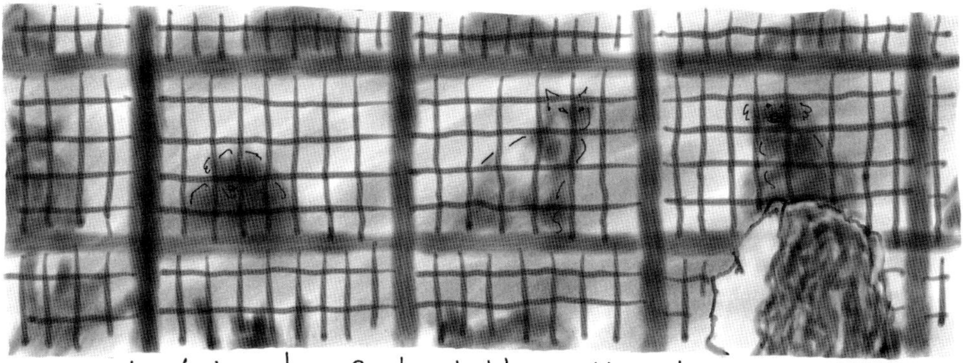

and volunteered at the city shelter.

Gradually, I stopped eating animals.

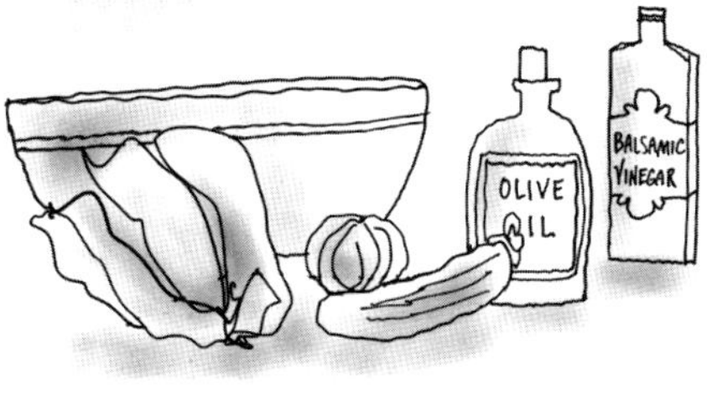
OLIVE OIL
BALSAMIC VINEGAR

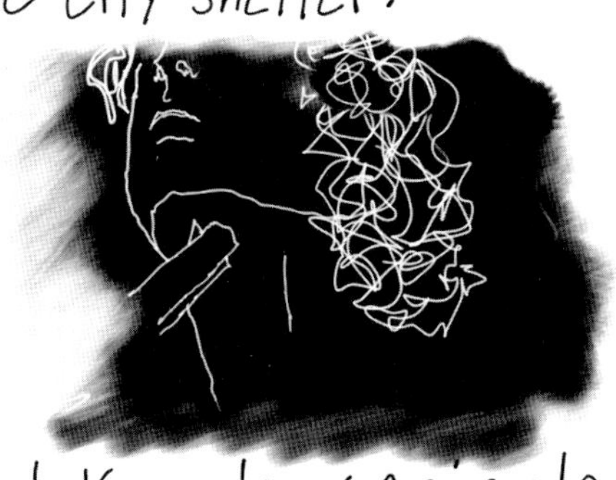

I knew how animals feel in a slaughterhouse.

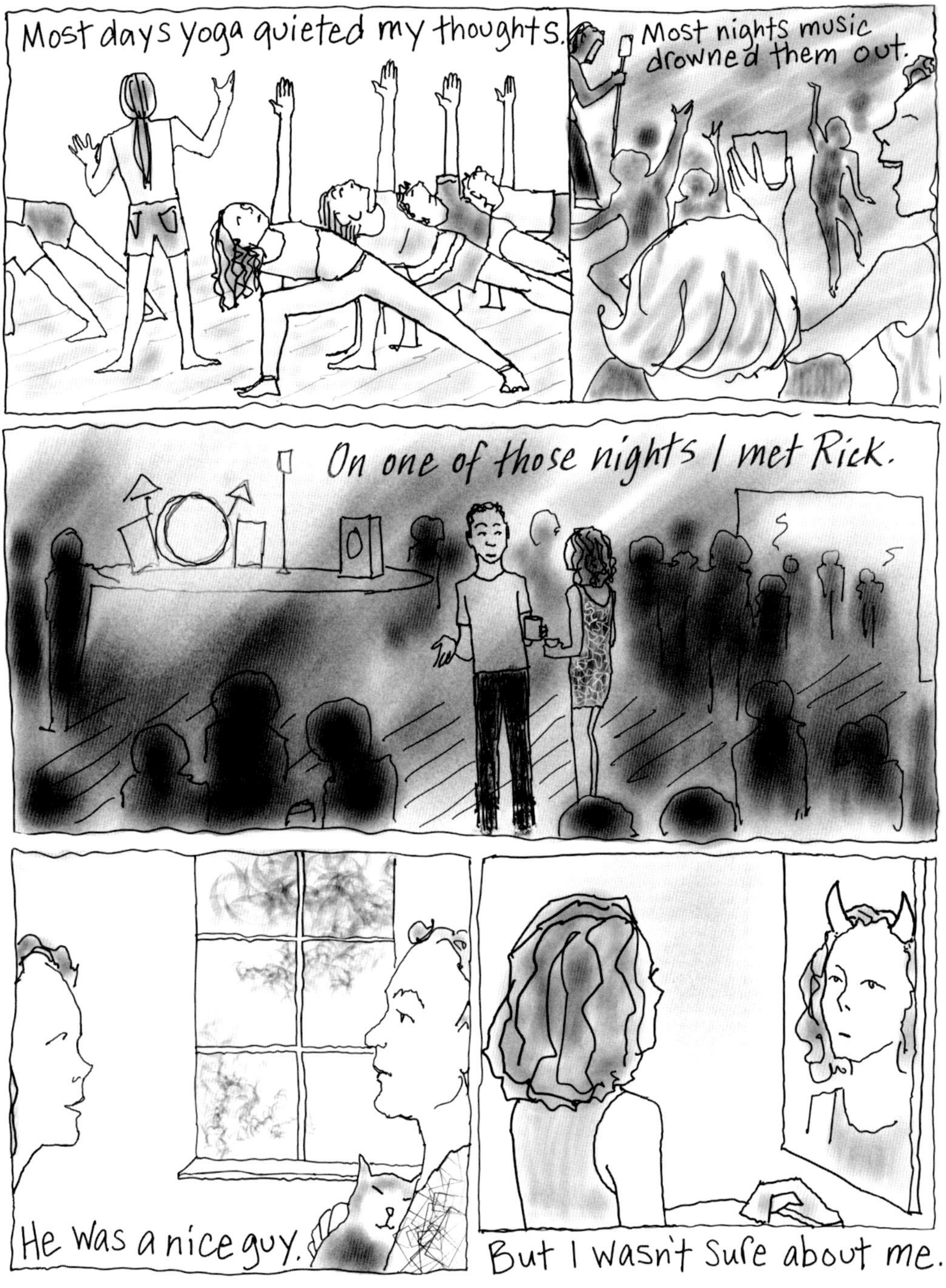

Most days yoga quieted my thoughts.
Most nights music drowned them out.
On one of those nights I met Rick.
He was a nice guy.
But I wasn't sure about me.

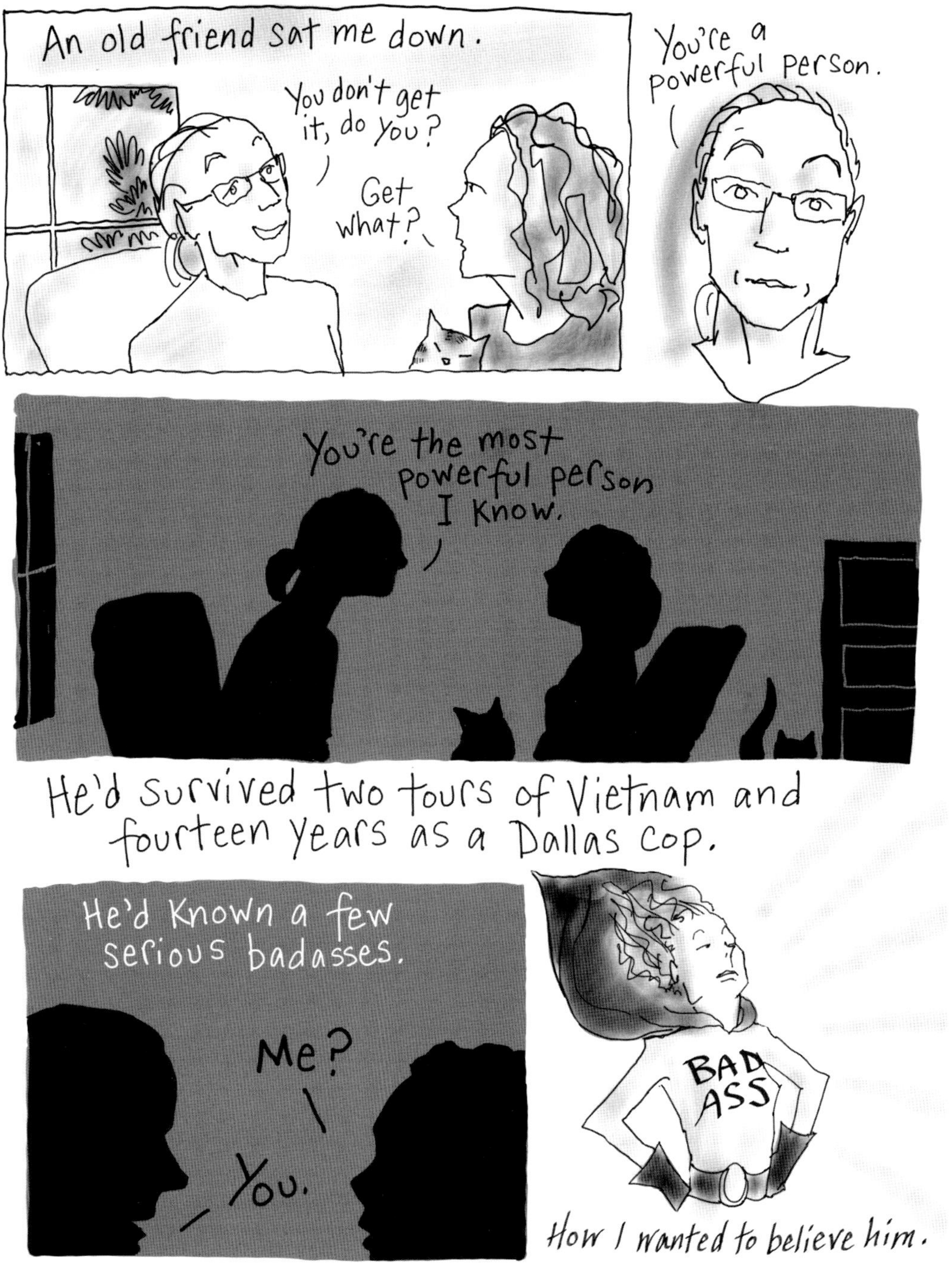
An old friend sat me down.
You don't get it, do you?
Get what?
You're a powerful person.
You're the most powerful person I know.
He'd survived two tours of Vietnam and fourteen years as a Dallas cop.
He'd known a few serious badasses.
Me?
You.
BAD ASS
How I wanted to believe him.

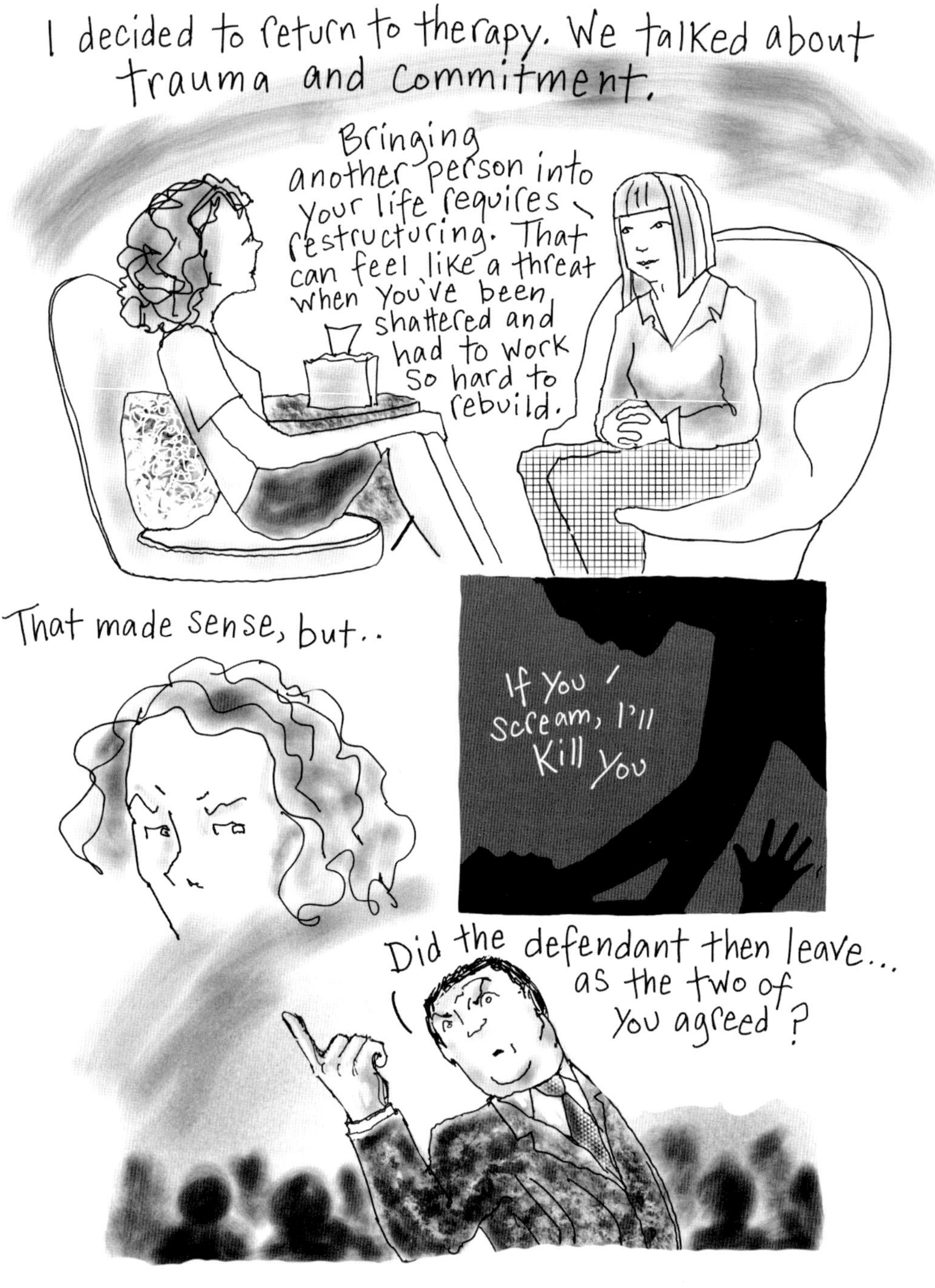
I decided to return to therapy. We talked about trauma and commitment.
Bringing another person into your life requires restructuring. That can feel like a threat when you've been shattered and had to work so hard to rebuild.
That made sense, but..
If you scream, I'll kill you
Did the defendant then leave... as the two of you agreed?

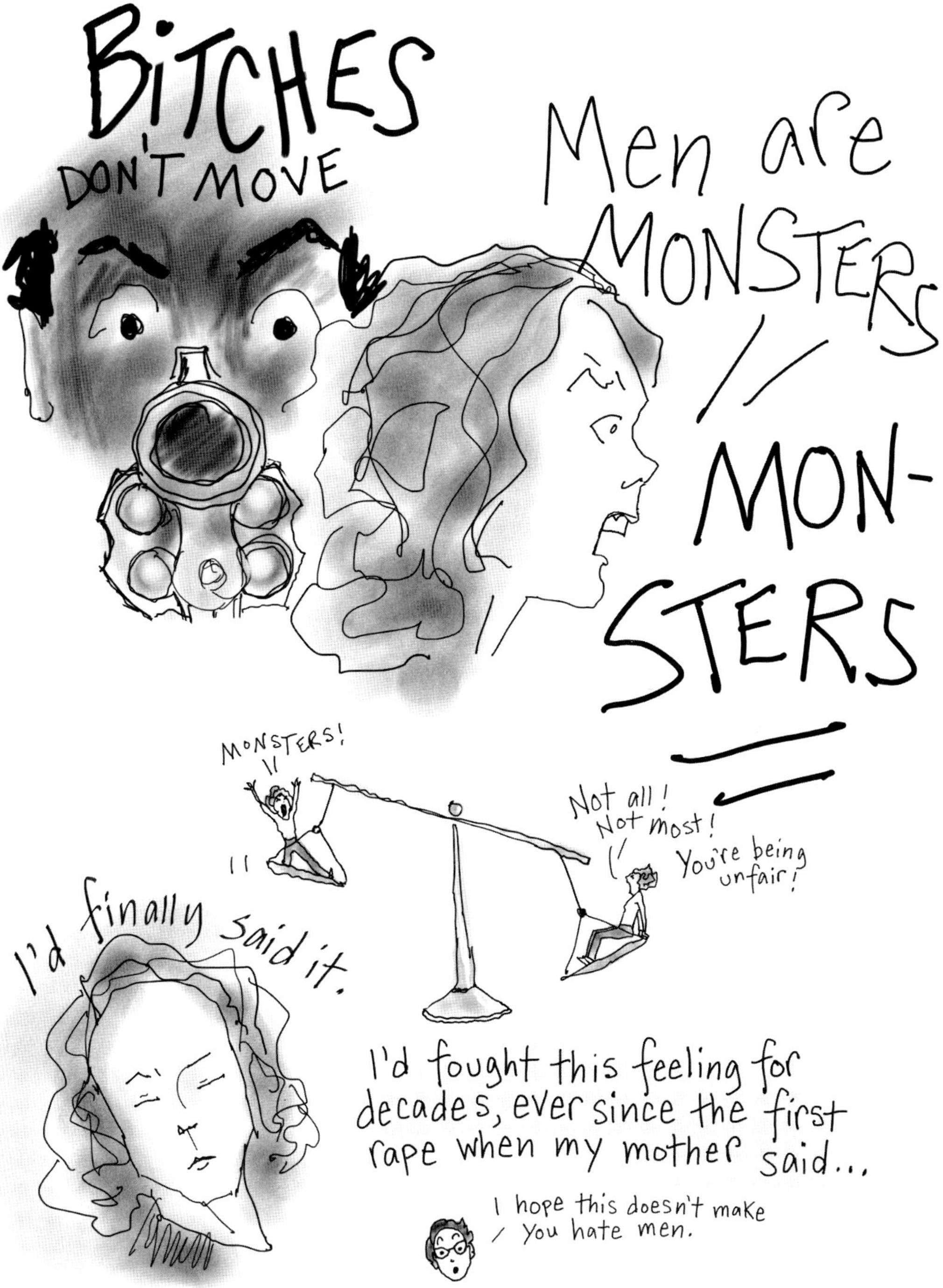
BITCHES DON'T MOVE
Men are MONSTERS
MON-STERS
MONSTERS!
Not all! Not most!
You're being unfair!
I'd finally said it.
I'd fought this feeling for decades, ever since the first rape when my mother said...
I hope this doesn't make you hate men.

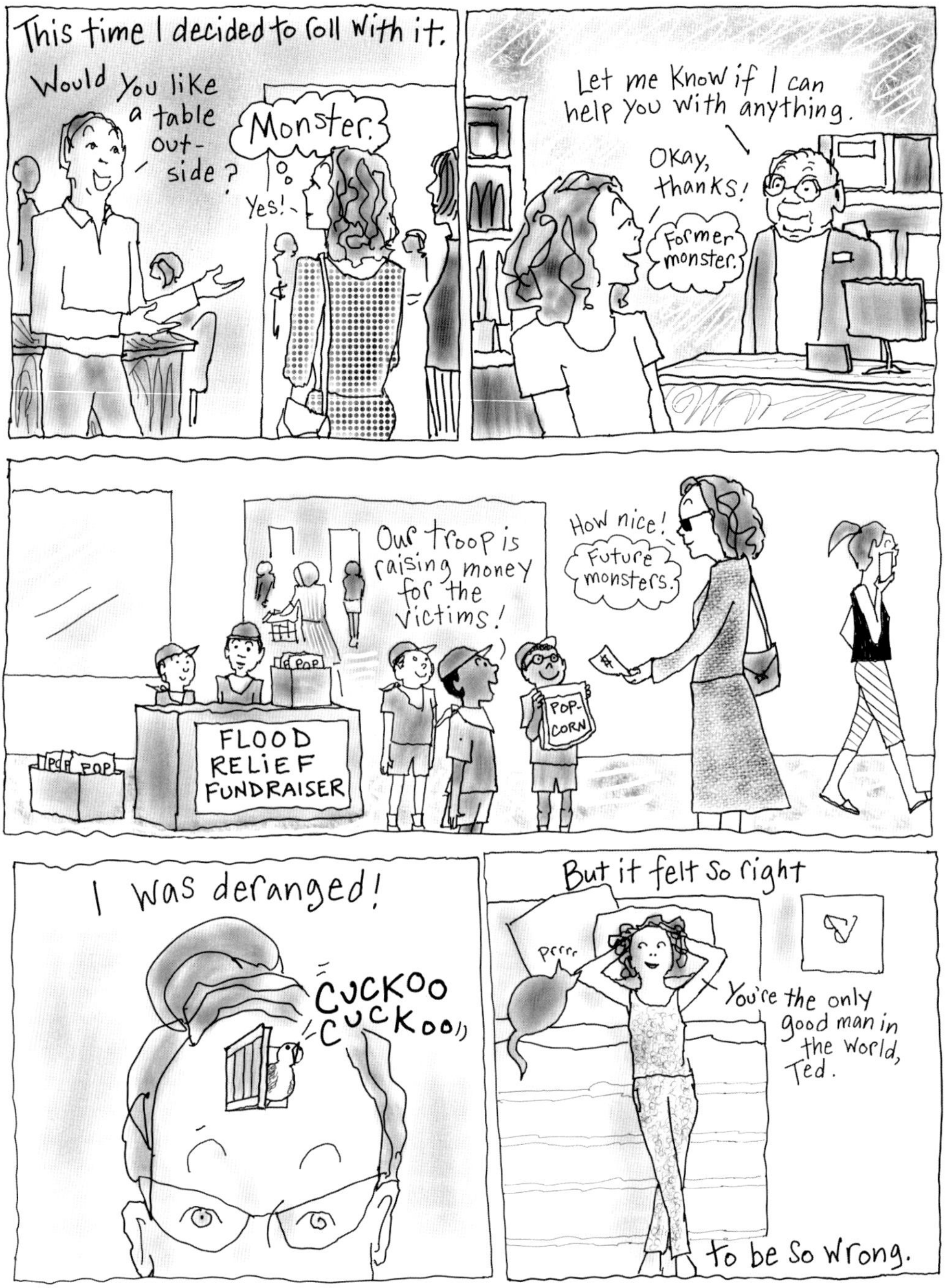
This time I decided to roll with it.
Would you like a table out-side?
Monster.
Yes!
Let me know if I can help you with anything.
Okay, thanks!
Former monster.
Our troop is raising money for the victims!
How nice!
Future monsters.
FLOOD RELIEF FUNDRAISER
POP-CORN
POP
I was deranged!
CUCKOO CUCKOO
But it felt so right
Prrrr
You're the only good man in the world, Ted.
to be so wrong.

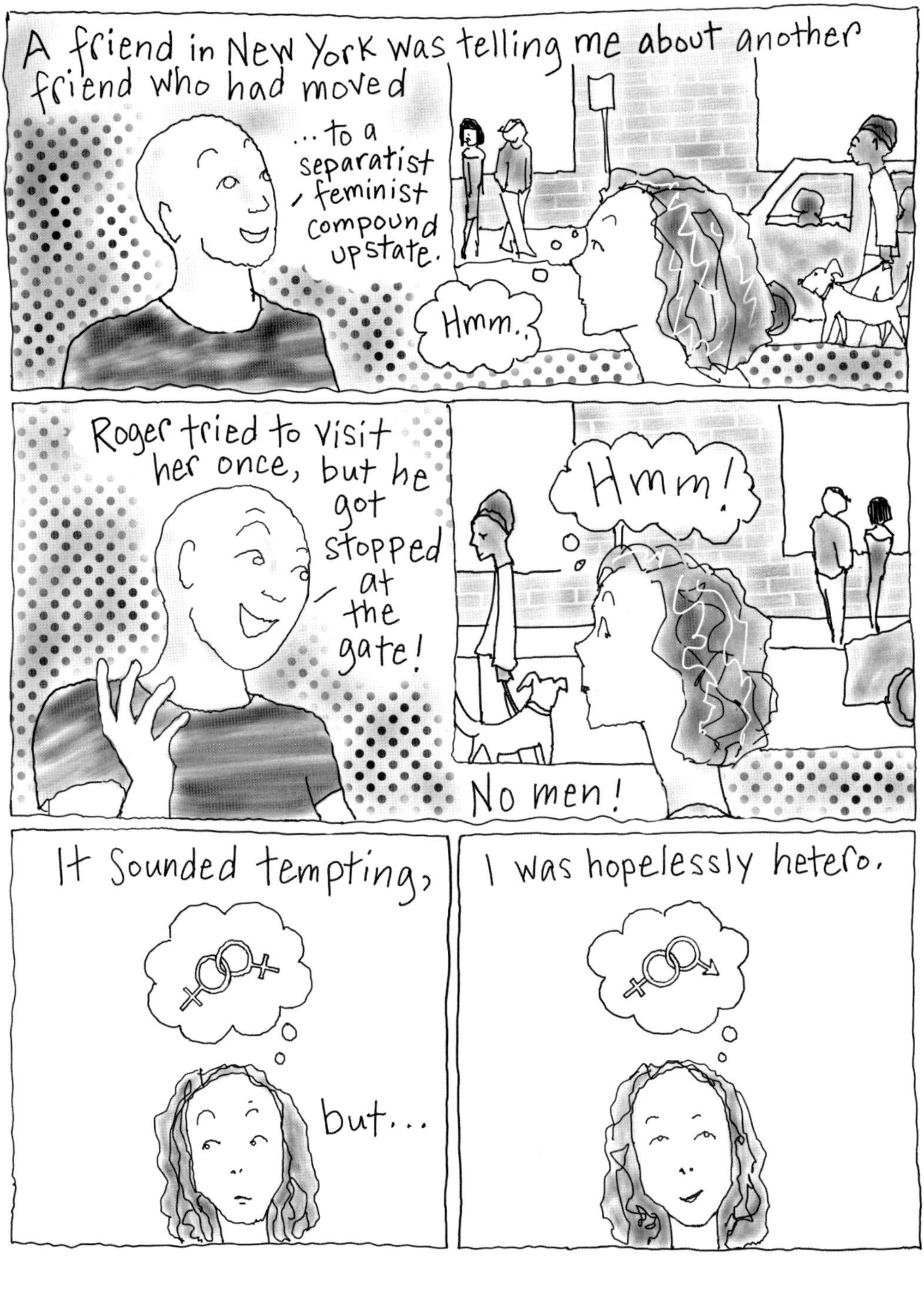

A friend in New York was telling me about another friend who had moved
...to a separatist feminist compound upstate.
Hmm..
Roger tried to visit her once, but he got stopped at the gate!
Hmm!
No men!
It sounded tempting,
but...
I was hopelessly hetero.

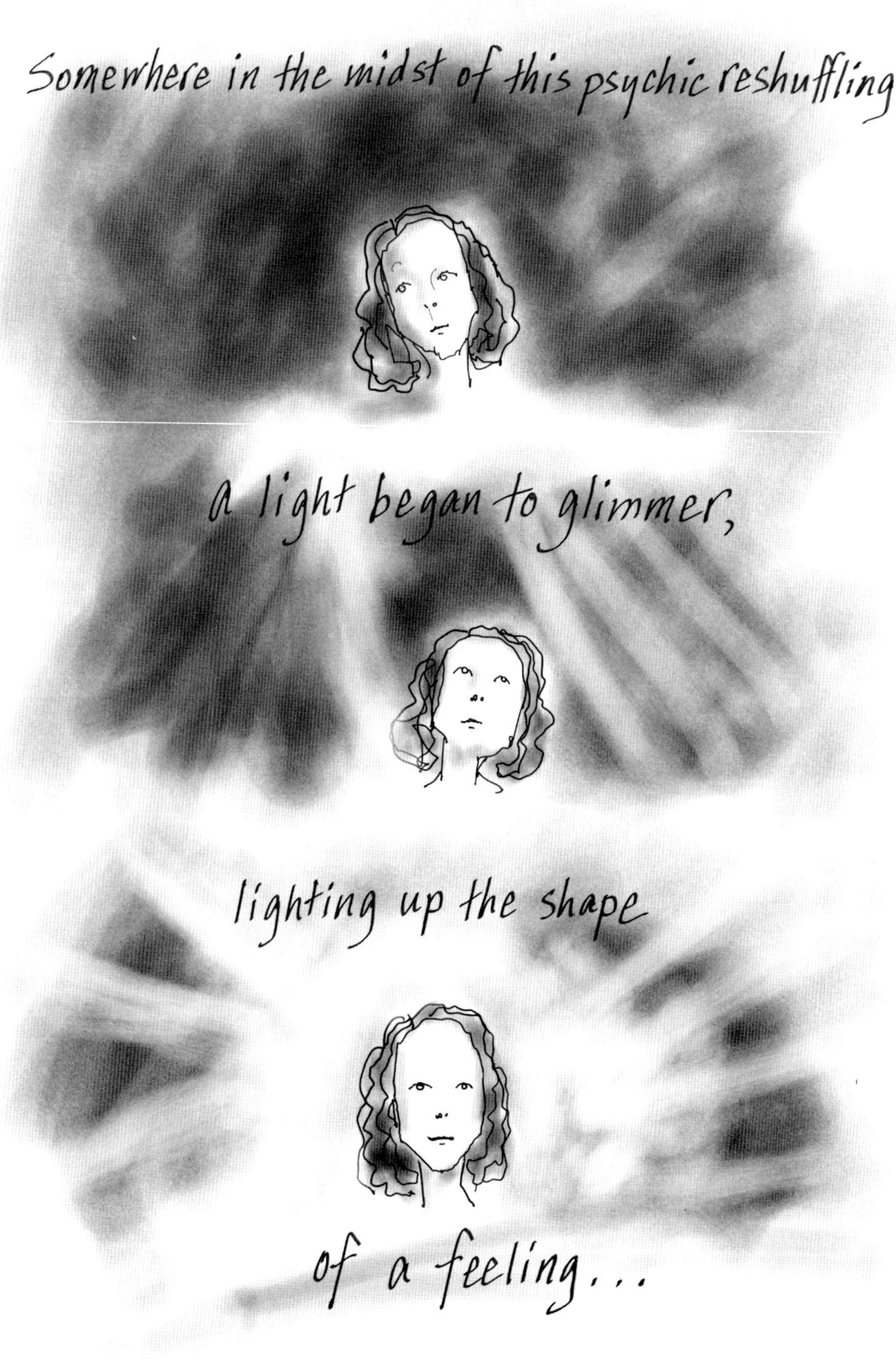
Somewhere in the midst of this psychic reshuffling
a light began to glimmer,
lighting up the shape
of a feeling...

a revelation...

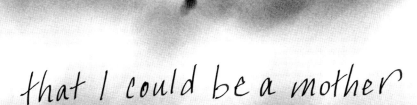

that I could be a mother

to a boy.

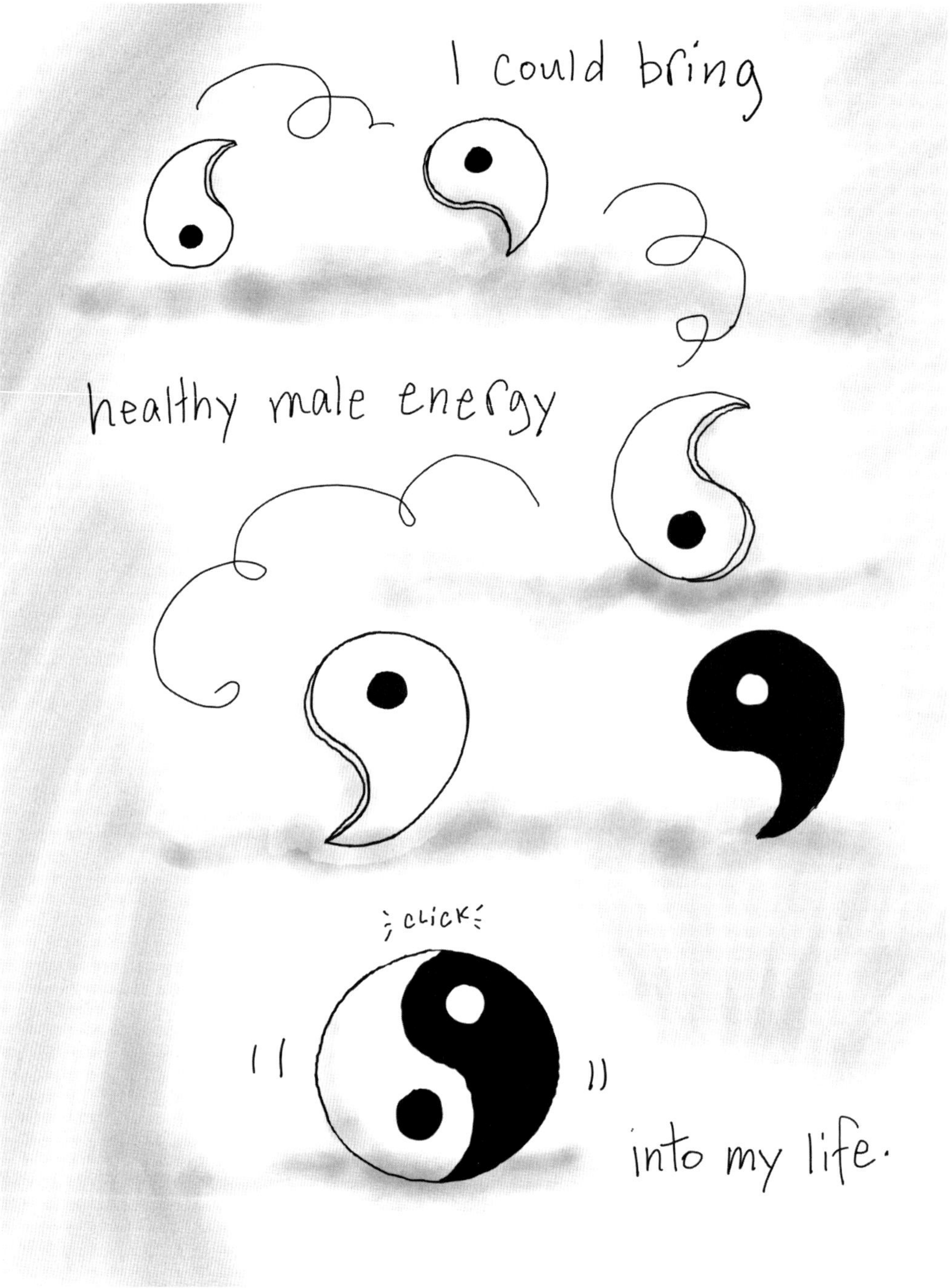
I could bring
healthy male energy
CLICK
into my life.

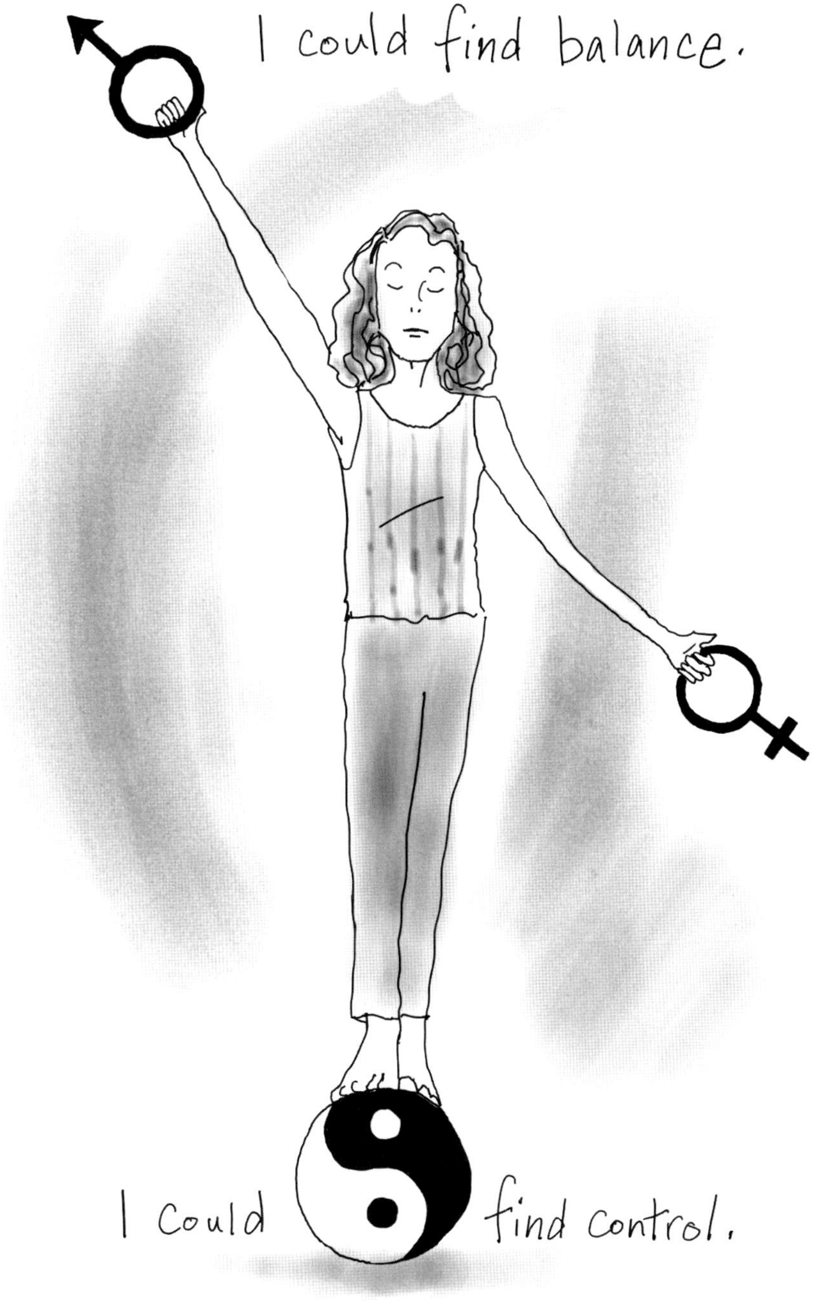
I could find balance.
I could find control.

So much control had
been taken away from me.

Every last shred of it...

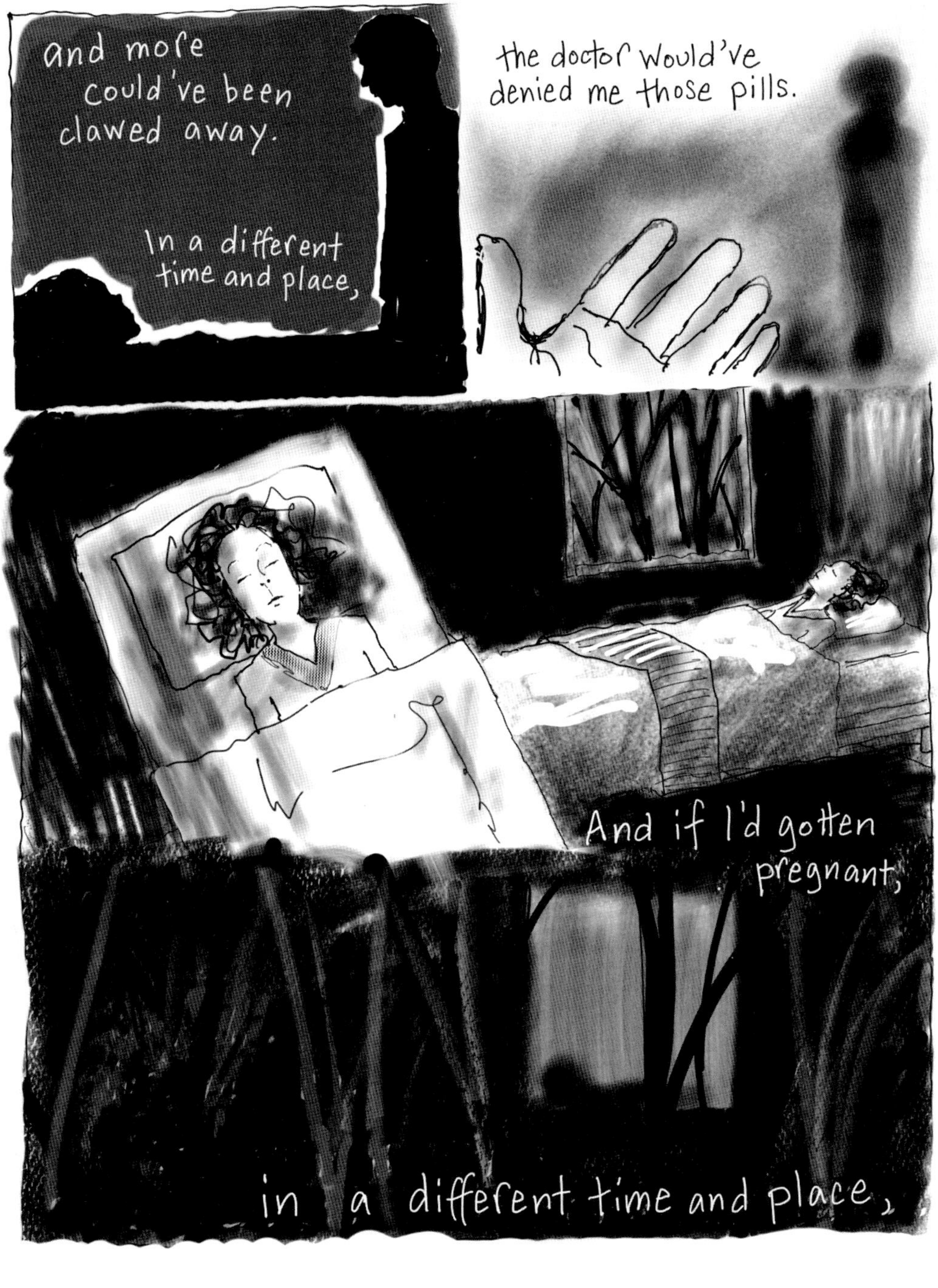
and more could've been clawed away.
In a different time and place,
the doctor would've denied me those pills.
And if I'd gotten pregnant,
in a different time and place,

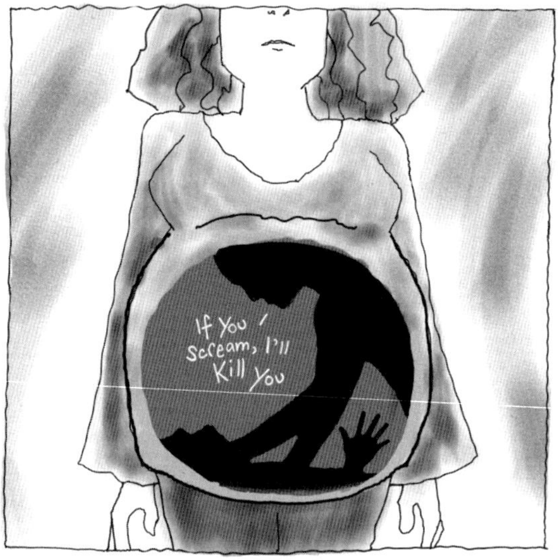
If you scream, I'll kill you

I would've been forced to carry a rapist with me.

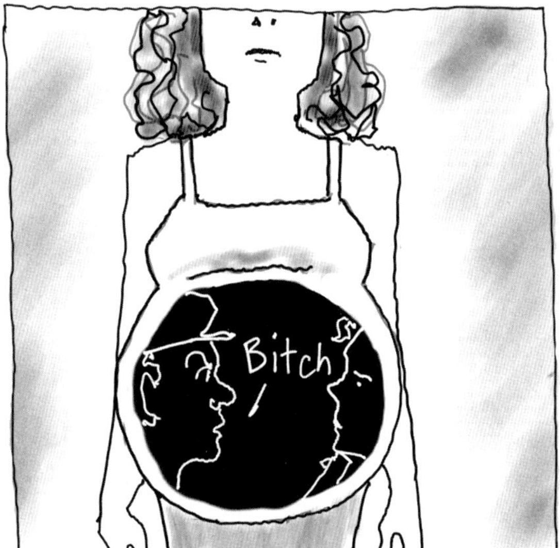
Bitch

For nine months. Forever.

But I'd had a choice.

My body was my own.

My future was mine for the making.

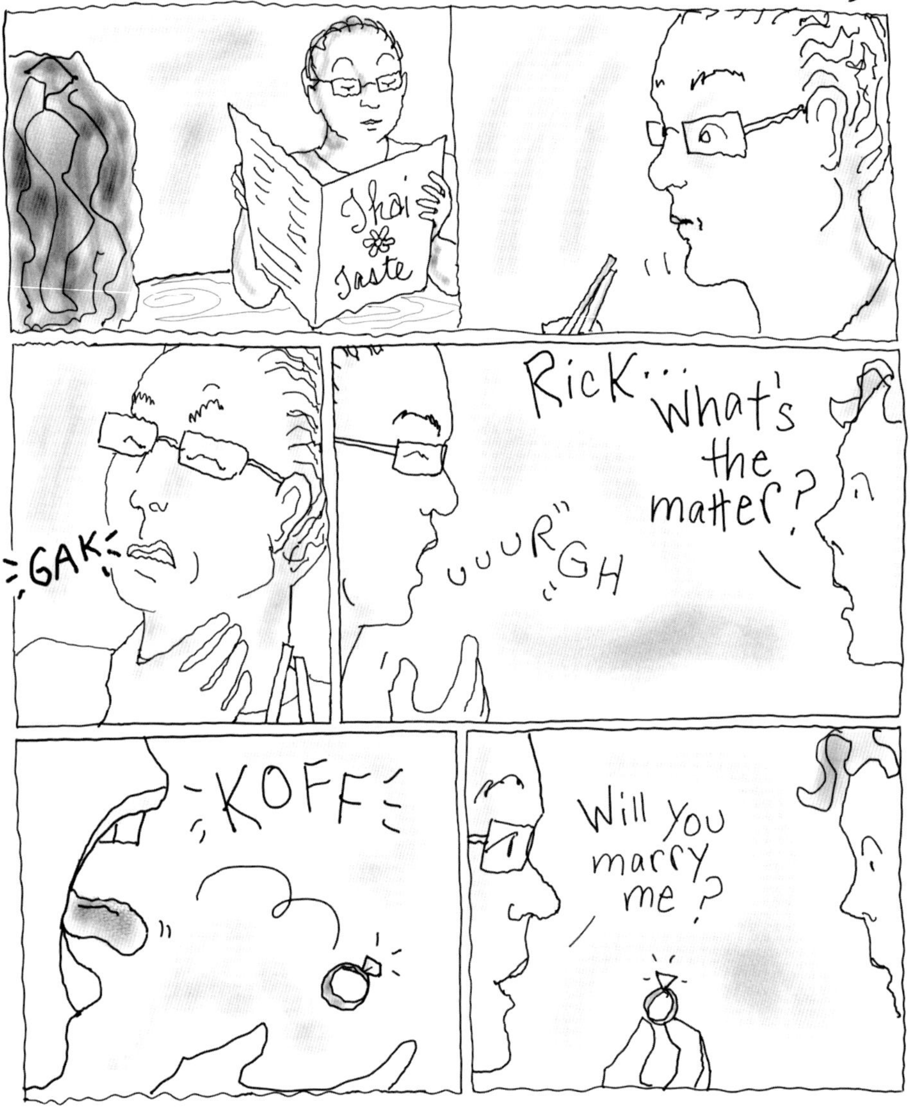
Thai Taste
GAK
Rick... what's the matter?
UUURGH
KOFF
Will you marry me?

My future was this kooky character.

And this little boy.

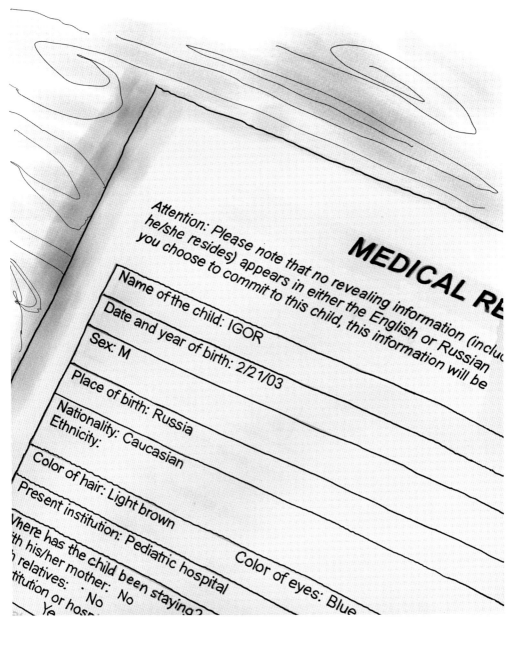

Attention: Please note that no revealing information (inclu
he/she resides) appears in either the English or Russian
you choose to commit to this child, this information will be

MEDICAL RE

Name of the child: IGOR

Date and year of birth: 2/21/03

Sex: M

Place of birth: Russia

Nationality: Caucasian
Ethnicity:

Color of hair: Light brown

Present institution: Pediatric hospital

Color of eyes: Blue

here has the child been staying?
th his/her mother: No
relatives: . No
titution or hosp
Ye

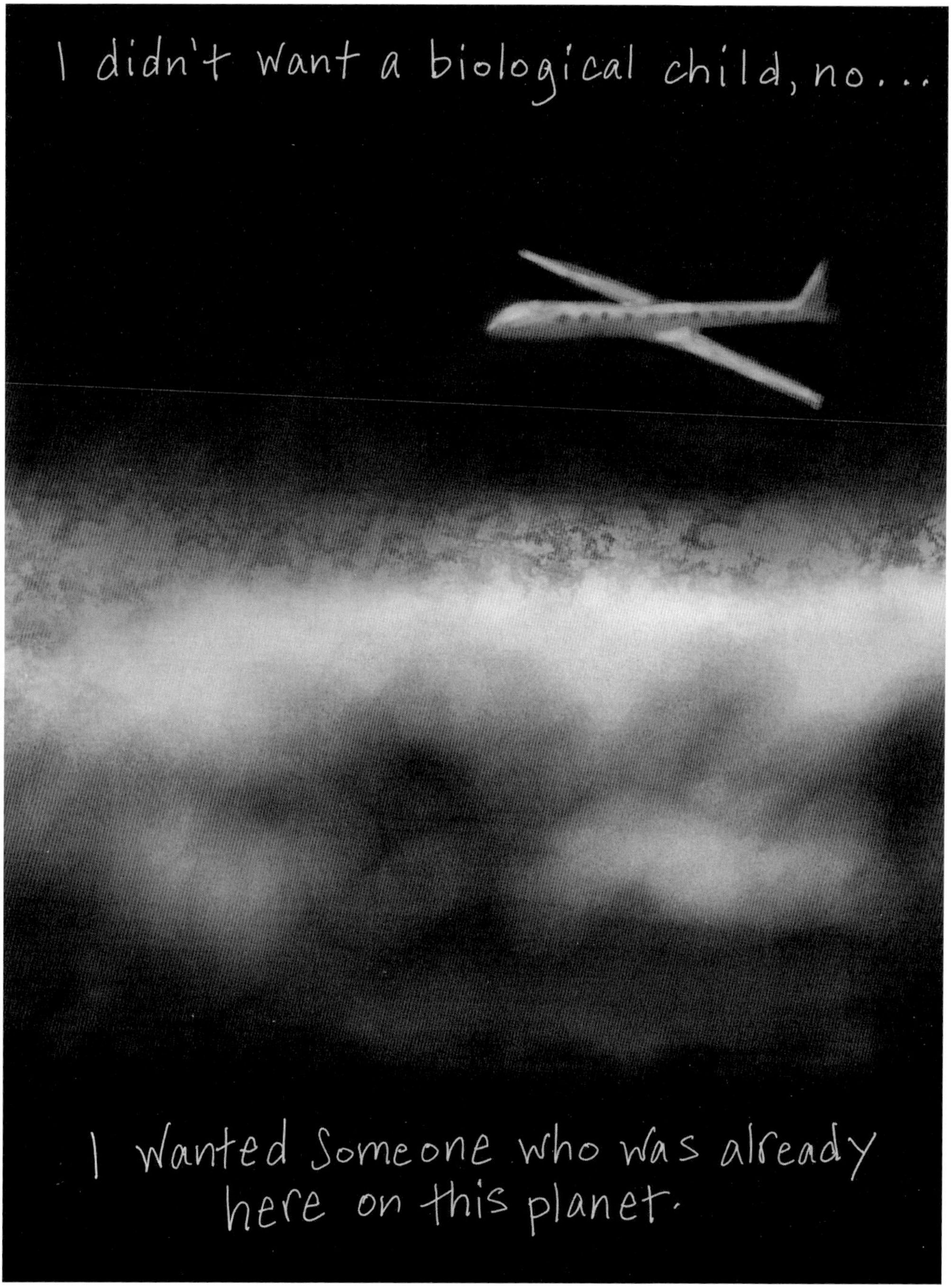
I didn't want a biological child, no...
I wanted someone who was already here on this planet.

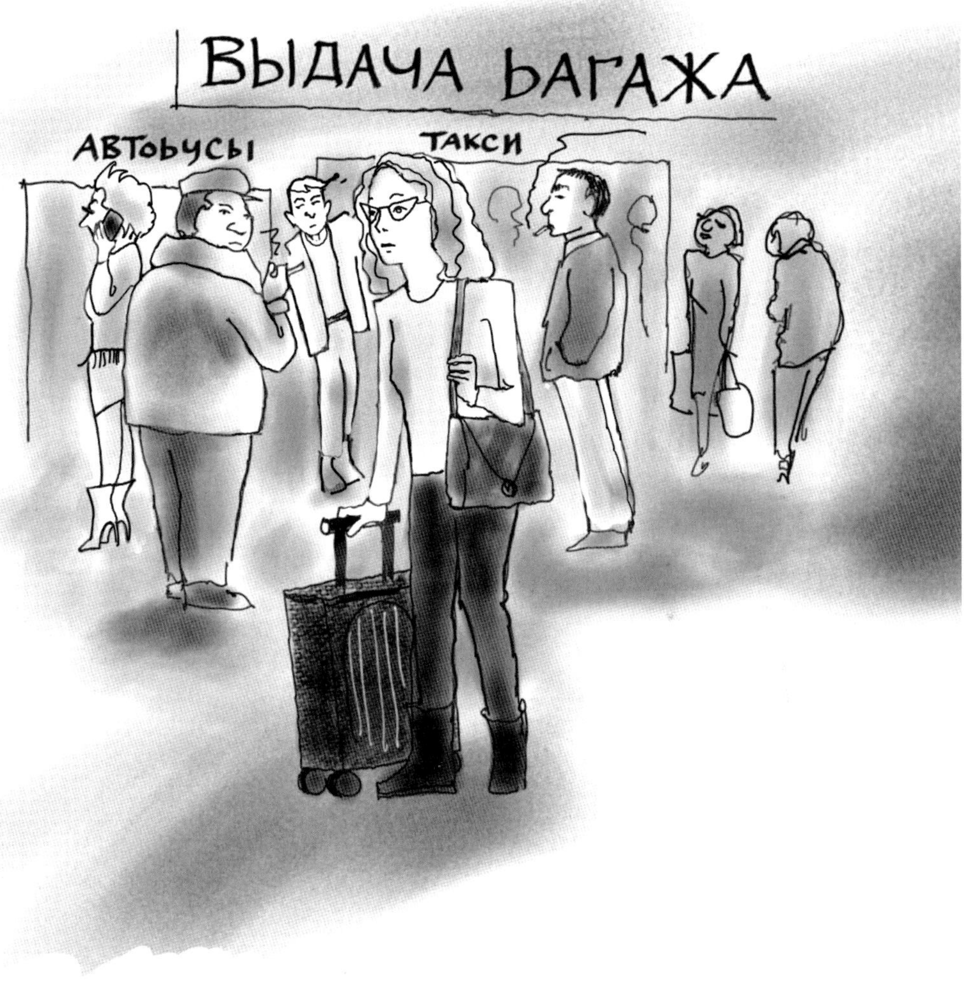
ВЫДАЧА ЬАГАЖА
АВТОЬУСЫ
ТАКСИ

Someone who needed
me now.

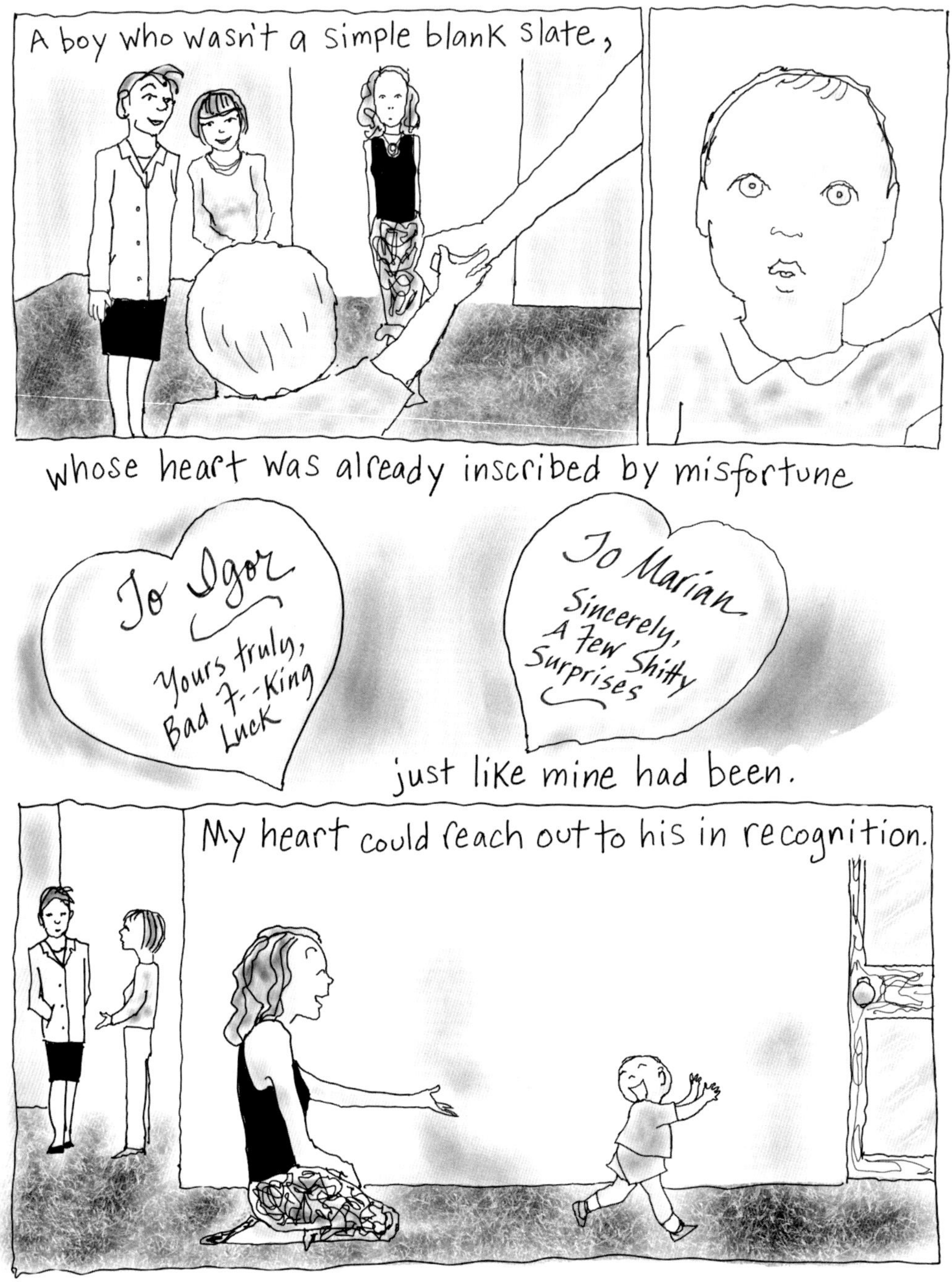
A boy who wasn't a simple blank slate,
whose heart was already inscribed by misfortune
To Igor
Yours truly, Bad F--King Luck
To Marian
Sincerely, A Few Shitty Surprises
just like mine had been.
My heart could reach out to his in recognition.

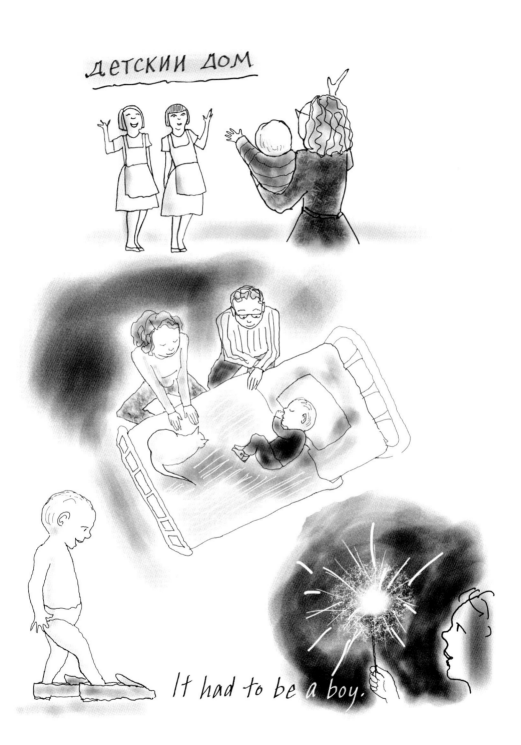

ДЕТСКИЙ ДОМ

It had to be a boy.

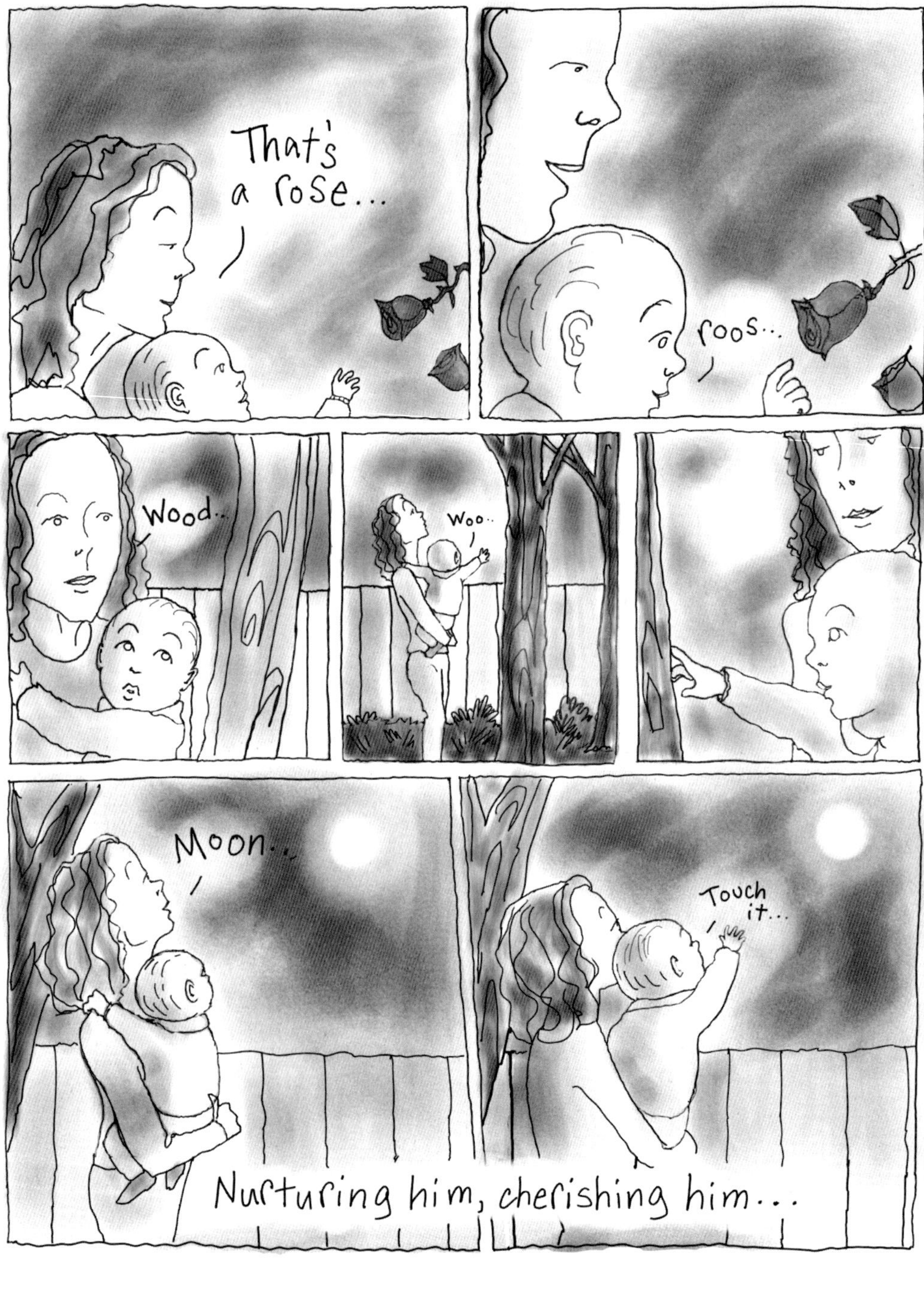
That's a rose...
roos...
Wood...
Woo..
Moon...
Touch it...
Nurturing him, cherishing him...

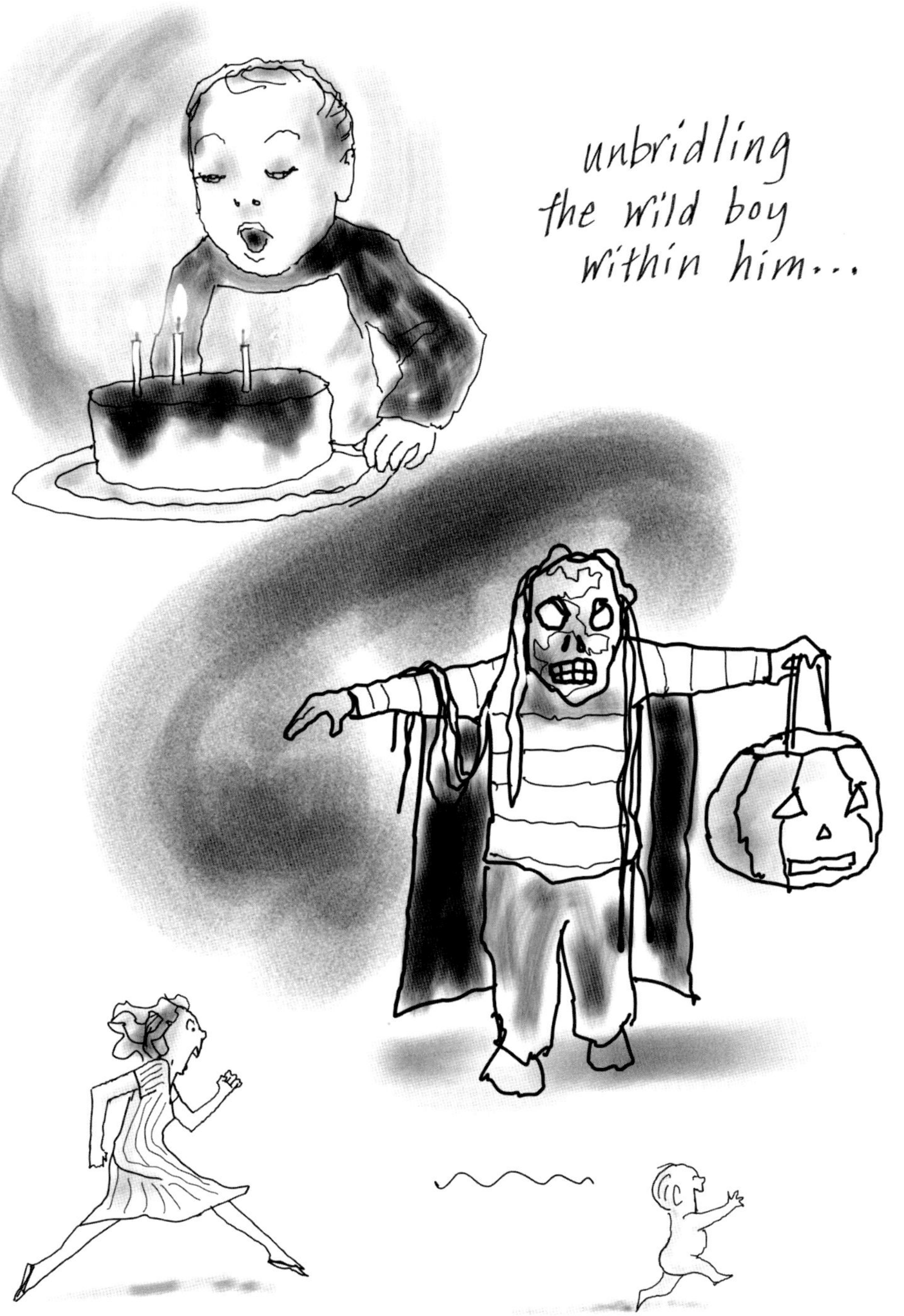
unbridling
the wild boy
within him...

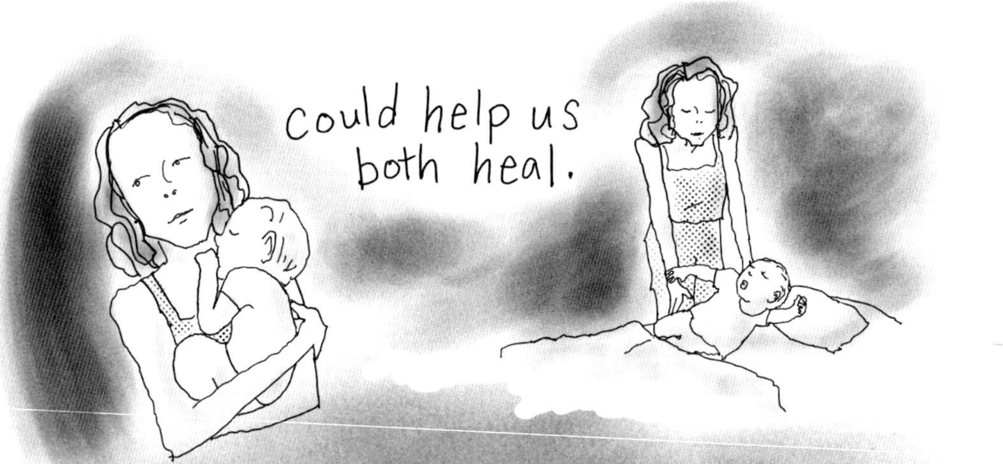
could help us
both heal.

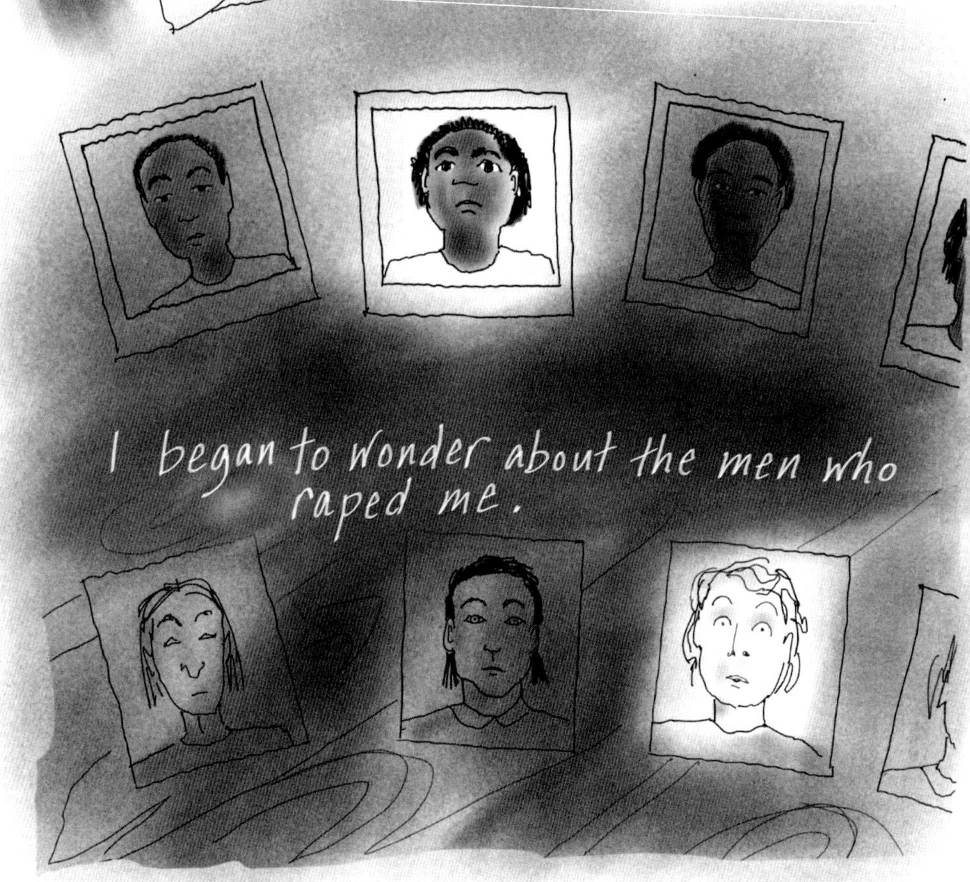
I began to wonder about the men who
raped me.

Had no mother loved them the way I loved William?

Mother love.

Father love.

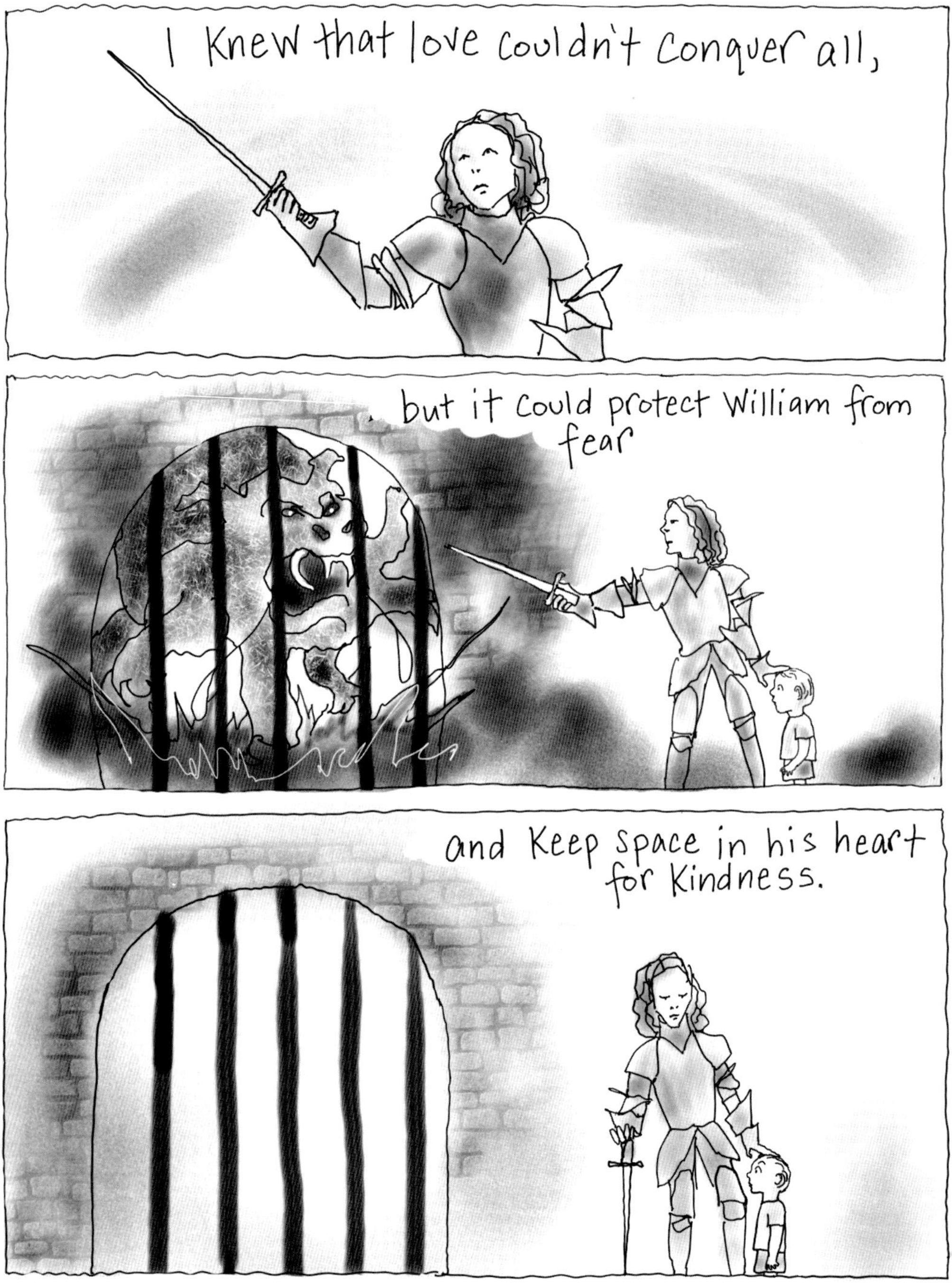
I knew that love couldn't conquer all,
but it could protect William from fear
and keep space in his heart for kindness.

The day came when I knew this had come true.

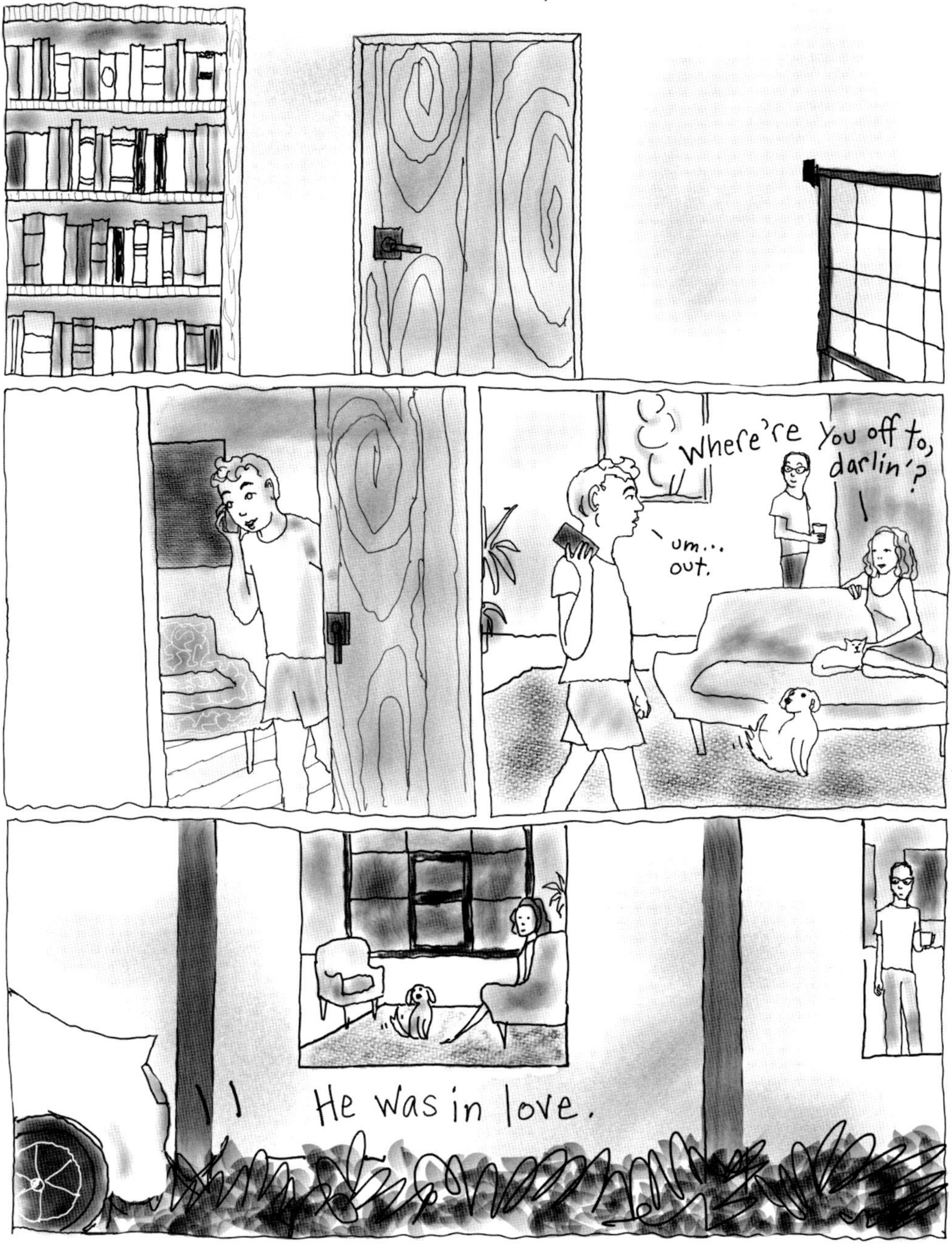
Where're you off to, darlin'?
um... out.
He was in love.

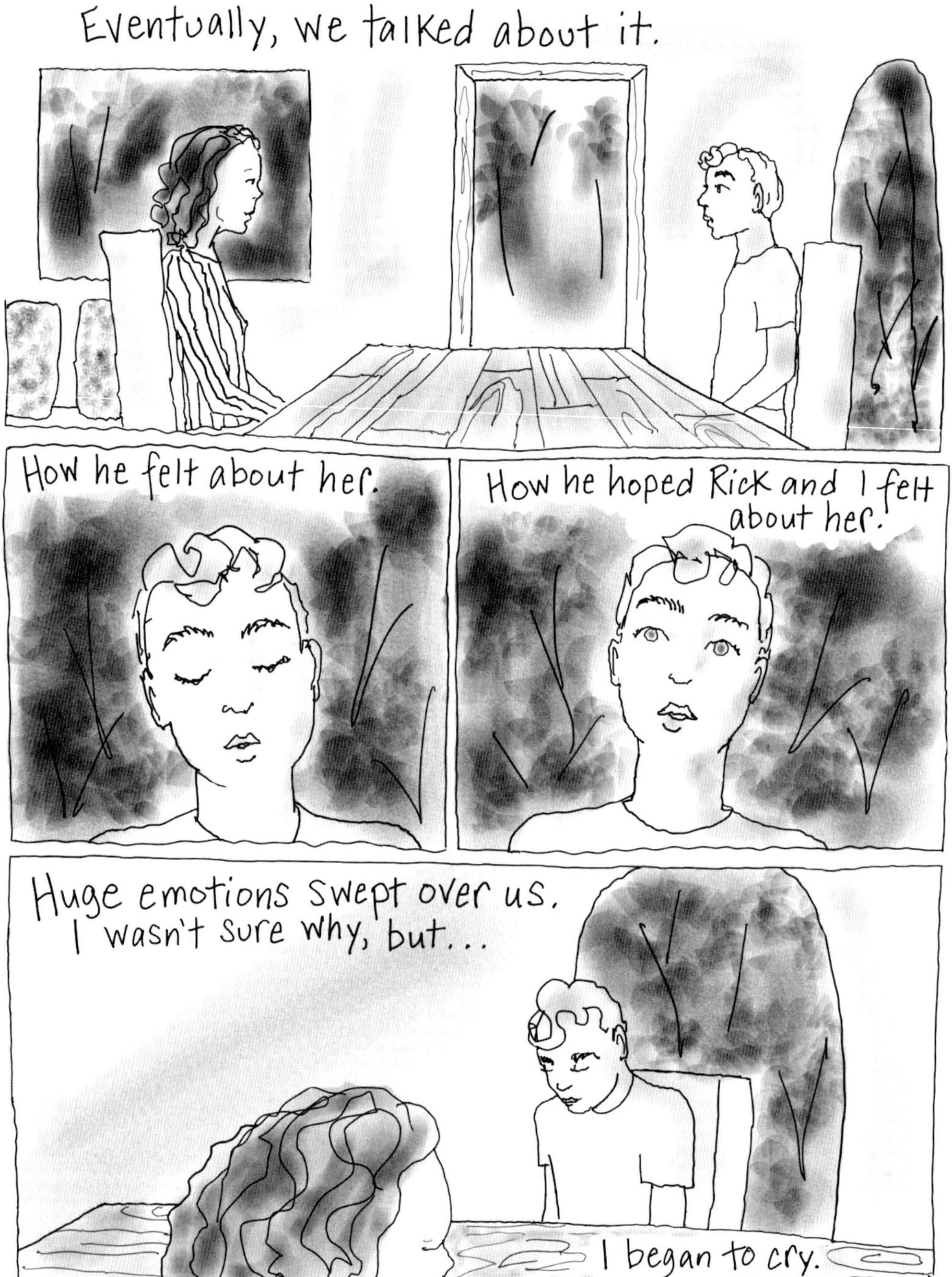
Eventually, we talked about it.
How he felt about her.
How he hoped Rick and I felt about her.
Huge emotions swept over us. I wasn't sure why, but...
I began to cry.

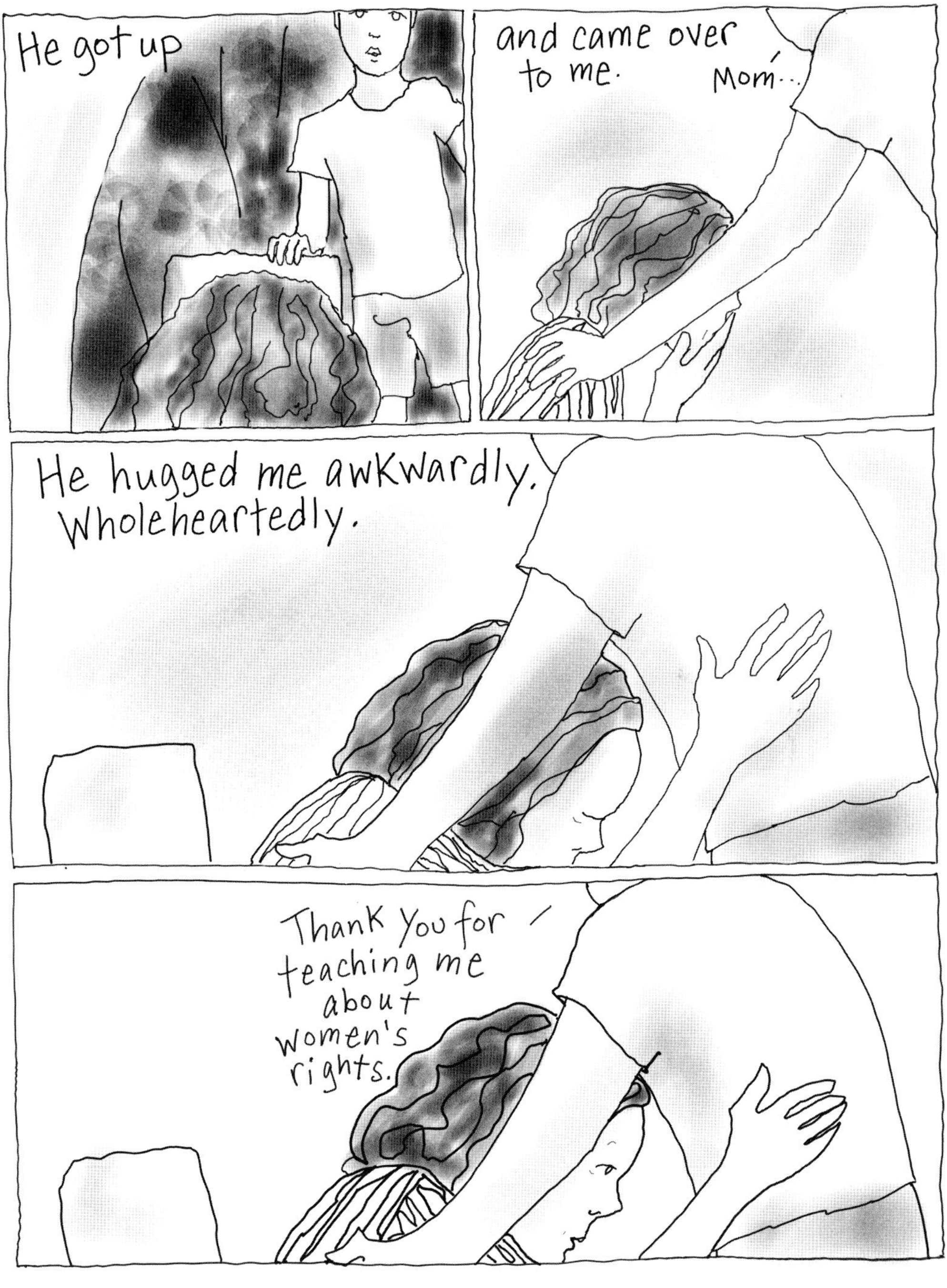
He got up
and came over to me.
Mom...
He hugged me awkwardly. Wholeheartedly.
Thank you for teaching me about women's rights.

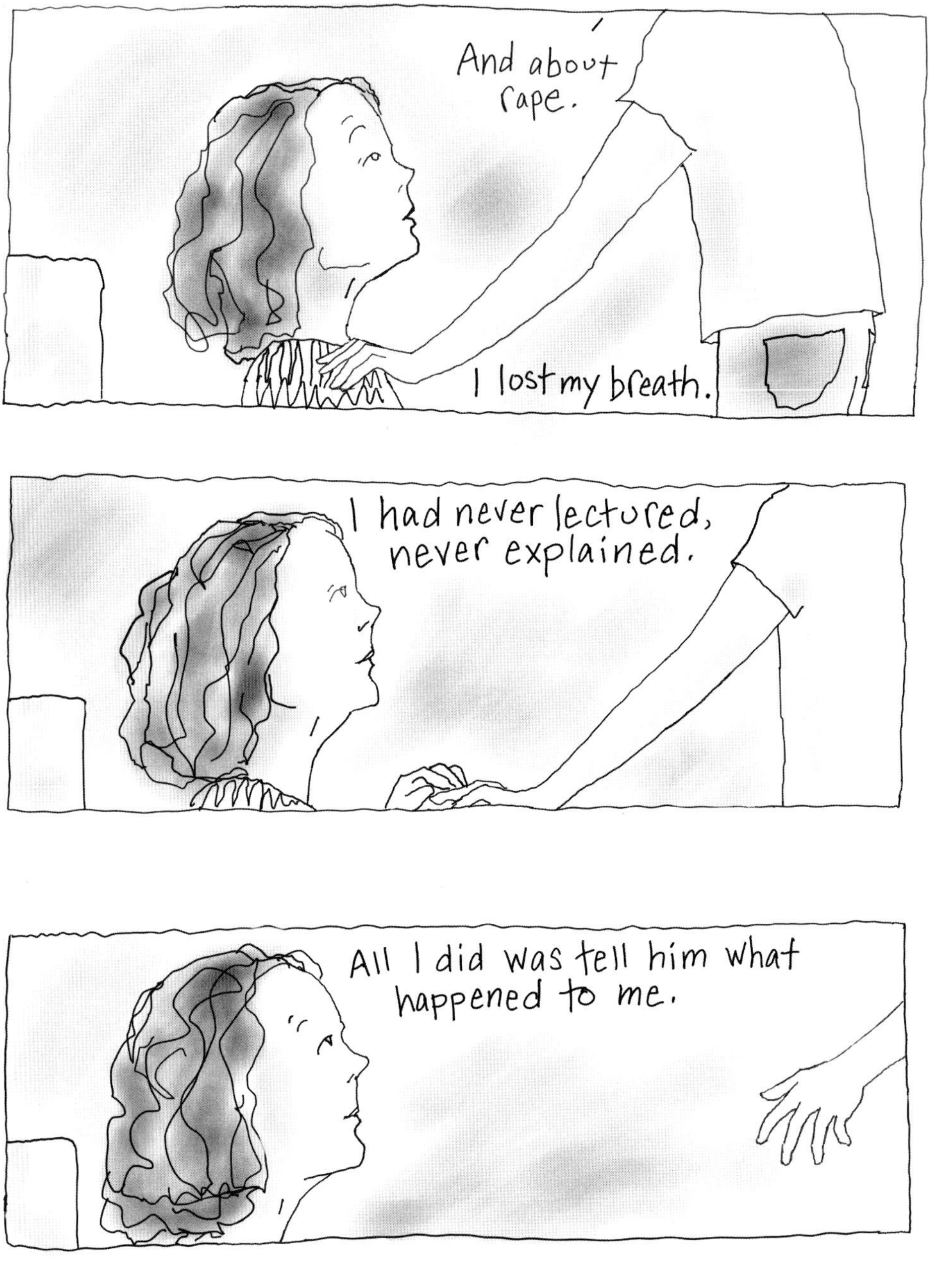
And about rape.
I lost my breath.
I had never lectured, never explained.
All I did was tell him what happened to me.

He had taken that

and made it into something meaningful to him,

Mom?

into something of his own.

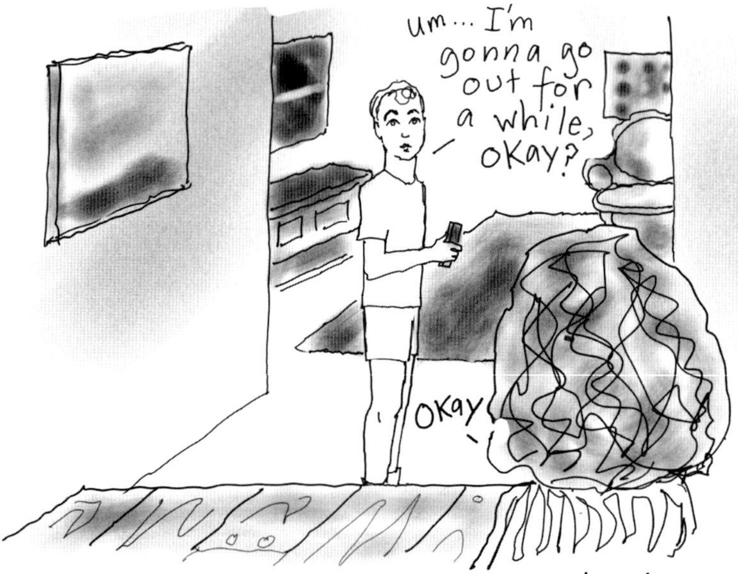
um... I'm gonna go out for a while, okay?
okay

When I looked at William,

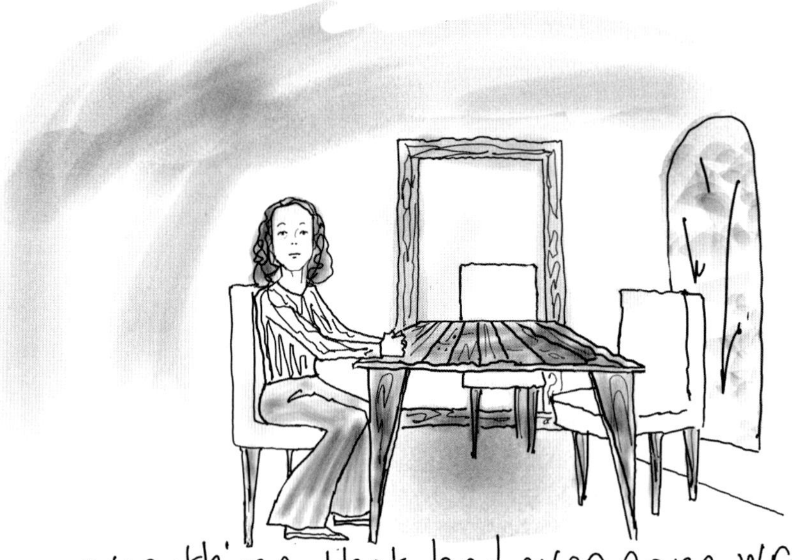

everything that had ever gone wrong

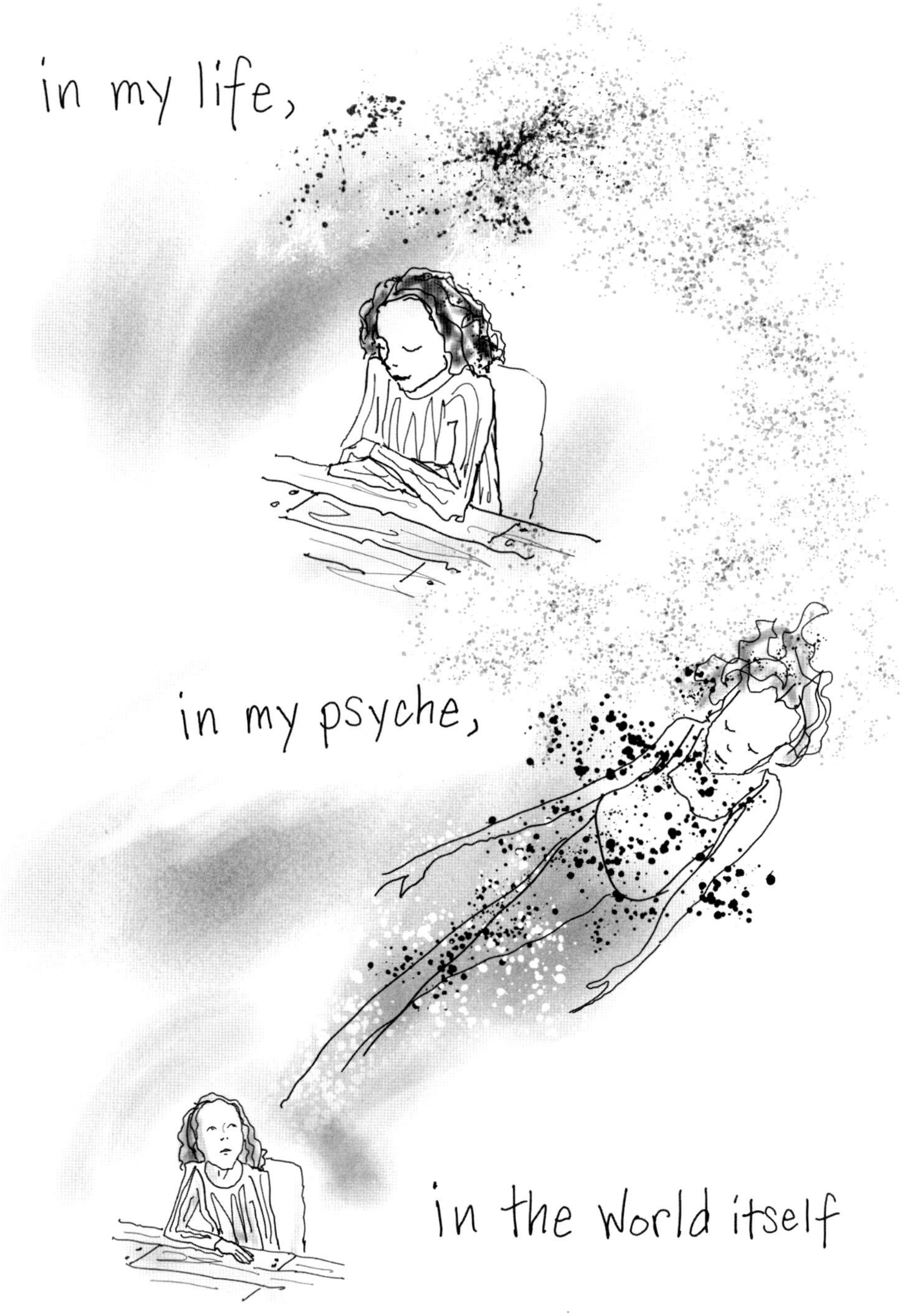
in my life,
in my psyche,
in the World itself

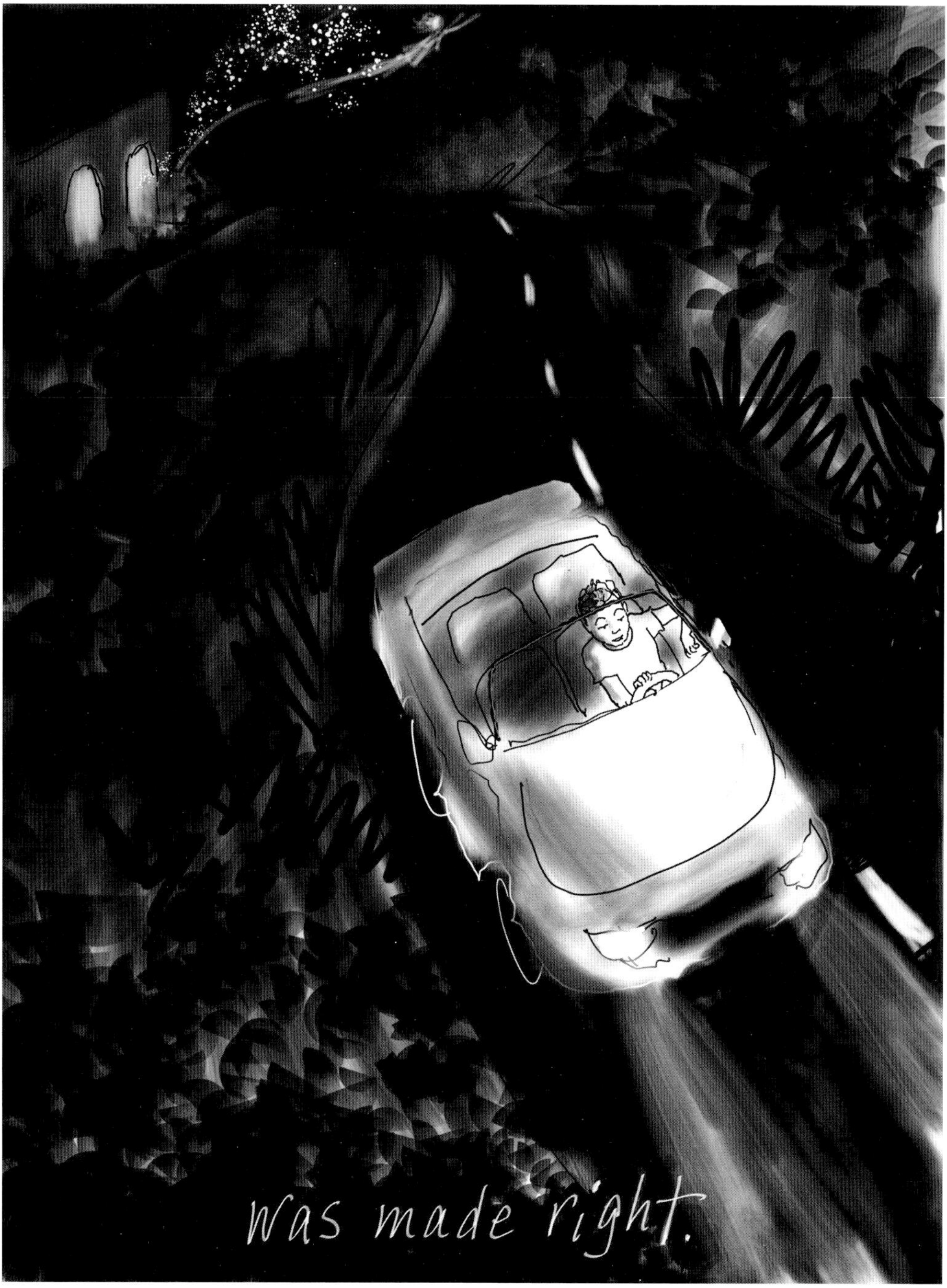
was made right.

Acknowledgments

For many years I tried, without success, to piece together into a story the shifting, scattering fragments of me that rape left in my life. At least two memoirs and a novel ended up in the dustbin, all too raw both emotionally and in technique to be publishable. But bad work can be good practice: I was building the foundation for this book.

Along the way, many people gave me generous reading time and even more generous feedback. It isn't easy to criticize someone's rape story, and I'm grateful for their tact and support. I owe more people than I can name, but I think you know who you are.

I want to thank my agent, Betsy Amster, for her guidance and commitment. We had setbacks, and no doubt she suspected this book would never land either of us in a deep tub of lucre. But she didn't waver. I also want to thank Lucas Wetzel, my editor, and the whole team at Andrews McMeel for their willingness to take on difficult material that, most likely, is not inside *anyone's* comfort zone.

When I was nineteen years old and alone in the courtroom being eviscerated by Mr. Crackerjack, I would not have believed that someday such kind allies would appear. Or that I would have you, the readers, to listen. And witness.

Thank you.

Finding the Light copyright © 2023 by Marian Henley. All rights reserved. Printed in China. No part of this book may be used or reproduced in any manner whatsoever without written permission except in the case of reprints in the context of reviews.

Andrews McMeel Publishing
a division of Andrews McMeel Universal
1130 Walnut Street, Kansas City, Missouri 64106

www.andrewsmcmeel.com

23 24 25 26 27 SDB 10 9 8 7 6 5 4 3 2 1

ISBN: 978-1-5248-8469-7

Library of Congress Control Number: 2023942380

Editor: Lucas Wetzel
Art Director and Cover Design: Diane Marsh
Production Editor: Meg Utz
Production Manager: Tamara Haus
Designer: Tiffany Meairs

ATTENTION: SCHOOLS AND BUSINESSES
Andrews McMeel books are available at quantity discounts with bulk purchase for educational, business, or sales promotional use. For information, please e-mail the Andrews McMeel Publishing Special Sales Department: sales@amuniversal.com.